BUILDING THE FLEXIBLE FIRM

Building The Flexible Firm

How To Remain Competitive

Henk W. Volberda

OXFORD UNIVERSITY PRESS
1998

Oxford University Press, Great Clarendon Street, Oxford OX2 6DP

Oxford New York

Athens Auckland Bangkok Bogota Bombay
Buenos Aires Calcutta Cape Town Dar es Salaam
Delhi Florence Hong Kong Istanbul Karachi
Kuala Lumpur Madras Madrid Melbourne
Mexico City Nairobi Paris Singapore
Taipei Tokyo Toronto Warsaw

and associated companies in
Berlin Ibadan

Oxford is a trade mark of Oxford University Press

Published in the United States
by Oxford University Press Inc., New York

British Library Cataloguing in Publication Data
Data available

Library of Congress Cataloging in Publication Data
Volberda, Henk Wijtze, 1964–
Building the flexible firm: how to remain competitive /
Henk W. Volberda.
p. cm.
Includes bibliographical references (p.   )
1. Organizational change.   2. Strategic management.
3. Competition.   I. Title.
HD58.8V638   1997   658.4'06—dc21   97–33638
ISBN 0–19–829090–X

10 9 8 7 6 5 4 3 2 1

Typeset by Hope Services (Abingdon) Ltd.
Printed in Great Britain
on acid-free paper by
Biddles Ltd.
Guildford & King's Lynn

To Anna and Lisa

FOREWORD
BY H. IGOR ANSOFF

It gives me great pleasure to introduce readers to Henk Volberda's outstanding book.

It arrives at a time when the environment of firms around the world is turbulent and unpredictable—and firms must respond with anticipatory, rapid and flexible behaviour. The book helps managements to succeed in several ways:

- It offers instruments which enable managers to determine whether their firm is flexible and prepared to succeed during the turbulent 21st century.
- The book offers an unusually comprehensive bibliography which comprises most of the literature on Strategic Management and in particular, literature on design and implementation of the design for flexible response.
- The book includes numerous useful diagrams and diagnostic instruments.

Some managers, who grew in the American tradition which says that 'if it 'aint simple it isn't right', might be reluctant to tackle Henk's massive work.

My advice to such managers, which I borrow from the great physicist Albert Einstein, translated into managerial language, says:

In the turbulent environment of the
21st century
the complexity of firms' response to the environment
must match the turbulence in the environment

Henk W. Volberda's book is a must for managers who aspire to be ahead of the competition during the turbulent 21st century.

H. Igor Ansoff
Distinguished Professor of Strategic
Management at United States
University, San Diego, California

The Igor Ansoff Award

The Igor Ansoff Strategic Management Award is an international award given to a person who has distinguished him- or herself by making an outstanding theoretical or practical contribution to the development of strategic management and strategic thinking. The award was established in The Netherlands jointly by Coopers & Lybrand and the Faculty of Technical Business Administration of the University of Twente.

The confinement of the award, in 1997 for the fifth time, is leading to a tradition in selecting a contribution of great importance to the continued development of this field of expertise from the numerous national and international entries submitted.

The founders of the award aim at underlining on one hand the importance of strategic thinking and strategic management as a basis for determining the policy of undertakings in a turbulent environment and in virtually all other sectors of social and business life. At the same time they want many organizations from both the profit and non-profit sector to benefit from the continued development of strategic thinking through the publication of these studies.

The first Igor Ansoff Strategy Award, which was conferred in 1991, was presented to Igor Ansoff himself in recognition of his contribution to the development and refinement of the principles of strategic management and strategic thinking as well as the application of these principles to turbulent environments. Ansoff is regarded as the founder of the concept of strategic management. His work can be seen as an extension of contingency theory, which focuses on the adaptation of corporate structures to altered environments.

In 1993, the Igor Ansoff Strategy Award was conferred on Henk W. Volberda for his work on 'Organizational Flexibility'. Volberda is fascinated by the dynamic relationship within organizations between the necessity of change and targeted planning and control. He postulates that flexibility is strategically important for many organizations. Further, he argues that strategic planning is generally insufficient for firms that operate in turbulent environments (short product life cycles, rapid technological developments, shifting competition relationships, strong fluctuations in turnover volumes, and so on). In such organizations, an unbalanced bias towards planning and control will lead quickly to rigidity and lack of innovation.

The Igor Ansoff Award

The future competitions will again lead to the selection of trendsetting studies which will help to create greater accessibility to innovations and developments in the field of strategic management.

Preface

As a researcher and consultant, I have studied a variety of organizations for more than ten years. In this voyage of discovery, I have been struck by the conflicting forces of change and preservation. How do firms promote order and control, while having to respond, innovate, and learn? As a new graduate in Business Administration, I was impressed by the highly sophisticated structures, the elaborate planning and control systems, the formal job descriptions, and strong corporate values of most of the companies I studied. None the less, these successful firms of the 1970s and early 1980s, still focusing on stability and preservation, had tremendous problems with accelerating competitive change. Some years later, I was surprised by the loose structures, emergent strategies, and weak corporate values of the consulting firms, universities, service firms, and research and development (R&D) institutions I worked for. Although they showed a remarkable capacity for change, innovation, and creativity, they did not have the strategic vision nor coherent culture to efficiently implement change. Despite the clear benefits of these extreme forms, I was convinced that there was a better way to organize that could combine the best of both worlds: the flexible firm. The flexible firm facilitates creativity, innovation, and speed, while maintaining coordination, focus, and control.

Nowadays, changing competitive environments are forcing companies in almost every sector to re-examine their organizational form. There seems to be a growing consensus among managers that the path to future forms of organizing leads away from traditional prescriptions advocating top-down control, rationality, and hierarchy. Managers and practitioners are heralding flexibility as the new hallmark of organizational excellence. Moreover, the business literature on organizational change is replete with prescriptions and directives with regard to the design and management of new organizational forms. Characteristics of such new forms seem to include flatter hierarchies, decentralized decision-making, greater tolerance for ambiguity, empowerment of employees, capacity for renewal, and self-organizing units.

Despite all the business literature offering these signposts for flexible forms, there is relatively little theory on flexibility. Managers in today's competitive environment are engaged in organizational experiments without the guidance of an appropriate theory or framework. Of course, numerous management gurus have

Preface

convincingly promoted the 'one and only' flexible form based on experience with one or a few successful firms. However, a theoretical framework for managing and understanding the conflicting forces of change and preservation that increasingly characterize the flexible firm of the future is lacking. By investigating the paradoxical nature of flexibility, this book develops a strategic framework of flexibility, which allows the reader to discover a variety of flexible forms. Furthermore, a management tool for building flexible firms is presented.

On this voyage of discovery of new flexible forms, I was in good company. I would like to thank the various partners and sponsors of this expedition. First of all, thanks to Charles Baden-Fuller for putting me in touch with Oxford University Press and giving me the opportunity to work on the basic ideas of this book in the autumn of 1995 at City University London. In addition, I want to thank Igor Ansoff for his support and encouragement in writing this book, and Frans van den Bosch of Erasmus University for his helpful comments and suggestions. Parts of this book are based on my Ph.D. dissertation. I owe many thanks to my supervisor Ton de Leeuw of the University of Groningen.

I am also indebted to Coopers & Lybrand for their financial support. Winning the Igor Ansoff Award for my Ph.D. dissertation allowed me to further develop my ideas on strategy and organizational design of the flexible firm. I owe special thanks to Simon Huyzer, initiator of the European Igor Ansoff Award, Willem Bröcker, and Louk Stumpel.

Of course, my colleagues in the Department of Strategic Management and Business Environment of the Rotterdam School of Management also deserve recognition for their valuable suggestions, for listening patiently to my grumbling, and for putting up with my hurried behaviour in the corridor. I especially want to thank the members of the research programme on Strategic Renewal in European-Based Corporations: Wietze van der Aa, Tom Elfring, Eva Meeusen-Henniger, Martin Wielemaker, and Thijs Spigt. The ideas presented in this book led to the development of this research programme.

I appreciate the enthusiasm and recognition I received from the companies involved in the flexibility audit and redesign project: the Dutch Postbank, Philips Semiconductors, the Dutch Gas Corporation, KLM Royal Dutch Airlines, the Dutch PTT Post, Van Ommeren Tank Storage, and Ericsson Telecommunication. They were all valuable in my search for new flexible forms of organization. In this connection, I want to mention some people without whom these flexibility studies could not have been conducted, namely, Joop Hendriks and Jan te Velthuis of the Postbank; Klaas Harms, Arjan Kastelein, and Thijs van Oord of Philips Semiconductors Stadskanaal; Jan Doelman, Simiko Misker, Gerard Reith, and the late Hip de Vries of the Gasunie; Jacques Ancher, Bouby Grin, Nico Giling, Hans Kooiman, and Leo van Wijk of KLM; Hennie Dijkhuis-Potgieser and Sjef Siero of PTT Research; Paul Govaert of Van Ommeren; and Piet Grootenboer, Joop van Troost, and Tom Paffen of Ericsson.

With each of these companies, we had at least twenty semi-structured interviews, two flexibility surveys, and three feedback sessions. Happily, several research assistants accompanied me on this flexibility expedition. I want to thank Judith Jeurissen, Marcel van Leeuwen, Jeroen Dubel, Jeroen Menting, Ronald Boers, Gerda Joppe, Mark Oskam, Carlo Jochems, Marjolijn Dijksterhuis, and especially Bert Flier. Bert Flier not only assisted in the flexibility studies, but also provided me with helpful feedback on this book and compiled the list of references.

Analysis of the data was performed with the software tool, FARSYS, which was particularly useful during the diagnosis phase in the graphical representations of the firm's flexibility. I owe many thanks to Ab Rutges and his research assistants Frits Bouma and Geert-Jan Ringerwöle for developing this system. I am also grateful to GITP International for their financial support in developing this software tool, especially Frank Hüsken, Hanke Lange, and Miel Otto.

My voyage of discovery of new flexible forms was enriched by the many pleasant and stimulating discussions I had with students in the Strategic Management Programme of the Rotterdam School of Management. The class discussions as well as the presentations of empirical group projects helped me fine-tune my line of reasoning and forced me to simplify the flexibility framework. In addition, the many interactions with managers participating in MBA executive and in-company programmes on strategy and organization design (e.g. Analytical Laboratory Management, Dutch Energy Distribution Companies, Dutch Institute on Management, Dutch Strategic Management Society, Dutch Tax Authority, Coopers & Lybrand, Ericsson, Fokker, Hewlett-Packard, KLM, Province North Holland, Rabobank) proved to be extremely useful in developing a framework for helping managers organize for flexibility.

The scientific debates I had with peers in the field, as well as comments from reviewers on previous work, served as the engine for progress. Parts of this book were presented at conferences and workshops of the Strategic Management Society (SMS), the European Institute of Advanced Studies in Management (EIASM), the European Group of Organization Studies (EGOS), European Management and Organizations in Transition (EMOT), Organization Science (OS), and Research in Entrepreneurship (RENT). In alphabetical order, the following academics have been very helpful: Paul Adler, Michiel de Boer, Jan Buijs, Gerrit van Bruggen, John Cantwell, Tim Craig, Yves Doz, Hock-Beng Cheah, Deborah Dougherty, Paul Evans, Charles Galunic, Anna Grandori, Aime Heene, Paul Hirsch, Martijn Hoogeweegen, Wim Hulsink, Marco Huygens, Dong-Jae Kim, Ard-Pieter de Man, Henry Mintzberg, Rudy Moenaert, Jaap Pauwe, Hans Pennings, Sjoerd Romme, Ron Sanchez, and Russel Wright. In addition, the insightful and thought-provoking comments of participants of the Whittemore Conference on Hypercompetition and New Flexible Forms organized by the Amos Tuck School and Organization Science resulted in a

Preface

substantial revision of the framework and typology of flexible forms provided in this book. I owe a great debt of thanks to the editors of a special issue on the subject of Organization Science, Richard D'Aveni, Anne Ilinitch, and especially Arie Lewin. Furthermore, I want to thank some of the authors who participated in this issue, Jon Hanssen-Bauer, Robert Grant, Julia Liebeskind, Anne Smith, and James Richardson.

I would also like to acknowledge the efforts of Wil Geurtsen and Sandra Everts for their help in drafting the complex illustrations. Somehow, they managed to make sense of my illegible handwriting and thumbnail sketches. Moreover, the revision of the English by John Lafkas greatly improved the quality of this book. His suggestions for argumentation were also very helpful. Furthermore, I want to express my gratitude to David Musson of Oxford University Press, who pressed me to set priorities and assisted me with the difficult chore of producing the final manuscript.

Finally, I am grateful to my closest partner in this endeavour, my wife Anna. During the voyage of discovery of flexible forms, she not only gave birth to our daughter Lisa, she also managed to build the flexible family: Anna and Lisa demonstrated flexibility, while I persevered with the manuscript. Many weekends and holidays were spent on this book. Nevertheless, Anna deliberately forced me to put the work I was doing into perspective, while Lisa unintentionally got me to relax by laughing, gurgling, and sometimes crying. This work would not have been accomplished without their support.

Henk W. Volberda

Rotterdam
April 1997

Contents

Contents

List of Figures

List of Figures

List of Tables

List of Tables

List of Abbreviations

ABACUS	Asea Brown Boveri Accounting and CommUnication System
ABB	Asea Brown Boveri
A-entrepreneur	Austrian entrepreneur
BT	British Telecom
CAD	Computer-Aided Design
CAM	Computer-Aided Manufacturing
CEO	Chief Executive Officer
CNC	Computer Numerical Control
CPD	Central Planning Department
DEC	Digital Equipment Corporation
Dutch PTT	Dutch Post, Telegraaf, Telefoon
EDI	Electronic Data Interchange
FAR	Flexibility Audit and Redesign
FARSYS	Flexibility Audit and Redesign SYStem
FFS	Flexible Fabrication System
FMS	Flexible Manufacturing System
FPA	Flexible Production Automation
GB	Glass-Bead Diode
GE	General Electric
GM	General Motors
HP	Hewlett-Packard
HRM	Human Resource Management
ID	Implosion Diode
IOR	Integrated Organization Renewal
ISO	International Standard Organization
IT	Information Technology
ITT	International Telephone and Telegraph

JIT	Just In Time
MBO	Management By Objectives
MIS	Management Information System
MPRS	Medium Power Rectifiers and Stacks
NC	Numerical Control
NCR	National Cash Register
OECD	Organization for Economic Cooperation and Development
OTB	Organizational Transition Board
PC	Personal Computer
PERT	Programme-Evaluation Review Techniques
PMC	Product-Market Combination
POS	Point Of Sale
PPBS	Planning, Programming, and Budgeting System
RBOC	Regional Bell Operating Company
RPS	Redesign Production Systems
S	Stack
S-entrepreneur	Schumpeterian entrepreneur
SWOT	Strengths, Weaknesses, Opportunities, and Threats
TI	Texas Instruments
UPS	United Parcel Services
VAS	Value-Added Services

1   Introduction

> In recent years there has been an amazing amount of verbiage instructing
> managers on how to become 'leading-edge', 'excellent', or 'innovative'—
> yet little of it attends to the practical questions of how to actually get things
> done in organizations. To be sure, there has been a lot of hoopla about the
> 1990s heralding a new area of progressive, nonbureaucratic organization,
> but these New Age ideas are often propounded in such a way as to make
> their translation into action frustrating or even impossible.
>
> (Eccles and Nohria, 1992: 1)

An extensive array of organizational experiments has been under way in many
corporations during the past decade: flattening and downsizing corporations;
re-engineering the business process; subcontracting and outsourcing of non-
core activities; creating multifunctional project teams; empowering employees;
increasing the workforce flexibility (multi-skilled workers); expanding the exter-
nalized workforce (temporary workers); replacing highly specialized machinery
for flexible manufacturing systems; developing multipurpose information
systems.

There is a shared sense among management gurus and practitioners that
these experiments characterize the rise of a new 'flexible firm' (Handy, 1995;
Kanter, 1994; Pasmore, 1994; Peters, 1987). These individuals argue that flexibility is required by every organization. Traditional bureaucratic firms severely
hamper an organization's ability to respond to accelerating competition.
Flexible firms, in contrast, can respond to a wide variety of changes in the competitive environment in an appropriate and timely way. Yet there is an unre-
solved sense about whether the above experiments are interrelated or the
precise ways that they transform contemporary corporations.

1.1 (Mis)conceptions of Flexibility

The concept of flexibility is not entirely new. More than twenty years ago, Steers
(1975) demonstrated, on the basis of seventeen organizational effectiveness
studies, that flexibility was the evaluation criterion mentioned most frequently.

Introduction

Although the issue of organizational flexibility has recently received much attention from researchers, management consultants, and practitioners, its meaning in relation to the functioning of an organization is still ambiguous. Managers intuitively understand flexibility to mean mobility, responsiveness, agility, suppleness, or litheness. The term has a positive connotation: flexible organizations are better. It seems to be the answer to the turbulent, competitive context that organizations face. However, the added value of the construct to the theory and practice of management is in many cases very restricted. We may rightfully ask ourselves if flexibility is used as a magic word or suggests a new business fad. What exactly is a flexible firm? How can flexibility be diagnosed or measured? How should a more flexible organization be developed?

From recent research on flexibility, we can broadly distinguish three distinct approaches to these questions: the general, the functional, and the actor approach. In the first, *general approach*, flexibility is defined by such words as adaptability (Toffler, 1985) or preparedness (Ansoff, 1978) and considered as an essential organizational property for survival. This approach assumes that effective organizations have to cope with acceleration of change in the business environment and need flexibility in order to adapt to the environment or to stimulate renewal and innovation processes. However, these propositions are rather simplistic. First, many organizations still function in a stable environment and are able to plan their activities. Secondly, although an innovation cannot be accomplished without some sort of change, not every change results in an innovation. Thus, flexibility is a necessary but not a sufficient condition for innovation. In this general approach, the discussion of the construct remains superficial and sometimes even results in instrumental slogans on how to improve the firm's flexibility, such as 'get lean and mean', 'make the assets sweat', 'get back to basics', or 'get rid of staff'. As a result, many large firms like IBM (ongoing reorganizations resulting in a 13% reduced headcount by 1993), Xerox (numerous reorganizations in the 1980s), and Philips (launching of the Centurion project in 1990 resulting in the elimination of 67,000 jobs over a three-year period) restructured themselves by using a slash-and-burn approach, cutting staff to the bone without thinking about how the work gets done and rationalizing their portfolios without supporting promising new lines of business. The enforced corporate anorexia made these companies thinner and more efficient, but did not really make them more flexible (Hamel and Prahalad, 1994: 11). Although the general approach has some intuitive appeal—large corporations have to be more responsive and willing to change—the underlying concept of flexibility is too abstract to have any descriptive or prescriptive value.

In the second, *functional approach*, organizational flexibility is reduced to certain aspects of the organization such as flexible employment contracts; flexible forms of financing; flexible production automation; flexible information systems; and the make or buy decision. This approach can be appropriate for well-structured problems. However, organizational flexibility cannot be divided into isolated functional elements. The whole as well as the parts are important; impeccable micro-logic may create macro-nonsense (Van de Ven, 1986). For instance, in many firms quantitative labour flexibility by adjusting the size of their workforce to shifts in demand has not really contributed to the flexibility of these firms, but only obfuscated and further maintained their inflexibility. Kanter (1983), Tushman and Romanelli (1985), and Peters and Waterman (1982) have shown that this 'segmentalistic logic' is severely flawed for managing highly complex and interdependent activities. Flexibility processes are never restricted to a certain aspect, area, or level of an organization. For example, improvement in the flexibility of a production process of a manufacturing organization like Philips Semiconductors makes totally different requirements of the layout (group technology); the assembly of components (modular production); the workforce (upgrading of personnel); stock control; suppliers and raw materials (just-in-time purchasing); and management. Within a service organization like the Dutch Postbank, the provision of more customized services may result in a necessary enlargement of the decision space of employees, an increase of the professional skills of the personnel, and more variable forms of employment (e.g. flexibility in working hours, pooling arrangements for temporary workers, flexible employment contracts). As these examples suggest, organization design for a flexible organization is not a discrete event, but a process for integrating all the essential functions, organizational units, and resources needed to manage the transition from less flexible to more flexible. It requires a significant departure from traditional approaches to organizational design. Flexibility has technical, managerial, organizational, and human resources implications and cannot be treated as an isolated phenomenon.

Finally, the *actor approach* highlights the important roles and traits of different stakeholders in developing flexibility, such as the character of the entrepreneur (uncertainty creating or reducing), management (risk rewarding or risk averse), employees (satisfaction by routines or variety), or customers (innovators, adopters, or laggards (Rogers, 1983; Gatignon and Robertson, 1985)). The personality-based approach to flexibility posits that actors' special personal traits make them prone to stimulating or restricting flexibility (cf. Pasmore, 1994: 47). Its list of traits includes internal locus of control, low aversion to risk-taking, aggressiveness, ambition, and a high need for achievement. This approach assumes that if we want flexible organizations we must first have flexible individuals (Gabor, 1969).

Two problems characterize the personality-based approach to explaining organizational flexibility. First, empirical research does not find strong evidence supporting a single 'flexibility' trait. In fact, it appears that flexibility is very much a contingent phenomenon. For example, flexible organizations need insurgent entrepreneurs (Schumpeter, 1934), mavericks, cowboys (Kanter,

1994), or promoter type of managers to create fundamental new opportunities, and conservative resource preservers, corpocrats, administrators (Kirzner, 1985), or trustee type of managers to exploit these opportunities to the full (Stevenson and Gumpert, 1985).

Secondly, the personality approach may substantially underestimate the impact of managerial and organizational traits, as it holds individual variables to be more important than structural and cultural variables and tends to see organizations in general as negative forces, with actions occurring despite the organization, through accidents, lucky breaks, and bootlegged funds. Kanter (1988) has drawn attention to the importance of 'structural, collective, and social conditions within the organization'. According to her (1988: 197), flexibility is an organizational rather than a purely individual variable. Organizational conditions—structure and social arrangements—can actively stimulate flexibility.

Each of these approaches illustrates that flexibility is perceived as an important phenomenon in management practice and theory. All, however, lack an integrated approach.

1.2 A Strategic Approach

As researchers by and large have either looked at aggregate trends such as downsizing, re-engineering, or empowerment (the general approach), or conversely studied single features of flexibility (the functional and actor approaches), we lack perspective on how these features influence one another. To what degree are these trends, commented on so widely yet empirically little studied, woven together into a coherent strategic approach? Is there just one type of flexible firm? Does every firm face the same competitive challenges? How should we design a flexible corporation?

Many one-time industry leaders that failed to keep up with the accelerating pace of industry change have started experimenting with new flexible forms. Large bureaucratic corporations like IBM, Philips, Xerox, GE, and Volkswagen undertook large-scale transformations in order to recover some of their flexibility. On the other hand, small flexible firms gave up some of their flexibility by participating in networks with other companies that provide complementary assets and skills. Simultaneously, management futurologists have tried to show us a rough sketch of the new flexible landscape, including the virtual corporation (Davidow and Malone, 1992); the hollow corporation; the dynamic network form (Miles and Snow, 1986); the hypertext organization (Nonaka and Takeuchi, 1995); the platform organization (Ciborra, 1996); and the shamrock organization (Handy, 1995). Most of these studies, however, have tried only to justify and rationalize successful adaptive organizational forms (e.g. Sun Microsystems' virtual organization, Dell Computer's dynamic network, Sharp's hypertext form, Olivetti's platform organization, or F International's electronic shamrock), rather than to define new flexible forms in general. None the less, the contributions from management practice and theory illustrate that the flexible form is not simply another business fad, another one-shot programme to be added to all the other things corporations are attempting to do. It represents a fundamentally different set of managing and organizing principles, a different way of conducting corporate life. However, a strategic framework that distinguishes the building blocks needed to analyse and develop flexible forms is lacking.

In this book, we will give the reader a more strategic, integrated approach to flexibility, based on new developments in strategy and organization theory, extensive interviews with practitioners, and detailed case studies of flexibility improvement within large corporations. On the basis of the results of the Flexibility Audit and Redesign Project (FAR project), an empirical study on flexibility improvement within three large Dutch companies (Philips Semiconductors, The Dutch Postbank, The Dutch Gas Company) and ongoing flexibility projects within KLM Royal Dutch Airlines, PTT Post, Van Ommeren Tank Storage, and Ericsson, we will elaborate a strategic framework which helps managers to organize for flexibility.

In this framework, changing competitive environments require fundamentally new management and organizing principles, resulting in alternative flexible forms (see Fig. 1.1). Competitive changes force firms to move more quickly and boldly and to experiment in ways that do not conform to traditional administrative theory. Although traditional organizational forms have worked well in the relatively stable environments of the past, the globalization of markets, rapid technological change, shortening of product life cycles, and increasing aggressiveness of competitors have radically altered the ground rules for competing in the 1990s and beyond. This book addresses the question of how firms should be organized to cope with these changing competitive environments. In their struggle for control, firms have to continuously identify and develop new advantages. This dynamic process requires new organizational forms that are able to explore new opportunities effectively as well as exploit those opportunities efficiently, that allow firms to change their strategic focus easily even while developing and maintaining some strategic direction, and which can change their dominating norms and values as well as correct deviations from essential norms and values. The paradoxical requirements of flexibility imply that balances must be struck if organizational forms are to remain vital. Organizations cannot survive without changes to adapt to changing conditions, yet they must also be stable enough to exploit the changes they have made. How can firms reconcile these conflicting forces?

The framework proposed here suggests two important tasks required to resolve the paradox of flexibility. First, it is argued that flexibility is a managerial

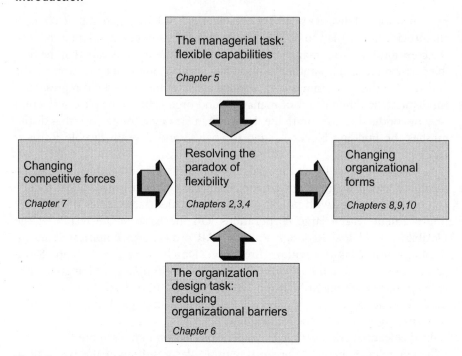

Fig. 1.1. A strategic framework of flexibility

task. Can managers respond at the right time in the right way? In this connection, the concern is with the managerial capabilities that endow the firm with flexibility (e.g. manufacturing flexibility to expand the number of products the firm can profitably offer in the market or innovation flexibility to reduce the response time for bringing new products to market). Secondly, the framework suggests that flexibility is an organization design task. Can the organization react at the right time in the directed way? The concern here is with the controllability or changeability of the organization, which depends on the creation of the right conditions to foster flexibility. For instance, manufacturing flexibility requires a technology with multipurpose machinery, universal equipment, and an extensive operational production repertoire (cf. Adler, 1988). Similarly, innovation flexibility requires a structure of multifunctional teams, few hierarchical levels, and few process regulations (cf. Quinn, 1985; Schroeder *et al.*, 1986).

Combining the managerial and organization design tasks involves a process of matching and resolving paradoxes. Management must develop dynamic capabilities that enhance flexibility, and the firm must have an adequate organizational design to utilize those capabilities. Consequently, management must cope with a constructive tension (Kanter, 1983) between developing capabilities and preserving organizational conditions, which can be considered the building blocks of flexibility. Different companies put these building blocks together in very different ways. From this framework we can therefore obtain several alternative flexible forms, each of which reflects a particular way of coping with the paradox of change and preservation.

1.3 Structure of the Book

The argument in this book is structured around the strategic framework shown in Fig. 1.1. In Chapter 2 we argue that flexibility is a fundamentally new strategic challenge that originates not only from competitive changes in the environment of many organizations, but also from changes in thinking about management and organization. Hence, besides competitive changes in the business environment, changes in dominant management-thinking are described. Both sets of changes are the basis for a postmodern management perspective adopted in this book.

Chapter 3 analyses the contributions of organization theory to the concept of flexibility. Various theoretical perspectives from the field of strategy, business environment, learning, innovation and entrepreneurship help to clarify the paradoxical nature of flexibility, in which change as well as stability is possible.

In Chapter 4, we try to grasp this paradox. First, from an evaluation of definitions of flexibility, essential elements of the concept are identified. Subsequently, on the basis of insights from theories of control, a more comprehensive definition of the concept is derived. In this definition, flexibility is a function of the interaction of two sets of variables: the repertoire of flexible capabilities of management (managerial task) and the potential for flexibility in the design of organizational conditions (organization design task).

Chapter 5 considers the managerial task, which involves the creation of capabilities for situations of unexpected disturbance. The managerial capabilities that endow the firm with flexibility are manifested in the flexibility mix. On the basis of the variety of these capabilities and speed of response, three types of flexibility are distinguished: operational, structural, and strategic flexibility.

The ability to initiate the repertoire of managerial capabilities depends on the design adequacy of organizational conditions, such as the organization's technology, structure, and culture. Those conditions determine the organization's responsiveness. Designing the appropriate organizational conditions requires identifying the types of technological, structural, and cultural changes necessary to ensure effective utilization of managerial capabilities. Chapter 6 provides a systematic discussion of how to analyse and reduce technological, structural, and cultural barriers to flexibility.

Introduction

Chapter 7 considers alternative ways to resolve the paradox of flexibility under various levels of competition. Management must reconfigure the flexibility mix and redesign the organizational conditions in line with future competitive changes (metaflexibility). The more turbulent the environment, the more difficult it is to handle the managerial and organization design tasks. In this chapter, the strategic framework is used to relate the composition of the flexibility mix and the design of organizational conditions to various degrees of environmental turbulence.

In Chapter 8, we study how organizations deal with the paradox of flexibility over time. The strategic framework provided in Chapter 7 helps to generate a rich typology of organizational forms, consisting of the rigid, planned, flexible, and the chaotic mode. None of the forms is a permanent solution of the flexibility paradox of change versus preservation. However, we can obtain from the typology trajectories for coping with competitive change. For many organizations, the transition from a chaotic state towards a 'rigid' organization may be regarded as a 'natural trajectory' or life cycle. Many large corporate giants such as General Electric (GE), IBM, and Philips realized years ago that they went too far with this process of routinization and created extremely rigid organizations. They want to be revitalized in more flexible or even chaotic forms. Some observers argue that older, larger corporations must die off, like dinosaurs, to be succeeded by a new breed better adapted to its environment, in much the same way that has characterized biological evolution. In contrast with this selection perspective, our organizational typology shows several successful trajectories through which large companies can mould themselves into flexible forms that balance corporate discipline with entrepreneurial creativity.

On the basis of the strategic framework and the developed typology, Chapter 9 provides tools and techniques for supporting management efforts directed towards 'revitalization' of mature or declining organizations and 'routinization' of chaotic organizations. In particular, this chapter describes a method for diagnosing organizational flexibility and guiding the transition process, the Flexibility Audit and Redesign (FAR) method. The method was applied in a longitudinal study consisting of three different organizations operating in different, changing environments, namely an administrative (Dutch Postbank), a production (Philips Semiconductors), and a professional organization (Dutch Gas Company). After this study, the method was used by management consultants of GITP International and in research projects of the Rotterdam School of Management of the Erasmus University. Some diagnostic findings of flexibility trajectories within large corporations are presented.

Finally, in Chapter 10, we discuss the managerial and theoretical implications of our framework and typology for the design of the flexible corporation of the future. In particular, we consider four ways to reconfigure the multibusiness corporation to improve its overall flexibility: the network, the dual, the oscillating, and the balanced corporation. Moreover, on the basis of corporate trans-formations in various multiunit corporations (Dutch PTT Post, KLM, Regional Bell Operating Companies), we will show effective dual trajectories of transfor-mation. These trajectories illustrate that there is managerial choice in building flexible firms.

1.4 Who should Read this Book?

The principal aim of this book is to develop a strategic framework and a method for improving organizational flexibility. The rationale for the development of such a method has a managerial, a scientific, a societal, and an educational basis. This book is therefore intended for managers, consultants, policy-makers, as well as management scholars and students.

From a *managerial* point of view, it contributes to the 'tool box' of practition-ers, increasing the practice of management as a profession. Aaker and Mascarenhas (1984) concluded, on the basis of fifty interviews with executives of twenty companies, that alternative ways to increase flexibility tended to be limited and ad hoc rather than comprehensive, systematic, or formal. Ansoff (1965) even declared that it is very difficult to achieve flexibility. In the same vein, Eppink (1978) argued that flexibility is regarded as the answer to the firm's prob-lems, but that the possibilities for enhancing it are largely unexplored. In addi-tion, the literature lacks a comprehensive structuring of the many alternative approaches to flexibility. Judgements about flexibility options tend to be subjec-tive and informal. Flexibility levels are rarely monitored or even measured. This book provides an integrated method for diagnosing organizational flexibility and for guiding the transition process. With the framework and related tools and techniques, managers as well as consultants can expand their range of skills in defining and solving flexibility problems.

From a *scientific* point of view, this book provides both theories and a further development and explication of the design methodology for solving the paradox of flexibility. How do firms reconcile the conflicting forces for change and sta-bility? How do they promote order and control, while having to respond, renew, and learn? Most of the research endeavours in strategy and organization are rooted in stability, not change (cf. Mintzberg, 1990). This book contributes new insights to the design of flexible organizations and strategic trajectories of change for dealing with highly competitive environments. It provides researchers in strategy and organization design with new concepts for exploit-ing the flexibility option in situations in which anticipation is impossible and strategic surprise likely.

From a *societal* viewpoint, this book provides new insights into developing public policies that increase the flexibility of firms for economic adjustment and industrial innovation (cf. Jessop *et al.*, 1991). Flexibility has become a prominent catchword in recent economic and political debates. Aspects of flexibility, particularly labour flexibility, are studied by governmental agencies, labour unions, trade associations, and business associations. Some economists and policy-makers have even heralded the coming of a 'high flex society', pointing to the new social policies required to increase business flexibility by helping individuals be more flexible in their job choices over their lifetimes. Others have pointed to the competitive virtues of small, focused companies participating in a network of other companies, a feature they call flexible specialization (Piore and Sabel, 1984). While this book focuses on a firm-level approach to flexibility, it can produce spin-offs to an industrial and a macro approach to flexibility. The strategic and integrated approach provided in this book, which stresses that there are more or even better ways to become a flexible firm than increasing labour flexibility, may be of interest for policy-makers, economists, human resources managers, and even politicians.

Finally, from an *educational* point of view, this book can be used as the main textbook in courses on strategic flexibility or new organizational forms and as a supplementary textbook in courses on strategy and organization design. The strongly theoretical background, the systematic framework, and the tools and techniques provided in this book make it suitable for both MBA and Ph.D. students in management. In the near future, many of them will find positions in the kinds of flexible companies discussed in this book.

2   A Revision of Management and Organization

Acceleration of change takes place in our minds as well as in our environment. . . . The most important change . . . is in the way we try to understand the world, and in our conception of its nature. However, the large and growing literature on change and its management focuses on its objective rather than subjective aspects. It assumes that most of the managerial problems created by change derive from its rate. This may be true, but it is apparent that we cannot deal with change effectively unless we understand its nature.

(Ackoff, 1981: 5).

In this chapter, the importance of flexibility is considered at length. It is argued that flexibility is a fundamentally new strategic challenge. Our explanation of this challenge is not limited to an illustration of the major competitive changes most organizations are struggling with, but also includes a concise description of the changes in our thinking about management and organization.

To begin, some objective competitive changes in the environment are portrayed (Sect. 2.1). They illustrate the importance of flexibility for organizational effectiveness. Moreover, our view of the world changes. We cannot cope effectively with change unless we develop an appropriate view of the world. While managers used to think of their organizations in terms of stability, order, optimality, and uniformity, they now prefer to associate them with change, chaos, creativity, diversity, and novelty. Hence, the changes in the dominant management-thinking in interaction with major management and organization theories are described (Sect. 2.2). From the examination of these objective and subjective changes, we then develop the perspective of management followed in this book (Sect. 2.3).

2.1 Acceleration of Competitive Change

While every competitive change is a specific case for an organization and requires a unique response by the management involved, there are some trends of the last three or four decades that are typical for many organizations. We do not mean to suggest that every organization is confronted with these specific challenges; our intention is to show that changes have occurred and that many organizations have had to deal with multiple and sometimes contradictory criteria of effectiveness.

New Competitive Demands

In the 1950s and 1960s, *efficiency* was the most important criterion for organizations. This development was dictated by a major change in technology: a far-reaching transition from craft work to mass production (Toffler, 1985). Productivity in terms of quantity was the key objective. It essentially meant doing more of the same things: by specialization in well-defined market segments, management wanted to exploit economies of scale or repetition effects. This so-called learning curve effect resulted in accumulated experience with decreasing per-unit costs. Learning by doing (Arrow, 1962)[1] was possible because most markets were sellers' markets and seemed to have unlimited growth potential.

Efficiency was obtained largely by standardization. In the past, the organization which could most effectively standardize all its processes would certainly outperform its competitors (Toffler, 1985). Management tried to optimize everything inside the organization and ignored the competitive environment. The increased standardization of jobs and specialization of management tasks resulted in a separation of thinking and doing and a further splitting up of individual management tasks and jobs. Attempts were made to achieve strong control and coordination in order to assure stability; coordination and control became distinct goals instead of means of reaching certain goals. This closed systems approach resulted in control-oriented organizations, with complex structures and simple, routine, monotonous tasks.

Then, in the 1970s, *quality* became an additional important criterion. Customers became more quality-oriented and required higher levels of 'service' and more 'value for their money'. Moreover, markets became more open as a result of decreased entry barriers and intensive international competition. There was no more elasticity or slack within the efficiency norms; further standardization did not cause further reductions in costs. The only way to distinguish an organization from its competitors was excellence. This situation implied doing more of the same in a perfect way; not only offering the right price, but also the best products and services.

Now, *flexibility* is a necessary complement to efficiency and quality. Managers in a broad array of industries agree that achieving low cost and high quality is no longer enough to guarantee success. In the face of fierce, low-cost competition and an army of high quality suppliers, companies are increasingly concentrating on flexibility as a way to achieve new forms of competitive advantage (Upton, 1995). According to Morgan: 'Changing circumstances call for different kinds of action and response. Flexibility and capacities for creative action thus become more important than narrow efficiency. It becomes more important to do the right thing in a way that is timely and "good enough" than to do the wrong thing well, or the right thing too late' (Morgan, 1986: 35). Figure 2.1 illustrates the accumulation of competitive demands and conflicting performance criteria. Consumer demands proliferate and are communicated more effectively and vigorously to firms; there is a shift from sellers' to buyers' markets. Various markets are saturated as a result of overcapacity. Product life cycles are often so short that organizations do not have sufficient time for learning by doing. Still, customers demand ever more choice. For example, organizations have to be able to offer a variety of products and services in small quantities within ever shorter delivery times. Furthermore, they have to cope with variable delivery times, tailor-made products and services, a broadly varying product and service range, and fast-changing lot sizes and sales volumes. Customers expect organizations both to satisfy their individual needs and to maintain a reasonable relationship between price and quality.

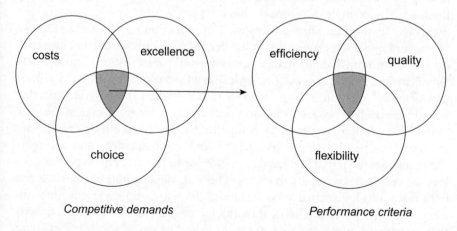

Competitive demands   *Performance criteria*

Fig. 2.1. Accumulation of competitive demands and conflicting performance criteria

Flexibility Gains

How do firms cope with the conflicting demands? According to Porter's generic strategies (1980), firms should choose to satisfy only one of these demands in order to achieve a sustainable competitive advantage. Firms that try to satisfy two or even three are significantly handicapped. More recently, however, management scholars have portrayed multiple-performance criteria as a staircase (Baden-Fuller and Stopford, 1994) or escalation ladders of competition (D'Aveni, 1994). Firms have simultaneously to compete on costs, excellence, and choice. They are under intense pressure to find new ways to increase efficiency, improve quality, and offer flexibility at the same time, as depicted by the intersection in Figure 2.1. Emphasis on only one criterion can trap an organization in an endless cycle of failure.

For instance, US automobile producers focused for a long time on achieving low costs and fell into the efficiency trap. In their mass-production systems, high quality required more checking and reworking of substandard parts. Toyota's lean production system approach to quality, however, showed that high quality may cost less (Womack *et al.*, 1990). Toyota's combination of efficiency with quality had a devastating effect on European and US car producers. While US car producers are now catching up on efficiency and quality, Japanese producers are setting new competitive hurdles relating to flexibility: breathtaking engine performance, razor-sharp handling, luxury, new design aesthetics, and product development aimed at lifestyle niches (Hamel and Prahalad, 1994).

Firms can also become trapped by focusing too much on quality. Such firms have spent much effort in mastering efficiency and quality at the cost of reduced flexibility. For example, McDonald's has long concentrated on its powerful formula of increasing efficiency and quality. Through a limited menu and a high set of standard operating procedures, it has been able to provide outstanding quality and superior price performance across its whole organization (Upton, 1993). Simplicity and limited range allowed McDonald's to concentrate on the process that delivered this range to its customers rather than the coordination that would have been necessary to accommodate a larger range. However, the saturation of its existing market, fierce competition from chains offering wider variety with competitive prices like Chili's and Olive Garden, and changing customer tastes required McDonald's to increase its product offerings. None the less, the emphasis on quality in terms of very detailed operations manuals and tight cultural rules made it very difficult to develop flexibility in meeting customers' changing needs. This quality trap forced McDonald's to stick narrowly to 'hamburgers' until growing complaints from McDonald's franchisees about the limited product range forced it to develop new menu items such as the Egg McMuffin, Chicken McNuggets, the McBarbecue, and the salad bar. Consequently, its original menu of nine items has become much more extensive (at least fifty-five items in 1992).

The same quality trap was experienced by the Dutch Postbank. Management's focus on efficiency and quality through tight production norms and quality norms had a negative influence on the firm's flexibility. The organization's aim was to reach zero per cent of errors in its service process. As a result, its employees could not make any exceptions to rules when providing financial services to clients. The detailed manuals and procedures, as well as the fear of making errors decreased workers' ability to quickly and easily provide custom-made services and contributed to longer delivery times.

These examples show that many firms are stuck with quality. Divisions of IBM, General Motors, and Digital Equipment Corporation (DEC) have all won the Baldrige award for quality, but providing excellent products is not enough. The one-sided attention to efficiency norms and quality standards (e.g. ISO 9,000 accreditation) in many firms creates barriers to improving flexibility. These firms have analysed and formalized the primary process in such a way that an increase in flexibility is possible only at the cost of efficiency or quality. For these firms, increasing flexibility is a zero-sum game; an increase in flexibility has to be compensated by a decrease in efficiency or quality.

Possibilities for Implementing Flexibility

But how can firms realize flexibility gains without losing efficiency and quality? The transitory nature of many competitive demands strongly indicates that flexibility in the face of change is, or ought to be, a defining characteristic of organizational effectiveness. There are two important enablers for implementing organizational flexibility without reductions in efficiency and quality levels.

First, changes in *production technology*, such as developments in computer-aided technology and information systems, promote the production of tailor-made products and services without the loss of economies of scale. In the past, flexibility and efficiency were considered to be mutually exclusive (Bowman, 1973; Eppink, 1978). This no longer has to be the case. Using multi-purpose machinery and equipment, like computer numerically controlled (CNC) machines, computer-aided design (CAD), and computer-aided manufacturing (CAM) systems, or robotics in the form of flexible fabrication systems (FFS), manufacturing firms have the possibility of increasing the variety of their products and of decreasing set-up times for these products. As a consequence, economies of scale can be reached within smaller lot sizes. The same possibility applies to service organizations, which may now extend and diversify their packages of services, instead of just supplying universal services, because of developments in information systems technology.

In addition, there are now new smart production concepts that firms can use to achieve flexibility even while they still employ old inflexible technologies (Morroni, 1991). For instance, applying the principles of just-in-time (JIT) purchasing, organizations can offer a large assortment and short delivery times without needing large supplies. Also, the modular production concept gives organizations the opportunity to combine economies of scale with increased choice; standard components can be produced in large series, while a variety of products can be assembled through changes in the configuration of components. Sony, for example, leveraged more than 160 Walkman models from five modular platform designs in the 1980s.

Secondly, changes in *labour markets* facilitate higher levels of flexibility. There is a growing social pressure to increase the quality of working life, which depends on the discretion or degree of self-control of organizational participants.[2] Self-control increases when participants are engaged in a wide variety of tasks associated with producing products and services, as well as when they gain more influence over these tasks (Mintzberg, 1979: 75). It results in an integration of thinking and doing, thereby reducing coordination and communication problems. Consequently, gains in flexibility can be reached without losses in quality and efficiency. Instead of eliminating individual autonomy and optimizing central control, flexibility thus requires a further extension of the worker's control capacity by making proper use of management's most valuable resources: the complex and multiple capacities of people. Instead of traditional production workers who are involved only in narrow repetitive production tasks or information workers who are processing small pieces of data, the workforce of the flexible firm is represented by the 'knowledge worker' (cf. Drucker, 1993; Nonaka and Takeuchi, 1995; Quinn, 1992). The core of a software company like Microsoft, a consulting firm like McKinsey, or a Dutch temping agency like Randstad consists mainly of these knowledge workers. They do not simply transform raw materials into products or data into information, but have unique skills to create new products and services. Because of their know-how (e.g. technological know-how, understanding of the customer, creativity) they are engaged in a variety of activities such as product development, product design, and marketing presentation. The higher level of education of an increasing number of participants in organizations supports this tendency. Flexibility may thus improve the quality of working life by giving participants more tasks, authority, and responsibility. Participants can influence the standard operating norms they are supposed to meet. Consequently, traditional structures are becoming less viable, not only because of their lack of flexibility, but also because of the changing professional needs of potential participants.

Of course, the exploitation of the above opportunities (flexible production, broader jobs) may lead to *new rigidities*. For example, in a study of flexible production automation (Boerlijst *et al.*, 1985), it was argued that FPA requires a more formal planning of work and results in an enlargement of the planning and control cycle. Decisions in one part of the organization strongly affect other parts of the organization. It is no longer possible to take ad hoc decisions to solve a problem without taking into account the consequences for these other parts; a small error in one department will have far-reaching consequences for other departments.[3] In addition, these new opportunities entail certain costs. New technologies and broader jobs require an upgrading of personnel; a higher level of autonomy for individual workers demands multiple skills and more comprehensive knowledge. Instead of complex structures with simple tasks, simple structures and complex tasks are required. Secondly, these new technologies and broad jobs require more individual authority and responsibility. More flexibility implies that one has to know which procedure has to be used in which situation. The following pronouncement of a worker in an assembly department of DAF Trucks illustrates this aspect: 'The stupid work is declining slowly but steadily. There is less dragging and grinding, because the supplies are low. However, we do need much more individual control in order to smooth the production process.' The more flexibility is introduced into the production facility, the more complex the production process becomes, thus requiring decision support systems to assist the workers in scheduling and controlling the system (cf. Muller *et al.*, 1987).

The opportunities and constraints of technology for organizational flexibility and the relationship between flexibility and efficiency will be further discussed in Chapter 6, where we will present technological barriers to flexibility. At this point, we wish only to emphasize that changes in technology and labour markets can contribute to increasing possibilities for flexibility gains without losses in quality and efficiency. As illustrated in Figure 2.2, there are three related forces explaining the growing needs and opportunities for organizational flexibility, namely market, labour, and technological forces.

First, market forces are responsible for a fast-growing de-standardization of customer needs (Toffler, 1985). Firms have to offer choice in order to cope with quantitative and qualitative changes on both the supply and demand side. At the same time, the further sophistication of technology makes possible greater customization of products and services. In addition, changes in labour such as the higher education levels of new entrants as well as their growing demands with respect to tasks and responsibilities facilitate higher levels of flexibility. If the need for flexibility is balanced by new technological and labour possibilities, flexibility can be built atop efficiency and quality. If not, flexibility gains have to be compensated for by efficiency or quality losses.

2.2 Changes in Dominant Management-Thinking

In addition to real changes, perspectives on management have changed. Changes in the competitive environment have had major consequences for our thinking about management and vice versa. It is hard to find managers who refer to their organizations as stable, orderly, and non-changing. There seems to be a growing consensus among managers that the path to future forms of

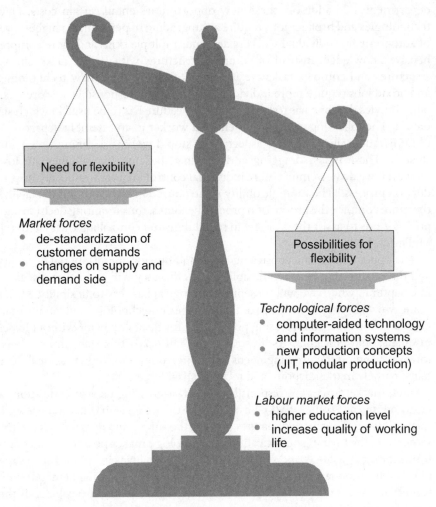

Fig. 2.2. Need for flexibility versus possibilities for flexibility

organizing leads away from traditional prescriptions advocating top-down control, rationality, and hierarchy as the hallmarks of organizational excellence. Furthermore, these perspectives are emerging at the forefront of the management literature (cf. Peters, 1992; Senge, 1990). By reconsidering the underlying management and organizing principles, we can analyse the changes in dominant perspectives on management.

The Classical Management Perspective

During this century, theoretical and practitioner-oriented thinking about management and organizations has been dominated largely by the normative propositions of classical theories. In the light of this pattern, it is interesting to note that the widespread application of the normative propositions of classical theories is a relatively new phenomenon. In the nineteenth century, both business and government operated with relatively flat organizational structures based on 'traditional' or 'patrimonial' authority relations (Perrow, 1986). In response to the weakening of primary institutions such as family and church, and the technological advances of the Industrial Revolution such as railways, telegraphs, and telephones, a new, 'classical', management perspective evolved that facilitated the rise of the bureaucratic organization with a focus on standardization and mass production (Lewin and Stephens, 1993). Recognizing that the 'new' classical management approach at the beginning of the twentieth century was itself a relatively recent invention makes it easier for us to consider the possibility that there may be other viable management perspectives of organization (Low, 1989).

There are four literatures that, taken together, provide both the intellectual substance and the legitimacy for the classical management perspective. They are (1) scientific management, (2) classical organization theory, (3) classical economics, and (4) bureaucratic theory.

Taylor (1911) was a crusader for '*scientific management*'. He argued that the old system, where management left it up to the workers to work out how to get the job done, was hopelessly inefficient. In response to traditional management, scientific management combined a study of the physical capabilities of a worker with an economic approach that viewed the individual as driven by fear of physical and mental starvation and the search for monetary rewards (Kilmann, 1977: 19). Management's function was to determine 'scientifically' the best procedures for performing every task, to select and train workers in following these procedures, and to provide financial rewards for compliance (Taylor, 1911: 59–60). However, it was not only, or even primarily, the lot of the workers that was to be altered by the introduction of scientific management; the role of management itself was also to be transformed (Scott, 1987: 36). Taylor's aim was to replace the arbitrary and capricious activities of managers with analytical, scientific procedures (Taylor, 1947: 189, 211). The activities of both managers and workers were to be rationalized; both were to be equally subject to the regimen of science.[4] The resulting contribution to the classical management approach was a perspective on job design that separates thinking from doing, focuses on the individual worker as opposed to the group, and stresses economic incentives as the sole source of motivation.

A Revision of Management and Organization

Whereas Taylor and his disciples proposed to rationalize the organization 'bottom-up' beginning with the individual job, *classical administrative theorists* worked 'top-down' (Scott, 1987: 37). Unlike scientific management, classical administrative management was concerned with the overall design of the organization, such as the process of dividing the organization into departments, coordinating the departments, managing the hierarchy, and so on (Kilmann, 1977: 20). Fayol suggested that managerial processes such as planning, organizing, directing, coordinating, and controlling are requirements for efficient and effective task fulfilment (Fayol, 1949; Kilmann, 1977: 19–20). He and his followers sought to develop 'principles' of rational organization, such as 'unity of command', 'span of control', 'exception', 'departmentalization', and the 'line-staff' principle. These principles increasingly came under attack for being mere truisms or common-sense pronouncements, and for being based on questionable premises. Their main weakness, however, was not so much that they provided an inadequate theory of motivation, or their prescriptive cast, as their failure to provide conditional generalizations, that is, statements that include the limits of their applicability to particular situations or types of organizations.

While scientific management and classical administrative theory have had a lasting effect on management practice, it was classical economic theory and Weber's theory of bureaucracy that provided intellectual legitimacy for the classical management perspective. *Classical economic theory* had its origins in the ideas of Adam Smith, who set forth the principles of specialization in his work entitled *An Inquiry into the Nature and Causes of the Wealth of Nations* (1776). Classical economics views the firm as having a single purpose, namely the maximization of profit. The firm is seen as the instrument of the entrepreneur, with all other organizational participants being supplied by the market at the going rate. This view of the organization as a solitary actor with a single objective or goal is a key part of the classical economic theory.[5]

However, it is Weber (1946) who provided the greatest insight into the classical management perspective, and perhaps did the most to legitimize it. He suggested that all organizations were moving towards an ideal type of structure, a bureaucracy characterized by a high degree of specialization or division of work at all organizational levels, a hierarchy of authority, the use of a set of rules and procedures for conducting daily organizational functions, and impersonality in decision-making (Kilmann, 1977: 18). The emergence of this 'rational-legal' ideal form of management and organization was seen as a response to the problems associated with the traditional and charismatic form of leadership. Rational-legal authority rests on a belief in the 'legality' of patterns of normative rules and the right of those elevated to authority under such rules to issue commands. By contrast, charismatic authority[6] is too transitory to result in the formation of a permanent organizational structure, and traditional authority[7] leaves an organization subject to the arbitrary and capricious acts of its leader.

By comparing bureaucracy based on rational-legal authority to the traditional structure, Weber provided the most sophisticated argument for the legitimization of the classical management perspective.

Taken together, the ideas of scientific management, classical administrative and economic theory, and bureaucratic theory provide the theory and rules for the practice of the dominant management perspective of this century. Scientific management provides the rationale for job design. Classical organizational theory provides the guidelines for overall design. Classical economic theory provides the rationale for pursuing the single goal of maximization of profits, which deals with employees as variable costs and deals with other firms on a transactional basis. Bureaucratic theory provides the rationale for hierarchical authority relations.

In this classical management perspective, organizations are considered as *machines*—single-purpose mechanisms designed to transform specific inputs into specific outputs, and capable of engaging in different activities only if they are explicitly modified or redesigned for that purpose (Morgan, 1986: 35). This machine metaphor has dominated the practice of management and organization: 'The universe was frequently compared to a hermetically sealed clock. This is a very revealing comparison, implying that it had no environment. Like a clock, its behaviour was thought to be determined by its internal structure and the causal law of nature' (Ackoff, 1981: 11).

According to Scott (1987: 99), the classical management perspective is a *closed rational approach*, which portrays organizations as tools designed to achieve preset ends and which ignores or minimizes the perturbations and opportunities posed by connections to a wider environment.

Some ideas in this perspective are still being reinforced under the guise of modern management. For example, classical management theorists recognized the necessity of reconciling the contrary requirements of centralization and decentralization to preserve an appropriate flexibility in different parts of large organizations. In recent years, the ability to achieve this kind of decentralization has been greatly advanced through highly technical management systems, such as management by objectives (MBO), planning, programming, and budgeting systems (PPBS), or programme-evaluation review techniques (PERT), all developed and widely adopted to facilitate rational decision-making within complex organizational systems. In particular,

MBO is now often used to impose a mechanistic system of goals and objectives on an organization. These are then used to control the direction in which managers and employees can take the organization, e.g., through the development of performance targets consistent with these goals. The same often happens with PPBS and other budgeting systems, with MIS being used to provide the detailed information necessary to implement the controls on a monthly, weekly, and even daily basis. (Morgan, 1968: 29)

Furthermore, successful companies such as McDonald's are basically extensions and improvements of the Tayloristic principles of division of labour and detailed work procedures (cf. Baden-Fuller and Stopford, 1994: 54), as they have perfected a method of delivering a standardized product at low cost. In addition, their emphasis on a common culture and on-the-job training has helped the company neutralize many negative consequences of the classical form. None the less, the whole thrust of the classical management perspective and its modern application is to suggest that organizations can or should be rational systems that operate in as efficient a manner as possible. This *technical rationality* consists of instrumental and economic criteria (Thompson, 1967: 14–15). The instrumental criterion requires that specified actions do in fact produce the desired outcome, whereas the economic criterion requires that results are obtained with the least necessary expenditure of resources. The economic dimension, however, can be considered only after the instrumental dimension is understood. Unfortunately, classical management sometimes gave more attention to the economic dimension than to the instrumental question.

The Modern Management Perspective

To say that this perspective and related issues of technical rationality have dominated our thinking about management is not to say that it had no critics (see Fig. 2.3). It has been revised several times since it first came under empirical scrutiny. For the moment, we will confine ourselves to a short outline of criticism from major schools in organization theory.

In the 1930s, the human relations movement founded by Elton Mayo emphasized the importance of social relations among organizational participants (Khandwalla, 1977: 133). By illustrating the inhumane aspects of classical concepts, the human relations movement challenged scientific management's basic assumptions about job design and motivation.

In the 1940s, Herbert Simon expounded the concept of bounded rationality, which asserted that the administrative decision-maker had limited reasoning, perceiving, and information-processing abilities. Simon thus attacked the perfect rationality assumptions of traditional economists and the universalistic prescriptive character of classical organization theory. In place of the 'economic man', motivated only by self-interest and completely informed about all available alternatives, Simon substituted a more human 'administrative man', who seeks to pursue his own interests but does not always know what they are, is aware of only a few of all the possible alternatives, and is willing to settle for an adequate solution instead of an optimal one (Scott, 1987: 45–46).

In 1950, Eric Trist of the Tavistock Institute of Human Relations brought the sociotechnical systems viewpoint to bear on organization behaviour. This

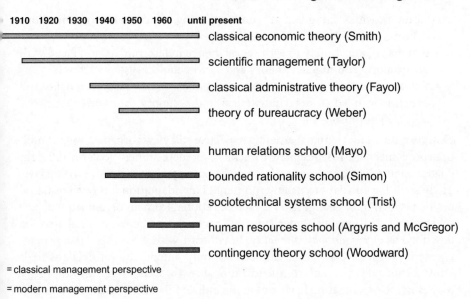

Fig. 2.3. The classical management perspective and major schools in reaction to it

stressed that a work group is subject to social, psychological, technical, and economic forces.

In the mid-1950s, Chris Argyris and Douglas McGregor developed their models of desirable organizations in which human needs would be more fully satisfied and a fuller use could be made of human capital. While the human relations school sought only to modify classical organizational theory (Mayo, 1933), the behavioural humanists have been inclined to seek radical change (Kilmann, 1977: 21). In reaction to numerous revisions of the classical approaches to design and management of organizations, they began to emphasize change in social systems processes for improving organizational effectiveness.

In 1958, Joan Woodward laid the basis for contingency theory, based upon the observation that differences in the structures of organizations depend on differences in the technology they employ. She revealed the inappropriateness of universal principles of organizations and brought out their situational character.

These schools of thought provide the basis of modern organization theory. Their insights into management and organization resulted in a new management perspective, which recognizes:

- that an organization possesses properties of a natural system[8] (human relations and human resources school) as well as of a rational system[9] (bounded rationality school): each approach gives some insight, but neither

23

alone provides an adequate understanding of complex organizations (Thompson, 1967: 8);
- that an organization is an *open system*, hence indeterminate and faced with uncertainty (contingency theory and sociotechnical systems school);
- that an organization is at the same time subject to criteria of rationality and hence is in need of determinateness and certainty (bounded rationality school; Thompson, 1967: 10).

However, the modern management perspective still views organizations as multipurpose mechanisms designed to achieve predetermined goals in different environments. The organization is viewed as an organism that strives to survive. To do so, it has to adapt to its environment. This adaptation, however, is based on the prediction of changes and therefore rational from an organizational perspective. The rationality underlying this revised perspective is what may be described as *organizational rationality*. In contrast with what the classical management perspective suggests, humans are only 'intendedly rational', as their limited capacities prevent complete rationality. In a larger sense, rationality resides in the organization itself, not in the individual participants—in rules that assure that participants will behave in ways calculated to achieve desired objectives, in control arrangements that evaluate performance and detect deviance, in reward systems that motivate participants to carry out prescribed tasks, and in the set of criteria by which participants are selected, replaced, and promoted. The concept of organizational rationality derives from the way people and jobs fit together in a fixed design. Just as in the classical management perspective, great emphasis is still placed on control by certain structural arrangements. The modern management perspective justifies these arrangements as being in the service of rationality: control is the means of channelling and coordinating behaviour so as to achieve specified goals.

Towards a New Management Perspective

The organizational rationality of the modern management perspective contrasts with the '*substantial rationality*' view of organizations, in which people are encouraged to determine whether what they are doing is appropriate, and to adjust their actions accordingly (cf. Clegg, 1990: 155; Morgan, 1986: 37). Substantial rationality implies that organizational participants are able to perceive or to experience reality as a meaningful and coherent whole, giving sense to their actions within the organization. Whereas under the control ethos, actions are rational because of their defined place within the whole, substantial rationality requires actions that are informed by intelligent awareness of the complete situation. Whereas intended rationality is in its roots mechanical, substantial rationality is reflective and self-organizing; firms built on substantial rationality possess an inherent ability to reorganize and renew themselves in meaningful ways.

It is possible to develop the concept of substantial rationality by using the brain as a metaphor for organization (cf. Morgan, 1986: 78; Garud and Kotha, 1994). The brain is a self-organizing system capable of responding rapidly to a broad range of external stimuli. To the extent that we build organizations on classical or modern principles, we develop technical or organizational rationality, respectively, where people are valued for their ability to fit in and contribute to the efficient operation of a predetermined structure. Such organizations encourage people to obey orders and keep their place rather than to take an interest in, challenge, and question what they are doing. This mode of organization is sufficient for performing a fixed task in stable circumstances or changing tasks in predictable circumstances. When these conditions are violated (as illustrated in Sect. 2.1), however, organizations designed along these lines encounter many problems. In situations of change, it is necessary to improve our ability to organize in a way that promotes flexibility. Under changing circumstances, it is important that participants of the organization are able to question the appropriateness of what they are doing and to modify their action to take account of new situations: 'This requires an organizing capacity that is "substantially" rational, in the sense that action manifests intelligence of the relations within which the action is set: substantially rational action is not undertaken blindly but in an awareness that it is appropriate' (Morgan, 1986: 78).

The principles underlying substantial rationality have been developed into a postmodern management perspective, which represents a set of organizing principles fundamentally different from those of bureaucracy. Whereas the modern management perspective was premised on an increasing functional differentiation in organizations (e.g. division of labour, line / staff distinction, hierarchical differentiation) and management as the central organizing principle, the postmodern perspective is characterized by a reverse process of integration: a blurring of the boundaries between what, under a modernist impulse, would have been recognized as distinct phenomena (Clegg, 1990: 11). In this perspective, the question of whether organizations are closed or open systems is not important. Instead, organizations tend to maintain their existence by opening up in particular ways to the environment. The sharp dichotomy between organizations and environments is misleading. Environments are as much part of organizations as production technologies, organizational structures, and cultures. If we put ourselves 'inside' such systems, we may come to realize that we are within a closed system of interaction and that the environment is part of the organization because it is part of its domain of essential interaction. This perspective may be necessary if we attempt to understand these systems' inner logic (Maturana and Varela, 1980). If we put ourselves 'outside' such systems,

TABLE 2.1. Changes in perspectives of management

Dominant management perspective	Rationality concept	Environmental approach	Organizational approach	Dominant metaphor
classical management	technical rationality	closed system approach	rational system approach	machine
modern management	organizational rationality	open system approach	rational/natural system approach	organism
postmodern management	substantial rationality	open/closed system approach	natural system approach	brains

we may come to realize that they are open systems. A recapitulation of the management perspectives discussed is presented in Table 2.1.

2.3 A Postmodern Management Perspective

On the basis of the perceived changes in the competitive environment and successive revisions of 'rationality', a new management perspective has evolved. Initially, order, stability, and control were emphasized. As a consequence of the overestimation of the controllability of the organization and the simultaneous underestimation of self-control and the impact of environmental uncertainties, management theory has been dominated by rational thinking, which was first technical and later organizational. At present, changeability, variability, instability, and agility are receiving more attention.

Inside the organization, with its traditional methods, people, and organizational structures, routine responses no longer work. Outside the organization, a totally new and unknown environment is emerging (Toffler, 1985). Moreover, the tensions between the complexity of the organization and the variability of the environment are becoming more visible. While the internal complexity of the organization, caused by technically and organizationally rational thinking, has a negative effect on the flexibility and controllability of the organization, these latter properties are of vital importance. As Haselhoff (1977) proposes, management is 'to give a free hand' instead of only 'intervening'.

Rosemary Stewart (1983: 82–97) described these changes in several dimensions on the basis of empirical research (see Table 2.2). Her picture, which has been built up from empirical studies of how managers behave, gives a very

TABLE 2.2. Changes in dimensions of management

From:	To:
• orderly	• disjointed, fragmented
• planned	• instinctive/reactive
• vertical relationships	• lateral relationships
• stable relationships	• developing and maintaining reciprocal relationships
• formal information	• informal, speculative information
• predetermined goals	• individual and group goals

Source: Adapted from Stewart (1983).

different impression from the traditional one that underlies many of the writings on management. Traditional descriptions of managerial functions include planning, organizing, and controlling. The emphasis in those descriptions, and in much writing on decision-making, is on logical, sequential processes. These characteristics are supposed to be applicable to all managerial activities. While the findings of these studies do not negate the traditional conceptions, they represent a major shift in emphasis.

As a consequence of this shift (see Table 2.3), rigid classical and planned modern organizations are being replaced by flexible postmodern organizations (Clegg, 1990: 181; Lewin and Stephens, 1993). Where classical and modern organizations were premised on mass production, the postmodern organization is premised on flexible specialization. Where classical and modern organization were premised on technological determinism, postmodern organization is premised on technological choices made possible through flexible manufacturing

TABLE 2.3. Towards a new management perspective

Classical	Modern	Postmodern
• mass production		• flexible specialization
	• technological determinism	• multi-purpose machinery and information systems
• highly differentiated, deskilled jobs		• multiskilled jobs
• tight employment relations		• networking and subcontracting

systems and multipurpose information systems. Where classical and modern organization and jobs were highly differentiated, demarcated, and deskilled, post-modern organization and jobs are highly de-differentiated, de-demarcated, and multiskilled. Where classical and modern organization were based on tight employment relations, postmodern organization develops more complex and fragmentary relational forms, such as subcontracting and networking.

Examples of firms with clearly postmodern characteristics are Asea Brown Boveri (ABB), a Swedish–Swiss conglomerate producing electrical and power-related products, Benetton, an Italian textile retailer-producer, Nike, a US-based company in the athletic footwear and clothing business, and Océ van der Grinten, a Dutch photocopier and office equipment manufacturer. The production of all of these companies is based largely on networks of small, flexible producers. For instance, 90 per cent of the components of Océ's copy machines are obtained from a regional network of suppliers and co-developers in the south of The Netherlands. In addition, these firms' production systems can respond quickly to changes in supply and demand, and they all have broad information systems that can be used for various purchasing, production, and distribution decisions. Benetton's rapid response factory systems and its real-time retailer information system enables it to introduce new products quickly and cheaply. ABB's fully automated ABACUS (Asea Brown Boveri Accounting and CommUnication) system provides accurate and timely information to field operations and helps group executives to evaluate performance. Moreover, all these companies have a core of highly educated knowledge workers and a peripheral flexible labour force consisting of part-time and temporary workers. Yearly, Océ invests 7 per cent of its turnover in research and development, the core of the corporation. This consists of highly qualified technicians, professionals, and managers. By contrast, 25 per cent of the assembling is done by temporary workers while a large part of the production workforce has one-year contracts. Nike's core consists of R&D and marketing experts. By heavily staffing itself with specialists in biomechanics, exercise physiology, engineering, and industrial design, Nike is able to stay at the forefront in athletic footwear research and development (Miles and Snow, 1994). Finally, instead of a vertical hierarchy, these firms employ a web of strategic partners in supply and distribution. For instance, Nike has long-established relationships with a broad network of suppliers and distributors around the world.

In Chapter 3, some theoretical contributions to this postmodern management perspective are examined. These theories on strategy, organization–environment relationships, learning, innovation and entrepreneurship may improve our understanding of flexibility and our ability to organize in a manner that promotes flexibility. This does not mean, however, that the classical and modern theories are no longer relevant. The success of McDonald's shows that there is much greater accumulation of knowledge within the discipline of management and organization than we think. By discussing these postmodern theories, we will illustrate the tensions within organizational theory. These tensions, which exist between alternative theories, will be constructively used in order to address the paradoxical nature of organizational flexibility.

Notes

1. Arrow characterized the learning that comes from developing skills in manufacturing as 'learning by doing'. The concept of improvement by learning from experience has been subsequently elaborated by the Boston Consulting Group and others to include improvements in production processes, management systems, distribution, sales, advertising, worker training, and motivation. This enhanced learning process, which has been shown for many products to reduce full costs by a predictable percentage every time volume doubles, is called the experience curve.

2. Quality of working life is defined here from a socio-technical systems perspective instead of an individual psychological perspective (De Vries and Van de Water, 1992). The latter approach considers only the subjective aspects of the quality of working life, without looking for changes in the structure (tasks and degree of control) of the individual job. By contrast, the former approach highlights the objective aspects of the task and how these can be improved in order to increase the quality of working life.

3. For example, the tolerances for the raw materials within the FPA concept are very limited. A small deviation from the norm means that the product cannot be produced.

4. Perhaps not surprisingly, managers in Taylor's day readily accepted the notion that workers' jobs should be programmed but found it unacceptable that the same principles should apply to themselves (Bendix, 1956: 280).

5. Classical economic theory legitimizes this perspective by arguing that, through the workings of the invisible hand, the single-minded pursuit of profit will result in maximum social welfare (Smith, 1957).

6. Charismatic authority rests on devotion to the specific and exceptional sanctity, heroism, or exemplary character of an individual person, and of the normative patterns or order revealed or ordained by him (Scott, 1987: 40).

7. Traditional authority rests on an established belief in the sanctity of immemorial traditions and the legitimacy of those exercising authority under them (Scott, 1987: 40).

8. In a natural system approach, organizations are conceived of as collectivities whose participants share a common interest in the survival of the system and who engage in collective activities, informally structured, to secure this end (Scott, 1987: 23).

9. In a rational system approach, organizations are considered as collectivities oriented to the pursuit of relatively specific goals and exhibiting relatively highly formalized social structures (Scott, 1987: 22).

3 Flexibility, the Hallmark of Postmodern Organization

> It is evident that organizations are admixtures of stability and change: Organizations are relatively stable, enduring features of life, yet when we look closely they do not appear stable at all. They are continuously changing, continuously being produced and renewed by member activities. Nevertheless, an argument can be made that stability is primary; any change is observable only in contrast to some stable state . . . Generally, however, organizational theories have emphasized either stability or change, slighting the other term . . . How can both faces of organizations be encompassed in the same framework?
>
> (Poole and Van de Ven, 1989: 564–5).

In the previous chapter, we described an acceleration of competitive change and the rise of a postmodern perspective of management in order to illustrate the increasing needs and opportunities for organizational flexibility. Moreover, some essential theories supporting the classical and modern management perspectives were briefly discussed. We argued that organizations designed and managed according to these perspectives and theories encounter many problems associated with contemporary competitive changes.

In response, managers and practitioners have heralded flexibility as the new hallmark of organizational excellence. Representatives of the classical and modern management era, such as Sears, IBM, General Motors, ICI, and Matsushita continue to have myriad difficulties against new-design flexible competitors, such as Wal-Mart, Compaq, Microsoft, and ABB. Other 'best-managed' firms of the 1970s and early 1980s, such as Xerox, GE, Motorola, and Philips have been partly successful in transforming their traditionally designed organizations. These examples seem to indicate that firms of the classical and modern management era, and the theories derived from them, will give way to firms and theories reflecting the postmodern perspective. Yet, while the business literature on organizational change is replete with prescriptions and directives with regard to the design and management of the new flexible firm (cf. Kanter, 1994; Peters, 1992; Peters and Waterman, 1982; Senge, 1990), there is relatively little theory on flexibility.

In this chapter, some recent developments within organization theories which contribute to the body of knowledge of the postmodern management perspective and our understanding of flexibility are examined. We consider in turn the developments regarding organizational flexibility in strategic management theories, contingency theories, organizational learning theories, and theories of innovation and entrepreneurship.

In theories of strategic management (Sect. 3.1), organizational flexibility is considered as a strategic asset in situations in which anticipation is impossible and strategic surprise likely. It consists of flexible resources and capabilities and broad strategic schemas. In dynamic contingency theory (Sect. 3.2), organizational flexibility is regarded as an organizational potential for maintaining a dynamic fit between the environment and the organization. This potential can be reactive as well as proactive. Organizational learning theories (Sect. 3.3) refer to organizational flexibility as a reflective capacity concerning the organization's learning system for creating a process of dynamic balance between single-loop and double-loop learning. These theories emphasize different levels of flexibility. In theories of innovation and entrepreneurship (Sect. 3.4), organizational flexibility is judged as an organizational ability to facilitate entrepreneurial activities and innovations. This ability refers to routine proliferation as well as routine destruction. Finally, the tensions between the developments within these various theories are further discussed (Sect. 3.5). New theories seem to stress change, while older theories prefer stability and preservation. We will argue that the concept of flexibility is inherently paradoxical; it requires change as well as preservation. Different approaches for dealing with this paradox are presented.

3.1 An Asset for Strategic Surprise

Over the past thirty years, strategic management has become established as a legitimate field of research and managerial practice. In the evolution of strategy research, a diversity of partly competitive and partly supplementary paradigms or models have emerged (cf. Elfring and Volberda, 1996; Mintzberg, 1990; Chaffee, 1985). For a long time, however, these models ignored the concept of flexibility. They focused instead on how firms should develop sound strategies by means of systematic forecasting, planning, and control. While it is true that organizations must pursue strategies for purposes of consistency, they must also discard their established competences in response to a changed environment. When environmental changes become increasingly undefined, fast-moving, and numerous, it is risky to rely upon conventional strategic management approaches. Therefore, more recent descriptive strategy perspectives consider organizational flexibility as a strategic asset in situations in which anticipation is impossible and strategic surprise likely (cf. Aaker and Mascarenhas, 1984;

Quinn, 1980; Sanchez, 1995). In this section, we will consider major developments within the strategy field and their contribution to flexibility.

The Linear Model: Rigidities of Strategic Planning

Historically, an organization's strategy has been thought of as an integrated plan. The most frequently cited definitions of organization strategy are provided by Andrews (1971) and Chandler (1962), and emphasize concepts such as goals, resource allocation, and especially plans. These concepts form the essential elements of the *linear model*[1] of strategic management (Chaffee, 1985), corresponding to what others have called the 'planning' (Mintzberg, 1973), 'rational' (Peters and Waterman, 1982), 'rational comprehensive', or 'synoptic' (Fredrickson, 1983) approach.

This model still pervades the literature on the process of strategic management. It characterizes the strategic process as a highly rational, proactive process that involves activities such as establishing goals, monitoring the environment, assessing internal capabilities, searching for and evaluating alternative actions, and developing an integrated plan to achieve organizational goals (Ansoff, 1965; Hofer and Schendel, 1978; Lorange and Vancil, 1977). In this sequential process, 'strategy formulation' precedes 'strategy implementation'. Emphasis is on planning 'what to do', rather than on planning 'what the organization might be capable of doing in the future'. As a consequence, the content of strategy (i.e. 'in which direction do we change the firm's position in the environment?') dominates the process in the linear model, while the process itself is often underestimated or oversimplified. The linear model assumes there are no problems with implementing strategy after it has been formulated.

Regarding strategy formulation, the role of the management is that of a 'rational actor' issuing directives from the seat of power. The model assumes that an exhaustive analysis can be undertaken[2] before action is taken, and requires that management holds a considerable amount of power and has access to complete information. Regarding implementation, the role of the management is that of an architect, designing administrative systems to orchestrate implementation and to push the organization towards goal achievement. By manipulating the systems and structures of the organization in support of a particular strategy, however, the management may be trading off important strategic flexibility: 'Should an unforeseen change in the environment require a redirection of the strategy, it may be very difficult to change the firm's course, since all the "levers" controlling the firm have been set firmly in support of a now-obsolete game plan' (Bourgeois and Brodwin, 1984).

Thus, where environmental uncertainty is high, it may prove effective in the long run to refrain from the linear model described above. Whereas in a stable environment we can permit deliberate formulation and execution of strategy, many situations now involve strategic surprises that do not give sufficient warning to permit deliberate planning (Burton, 1984). A stable environment increases the likelihood that the critical variables can be identified, and it allows plans to be developed regarding the relationship between those variables and the organization. On the other hand, a highly unstable environment makes it difficult to achieve the level of certainty needed for rational models to be effective.

According to the linear model, however, increased environmental uncertainty can be addressed by a more comprehensive decision process. Instead of relatively fixed strategic programmes, which are in essence extrapolations of former trends, management has to develop action strategies and to concentrate on certain essential strategic issues, both of which have to be regularly revised (Ansoff, 1980: 132–48). In addition, in situations of more extreme uncertainty, management has to develop contingency plans in which decisions that deviate from decisions which are part of the long-term plan are assessed and prepared (Linneman and Chandran, 1981). Contingency plans are complementary plans: that is, they are based on developments that are relatively unlikely, but are very important should they occur. These 'what if' approaches are widely understood and they are growing in technical sophistication as a result of computer modelling (Burton and Naylor, 1980). Indeed, these various planning tools are able to cope with more uncertainty. Yet they are not sufficient to assure the viability of the organization. There is a limit to an organization's planning repertoire, due to organizational inertia. A firm can change its plan yearly, monthly, or daily, but the one-sided focus on planning is insufficient and leads in many cases to organizations becoming ever more rigid. For instance, an increase in the number of planning forecasts of the Central Planning Department of Philips Semiconductors in Eindhoven resulted only in larger inventories and higher prices for the plants. It has been suggested that even if an organization has significant resources, attempting to be comprehensive may result in achieving tomorrow's solution to yesterday's problem (Braybrooke and Lindblom, 1970: 121).

The empirical research of Fredrickson and Mitchell (1984) and Fredrickson (1984), which analysed the degree of comprehensiveness of the decision process of firms in stable and unstable environments, supports this view. It defined comprehensiveness as the extent to which an organization attempts to be exhaustive or inclusive in making and integrating strategic decisions. The researchers concluded that a comprehensive decision process will result in superior performance in an environment that can be well understood. On the other hand, a non-comprehensive planning process leads to superior performance[3] in an unstable environment: 'Its decision speed and flexibility allow fast, low-cost action that can exploit and overcome a changing list of opportunities and threats that defy thorough understanding' (Fredrickson and Mitchell, 1984: 405).

Flexibility and the Postmodern Organization

Moreover, Mintzberg (1973, 1994) argued that planning is not a panacea for the problems of strategy-making: 'The repetitive nature of the annual planning process can easily become a mechanical extrapolation of information. That kind of exercise, like "crying wolf too often", may actually desensitize top managers of strategic issues, so that the need for substantive change may not be recognized when it does arise' (Mintzberg, 1994: 179). In the same way, Kanter (1983) suggested that the art and architecture of change work through a different medium than the management of the ongoing, routinized side of an organization's affairs: 'Most of the rational, analytical tools measure what already is (or make forecasts as a logical extrapolation from data on what is). But change efforts have to mobilize people around what is not yet known, not yet experienced' (Kanter, 1983: 304).

Attitudes towards planning and analysis should therefore be biased towards new ways of thinking in order to compensate for the one-sided tendency of corporate planners to produce highly formalized and ritual-like planning procedures. In this context, Pennings (1985: 20) and Starbuck (1983) warned against the institutionalization and routinization of formal planning systems which might lead a life of their own, uncoupled from relevant strategic events. In such circumstances, strategy becomes the job of an increasingly specialized planning department that is divorced from the everyday business. Numerous examples can be found in the public sector where planning systems are imposed upon the organization by legislative moves or, in large private corporations, where planning systems are imposed by executive order. For instance, in the 1970s and early 1980s, strategic planning was the gospel at GE. The company's elaborate controls ranged from detailed monthly budget approvals to an annual strategic planning review that required six to eight months of preparatory research and analysis (Tichy and Sherman, 1994). Jack Welch's success started when he dismantled this rigid strategic planning system and slimmed down the corporate planning group. Instead of directing a business according to a detailed GE-style strategic plan, Welch believes in setting only a few, clear overarching goals.

Considering these arguments, we might conclude that planning and analysis are necessary but not sufficient, and need to be understood as mechanisms for problem and opportunity identification and strategy evaluation, rather than as mechanisms for radical change (Johnson, 1988). Planning requires unrealistic stability in the environment and can be very expensive.[4] These caveats do not mean that planning is useless; rather they suggest that the planner must become more realistic about the limitations of planning. In the linear approach, there is no room for flexibility. At most, flexibility represents a management capacity for quickly developing plans to anticipate new developments. However, we argued that in situations of radical change, attempts to adopt planning would only paralyse the organization (Burton, 1984). The annual planning rituals within corporations restrict their creative potential; options are fixed and new options are not noticed. In other words, planning is the least flexible of the strategy-making modes. Its obsession with rationality leads to a further refinement of the planning mechanism that is the cause of the problems.

The Adaptive Model: Opportunistic Behaviour and Flexible Resources and Capabilities

Surprisingly enough, it was Ansoff (1978), one of the founders of the linear model, who suggested that the level of environmental change was increasing and giving rise to strategic surprises, making strategic anticipation and strategic planning of the sort that proceeds in an outside-in, market-to-product development manner no longer useful. According to Ansoff, the planning concept of strategy had to be re-examined because uncertainty limits the ability of the organization to preplan or make decisions about activities in advance of their execution. Because of this effect, organizations must develop flexibility. The more uncertain the situation, the more an organization will need flexibility as a complement to planning (cf. Eppink, 1978: 59–61; Thompson, 1967: 148). Therefore Ansoff (1978) asserted that in these situations the use of traditional action strategies ('in which direction do we change the firm's position in the environment?') would be increasingly supplemented and sometimes replaced by preparedness or flexible configuration strategies ('how do we configure the resources of the firm for effective responses to strategic surprises?'). Rather than adhering single-mindedly to a predetermined set of goals and course of action, it is better to be capable of adapting to a variety of possible events, exigencies, or unpredictable states of nature (Burton, 1984; Hrebiniak and Joyce, 1986).

In line with this approach, Mintzberg and Waters (1985) argued that the focus should not be placed on deliberate planning and control, but on developing an organizational capacity for strategic thinking and learning, which means being open and responsive. From this capacity, strategies emerge which are not guided by explicit a priori intentions. Patterns or consistencies are realized despite, or in the absence of, intentions. Nevertheless, the emergence of these *ex-post* strategies does not mean that management is out of control, only that it is open, flexible, and responsive: 'Such behaviour is especially important when an environment is too unstable or complex to comprehend, or too imposing to defy. Openness to such emergent strategy enables management to act before everything is fully understood—to respond to an evolving reality rather than having to focus on a stable fantasy' (Mintzberg and Waters, 1985: 271).

As an example, Mintzberg and Waters (1985) proposed that a distinctive competence cannot always be assessed on paper a priori; often, it has to be discovered empirically by taking actions that test where strengths and weaknesses really lie.

Flexibility and the Postmodern Organization

The different modes of strategy discussed above are depicted in Figure 3.1. The relationship between environmental turbulence and comprehensiveness of planning activities is presented as a reversed U-form. In a relatively stable environment, strategic management can be limited to the development of strategic programmes, which are based on the extrapolation of trends. There is no need to change the organization. When the environment becomes more unstable, strategic programmes are insufficient and have to be supplemented with strategic issue management or even contingency planning. Besides strategic programmes, management has to focus on certain relevant issues and initiate organizational activities regarding these issues. If these programmes and issues have to be revised too often, contingency planning is more suitable. For every possible change, a plan has to be developed and the organization must be well organized in order to anticipate these various plans. However, in a highly unstable environment, planning activities create more problems than they solve. The associated uncertainty is not amenable to formal objective assessment. Therefore, organizational activities are substituted for planning activities in order to create a flexible configuration of resources.[5] These preparedness strategies result in a more spontaneous organization. Figure 3.1 shows that in situations of high environmental uncertainty, deliberate planning becomes less important while organizing for flexibility becomes more important.

Preparedness strategies are part of the *adaptive model*[6] of strategic management, a term also used by Mintzberg (1973) and Chaffee (1985). In this model, strategic management is depicted as a messy, disorderly, and disjointed process around which competing factors contend. Lindblom (1959), Mintzberg (1978), and Quinn (1980) contributed substantially to this approach by doing more descriptive strategy research instead of prescriptive research. Their contributions are founded largely on the notion of the cognitive limits of rationality as described in the early work of Herbert Simon and James March (Simon, 1947; March and Simon, 1958).

On the basis of these insights, it was Lindblom (1959) who first claimed that policy-making in government is an incremental process of 'muddling through' that is distinct from the linear rational perspective, since different subunits display a disorderly proliferation of preference orderings and divergent views of cause-effects relations. Lindblom's arguments have generally been supported by other management scientists. For example, in his ground-breaking *Harvard Business Review* article, 'Good Managers Don't Make Policy Decisions', Wrapp (1967) argued that disjointed incrementalism is also found in business firms. Years later, Quinn (1980) concluded that this 'non-rational' incrementalism is logical because of the inherently iterative nature of strategic decisions and the resultant need to make and remake them. In his in-depth study of nine large corporations facing major changes, Quinn concluded that the successful firms were those in which the strategist was able to adjust incrementally to changes

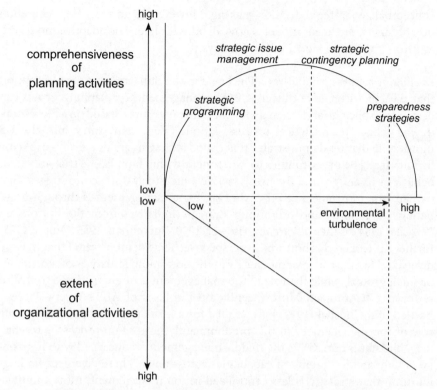

Fig. 3.1. Different modes of strategy depicted as a constellation of the degree of environmental turbulence, the comprehensiveness of planning activities, and the extent of organizational activities

Note:

- Strategic programming: extrapolation of trends without changing the organization.
- Strategic issue management: besides programmes, also focusing on relevant issues and initiating activities in line with these issues.
- Strategic contingency planning: developing plans for every possible change and transforming the organization in order to anticipate possible developments.
- Preparedness strategies: decreasing planning activities, and increasing organizational activities in order to get more strategic mileage out of the organization in case of strategic surprises.

in customer needs or in which the internal structures and processes were appropriate.

The arguments presented above do not imply that the rational, comprehensive prescriptive model of strategic management is not important or useful. It provides a general model through which other scholars have been able to conceptualize strategic decision-making. However, as an accurate representation of reality, the linear model is now all but obsolete. The adaptive model differs from this linear model in several ways.

Facilitating bottom-up initiatives   The linear model still works on the assumption that the chief executive officer (CEO), management, or planning group can design an explicit 'grand' strategy for the entire enterprise based on a highly top-down, deliberate, analytical process. Honda's successful entry into the US motorcycle market demonstrates that sound strategies are not always explicitly formulated. The opportunities to experiment within Honda, the trial-and-error behaviour in design, and the firm's lack of a hierarchical structure suggest that perhaps the most effective process of strategic management is through originating, developing, and promoting strategic initiatives from the bottom up (Pascale, 1984). Other researchers (Bower, 1970; Burgelman, 1983; Quinn, 1985) further developed this bottom-up perspective. They demonstrated that in large diversified firms, strategy emerges from the bottom-up initiatives of individuals or small groups, while the role of top management is often restricted to that of retroactive legitimizer. More recently, on the basis of ABB's recent success, Bartlett and Ghoshal (1993) have argued for a more proactive perspective; the role of top management in this predominantly bottom-up process is to challenge the status quo, while the middle management is concerned with horizontal linking and leveraging of capabilities across units. These divergent findings illustrate that strategy is less centralized in top management, more multifaceted, and generally less integrated than in the linear model. The adaptive model therefore asserts that strategic management is an organization-wide activity in which each management level has to contribute in its own way (Van Cauwenberg and Cool, 1982).

Keeping options open   A second difference follows from the relative unimportance of advance planning in the adaptive model. Top management initially formulates guidelines in more general terms. These are designed to steer the organization in the increasingly turbulent and therefore uncertain environment and to maintain a flexible position *vis-à-vis* the large number of unknown future events. Specific proposals formulated in technical and economic terms typically emanate from front-line management, while middle management faces the difficult task of integrating both activities. Since the formulation and the implementation of specific strategic initiatives do not originate at the same hierarchical level, and since different hierarchical levels are found to be relatively independent, it is inevitable that strategy can develop only in an incremental way. Strategic management is necessarily a fragmented process, whereby initiatives arise from different subsystems and top management defines strategies as broadly as possible and leaves options open as long as possible.

Maintaining flexibility of resources and managerial capabilities The adaptive model does not deal with decisions about goals as emphatically as the linear model. Instead, it tends to focus the manager's attention on resources and capabilities, and the goals are represented by alignment of the organization with the environment. If markets are in a state of flux, then the internal resources and capabilities of a firm appear to be a more suitable basis for strategy formulation than the external environment (Grant, 1996). For instance, Honda had no superior strategy for entering the US motorcycle market, but it had unique dealer-network capabilities and superior engine expertise. In this conception, organizational flexibility depends on the inherent flexibility of resources available to the firm and on the firm's managerial capabilities in applying these resources to alternative courses of action (Sanchez, 1995). Honda was able to apply its engine expertise in different end-products like motorcycles, cars, snowblowers, and lawnmowers. Similarly, Citibank is able to move rapidly to acquire other banks' portfolios and credit cards, adjust rates and prices, and target specific customer niches in promotional campaigns largely because of its continuing investment in general-purpose information processing capabilities (Boynton and Victor, 1991). In the linear model, such investments in flexible and general-purpose processing capabilities without known specific product returns would be considered to be signs of inefficiency. In the adaptive model, however, such investments create an asset for strategic surprise.

The emphasis on the flexibility of resources deployed and managerial capabilities are further developed in the resource-based theory of the firm (Penrose, 1959; Learned *et al.*, 1969). This approach does not consider the firm as a black box guided by the strategist, but as a bundle of firm-specific 'resources' which can lead to superior 'performance'. Although most of the proponents of the resource-based approach originally considered only pure physical resources, a shift can be seen towards more interest in 'intangible resources', 'tacit knowledge', and 'capabilities' (cf. Quinn, 1992; Itami, 1987; Teece *et al.*, 1997). The more a firm can exploit its resources in various end-markets, create access to a broad knowledge-base, and build up a variety of capabilities, the more flexible it becomes.

In summary, the adaptive model of strategic management requires an a priori flexible configuration of resources in order to facilitate *ex-post* emergent strategies. In situations of fundamental uncertainty, the management has to keep options open and to build in flexibility in order to adapt to and successfully handle unforeseen contingencies and exogenous shocks. In this regard, organizational flexibility is a strategic asset for facilitating effective responses to 'unanticipated' changes.

The Interpretative Model: Varying Strategic Schemas

Some questions remain about the nature of incrementalism within the adaptive model. What exactly drives adaptation? How can small, resource-limited firms successfully adapt to competitive change while some corporate giants with plentiful resources and many strategic options cannot? For instance, how could a smaller company like Cannon manage to make such a huge dent in Xerox's market share? Why was Sharp more successful in the electronic calculator business than Texas Instruments? Apparently, strategic options and flexible resources are not a sufficient basis for adaptation. The explanations for what drives adaptation range from those who see adaptation as a result of cognitive schemas (Weick, 1979), to paradigms (Johnson, 1987), or cultural idea systems (Smircich and Stubbart, 1985).

Adaptation requires that participants are able to make sense of their environment and know what to adapt to. In other words, the question of what drives adaptation depends on the socially constructed reality of organizational participants. That is, reality is defined through a process of social interchange in which perceptions are affirmed, modified, or replaced according to their apparent congruence with the perceptions of others. Weick (1979) described this process as enactment. Members of organizations actively form or enact their environment through their social interaction. A pattern of enactment establishes the foundation of organized reality, which in turn has effects in shaping future enactments. Strategy in this *interpretative model*[7] might be defined as strategic schemas or frames of reference that allow the organization and its environment to be understood by organizational stakeholders (cf. Bettis and Prahalad, 1995; Chaffee, 1985: 93; Prahalad and Bettis, 1986). These strategic schemas lead to calculated behaviour by participants in non-programmed situations (Van Cauwenberg and Cool, 1982). As such, stakeholders are motivated to believe and act in ways that are expected to produce favourable outcomes for the organization.

The most essential question for management becomes one of how to develop adequate strategic schemas that enable the firm to create or adapt to competitive change. The choice of schemas and interpretations becomes a creative and political art. Novel and interesting schemas may stimulate novel and interesting environments that can in turn preface novel and interesting strategic initiatives. For instance, when Sharp entered the electronic calculator business, it did not have an established strategic schema in the home appliance business, its main business. The calculator division of Sharp thus enjoyed a high degree of freedom in the strategy formulation process and was able to refine its strategic schema independently. While Sharp was able to refine its strategic schema, Texas Instruments could not change its schema. In TI, there already existed a sophisticated strategic schema in the semiconductor business, and its electronic calculator business was heavily dependent on the semiconductor division. When applied to the new business, the strategic schema, which worked so well for TI in the semiconductor business, led to failure.

Smircich and Stubbart (1985) argued that companies might be able to enlarge their capacities for novel interpretations by varying schemas systematically. Strategic management in this approach involves creating and maintaining systems of shared meaning that facilitate organized action. Similarly, Hamel and Prahalad (1994) discussed the concept of strategic intent: ambitious goals that stretch far beyond the temporal bounds of strategic plans. According to them, successful firms simply have more foresight, and are capable of imagining products, services, and entire new businesses that do not yet exist.

It is important to understand that a strategic schema is not purely a system of beliefs and assumptions, but that it is preserved and legitimized in a 'cultural web' of organizational actions in terms of myths, rituals, and symbols (Johnson, 1988). Therefore, a powerful tool in the hands of top management for creating, maintaining, and changing frames of reference is the organizational culture: 'This aims at inducing a sufficiently coherent set of values in the participant's behaviour. As such their calculated behaviour in new situations is thus directed in a desired way and some inadequate initiatives are ad initium sorted out' (Van Cauwenberg and Cool, 1982: 254).

None the less, too much control or too narrow an organizational set of beliefs and assumptions can prevent valuable strategic initiatives from rising from the front line, while too little guidance can result in destructive chaos. Organizations with very strong cultures usually suffer from xenophobia (Ouchi, 1981). That is, they resist deviance, retard attempts at change and tend to foster homogeneity and inbreeding. IBM is an excellent example of a strong culture. Its strategic schema revolved around a set of unseen assumptions about the centrality of the mainframe business. This mainframe logic was strongly preserved in IBM's culture. The resulting cultural blocks hampered IBM's efforts to refashion its basic beliefs and assumptions in line with changes in the computer business.

Usually, top management views the tools for eliminating cultural blocks in technical terms like structure, systems, and procedures, rather than symbolic terms. According to Smircich and Stubbart, the technical aspect is only the surface architecture of organization: 'Rather than concentrating on decisions or design of decision making structures, a strategic manager would concentrate on the values, symbols, language, and dramas that form the backdrop for decision making structures' (Smircich and Stubbart, 1985: 731).

Culture does not succumb to push-button control: it is far too complex and multifaceted. As Green (1988) said: 'You do not control culture, at best you shape it.' This shaping can be accomplished through values and their symbolic expression, dramas and language. This management of meaning depends heavily on symbols and norms.

As the above arguments imply, flexibility means that strategic schemas must be broad enough to encourage strategic initiatives and narrow enough to suppress counterproductive actions. In this sense, a flexible organization is an organization with a core set of beliefs of a relatively high order and yet a rather heterogeneous sets of beliefs at other levels (Peters and Waterman, 1982). In other words, there must be a 'constructive tension' between that which it is necessary to preserve and that which must be changed (Kanter, 1983), such as that between the need for managers to question and challenge and the preservation of core values and the organizational 'mission'. This view is supported by Meyer (1982), who argued that organizations are more likely to adopt strategies that are more divergent from their previous strategies if they have a more heterogeneous organizational 'ideology', as manifested in terms of organizational images and symbols.

Flexibility from a Strategic Perspective

On the basis of these developments in strategic management, flexibility has become a strategic asset in strategic management theories. In Table 3.1 these developments within strategic management are illustrated.

Traditionally, a strategic manager is portrayed as a planner, an implementer of structure, and a controller of events who derives ideas from information. However, in a highly turbulent environment, the prescriptive assertions of the linear model are no longer tenable. As a consequence of more descriptive strategy research, the strategist's task is defined as organizational in the adaptive model and imaginative in the interpretative model. These developments have contributed substantially to the concept of organizational flexibility, which from a strategic perspective means creating a flexible configuration of resources for facilitating emergent strategies and creating strategic schemas which enhance the creation of multiple interpretations. This results in a process of the management of 'unintended order' (Mintzberg and Waters, 1985) or 'controlled chaos' (Quinn, 1985), in which change as well as stability is possible. That is, the organization can respond to surprises and initiate novel actions, but is also able to resist certain changes or to squash destructive initiatives.

3.2 Maintaining a Dynamic Fit

We argued that flexibility is an asset for strategic surprise. But how much flexibility must be built in the organization in terms of flexible resources, manager-

T ABLE 3.1. Developments within strategic management and their contributions to organizational flexibility

Strategic management		
Linear model	Adaptive model	Interpretative model
planning strategies	flexible configuration strategies	strategic schemas
In which direction do we have to change the firm's position in the environment	How do we have to configure the resources of the firm for effective responses to unanticipated changes?	How do we give meaning to our activities for participants and stakeholders?
problem area: establishing long-term goals	problem area: developing flexible resources and capabilities	problem area: creating and maintaining broad strategic schemas
methods: long-term planning, SWOT analysis, determination of sustainable competitive advantages	methods: analysing firms' resources and managerial capabilities	methods: managing culture by concentrating on values, symbols, language, and dramas
flexibility is a management capacity for quickly developing plans	flexibility is an organizational capability for facilitating emergent, spontaneous strategies	flexibility is an imaginative capacity for creating strategic schemas broad enough to encourage strategic initiatives

ial capabilities, and broad strategic schemas? The answer strongly depends on one's conceptions of the environment and perspective of the organization–environment relationship. In this section, three theories dealing with the organization–environment relation are considered: static contingency theory, population-ecology theory, and dynamic contingency theory. These theories may clarify the crucial role of the environment in the concept of organizational flexibility.

Static Contingency Theory: Reactive Flexible Forms

The first contingency approach was based on the assumption that organizations react in predictable ways to the conditions which surround them, adjusting their purpose and shape to meet market and other environmental characteristics (Miles and Snow, 1978). This assumption is an elaboration of the biologist's functional view of the adaptation of living forms to their environment, which considers organizations as open systems (Khandwalla, 1977). In this approach, survival is seen as the key aim or primary task facing an organization.[8] Environmental conditions are regarded as a direct source of variation in organizational forms. As a consequence, management must be concerned, above all else, with achieving 'good fits'. There is no one best way of organizing. The appropriate form depends on the kind of task or environment with which one is dealing. To perform different tasks within the same organization, different approaches to management may be necessary, and quite different types or 'species' of organization are needed in different types of environments. The ideas underlying the static contingency approach to organization have become established as a dominant perspective in organizational analysis, in which environmental factors came to be viewed as an important influence on the behaviour of organizations.

The most influential studies establishing the credentials of this approach were conducted by Burns and Stalker (1961) and Woodward (1965). Focusing on firms in a variety of industries, Burns and Stalker illustrated that when change in the environment becomes prevalent, open and flexible styles of organization and management are required. On the basis of their qualitative research, they identified a continuum of organizational forms ranging from mechanistic to organic. They postulated that the latter, more flexible forms are required to deal with changing environments, while mechanistic or highly bureaucratized forms are more appropriate for stable environments.

Moreover, Woodward, in a study of manufacturing firms, discerned a relationship between technology and the structure of successful organizations. She demonstrated that the principles of classical management theory were not always the right ones to follow, since different technologies impose different demands on individuals and organization, which have to be met through appropriate structures. Hence, Woodward developed a technological scale ranging from unit or small-batch production, through large-batch or mass production, to continuous-process production. She concluded that a mass production technology requires a highly functionalized structure and a large administrative component with a wide span of control, whereas a unit technology is usually accompanied by a flexible organization structure that has a small administrative component, few hierarchical levels, and a moderately broad span of supervising control. Most of the employees who operate this latter type of technology have general as opposed to specialized skills, and the unit technology may be adjusted with comparative ease to permit experimentation with new products and work processes. The structure compatible with a continuous-process technology has the largest administrative component, the highest number of hierarchical levels, and the most narrow span of control. This technology requires comparatively few individuals to monitor the machinery, but such employees must have high levels of judgement and technical skill.

The above studies were static in that they overemphasized reactive adaptation and ignored the opportunity firms have to influence their environment. None the less, Burns and Stalker and Woodward made a similar point in stressing that there was absolutely no guarantee that firms would find the appropriate mode of organization for dealing with their environment. They emphasized that successful adaptation of organization to environment depended on the ability of top management to interpret the conditions facing the firm in an appropriate manner, and to adopt relevant courses of action.

Subsequently, Lawrence and Lorsch (1967) gave precision and refinement to the general idea that certain organizations need to be more organic or flexible than others, suggesting that the degree of flexibility required varies from one organizational subunit to another. They studied high- and low-performance organizations in the standardized-container industry, the food industry, and the plastics industry which were respectively experiencing low, moderate, and high rates of growth, technological change, and market change. They found that successful firms in uncertain environments (plastics industry) required high differentiation between functional subunits and the use of elaborate integrative mechanisms to coordinate subunit activities. Conversely, they found that success in more certain environments (container industry) required less differentiation and less elaborate integrative mechanisms.

Many other researchers have focused on change as a key environmental dimension, supporting the conclusion of the above studies that the more variable and unpredictable the task environment, the more flexible organizational structure and process must be (Dill, 1958; Thompson, 1967; Duncan, 1972). The resulting static contingency perspective served to popularize the idea that in different environmental circumstances some species of organizations are better able to survive than others, and that since the relations between organization and environment are the product of human choices, they may become maladapted. In such cases, organizations are likely to experience many problems both in dealing with the environment and in their internal functioning. Consequently, researchers have tended to search for those environmental factors which shape organizational behaviour. Most empirical studies on this topic, however, have undertaken little beyond establishing statistical associations between uncertainty and organizational variables. These studies generally adopted the most straightforward causal assumption that uncertainty determines the observed organizational characteristics. The organization was presented as only reacting to environmental conditions and never initiating change in their relevant environments.[9] Hence, adaptation in static contingency theory stands for reaction to environmental forces or demands, and depends on appropriate managerial actions.

Recent studies which argue that there is 'a best way of organizing' unintentionally reinforce the ideas of the static contingency theory. For instance, the study of Peters and Waterman (1982) documented the characteristics of US companies they regarded as excellent. Most of these firms had adopted organizational designs that have much in common with organic forms of organization. Furthermore, Kanter (1983) identified the characteristics of successful corporations dealing with changing environments, and distinguished between 'segmentalistic' and 'integrative' organizations. Her typology parallels the one Burns and Stalker developed for classifying 'mechanistic' and 'organic' organizations. Similarly, Lammers (1987) argued that these so-called 'excellent' types of organization are quite similar to Mintzberg's 'missionary form', Ouchi's 'type J', and Touraine's 'representative' organization, and can be seen as subtypes of the organic organization. Thus, even though many of these more recent studies do not devote much attention to the contingency theorist's dictum that successful organization rests in a fit between organization and environment, they constitute a valuable addendum to the static contingency perspective.

To sum up, static contingency theory and recent revisions have contributed valuable insights to the flexible form as part of an organizational typology, and illustrated the conditions under which this form is appropriate. In this perspective, organizational flexibility is considered as a *reactive capacity* of organizations to turbulent environments. This work neglects, however, the process of creating and maintaining flexible forms.

Population-Ecology Theory: Anti-Flexible Forms

The static contingency theory has received much criticism from theorists and researchers who support population-ecology theory. According to population ecologists such as Aldrich, Freeman, and Hannan, most organizations flounder helplessly in the grip of environmental forces. Consonant with static contingency theory, they believe that environments are relentlessly efficient in weeding out any organization that does not closely align itself with environmental demands. They doubt, however, that many organizations can self-consciously change themselves very much or very often, or that the conscious initiatives by management are likely to succeed. In criticizing the reactive 'managerial adaptation' view of organization, they have highlighted the importance of inertial pressures that often prevent organizations from changing in response to their environments. The concept of inertia, like that of fitness, refers to a correspondence between the behavioural capabilities of a class of organizations and their particular environments (Hannan and Freeman, 1984: 152). It is a result of the structural and procedural baggage that organizations accumulate over time. The speed of an organization's response relative to competitors reflects this inertia. For instance, specialization of production plants and personnel, internal political constraints, and established ideas of organizational participants and 'mindsets' of top managers may make it impossible for organizations to engage in timely and efficient changes (Hannan and Freeman, 1977).

A widely cited example of organizational inertia is General Motors, once the world leader in automobile production efficiency (Rumelt, 1995). Despite a joint venture with Toyota in which world-class methods were used, the company has been unable to substantially change its overall productivity. In fact, many GM plants became less productive during the 1980s while Chrysler and Ford made significant gains. GM's challenge is not really competition, but its own inertia.

The population-ecology perspective originated from evolutionary biology. It builds on a cyclical model that allows for the variation, selection, and retention of species characteristics. This three-stage model was intended to account for long-run transformations rather than short-run changes, which are temporary responses to local conditions (Aldrich and Pfeffer, 1976). In the first stage, variations may occur for whatever reason, planned or unplanned. The population-ecology perspective is indifferent regarding the source of variation or change. The general principle is that the greater the heterogeneity and number of variations, the richer the opportunities for a close fit to the environmental selection criteria. In the second stage, selection is accomplished by differential survival rates of structural forms. In the final stage, retention, the opposite of variation (Weick, 1979) is accomplished through organizational stability, manifested in the use of unchanging standard operating procedures or formal rules. Positively selected variations survive and reproduce other similar forms, which then form the starting point for a new round of selection.

The population-ecology approach has been developed to counteract the reactive adaptation bias generated by static contingency theory. The population ecologists believe the idea that organizations can adapt to their environment attributes too much flexibility and power to the organization and too little to the environment as a force in organizational survival. They focus instead on the way environments select organizations, emphasizing resource scarcity and competition. The analysis of this selection process is most appropriately applied at the level of organizational populations, as it is not the fitness of any single organization, but rather the distribution of fitness across the population of organizations that is of interest. In population-ecology theory, there is no place for flexibility; rather population ecology emphasizes the *anti-flexibility* of organizations, which are asserted to be highly inert, inherently inflexible and slow in responding to changing environmental opportunities and threats, and rarely able to engage in transformations. Further, transformations are believed to reduce organizations' chances of survival. According to the population ecologists, adaptation is not a managerial process, but caused by selection of the environment of populations of organizations. In their view, the fact that bureaucracies may give way to more flexible forms is not a result of managerial adaptation but a consequence of environmental selection and retention of flexible forms.

The application of the population-ecology perspective, however, brings about a number of problems. First, it requires a system of classification of organizational forms analogous to the system of classification of species in biology (Aldrich and Pfeffer, 1976). No such system exists in the study of organizations. Forms are currently identified through various typologies, such as mechanistic-organic or bureaucratic-professional, or through empirically developed typologies that are often not sufficiently developed to permit a very comprehensive ecological analysis. As a consequence, the difference between structural modifications and the emergence of fundamentally new organizations is frequently unclear.

In addition, the criterion of successful adaptation to the environment is changed by some researchers from the easier-to-observe survival or failure to the more problematic criterion of structural change or stability. Rather than being able to observe a population of organizations adapting by the selective elimination of the less fit, we may find that almost all survive, but that each undergoes significant internal transformations of structure. This addition may violate the theories borrowed from biology and ecology (Perrow, 1986).

Some population-ecology theorists admit the structural change of units. Recently, researchers (Barnett et al., 1994; Burgelman, 1991, 1994; Galunic and Eisenhardt, 1996) have tried to explain corporate change by applying the population logic on the level of analysis of the firm. For instance, in his study of strategic business exit within Intel Corporation, Burgelman (1994: 50) argued that it was not the corporate strategy but the internal selection environment that caused a shift from memory chips towards the microprocessor business. He conjectured that the higher the correspondence between the internal selection criteria within the multiunit firm and external selection pressures, the more the population logic guarantees that the most promising business ventures will be selected.

While some researchers have thus tried to address the stability question by admitting structural change, the general fatalistic tendency of population ecology results in more fundamental criticism. Its underlying theories represent a view of individual–organization interactions that are grounded in the assumption that the human role in organizations is essentially passive and pathological (Perrow, 1986: 213–14; Bartlett and Ghoshal, 1993: 43). This assumption about human agency is manifest in population ecology (Hannan and Freeman, 1984). If we accept population ecology at face value, then in the long run it really does not matter what managers and decision-makers do.

Further, the view of population ecologists has tended to be rather one-sided, emphasizing resource scarcity and competition, which lie at the basis of selection, and ignoring the facts that resources can be abundant and self-renewing and that organizations not only compete but collaborate as well. Their tendency to take inertial forces for granted has led population ecologists to overlook the processes by which individual firms adapt to fundamental environmental shifts and to concentrate instead on the study of the birth and death rates of structural forms (Ginsberg and Buchholtz, 1990: 467). Evidence from rejuvenators such as Richardson in knives, Edwards in high-vacuum pumps, and Hotpoint in the European appliance industry shows that change can be a purposeful action for achieving leadership from a position of maturity (Baden-Fuller and Stopford, 1994). Furthermore, companies like Swatch were able to recreate their past, change the rules of their sectors, and unlock hidden values. These firms combined novel approaches with stretched resources to create leading positions. These examples illustrate that we need to consider more dynamic theories by which firms change and adapt.

Dynamic Contingency Theory: Proactive Flexible Forms

Relaxing some of the unrealistic assumptions of the static contingency and pure population-ecology perspectives, and enlarging them with more social, rather than biological dynamics, makes their insights more productive. Static contingency and population-ecology perspectives have some major limitations, most of which are associated with their conception of the environment. Both incorporate the assumption that 'organization' and 'environment' are real, material, and separate just as they appear to be in the biological world (Smircich and Stubbart, 1985). Given this axiom, research proceeds directly to find the successful combinations of organization and environment. It does not question the pivotal notion of environments as independent, external, and tangible entities.

What people refer to as their environment, however, is generated not only by their imperfect perceptions of the material objective environment but also by their actions and accompanying intellectual efforts to make sense of them. That is, organizations and their environments can, to some extent, be understood as socially constructed phenomena. Organizational environments can be seen as a product of human creativity, since they are made through the actions of the individuals, groups, and organizations that populate them.

It is thus misleading to assume that organizations need to adapt to their environment, as static contingency theorists suggest, or that environments select the organizations that are to survive, as the population ecologists assert (Morgan, 1986: 74). Both views tend to make organizations and their members dependent upon forces operating in an external world, rather than recognizing that they are active agents operating with others in the construction of that world. They posit an optimal fit between the organization and its environment. However, organizational scholars have become increasingly disenchanted with this mechanical, deterministic conception of the organization–environment relationship because its strong deterministic bias largely ignores the important variable of *managerial choice*. Consequently, less is known about the managerial *processes* than about the surface characteristics that they generate, and causal effects have been attributed to variables that are, in fact, only indirectly related (Miles and Snow, 1978; 1994).

It was Thompson (1967) who presented a contingency approach in the form of an integrated model, which suggests how the dynamic organization, through the actions of some decision-makers or the dominant coalition, develops structures and processes that take both environment and technology into account. Following Thompson, other theorists have disagreed with the view that organizational characteristics are fully preordained by technical considerations or environmental conditions. They too have emphasized the importance of decision-makers who serve as a link between the organization and its environment and rejected the environmental determinism implicit in most static contingency theories and population-ecology theories.

It was Child (1972) who most explicitly argued for a less rigid view of the interaction between organizations and their environment that takes into account the dynamic interchange between the two forces. He called for a more voluntaristic or 'strategic choice' approach to organization–environment relations because decision-makers have more autonomy than is implied by the perspective of environmental determinism. If there is some freedom of manoeuvring with respect to environmental factors, standards of performance, and structural design, then there is some choice as to how the organization as an ongoing system will be maintained. This slack weakens the general proposition that environmental factors will exert a high degree of constraint upon the choice of structural design. Cyert and March (1963) proposed that there is typically slack in organizational operations and that few, if any organizations operate at the limits of efficiency. This possibility implies that there may be a variety of organizational forms that are viable in a given environment.[10]

In addition, Child and many others have argued that organizations are not always passive recipients of environmental influence but also have the power to reshape the environment. In this context, Weick (1979), for instance, introduced a famous concept which he called environmental enactment: organizational environments are acts of managerial invention rather than discovery. Hrebiniak and Joyce (1985), Khandwalla (1977), Mintzberg (1979), and many other neo-contingency theorists asserted that adaptation is a dynamic process that is both managerially and environmentally inspired. Static contingency and population-ecology theory focused on what 'fits' were most effective and not on the process by which they were achieved. This emphasis on fits between organizations and environments led to static interpretations. Too much fit breeds complacency. IBM became overadapted to the mainframe business and therefore failed to recognize the opportunities of the PC market. Moreover, the fact that Peters and Waterman's statements are based on this static approach, namely universal commandments for successful organizations, may explain that one year later many of their forty-three excellent companies were not successful any more. Organizations travel in changing environments, so fit has to be a dynamic concept. Instead of tight fits, organizations have to look for loose fits in which there is some stretch for change (Hamel and Prahalad, 1994).

The above arguments against environmental determinism resulted in a *dynamic contingency perspective*,[11] which can be characterized as one that (1) views managerial choice or strategic choice as the primary link between organization and its environment, (2) focuses on management's ability to create, learn about, and manage an organization's environment, and (3) encompasses the multiple ways in which organizations interact with their environments through the process of mutual adaptation between organization and its environmental domain. In this perspective, flexibility does not result in suboptimal use of firm resources, thus leaving the firm vulnerable to competitors with cost focus or differentiation focus strategies. Rather, it can stabilize firm performance and increase the probability of firm survival when environments are changing and uncertain.

Therefore, on the basis of the assumptions of the dynamic contingency theory, hundreds of research studies have further addressed the job of specifying organizational characteristics and their success in dealing with different environmental conditions. These studies replaced those in which specific relations between one organizational variable and one environmental variable were compared. For example, Khandwalla (1971) found not a single significant correlation between any single structural variable and performance, but he uncovered a number of significant correlations within the set of structural variables, especially for the sample of high performers. In other words, success seemed to stem not from the use of any single structural device, such as management by objectives, decentralization, or a planning system, but from the combination of appropriate ones. In line with Khandwalla's findings, Mintzberg (1979) searched for unique clusters or configurations of organizational characteristics (design parameters) related to clusters of environmental factors. He identified five organizational configurations: the machine bureaucracy, the divisionalized form, the professional bureaucracy, the simple structure, and the adhocracy. The machine bureaucracy resembles the mechanistic organization, while the adhocracy corresponds to the organic organization. These and many other studies have added rich insights to and further extended the mechanistic-organic typology developed by Burns and Stalker.

Besides the search for various clusters of organizational characteristics, the emphasis on strategic choice or slack resulted in an increase in descriptive strategy research as described in Section 3.1. Maintaining flexibility in resources and capabilities and creating broad strategic schemas can be considered as particular ways to create slack. It has long been an article of faith among administrative reformers that slack in terms of ambiguous work roles and redundancy constitutes a wasteful use of organizational resources. On these grounds, as was suggested in planning strategies of the linear model of strategic management, ambiguity and redundancy should be eliminated. Landau's (1969, 1973) exposition of the functions of redundancy in self-organizing systems, however, provides a more useful starting point. He showed that duplication and overlap contribute to both problem solving and problem setting and widen the range of environmental conditions in which organizations can operate. Furthermore, Morgan (1986) argued that redundancy is crucial for creating potential and for ensuring flexibility in operation. It facilitates the process of self-organization whereby internal structure and functioning can evolve along with changing circumstances: 'Any organization with an ability to self-organize must have an element of redundancy: a form of excess capacity which, appropriately designed and used, creates room to manoeuvre' (Morgan, 1986: 98).

A company in which duplication abounds is 3M. Duplication is deliberately created by such means as the 15 per cent rule that tells researchers to spend that much of their time working on something other than their primary project, the 'Genesis Grant'—money that is not allocated by management but by a panel of fellow scientists—or the many overlapping research laboratories (*Fortune*, 1996). The company also encourages the informal exchange of information. As a consequence, it has constant self-organization and self-redesign without the need for major coordination efforts across the company. Overlapping work roles or redundancies in functions (Emery, 1969), ambiguous goals and responsibilities (Burns and Stalker, 1961), and informal communication channels can increase the organizational potential to deal with emergent problems in the form of expanded search and a higher level of organizational curiosity (Hedberg, 1981: 15).

Even more important than slack for flexible resources and self-organizing capabilities is the slack in strategic schemas, sometimes called mental flexibility. Constructive responses to emerging changes depend on the degree to which these changes can be interpreted within a firm's strategic schema, that is, the collection of shared beliefs. It is important for any organization that this strategic schema changes sufficiently to interpret a changing world, yet remains sufficiently shared and stable to mediate mutual understanding and common action and to help organizational participants make sense of personal experience (Metcalfe, 1981: 507).

Flexibility from an Environment–Organization Perspective

In sum, organizational flexibility from a dynamic contingency perspective is a proactive and reactive organizational potential for maintaining a dynamic fit between organization and environment. As was already explained in Section 3.1, flexible configuration strategies and broad strategic schemas are required in order to develop this potential. A brief overview of the developments within conceptions of the environment and their contributions to organizational flexibility is presented in Table 3.2.

TABLE 3.2. Developments within conceptions of environment and their contributions to organizational flexibility

Organization–environment perspective		
Static contingency theory	Population-ecology theory	Dynamic contingency theory
objective/perceived environment	objective environment	perceived/enacted environment
deterministic approach	deterministic approach	deterministic and voluntaristic approach
static fit	tight fit	dynamic fit: fit and stretch
reactive adaptation	environmental selection	mutual adaptation
flexibility is reactive capacity	anti-flexibility in the form of inertia	flexibility is proactive and reactive organizational potential

3.3 A Capacity to Reflect on the Learning System

In considering strategic management and contingency theories, we contended that organizational flexibility requires organizational potential, created by a flexible configuration of resources and broad strategic schemas, for maintaining a dynamic fit between organization and environment. None the less, this conception of flexibility is still incomplete. How can this potential be maintained and further developed? How could Honda remain agile and adaptive while GM clearly could not? Honda employed ingenious means to trigger self-questioning and learning. To align themselves with their environments firms must have some unique skills to learn, unlearn, or relearn on the basis of their past behaviour. Learning theories, therefore, prescribe that organizational potential in the form of redundancy, ambiguity, and slack in idea systems must be allocated to organizational learning: 'What the organizations and systems to which we belong now require is a new capacity, enabling us consciously to face up to more direct and much clearer contradictions. This organizational capacity does not exist naturally, it is a human conquest, the fruit of a long learning process' (Crozier, 1973: 160).

In this context, organizational learning or reflective change concerns the development of insights, knowledge, and associations between past actions, the effectiveness of those actions, and future actions (Fiol and Lyles, 1985: 811). Learning may take place when organizations interact with their environment, in situations when organizations increase their understanding of reality by observing the results of their actions. This learning process is both adaptive and manipulative in the sense that organizations adjust defensively to reality and use the resulting knowledge offensively to improve the fits between organization and environment (Hedberg, 1981: 3). In other words, organizations map their environment and use their maps to alter their environment. This learning process is depicted in Figure 3.2.

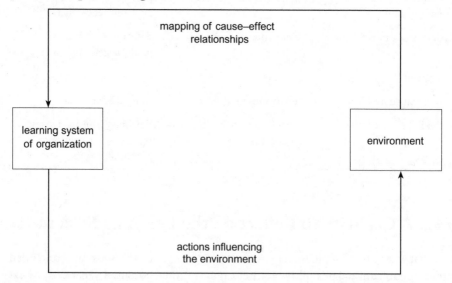

Fig. 3.2. Learning as an adaptive-manipulative relationship between the organization and its environment
Source: based on Hedberg (1981: 5)

Organizational learning must be distinguished from non-organizational learning, that is, unreflective change. In the latter case, the organization is unable to reap the fruits of its potential. As a consequence, the organization floats with its surroundings, almost unable to learn from and control its development.

Many firms have invested huge amounts of money in learning. SmithKline Beecham started training cascade-down its whole staff as a part of its change programme 'Simply Better Way' (Coyle and Page, 1994). Similarly, Motorola believes that its most crucial weapons will be responsiveness and adaptability and therefore dramatically increased training of all employees, from the factory floor to the corner office (*Business Week*, 1994). None the less, the crucial question of how to accomplish and facilitate collective learning in order to develop and maintain an appropriate organizational potential remains. The answer depends largely on the kind of learning discussed. In this section, three types of learning and the ways in which they contribute to the concept of flexibility are examined.

Single-Loop Learning: Limited Search

Whenever an organizational error, deviation, or problem is detected and corrected, or solved without questioning or altering the underlying values and norms of the organization, the learning is 'single-loop' (Argyris and Schön, 1978). This learning mechanism can help the organization to exploit previous experiences, to detect causalities, and extrapolate to the future. As a result, problem-solving skills may improve, formal rules may be modified, individual assumptions may be discarded in favour of others yielding different behavioural outcomes, but no cognitive change takes place in the organization. These learning mechanisms permit the organization to persist in its set policies and achieve its formulated objectives.

Based on *repetitive reinforcement* of associations between input and output, single-loop learning is very common in organizations. Many organizations have become proficient at this way of learning, developing an ability to scan the environment and to monitor the general performance of the organization in relation to its objectives (Morgan, 1986: 89). Xerox has mastered single-loop learning on a company-wide scale (Garvin, 1993). In 1983, senior managers launched the company's 'Leadership Through Quality' initiative. Since then, all employees have been trained in small-group activities and problem-solving techniques. A systematic problem-solving approach is used for virtually all decisions. The result of this process has been a common vocabulary and a consistent, company-wide approach to problem solving.

Single-loop learning goes together with the development of routines in the form of standard operating rules, which are often institutionalized in the planning and control systems and shared values of the organization. Organizations have many such stabilizers, but quite often lack proper destabilizers (Hedberg and Jönsson, 1978). Drifting into changing environments, they react with delayed and improper responses. Thus, when the fundamental norms and values are no longer appropriate, single-loop learning and the resulting use of standard operating procedures introduce significant response delays into organizations' decision systems. This is what actually happened with GM's learning system throughout the 1980s and early 1990s. It reinforced the mistaken belief that cars are status symbols and that styling is more important than quality. Further, finance exerted a tremendous dominance over the entire organization. The emergence of one dominant elite narrows the frame in which learning occurs (Pascale, 1990). This kind of learning hampers organizational search and filters away significant amounts of relevant uncertainty, diversity, and change signals. Consequently, the organization is motivated to transform ill-defined problems into a form that can be handled with existing routines (Miles and Snow, 1978: 156). GM's learning system rewarded only volume and simply ignored quality. The inability of the organization to solve new, significantly different problems derived from this retardation of organizational learning. Mistaken perceptions of the customer and the tight financial instruments led to complacency, myopia, and, ultimately, decline. Money became a substitute for innovation, past success turned into dogma, and maintenance of the status quo became the measure of success (*Fortune*, 1994; 1995). In a sense, single-loop learning may have the unintended consequence of building inertia that threatens organizational survival (Metcalfe, 1981: 507).

In this context, organizational flexibility is the ability of an organization to detect deviations from existing norms and values and the rapidity by which these deviations can be corrected. The resulting routines and standard operating rules, however, eliminate the organizational potential; the organization is doing what it has already been doing more efficiently (distinct competences), but is unable to question the appropriateness of what it is doing. The existing configuration of resources and capabilities and tight strategic schemas is reinforced, which gradually results in planning strategies (see Figure 3.3). These strategies may yield some organizational slack, which again stimulates limited search and reinforces the planning strategy (Bourgeois III, 1981). This vicious circle leads to a static fit. It is a self-reinforcing cycle in which conditions for error in organizational basic beliefs and norms provoke individual members to behaviour which reinforces those conditions. So long as these errors in beliefs and norms remain in force, individuals are unable to function effectively as agents of organizational learning. As a result, the organization is dominated by a tendency towards conservatism, delay in decision-making and implementation, and ossification. The process of allocating organizational potential to single-

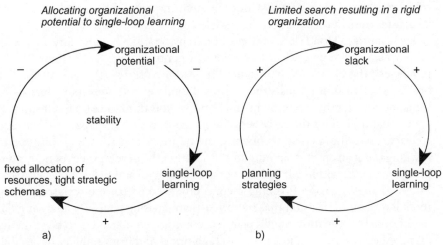

Fig. 3.3. The effects of single-loop learning

Note:
+ = the two connected events change in the same direction.
− = the two connected events change in the opposite direction.

loop learning is depicted in Figure 3.3*a*. The even number of negative signs implies that it is a deviation-amplifying loop; the organization will gradually develop into a rigid organization (see Fig. 3.3*b*) that will fall apart unless another type of learning occurs.

Double-Loop Learning: Expanded Search

How can the potential for expanded search be developed and maintained? At the same time that an organization develops its distinctive competence on the basis of limited search (single-loop learning), it exposes itself to risks associated with the things it does not do well. In order to expand its set of effective searches, double-loop learning, in which present behaviour and its underlying causes are directly confronted, must occur. This type of learning refers to those sorts of organizational inquiries which resolve incompatible organizational norms by setting new priorities and weighting norms, or by restructuring the norms themselves (Argyris and Schön, 1978: 24). It is a double feedback loop which connects the detection of error not only to procedures for effective performance, but to the very norms which define effective performance. It hinges on the ability to remain open to changes occurring in the environment, and on the ability to challenge operating assumptions in a fundamental way. Organizations must increasingly develop the capacity to redefine the problems they seek to solve, redesign their relations with their environments, and discard established structures in the process (Metcalfe, 1981: 526).

For example, Honda discourages hierarchy, grants responsibility to young employees, and supports confrontation. In contrast with GM's 'Rank has its privileges', the Honda Way preaches 'To lead is to serve' (Pascale, 1990). The boss's job is to free up his subordinates. Honda encourages individualists to think independently, experiment, and improve. It is this kind of self-questioning ability that underpins the activities of organizations that are capable of learning to learn and self-organize. Frequently, the desired consequence of this type of learning is not any particular outcome, but rather the development of new interpretive schemas within which to make decisions (Fiol and Lyles, 1985: 808). For instance, Shell's Group Planning reconceptualized its basic tasks as changing mental models of decision-makers rather than devising plans. By analysing different possible scenarios, Shell's planners conditioned managers to be mentally prepared for a shift from low prices to high prices and from stability to instability.

Most organizations do quite well in single-loop learning, but have great difficulties in double-loop learning. Further, organizations tend to create learning systems that inhibit double-loop learning, which calls into question their norms, objectives, and basic policies. Standard operating procedures, however, must be unlearned if new potentials are to be utilized. Before IBM could begin developing a new strategy, the mainframe logic needed to be partially unlearned or forgotten. The need for unlearning implies that firms have to reduce or abandon past routines to become more receptive to new possibilities. Totally new values and norms are required and past experience may not provide any advantage.

Regarding double-loop learning, organizational flexibility is the capacity of an organization to adjust its overall rules and norms, rather than specific activities or behaviours, and the rapidity with which these changes can be implemented. It occurs through the use of heuristics, skill development, and fundamentally new insights. It is therefore a more *cognitive process* than is single-loop learning, which is often the result of repetitive behaviour. The associations that result from double-loop learning have long-term effects and impacts on the organization as a whole (Fiol and Lyles, 1985: 808). It goes together with the emergence of a new configuration of resources and capabilities and new frames of reference. These emergent strategies are able to tap new potentials (see Fig. 3.4). For example, Honda's successful introduction of the Honda Supercub in the US market was a result of its ability to learn from failure and consistently reconfigure its resources and develop new strategic schemas. Due to technical problems with the larger motorcycles and limited cash reserves, it was able to discard its cognitive ideas that Americans are interested only in the larger 250cc and 305cc motorcycles and that 50cc motorcycles would harm its image in a heavily macho market (Pascale, 1984). It invested heavily in 50cc motorcycles, in

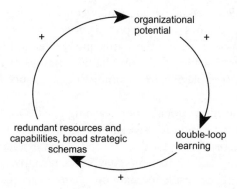

Fig. 3.4. Allocating organizational potential to single-loop learning

Note:
  + = the two connected events change in the same direction.
  − = the two connected events change in the opposite direction.

new retailers like sports-goods stores instead of traditional motorcycle dealers, and in new non-traditional marketing programmes such as 'You meet the nicest people on a Honda'.

However, double-loop learning can have dysfunctional effects. 3M, a company with a superior track record of double-loop learning, has found important drawbacks to this learning: idle financial and intellectual resources, an environment that encourages people to work around and even defy their superiors, and a determination to let the company follow where its scientists and customers lead (*Fortune*, 1996). The company does not have a clear strategy; the development and introduction of a product merely evolves. Patience, for example, has cost 3M dearly in the magnetic-storage business (diskettes, videotape, and audio tape). Still, 3M held on because the business supported technologies it needed elsewhere. A well-articulated strategy could have helped 3M work its way to a quicker and less drastic resolution of the long-simmering problems in its imaging and electronic storage businesses.

The attention to the incompatibility of norms and objectives, which cannot be resolved by a search for the most effective means, may produce low trust or defensive behaviours and lead to avoidance or bypass tactics (cf. Argyris and Schön, 1978, Van de Ven, 1986: 579). It may create forms of incomplete learning, such as superstitious or ambiguous learning. Superstitious learning may result during good times, when even the most inappropriate behaviour leads to favourable outcomes, or during bad times when optimal choices lead to disappointing results (March, 1981). Ambiguous learning refers to situations in which strategic schemas are conserved in the face of experience which radically contradicts them. For instance, leaders may consequently encourage the formation of strategic schemas that interpret experience as confirming the success of their own actions or conserve the status quo (Miller and Ross, 1975). These forms of incomplete learning focus on identifying ways of not changing, not experimenting; of game-playing, maintaining the status quo, and avoiding problems.

Furthermore, too much double-loop learning creates instability as a consequence of overreactions and excessive information searches. The organization exaggerates the importance of local errors and becomes overresponsive to fads and fashions. Continuous adjustments may waste resources on 'noise' in environmental signals. They result in chaotic organizations that cannot retain a sense of identity and continuity over time (Weick, 1979: 215). Chronic double-loop learning destroys the identity or shared idea system of the organization. It creates a vicious circle that results in an organization characterized by potentially serious problems with conflict of authority, unclear responsibilities, inadequate controls, lack of direction and shared ideology, and, consequently, greater scope for chaos and inefficiency (Volberda and Cheah, 1993). The decline of Apple Computer, once the hip standard-bearer of high tech, is illustrative (*Business Week*, 1996). Apple created the legend of two kids in a garage inventing a computer and then building a company where the old corporate rules were scrapped: no dress or hair codes, no formal meetings. This anarchic culture facilitated double-loop learning, and fostered chaos and conflict. It led to many clashes between the creators, or the 'technical wizards', and the experienced managers hired to run marketing and finance. Year after year, key decisions such as licensing the Mac operating system were postponed, reversed, or avoided completely as various executives and factions tried to push their own agendas.

Deutero-Learning: Balancing Single-Loop and Double-Loop Learning

An organization needs limited search in order to develop competences, but at the same time it must remain open for expanded search. Or, in Argyris and Schön's terminology, organizations need single-loop learning to accomplish some of their most important functions, such as creating continuity, consistency, and stability. On the other hand, organizational designs are imperfect and incomplete and thus require continual reflection and monitoring to meet challenges from both the changing external environment as well as counterproductive activities within the internal environment.

These paradoxical requirements imply that there are balances to be struck if learning is to remain vital (Hedberg *et al.*, 1976). Single-loop learning, where existing norms and values are not questioned, creates a rigid organization. By contrast, a wholesale discrediting of norms creates a chaotic organization. Neither form is flexible for long. It appears the extent to which organizations' exploration of unknown futures and their exploitation of the known past balance each other is of crucial importance to effective learning (Hedberg and Jönsson, 1978: 50). These forms of learning need not be contradictory processes. They can be opposites and yet complements. Therefore, the organization needs to learn how to carry out both of them. Following Bateson, Argyris and Schön called this learning to learn 'deutero-learning'. When an organization engages in deutero-learning, it reflects on and inquires into previous contexts for learning. It may evolve new ways of seeing that enhance its capability for learning across a range of situations. The most important function of organizational deutero-learning consists of reflection on those processes by which the learning system inhibits inquiry.

The difficulties of effective deutero-learning are illustrated by tensions between the two main divisions of KLM Royal Dutch Airlines, the KLM Passenger and KLM Cargo divisions. KLM is a one-system company, that is, its divisions share the same resources, namely aeroplanes. Within the passenger division, the focus is on single-loop learning: achieving tight cost reductions by essentially doing more of the same activities. By contrast, within the cargo division the emphasis is on double-loop learning. This means doing new things in new businesses such as offering an increasing number of added-value services to customers (transporting dangerous goods, live animals, or expensive paintings), attracting new customers, and providing non-transport-related logistic services (subassembly of components, stock maintenance). According to Jacques Ancher, Executive Vice-President of KLM Cargo, 'Our greatest challenge is to let go; there is no place for a command and control culture. We have to be prepared for mistakes, and be prepared to learn from them. This requires an entirely different mindset to the one we had last year: it demands nothing short of fundamental change.' The KLM board, however, faces the question of how to reconcile single-loop (tight cost reductions) and double-loop learning (new businesses) in one single company: by some form of compromise response, by alternation between single-loop and double-loop learning, or by the simultaneous expression of both tendencies in different portions of the organization. The latter two increase organizational flexibility, the former limits the organization's flexibility. Unfortunately, compromise responses usually dominate everything else since they seem to be acceptable to those with competing interests: 'The fact of acceptability is not what's crucial here. The crucial point is that, in effecting the compromise solution, important adaptive responses have been selected against and nonadaptive, moderate responses have been preserved' (Weick, 1979: 220).

The new cost-cutting programmes initiated by chairman Pieter Bouw seem inescapable in the airline industry but have the negative effect of eliminating double-loop learning. Flexibility is maintained, however, if opposed responses can be preserved. On the basis of reflections on the learning system, deutero-learning may help the organization to develop both learning mechanisms for exploiting previous experiences and to detect causalities, and unlearning mechanisms so that it can do away with obsolete knowledge and behaviour.

Flexibility from a Learning Perspective

In this section, two types of flexibility related to single-loop and double-loop learning have been distinguished. Deutero-learning implies that reflecting on the learning system may help organizations create adequate balances of single-loop and double-loop learning. It thereby emphasizes a higher level of flexibility, namely metaflexibility. In this context, metaflexibility is a reflective capacity concerning the organization's learning system for creating a process of dynamic balance, allowing single-loop and double-loop learning to operate in a predominantly complementary or simultaneous fashion. Table 3.3 demonstrates the different types of learning and their contributions to our understanding of flexibility.

3.4 Facilitating Entrepreneurial Behaviour and Innovation

So far, we have argued that organizational flexibility requires organizational potential, which is created by flexible configuration strategies and broad strategic schemas, and which has to be allocated according to a proper balance of single-loop and double-loop learning. None the less, we are still unsure about the outcome of such an allocation.

In recent years, several scholars and practitioners within the fields of innovation and entrepreneurship have contended that organizational flexibility is one of the most important factors which contribute to successful entrepreneurial activities and innovation. According to Kanter (1988), for instance, innovations are most likely to flourish when organizational conditions allow flexibility. In her conception of the innovation process, flexibility is a requirement for idea realization; the unpredictable nature of innovation demands flexibility if the organization is to persist with a new idea, project, or product. Moreover, Kanter's (1982) research indicated that internal entrepreneurship cannot thrive in the absence of a flexible management style. Further, Quinn (1985) found in a sample of well-documented small ventures and large US, Japanese, and European companies that multiple approaches, flexibility, and quickness are

TABLE 3.3. Types of learning and their contributions to organizational flexibility

Type of learning		
Single-loop learning	Double-loop learning	Deutero-learning
learning to detect and correct errors from existing norms and values	learning to detect and correct errors in norms and values themselves	reflecting on and inquiring into previous contexts for learning
limited search based on routines	expanded search based on heuristic and non-routines	monitoring of learning system
eliminating organizational potential	creating new organizational potential	managing organizational potential
self-reinforcing configuration of resources and strategic schemas	emergent configuration of resources and strategic schemas	self-reinforcing and emergent configuration of resources and strategic schemas
flexibility is the ability to detect deviations from existing norms and values and the rapidity by which these deviations can be detected	flexibility is the ability to adjust the overall norms and values and the rapidity by which these adjustments can be implemented	flexibility is reflective capacity on the organization's learning system in order to create appropriate balances between single-loop and double-loop learning

necessary for innovation because of the advance of new ideas through random and often highly intuitive insights, as well as the discovery of unanticipated problems. Innovative companies keep their programmes flexible for as long as possible and freeze plans only when necessary for strategic purposes such as timing. In the same vein, Quinn noted that innovation requires a flexible entrepreneurial atmosphere. Furthermore, Utterback and Abernathy's (1975) dynamic model of process and product innovation suggests that innovation can start only within flexible organizations that can easily respond to environmental change, have 'slack', and are to some extent 'inefficient'. More extremely, Bolwijn and Kumpe (1990) argued that organizations must first manage flexibility well before they can realize innovations at all. In their view, flexibility is a necessary condition for innovation.

Flexibility and the Postmodern Organization

In sum, the basic assumption of these 'theories in use' is that organizational flexibility stimulates entrepreneurial activities and facilitates innovation. However, this proposition is rather simplistic. Although entrepreneurship and innovation cannot be accomplished without some sort of change, not every change results in the same kind of entrepreneurship and innovation. Therefore, we will more closely examine the relationship between organizational flexibility and different kinds of innovations and modes of entrepreneurship. In fact, we will argue that significantly different conceptions of flexibility are related to these different kinds of innovation and modes of entrepreneurship.

Incremental Innovations Promoted by Austrian Entrepreneurs

Organizations accumulate know-how in the course of their existence. They become repositories of skills which are unique and often difficult to transfer. These skills are the source of both inertia and distinctive competence. The inertia results from sunk costs in past investments and entrenched social structures, and also to organization members becoming attached to certain cognitive styles, behavioural dispositions, and decision heuristics. The accumulated skills which render firms inert also provide opportunities for strengthening their unique advantages and further improving their know-how. The potential benefits include greater reliability in delivering a sound and comprehensible product and many economies of efficiency and routine (Miller and Chen, 1994: 1). In this view, innovation hinges on the proximity to prior and commensurate skills. As a consequence, improvements occur slowly and incrementally.

Among the best-known proponents of the incremental view are evolutionary theorists as well as researchers within the resource-based theory of the firm. In their *Evolutionary theory of economic change*, Nelson and Winter (1982) present firms as *repositories of routines* which endow them with a capacity to search. Yet the same routines suppress attention span and the capacity to absorb new information by spelling out behaviour that permits search only for new ideas that are consistent with prior learning. In a similar way, the firm in the *resource-based theory* is seen as a bundle of tangible and intangible resources and tacit know-how that must be identified, selected, developed, and deployed to generate superior performance (Penrose, 1959; Learned *et al.*, 1969; Wernerfelt, 1984). These scarce, firm-specific assets may lead to a core competence with a limited capacity to change. Just as with the evolutionary theory of economic change, the resource-based theory assumes that firms are stuck with what they have and have to live with what they lack.

The most significant part of these theories is the notion that *routines play a large role in creating innovations*. Innovations are not radically different from previously followed routines, but are more often novel combinations of old routines. The old routines are a necessary element of innovations, whether they are technological or administrative. Organization search processes do not extend very far beyond the routines which are currently shelved by the organization. By this view, innovations have an inner logic of their own. Therefore, Nelson and Winter (1977) conjectured that there are powerful logics that apply when a technology is advanced in a certain direction, and payoffs from advancing in that direction under a wide range of demand conditions. The knowledge of potential and existing constraints gives rise to what Nelson and Winter call 'natural trajectories'. For example, advances in memory devices have been cumulative along a particular technological trajectory, from 1K to 4K to 64K to 256K to 1 megabyte, and so on. Given the tacit and cumulative nature of knowledge, experience with previous generations of a technology is often essential for future innovative success (Cohen and Levinthal, 1990).

On the other hand, the 'switching costs' or the costs of changing trajectories and acquiring knowledge unrelated to the asset base can be quite high. Rosenberg (1972) talked of 'technological imperatives' as guiding the evolution of certain technologies, such as bottlenecks in connected processes, obvious weak spots in products, or clear targets for improvement. The natural trajectories, as stated above, are based upon refinements or extensions of existing concepts or approaches. According to Clark (1985: 249), 'Innovation of this kind strengthens and reinforces existing commitments. The organization becomes more conservative in nature'. Consequently, the operational difficulties tend to become routine, capable of being solved on the basis of acquired experience. In this connection, the management task tends to become a matter of optimization (Simon, 1960). Incremental innovations also occur through imitation and extrapolation. The risks of these forms of 'single-loop learning' were discussed in Section 3.3.

Incremental innovations are promoted by Austrian (A) entrepreneurs, who seek to *exploit presently available knowledge and existing opportunities*. Drawing upon the work of Kirzner (1973) of the neo-Austrian school, Austrian entrepreneurship stems from the discovery of the existence of profitable discrepancies, gaps, mismatches of knowledge and information which others have not yet perceived and exploited. This concept of entrepreneurship is closely linked to arbitrage and the ability to correctly anticipate where these market imperfections and imbalances will be. Austrian entrepreneurs therefore increase knowledge about the situation, reduce the general level of uncertainty over time, and promote market processes which help to reduce or to eliminate the gap between leaders and followers. They tend to develop appropriate routines to reduce uncertainty to a minimum, and to enable the organization to operate as efficiently as possible. As a result, the organization becomes very concerned with 'doing things right'. By developing certain routines, the organization tries to adapt to certain demands in the environment. Its growing concern is, therefore, to achieve stability and equilibrium. In this connection, the A-entrepreneur acts only when he or she is able to assess the risks attached to an opportunity. Although opportunities for the A-entrepreneur can be very dynamic and complex, they are predictable to a large extent, and various routines (ranging from simple to very sophisticated) can be developed. Consequently, the A-entrepreneur devotes substantial resources to formal planning, analysis, and evaluation of an opportunity and its associated risks before arriving at a decision about it.

To sum up, in this incremental view of innovation as combined with the Austrian mode of entrepreneurship, flexibility is conceived of as an organizational ability to create a repertoire of routines for alertly exploiting available opportunities. Routines are used here in a flexible way, in much the same way as a program is used in discussions of computer programming. This type of flexibility promotes routine learning by entrepreneurs and facilitates changes that are realized step by step, balancing small winnings and mistakes in the form of natural trajectories.

Radical Innovations Promoted by Schumpeterian Entrepreneurs

In the incremental view of innovation, it is assumed that the gap between the current know-how (and its associated inertia) and the required know-how, which lies at the heart of the quest for renewal, can be bridged. If the distance is large, however, it can be assumed that incremental efforts at renewal are less likely to succeed (Pennings and Harianto, 1992). Furthermore, Teece (1984: 106) has argued that a *limited repertoire of available routines severely constrains a firm's strategic choice.* While the suppression of choice is probably a condition for the efficient exploitation of a core competence, many studies show that in highly competitive environments a core competence can become a core rigidity (Leonard-Barton, 1992; Burgelman, 1994; Barnett *et al.*, 1994) or competence trap (Levitt and March, 1988; Levinthal and March, 1993). Firms develop core rigidities together with highly specialized resources and routines to enhance profits at the price of reduced flexibility (Volberda, 1996*b*). GM, IBM, and DEC have encountered these traps. They have become prisoners of their deeply ingrained routines and irreversible, fixed assets, turning their formerly distinctive competences (big cars, mainframe computers, minicomputers) into new problems to be resolved.

Teece *et al.* (1997), therefore, have suggested that the relative superiority and imitability of firm-specific resources and routines cannot be taken for granted and that, from a normative perspective, the firm must always remain in a dynamic capability building mode, in which the firm retains its capacity to renew, augment, and adapt its core competence over time. Similarly, Utterback and Abernathy's (1975) model posits that a firm which does pursue the evolution of its processes and products to the extreme may find that it has achieved the benefits of high productivity only at the cost of decreased flexibility and innovative capacity. It must face competition from innovative products that are produced by other flexible firms. NCR's focus on its established line of business, electromechanical cash registers, and ignorance of electronic machines is illustrative. From 1972 to 1976, it lost 80 per cent of the market for cash registers to more flexible manufacturers of electronic products. Likewise, GM was reluctant to design and build compact cars for fear this niche would cannibalize its big-car business.

Using an interpretative perspective on product development within five large firms, Dougherty (1989) demonstrated that routines tend not to include the intensive interactions and creative learning necessary to produce innovation. By relying on routines, which work like well-worn grooves to channel activities, organizational units concentrate on their own specialized areas and avoid the need to construct their notion of the whole for new activities. Their routines, in effect, gloss the outer processes of knowledge development, closing off the firm as a whole from an evolution of its competences. Not surprisingly, successful innovation efforts violate the established routines, while unsuccessful efforts follow them. In the latter case, the routines exacerbate the separation of 'thought worlds', impede learning processes by dictating relationships, and further restrict the development of new knowledge and continued competence by imposing old understandings.

The findings of the Minnesota Innovation Research Program, based on seven longitudinal case studies, reveal that the process of innovation often elapses ad hoc, discontinuously, and by fits and starts, and relates to multiple organization levels (Schroeder et al., 1986). This *discontinuous process of innovation* implies that renewals are rarely predictable. Certain unexpected shocks, either internal or external to the organization, stimulate innovations. When these impulses reach a certain threshold of necessity, opportunity, or dissatisfaction, they may lead to innovative behaviour by organizational participants. Therefore patterns of actions and decisions can be observed only *in retrospect*. In this context, the development of a priori routines is not useful. One-sided planning of discontinuous processes may paralyse processes of renewal. Rather, discontinuous innovations go together with unplanned change.

The modification of skilled performance and routines by choice greatly expands the potential diversity, flexibility, and adaptability of an organization. Increased choice promotes radical innovations, instead of incremental or adaptive innovations. These innovations are associated with departures from existing approaches, destroying the value of established commitments and competence, and requiring new resources and skills (Clark, 1985). While the liability of newness plagues new firms confronting incremental innovations within well-established markets, liability of age and tradition constrains existing successful firms in the face of radical innovations (Tushman and Anderson, 1986; Stinchcombe, 1965). Instead of building on existing skills and know-how, radical innovation requires fundamentally new skills and competences. In this context, 'double-loop learning' by trial and error is essential. As was argued in Section 3.3, the expansion of choice by abandoning routines also results in certain opportunity costs in terms of foregone uses of conscious attention. As a consequence, some hesitation and awkwardness is introduced into an otherwise smooth process.

The development of 'breakthrough' innovations (Hisrich and Peters, 1989) requires a totally different mode of entrepreneurship than 'ordinary' innovations, where the desire for or expectation of change is limited and predictable. Radical innovations are facilitated by the disequilibrium-generating activities of the Schumpeterian (S) entrepreneur,[12] who is capable of 'breaking new ground', pioneering new fields, promoting radical diversification efforts and innovations, and partially or completely transforming the organization, its products, its technology, and its markets in the process. These innovative activities lead to 'the discovery of an intertemporal opportunity that cannot, even in principle, be said to actually exist before the innovation has been created' (Kirzner, 1985: 85), and this circumstance causes disruption and transformation of the pre-existing equilibrium situation. Thus, a Schumpeterian opportunity is one where the *associated uncertainty is not amenable to formal objective assessment, and against which no insurance is possible*. Therefore, S-entrepreneurs will tend to act despite an inability to formally and carefully assess the risks associated with the opportunity. Owing to the inherent uncertainties in the development process, Schumpeter asserted that, in addition to technical skills and expertise, the exercise of choice was of particular importance. He pointed out that the entrepreneur, in undertaking innovation,

must still foresee and estimate on the basis of his experience. But many things must remain uncertain, still others are only ascertainable within wide limits, some can perhaps only be 'guessed'. . . . As military action must be taken in a given strategic position even if all the data potentially procurable are not available, so also in economic life action must be taken without working out all the details of what is to be done. Here the success of everything depends upon intuition, the capacity of seeing things in a way which afterwards proves to be true, even though it cannot be established at the moment, and of grasping the essential fact, disregarding the unessential, even though one can give no account of the principles by which this is done. (Schumpeter, 1934: 85)

Consequently, the S-entrepreneur would rely on informal ('rules of thumb') methods of assessment to a greater degree, and devote relatively few resources to the formal assessment of an opportunity or of the uncertainty associated with it, prior to committing himself.

To recapitulate, in this radical view of innovation together with the Schumpeterian mode of entrepreneurship, flexibility is conceived of as an organizational ability to abandon routines in order to improve adaptability for exploiting future opportunities.

Oscillating, Balanced, or Simultaneous Modes of Innovation and Entrepreneurship

At its very root, the entrepreneurial process of radical innovation, where fresh insights and bold creativity may be required, is at odds with the incremental process of innovation, where stability, consistency, and alert planning may be essential to regular improvement. This tension is addressed by Weick (1982) in terms of a trade-off between adaptation (incremental innovation) to exploit present opportunities (Austrian entrepreneurship) and adaptability (radical innovation) to exploit future opportunities (Schumpeterian entrepreneurship). Within research into entrepreneurship and innovation, most theories and classification models deny this *contradictory element*. They avoid the challenge of including both approaches in the process of innovation. That is, they stress either the incremental or radical view of innovation. More recently, however, many scholars have asserted that incremental and radical innovations and their associated entrepreneurial processes need not be contradictory.

For instance, Utterback and Abernathy (1975) suggested that the dominant type of innovation, whether technologically complex or simple, and whether applied to product or process, depends upon the *stage of development*. In the early stage of the production process and product life cycle, when the process is fluid with loose and unsettled relationships (uncoordinated) and when the firm emphasizes unique products and product performance (performance-maximizing), fundamental or radical innovations dominate (Clark, 1985). In this situation, production capacity will be flexible, permitting easy variation in production input, and will tend to be located both near affluent markets and where a variety of production inputs are available. As a result, the rate of product change is expected to be rapid and margins are expected to be large. However, as the process becomes more highly developed and integrated, and investment in it becomes large (systemic stage), radical innovation will be increasingly more difficult. The process becomes so well integrated that major changes are very costly because they require changes in other elements of the process and in the product design. Isolated radical innovations, even those of major significance, seldom gain ready acceptance. Innovation at this stage is likely to alter only a small aspect of the basic product, and any changes introduced serve to refine the established design. On the process side, work flow is rationalized, integrated, and linear, unlike the fluid and flexible job shop of the early period. Further, general-purpose machines and skilled workers are replaced by dedicated, highly specific equipment. During this stage, incremental innovations dominate.

Furthermore, the study of Tushman and Anderson (1986), on the basis of a number of product-class case studies, indicates that technology progresses in stages through relatively long periods of incremental, competence-enhancing innovation elaborating a particular dominant design. None the less, these periods of increasing consolidation and learning-by-doing may be *punctuated* by radical competence-destroying technological innovations.

This postulated complementarity of incremental and radical innovations in the development process also pertains to the associated entrepreneurial activities. For example, Johannisson (1987) argues that successful entrepreneurs are both anarchists and organizers. Moreover, Volberda and Cheah (1993) assert that Schumpeterian and Austrian entrepreneurship are *interdependent* in the overall development process. Specifically, it is the activities and processes generated by Schumpeterian entrepreneurs which, over time, increase the scope for Austrian entrepreneurs, and vice versa. The launching of a radical innovation by Schumpeterian entrepreneurs produces systemic change(s) that destroy the existing equilibrium and re-create uncertainties, mismatches of information, and a proliferation of new, unexploited opportunities within a particular situation. Through the exploitation of those opportunities, the specific function of Austrian entrepreneurs is to help to define the full potential and approximate limits of this radical innovation. When Austrian entrepreneurs establish the limits of the previous radical innovation, an equilibrium is created which serves as the foundation for subsequent Schumpeterian entrepreneurs to use that knowledge as the new foundation from which to launch the next radical innovation.

In sum, the process of innovation is considered as a *dynamic alternation* between incremental innovations undertaken by Austrian entrepreneurs and radical innovations undertaken by Schumpeterian entrepreneurs over time. This process of alternation of hegemony between radical and incremental innovations and their associated entrepreneurial activities creates significantly different situations, in response to which organizations have to alter their systems of organization and managerial practice. The real question, therefore, is not what technology, structure, or culture to put in place to encourage innovation, but how the dichotomy between the routinized current activities and the disorganized activities can be managed. One may move towards diversity and openness or towards homogeneity and tightness, but either choice leads to a theoretical stalemate because of the trade-offs between enhancement of radical innovation and enhancement of incremental innovation (Becker and Whiskler, 1967).

In response to firms' need for both alternatives, many scholars have speculated on the possibility of an *oscillating organizational mode* in line with the ideas of Burns and Stalker (1961), who described a process in which the organization is sequentially being manipulated into the loose, open diverse state that stimulates proposal of radical innovations and then back into the tight homogeneous state that enhances adoption of incremental innovations. In Weick's terms (1982), loose coupling is the source of adaptability to exploit future opportunities in organizations, whereas tight coupling is the source of adaptation to exploit present opportunities. Loosely structured, decentralized, complex, and heterogeneous organizations enhance radical innovation, but inhibit incremental innovation. On the other hand, tightly structured, centralized, highly formalized, homogeneous organizations facilitate incremental innovation (Duncan, 1976; Cohn and Turyn, 1984; Shepard, 1967). Duncan (1976) referred to the bifurcated organization as the ambidextrous organization, which is able to shift its technology, structure, and culture as it moves through various stages of innovation, while Shepard (1967) called it the two-state organization. Large capital-intensive corporations such as DSM Chemicals, Shell, and Unilever, which operate in cyclical industries, are still successful because they have managed to alternate cycles of convergence (centralization and formalization) with cycles of divergence (decentralization and autonomy).

Others (cf. Gresov, 1984) have argued for a simultaneous *balancing* of these two organizational modes. For example, an organization can choose to compensate for the proven adoptive incremental capacity of its mechanistic structure by encouraging and promoting cultural heterogeneity. If, on the other hand, an organization wants to compensate for the proven radical adaptability of its organic structure, it can seize upon the various devices used to solidify and extend a more homogeneous cultural pattern. Some large corporations have developed structures and cultures to achieve this balancing act. 3M, for example, continually reassesses the barriers to innovation that tend to develop over time. In order to overcome core rigidities, 3M has a formal goal of having 30 per cent of its sales derived from products that are new or have been substantially modified in the past four years. HP and Motorola are also pursuing structures and cultures that are more focused on building new competences. Like 3M, these companies decentralize decision-making at the team and divisional level, and encourage spin-off projects. In addition, they constantly seek ways of making their current technology obsolete in order to push the innovation envelope of their assets. For example, 70 per cent of HP's sales are represented by products introduced or substantially modified in the past two years. Similarly, the development of the Motorola Integrated Radio Services is projected to effectively supplant Motorola's lucrative cellular handset business.

Weick (1982) suggested that the firm may also *simultaneously* express the two organizational modes (loose and tight coupling) in different portions of the system. The simultaneous expression of the two necessities results in organizational asymmetry (Fast, 1979). In almost every diversified firm, one sees examples of asymmetry. For example, at the simple level, there is the asymmetry between high growth businesses and older, mature operations. More deliberate ways to create asymmetry are various modes for innovation, such as joint ventures (Powell, 1987), skunk works (Peters and Waterman, 1982) or internal corporate venturing (Fast, 1979, Burgelman, 1983). The development of the IBM personal computer is illustrative. Isolated from the bureaucratic IBM organization, a team of people managed to quickly develop an IBM PC. The downside of this organizational asymmetry was that once the PC business was integrated in the traditional IBM structure, it lost much of its momentum. Similarly, Eastman Kodak, Philips, and Xerox have had only modest success from their internal venturing and new business development programmes. More extreme examples of simultaneous structures are the alloplastic organization (Nicholls, 1980) or more recently the hypertext form (Nonaka, 1994). Based on successful Japanese companies, the hypertext organization is a parallel structure that combines the efficiency and stability of a hierarchical bureaucracy with the dynamism of the flat, cross-functional task force. For instance, Sharp has a hierarchical business layer, but the company exploits its project-team layer, which is a completely independent, parallel structure when it comes to new-product development.

Flexibility from a Perspective of Innovation and Entrepreneurship

On the basis of recent developments within theories of innovation and entrepreneurship, two different conceptions or types of flexibility have been discussed. The first conception of flexibility, creating an appropriate repertoire of routines in order to be alert to exploit presently available opportunities, promotes Austrian entrepreneurship and results in incremental innovations. The second conception of flexibility, abandoning routines in order to create new opportunities, promotes Schumpeterian entrepreneurship and facilitates radical innovation.

Furthermore, the process of innovation has been conceived of as a dynamic alternation between incremental and radical innovations and their associated entrepreneurial activities. This conception implies that the organization has to (1) oscillate between loosely coupled and tightly coupled organizational modes and the related types of flexibility, (2) simultaneously implement these two modes and types of flexibility in different portions of the system, or (3) balance these two types of flexibility in terms of a mechanistic structure and a heterogeneous culture, or an organic structure and homogeneous culture. The contributions to our understanding of flexibility that come from the two different views of innovation and associated modes of entrepreneurship are illustrated in Table 3.4.

TABLE 3.4. Innovation and associated modes of entrepreneurship and their contributions to organizational flexibility

Innovation and entrepreneurship	
Incremental innovation	Radical innovation
innovation hinges on the proximity to prior and commensurate routines/skills	innovation depends upon the ability to reduce/abandon routines
accumulation of routines results in natural trajectories	routines dictate relationships and restrict the development of new knowledge and continued competence by imposing old understandings
the suppression of choice associated with routines is a condition for core upgrading	the expansion of choice associated with abandoning routines is a condition for core renewal
innovations are promoted by Austrian entrepreneurs who seek to exploit presently available knowledge and existing opportunities	innovations are promoted by Schumpeterian entrepreneurs who seek to exploit future opportunities
the entrepreneur devotes substantial resources to formal planning, analysis, and evaluation of an opportunity and associated risks	the entrepreneur relies to a greater degree on 'rules of thumb'
flexibility is an organizational ability to create an appropriate repertoire of routines in order to improve adaptation to exploit present opportunities	flexibility is an organizational ability to abandon routines in order to improve adaptability to exploit future opportunities

3.5 Tensions within Theories: Change and Preservation

The analysis of relevant developments in theories of strategic management, organization–environment theories, learning theories, and theories of innovation and entrepreneurship and their contributions to flexibility reveals that:

Flexibility is an organizational potential, created by flexible configuration strategies and broad strategic schemas, which has to be allocated to a proper balance of

Flexibility and the Postmodern Organization

single-loop and double-loop learning and results in incremental as well as radical innovations.

While the above assertion is a 'garbage can' definition originating from various, partially overlapping, theories, all these theories describe parallel developments and emphasize tensions between these developments. The opposing attributes of management and organization which create these tensions are enumerated in Table 3.5.

TABLE 3.5. Tensions within the concept of flexibility

	The paradoxical nature of flexibility	
	Morphostasis	Morphogenesis
strategy mode	deliberate planning (fixed allocation of resources and limited strategic schemas)	emergent spontaneous strategies (redundancies and broad strategic schemas)
organization–environment relationship	achieving a static fit (deterministic)	achieving a dynamic fit (voluntaristic)
type of learning	facilitating single-loop learning (limited search)	facilitating double-loop learning (expanded search)
type of innovation and entrepreneurship	resulting in incremental innovations; Austrian entrepreneurs	resulting in radical innovations: Schumpeterian entrepreneurship

The attributes on the left-hand side of Table 3.5 lead to *morphostasis*, while those on the right lead to *morphogenesis*. Morphostatic organizations treat disturbance as external noise to be blocked out or adjusted to (Smith, 1982: 370). In this type of transition, order is preserved. By contrast, morphogenetic systems treat disturbance as information about internal conditions and respond by altering their orders. Such changes, once they have occurred, eliminate the possibility of an entity returning to the condition it was in before the change.

These tensions between preservation and change can be regarded as paradoxes. Van de Ven and Poole (1988: 21) defined a paradox as the simultaneous presence of two mutually exclusive assumptions or statements; taken singly, each is incontestably true, but taken together they are inconsistent. In this sense, organizational flexibility is inherently paradoxical. To be flexible, an organization must possess attributes that are simultaneously contradictory, even mutually exclusive. A paradox differs from similar concepts such as dilemma, irony, inconsistency, dialectic, ambivalence, or conflict in that no choice needs to be made between two or more contradictions (Cameron, 1986: 545). Both contradictions of the paradox of flexibility are accepted and present. Both operate simultaneously. In her study of high-tech firms in the Silicon Valley, Bahrami (1992) showed that emerging flexible enterprises were able to manage opposing tensions. They facilitated creativity, innovation, and speed while maintaining coordination, focus, and control. They could accommodate opposing tendencies and yet function as coherent and cohesive firms. Similar tensions also seem to confront many established corporations (cf. Bartlett and Ghoshal, 1988). Percy Barnevik, CEO of ABB, describes the firm's challenge as dealing with tensions such as global versus local, big versus small, and centralized versus decentralized. British Petroleum's challenge is how to reinforce corporate control while allowing its constituent businesses much greater speed and response. In this connection, Andrew Grove of Intel introduced the metaphor 'agile giant': big enough to win global wars of products, technology, and trade, while moving like a small company.

Change and Preservation: The Risk of Schismogenesis

Without the tensions that exist between preservation and change in organizations, unproductive *schismogenesis* occurs. Schismogenesis is a process of self-reinforcement in which attributes of the organization perpetuate themselves until they become extreme and therefore dysfunctional. Schismogenic interaction between attributes, generating patterns of activity based upon positive feedback, has been most clearly developed in the work of Bateson (1936) and subsequently applied to organizations by Morgan (1981) and Cameron (1986). In analysing the above-mentioned theories with respect to flexibility, we have distinguished two self-reinforcing cycles which lead to schismogenesis (see Fig. 3.5). The first vicious circle ends in organizational rigidity (Fig. 3.5a). By focusing on planning, the organization eliminates all strategic choice. Once an optimal fit is achieved, search for new strategies tends to decline. The organization's slack permits a reduction of criteria by which an alternative is considered feasible. Hence, the organization accumulates repertoires of programmes, and grows insensitive to change signals. The limited search of single-loop learning facilitates the development of a set of 'distinctive competences' that allow the organization to develop incremental innovations. Its routines and standard operating rules, however, eliminate organizational potential: the organization is doing what it had been doing more efficiently, but is unable to question the appropriateness of its actions. Consequently, planning strategies are reinforced and errors in beliefs and norms remain. The organization is dominated by a tendency towards conservatism, delay in decision-making, and ossification. The

Flexibility and the Postmodern Organization

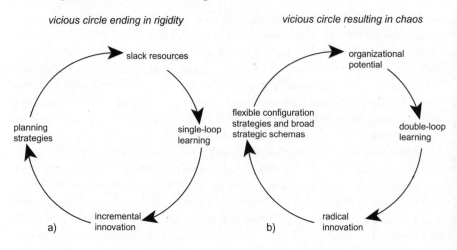

Fig. 3.5. Schismogenesis: self-reinforcement of preservation or change

accumulated organizational inertia may well be so significant that it threatens the organization's survival when environments change irreversibly.

On the other hand, flexible configurations of resources and broad strategic schemas may increase the organization's potential to deal with emergent problems in the form of expanded search and a higher level of curiosity (see Fig. 3.5*b*). The associated double-loop learning, which goes together with totally new values and norms, encourages radical innovations. None the less, the focus upon destroying the value of existing approaches may result in instability as a consequence of overreactions and excessive information searches. Continuous adjustment of strategic schemas and reallocations of resources may waste energy on 'noise' in environmental signals. Consequently, the organization is transformed into a chaotic organization that cannot retain a sense of identity and continuity over time.

To sum up, extremity in either direction of the paradox between change and preservation creates dysfunction in the form of rigidity or chaos. In a study on organizational failure, Hambrick and D'Aveni (1988) found that failing organizations displayed either extremely rigid or extremely chaotic behaviour in the years preceding a bankruptcy. By contrast, the creative tension arising from paradoxical attributes helps to foster organizational flexibility: it is the presence of balanced paradoxes that energizes and empowers organizational flexibility.

Four Generic Ways of Dealing with the Flexibility Paradox

As we have shown, most sub-theories within the field of strategic management, organization–environment, organizational learning, and innovation and entrepreneurship have emphasized either preservation or change. As Van de Ven and Poole (1988) argued, there is pressure to elevate one term and to subordinate the other. Therefore most theories within these fields represent defensive approaches that basically revoke the paradox's contradictory element. They all utilize either/or rather than both/and approaches. They escape the challenge of including both extremes. Hence, they have limited explanatory potential. However, we illustrated above that the tensions and contradictions between recent developments in the various fields provide important opportunities for developing a better and more encompassing understanding of flexibility. In other words, flexibility requires planning as well as redundancies for multiple allocations of resources, and broad strategic schemas for facilitating new interpretations. It helps in achieving a reasonable fit at a certain point in time (adaptation), but also facilitates the potential to create new fits in the near future (adaptability). While it cannot be accomplished without the ability of the organization to correct deviations from essential norms and values, the organization must have the ability to change these norms and values themselves. Finally, flexibility is often restricted to minor changes, but sometimes goes together with radical changes.

Thus, instead of suppressing or dismissing the apparent paradox of flexibility deduced from a comparison of one-sided theories, these opposing sub-theories form a basis for theoretical discourse which is potentially richer than either theory by itself. The problem is how best to mine this rich vein of insight. How can both faces of flexibility be encompassed in the same framework?

Poole and Van de Ven (1989) proposed *four generic ways of dealing with paradoxes*. In their view, paradoxes within management and organization differ from logical paradoxes. Whereas logical paradoxes exist in timeless, abstract thought, organizational paradoxes take place in a real world, subject to its temporal and spatial constraints. This fact opens the possibility of dealing with the paradox of flexibility not only through logical solutions, but through taking into account the temporal or spatial nature of organizations. Therefore, Poole and Van de Ven (1989) suggested that the paradox (1) be accepted and used constructively *(opposition)*, (2) be resolved by clarifying levels of reference *(spatial separation)*, (3) be resolved by taking time into account in exploring when each contrary assumption or process exerts a separate influence *(temporal separation)*, and (4) be dissolved by introducing new concepts which either correct flaws in logic or provide a more encompassing perspective *(synthesis)*.

The first response acknowledges the paradox of preservation and change and

Flexibility and the Postmodern Organization

learns to live with it. This strategy was applied above, when our analysis of theories and their contributions to flexibility resulted in the discovery of the underlying tensions within the concept of flexibility. When kept distinct, as opposed to being subsumed under a unified perspective, these sub-theories sensitize researchers to critical issues and divulge their weak points. However, living with the paradox of change and preservation has its costs. The separate pursuit of contrary perspectives may result in segmentation of knowledge and counterproductive bickering among proponents of the 'correct' horn of the paradox. Nor is it always clear just what sort of relationship 'tensions between opposing positions' constitutes. This relationship must be clearly defined or analysis can become sloppy (Van de Ven and Poole, 1988: 23).

The second response resolves the paradox by clarifying levels of reference and the connections between them. This approach assumes that one horn of the paradox operates at one level of analysis, while the other horn operates at a different level. For instance, we suggested that single-loop learning is mainly a lower-level learning process within organizations, involving the correction of deviations from norms. By contrast, double-loop learning is primarily a higher-level learning process, occurring through the use of heuristics, skill development, and fundamentally new insights. Similar to the distinction between levels is spatial separation. Each horn of the paradox is assumed to operate in different physical loci. We have demonstrated that organizations may simultaneously accomplish incremental and radical innovations and their associated modes of entrepreneurship in different portions of the organization. For example, mature divisions, operating in the Austrian mode of entrepreneurship, may promote incremental innovation, whereas new ventures, operating in the Schumpeterian mode, may promote radical innovations. The problem with this separation approach involves the difficulty of spelling out inter-level relations. According to Van de Ven and Poole (1988), many researchers have ignored these inter-level relations while advancing only partial and tentative solutions.

The third approach resolves the paradox over time. One horn of the paradox is assumed to hold during one time period and the other during a different time period. Consequently, several types of temporal relationships may exist among contrary forces. An example is the above description of the process of innovation as a dynamic alternation between incremental innovations undertaken by Austrian entrepreneurs and radical innovations undertaken by Schumpeterian entrepreneurs over time. These so-called punctuated equilibrium models, most explicitly discussed by Tushman and Romanelli (1985), posit alternating cycles of preservation, 'which elaborate structures, systems, controls, and resources toward increased coalignment', and cycles of fundamental change, 'periods of discontinuous transition where strategies, structure, and systems are fundamentally transformed towards a new basis of alignment'. However, the punctuation process itself remains underdeveloped (Van de Ven and Garud, 1988).

When does preservation stop and change begin? Most attempts at temporal resolution have glossed over the issue of transition points and focused instead on the periods of relatively pure action of either preservation or change.

The resolution of the paradox of change and preservation by distinction between levels or temporal analysis leaves each set of assumptions or processes basically intact. However, it is also possible that the paradox stems from conceptual limitations or flaws in theory or assumptions. A new framework of flexibility may dissolve the paradox that has so far been taken for granted. On the basis of the analysis of new theories and their contributions to flexibility, we may conclude there is a need for an overall framework of organizational flexibility, which (1) has to include the contradictory attributes of the preservation–change paradox, and (2) allows the deduction of different types of flexibility corresponding to those developed with respect to strategic management, organization–environment, organizational learning, and innovation and entrepreneurship, and (3) distinguishes effective trajectories for handling the paradox of flexibility.

Notes

1. Considering Mintzberg's schools of thought of strategic management (1990), the linear model of strategy comprises the prescriptive schools, namely the design (Andrews, 1971), the planning (Ansoff, 1965), and the positioning school (Porter, 1980).
2. According to Andrews (1971), these analyses had to be kept simple and informal and conducted by the CEO, while Ansoff (1965) argued that these analyses had to be exhaustive and conducted by the planning staff of the organization.
3. By analysing decision scenarios that depicted a hypothetical forest-product firm faced with a major problem (an inability to obtain timber for two years), and that were worked out by forest-product firms in an unstable environment, a negative relationship was found between comprehensiveness and performance (Fredrickson and Mitchell, 1984). Moreover, by analysing decision scenarios that depicted a hypothetical paint and coatings manufacturer faced with a major problem (a 16% decline in sales in eleven months), and that were worked out by paint and coatings manufacturers in a stable environment, a positive relationship was found between comprehensiveness and performance (Fredrickson, 1984). This implies that a comprehensive decision process will result in superior performance in an environment that can be well understood. A non-comprehensive process, with its speed and flexibility, will have a similar effect in an unstable environment.
4. Aharoni et al. (1978) found that managers do not attempt a comprehensive search as it is too costly.
5. Ackoff (1981) still calls this responsiveness planning; it consists of building flexibility into an organization. In our terminology, however, we will call this organizing instead of planning.

Flexibility and the Postmodern Organization

6. Using Mintzberg's classification of schools of thought (1990), we could argue that the adaptive model of strategy comprises most of the descriptive schools such as the learning school, the political school, and the environmental school.
7. The interpretative model of strategy includes Mintzberg's (1990) entrepreneurial, cognitive, and cultural school.
8. This perspective contrasts with the classical management's focus on specific operational goals, where goals are often targets or end-points to be achieved.
9. In a review of his own research, Lawrence (1981) admits this passive picture regarding organization–environment relations.
10. In open systems theory, this principle is called equifinality, that is, a dynamic equilibrium can be achieved in multiple ways, with different resources, diverse transformation processes, and various methods and means.
11. Miles and Snow (1978, 1994) call this the neo-contingency approach, while others call it modern contingency theory (Morgan, 1986).
12. The distinction made here between Schumpeterian and Austrian entrepreneurs has some parallels with those made earlier by Penrose (1959), Zaleznick (1977), and more recently by Stevenson and Gumpert (1985), Stevenson and Sahlman (1986), and others, of entrepreneurs or leaders versus administrators or managers. Similarly, Ansoff (1988) distinguished between entrepreneurial behaviour associated with the creation of new profit potential and competitive behaviour associated with the exploitation of available profit potential.

4 Grasping the Paradox of Flexibility: A Multidimensional Concept

> Developing flexible organizations is critical for business enterprises in the 1990s. Flexibility is a multi-dimensional concept—demanding agility and versatility; associated with change, innovation, and novelty; coupled with robustness and resilience, implying stability, sustainable advantage, and capabilities that may evolve over time.
>
> (Bahrami, 1992: 48)

In the preceding chapter we examined various theoretical perspectives and their contributions to the concept of organizational flexibility. This exercise provided rich insights concerning the paradoxical nature of flexibility, the distinctions among several types of flexibility, and the differentiation of trajectories for handling the paradox.

On the basis of these insights, which function as conditions for an appropriate definition of organizational flexibility, we are able to judge the value of existing definitions of flexibility. In this chapter several integrated definitions of organizational flexibility are compared (Sect. 4.1). This review illustrates the diversity of the definitions and also the ambivalence with respect to the terminology used. In addition, we will focus on the rough similarities and differences between these definitions. From this evaluation, essential dimensions of organizational flexibility are obtained (Sect. 4.2).

Subsequently, we develop a clearer and more encompassing formulation of the concept of flexibility (Sect. 4.3). On the basis of insights drawn from control theories, it is argued that organizational flexibility derives from the control capability of the management and the controllability of the organization. This two-dimensional conception of flexibility is portrayed in our basic framework; it shows the managerial and organization design tasks as the two most important building blocks of flexibility. These tasks constitute distinct and equally important challenges that have to be resolved if flexibility is to succeed. The managerial task of flexibility is concerned with the promotion of management's control capacity, especially in situations of unexpected disturbances. Management's ability to allocate this capacity, however, is dependent upon certain organizational conditions. The organization design task therefore involves the creation of the appropriate organizational conditions to foster flexibility.

4.1 An Inquiry into Definitions of Flexibility

In Webster's Collegiate Dictionary, flexibility is defined as the quality of being capable of responding or conforming to changing or new situations. Of course, this definition says nothing specifically about organizational flexibility. In general, we often know intuitively what flexibility must encompass, but its translation with respect to an organization is still ambiguous. The variety of definitions of organizational flexibility highlights this ambiguity and suggests closer examination of these definitions is required to obtain a clearer grasp of the concept.

As was argued in Section 1.1, organizational flexibility is often used as a general and abstract term without any additional clarification (general approach). Not surprisingly, an explicit definition is more often than not omitted. Rather, flexibility is reduced to certain aspects of the organization (functional approach) or related to certain stakeholders in the organization (actor approach). As a part of these partial approaches, one may find definitions in terms of flexible manufacturing (e.g. Bolwijn and Kumpe, 1990; De Meyer *et al.*, 1989; Nemetz and Fry, 1988; Swamidass and Newell, 1987; Wheelwright, 1984); flexible production automation (e.g. Buzacott and Yao, 1986; Lei *et al.*, 1996; Parthasarthy and Sethi, 1992; Piore and Sabel, 1984; Upton, 1995); flexible information systems (e.g. Boynton and Victor, 1991; Wortman, 1989); flexible financial control systems (e.g. Ittner and Kogut, 1995); labour flexibility (e.g. Appelbaum and Schettkat, 1990; Davis-Blake and Uzzi, 1993; Kopp and Litschert, 1980; Smith, 1994); flexible management styles (e.g. Khandwalla, 1977); and flexible organizational participants (e.g. Hage and Dewar, 1973).

Multidimensionality

Although some of these scholars start with a more general definition of a flexible organization, most of them focus directly on certain dimensions of the organization. Furthermore, many assume that a flexible organization can be accomplished only by optimizing the flexibility of these dimensions. For instance, in response to the Japanese, it was argued by many scholars that Western firms should optimize the flexibility of their manufacturing systems. None the less, US manufacturing firms still exhibit an astonishing lack of flexibility despite having invested in flexible manufacturing systems (Jaikumar, 1986). Even though manufacturing flexibility is now technologically feasible, it remains largely unrealized in US firms (Garud and Kotha, 1994). Although many bought flexible automation, few have added to this the human resource management practices and organizational structure that are needed to use flexible equipment effectively. As a result, Jaikumar found that the average number of parts made by FMS in the US was ten, while in Japan the average was ninety-three.

Similarly, the *National Platform Globalisation* (1994) and the *Competitiveness Audit* (1996), both organized by the Dutch Minister of Economic Affairs, as well as the OECD, *Employment Outlook* (1994), conjectured that labour flexibility had to be increased in order to achieve more flexible organizations. None the less, as the paradoxical nature of flexibility suggests about the dual needs for change and preservation, it is plausible that some flexible organizations require less flexible individuals or more stable employment contracts. For instance, Japanese firms were able to develop high levels of functional labour flexibility (such as increasing the variety of workers' skills) for transferring employees to various tasks within the organization only by limiting their workers' external mobility (numerical labour flexibility): they guaranteed their employees lifetime employment (Morroni, 1991). In the opposite case, in European companies many types of numerical labour flexibility for adjusting the size of the workforce to shifts in demand (such as flexible working times or flexible employment contracts) are compensated for by a rigid social system that guarantees a network of protection such as unemployment benefits and opportunities for retraining. Increasing functional labour flexibility in European firms therefore requires a higher commitment by these firms to their employees (Handy, 1995).

These examples illustrate that achieving truly effective flexibility is a challenging and elusive goal. Fifteen years ago, quality was much like flexibility is today: vague and difficult to improve yet critical to competitiveness. Flexibility is only beginning to be explored. Clearly, flexible manufacturing and labour flexibility are part of the answer, but technology or labour alone will not create flexibility. Furthermore, the examples of flexible rigidities in Japanese firms show that flexibility requires a constructive tension between dimensions, for example, flexible manufacturing systems that go together with tight employment relations. Thus, attempts to achieve flexibility cannot be described in monolithic, unidimensional terms, as simple recipes and either/or solutions: flexibility is a multidimensional concept (cf. Ackoff, 1977; Bahrami, 1992). However, little agreement exists on which dimensions to include (Gerwin, 1993). In this section we therefore analyse underlying dimensions of flexibility on the basis of various definitions. We will limit our search to integrated definitions of organizational flexibility in which flexibility is considered as an organizational property. First, several integrated definitions of organizational flexibility are reviewed (Sect. 4.1). After that, the similarities and differences between these definitions are evaluated (Sect. 4.2).

A Review of Definitions

Even if we leave out the definitions of the functional and actor approach and limit ourselves to those that consider flexibility as a quality of an organization (see Sect. 1.1.), it is still impossible to present all of them. Therefore only the most essential definitions are considered here in chronological order to give a representative overview of the various dimensions of the concept of flexibility.

Ansoff was one of the first authors to probe more deeply into the concept of flexibility. He suggested that firms need *internal* and *external* flexibility to cope with unforeseeable contingencies. According to him, 'external flexibility is best described by the maxim of not putting all of one's eggs in a single basket' (Ansoff, 1965: 55). This type of flexibility can be achieved *defensively* through a product–market posture which is sufficiently diversified to minimize the effect of a catastrophe and/or *offensively* by putting the firm into areas in which it can benefit from likely breakthroughs. Offensive external flexibility is more elusive and harder to implement than defensive external flexibility, but it maximizes the chance of participating in breakthroughs.

In contrast with these types of external flexibility, internal flexibility 'is as old as business itself . . . it seeks to provide a cushion for response to catastrophe' (Ansoff, 1965: 57). Instead of influencing contingencies, internal flexibility tries to respond to contingencies. In Ansoff's *Corporate Strategy*, however, this response is restricted merely to increasing the liquidity of a firm's resources.

Eppink (1978) rightly remarked that flexibility is used here by Ansoff in a *passive* context because it is defined in terms of limiting the impact of environmental change on the organization. This passive connotation does not result in fundamental changes to the organization; it makes adaptations of existing structures superfluous. For instance, one can think of changing the purchasing policy (multi-sourcing) or designing a defensive approach to existing markets (alliances or formation of trusts). In these situations, the turbulent environment is considered as a source of disturbances which must be closed off from the organization. By buffering the organization, the uncertainty is reduced to an acceptable level.

According to Eppink, a more *active* conception of flexibility includes the factors that make the firm responsive in the proper sense of the word. For instance, a more active definition of flexibility is given by Scott (1965), who emphasizes the ability to adjust or adapt to change, or Kieser (1969), who focused on the ability to adapt through internal changes to a changing environment and/or to take advantage of existing environmental changes. Eppink's own definition incorporates both the active and passive components of flexibility: 'flexibility can be seen as a characteristic of an organization that makes it less vulnerable to unforeseen external changes or puts it in a better position to respond successfully to such a change' (Eppink, 1978: 42).

By contrast, many scholars (e.g. Ackoff, 1971; Reichwald and Behrbohm, 1983) relate passive flexibility to the acceptance of the unchangeability of the environment and the need for the organization to adapt, whereas their interpretation of 'active' refers to trying to change the environment itself. Therefore we suggest that it is more adequate to use the term external flexibility for Eppink's passive notion and the term internal flexibility for Eppink's active notion. Internal flexibility goes together with self-adaptation, while external flexibility requires others to adapt.

It is important to note that Eppink explicitly related flexibility to *unforeseen change*. For the ability to respond to foreseen changes, he used the word 'adaptiveness'. The total responsiveness of an organization would then consist of adaptability and flexibility. He suggested that there may be some overlapping between the two, but does not explain this point further.

Finally, on the basis of a classification of external change and Ansoff and Brandenburg's (1971) criteria of organizational effectiveness, Eppink distinguished three *types* of flexibility, each related to one type of change:

- *operational flexibility*: flexibility required for changes which are familiar and often lead to a temporary change in the level of activity of the organization. In the case of operational flexibility, there is no substantial shift in the relationship between an organization and its environment;
- *competitive flexibility*: flexibility which is necessary to react to changes in the direct environment. In contrast with operational change, competitive changes cause a major transformation in the market position of a firm or an industry, such as the introduction of a really new product with a substantial market impact or the market entry of new competition;
- *strategic flexibility*: flexibility necessary to compensate for strategic changes which originate in the indirect environment of the organization and reach it via the components of its direct environment. These changes possess a high degree of unfamiliarity and are very dynamic and urgent. They require immediate attention to prevent the organization from being seriously affected. Examples of strategic change are the emergence of a radically new technology, the oil crisis, the Gulf War, and so on.

Eppink concludes that strategic flexibility is a new area, but that organizations are increasingly being confronted with strategic change.

Krijnen (1979) noted that firms functioning in a turbulent environment are increasingly confronted with uncertainty to the extent that the consequences of their actions are less predictable. It becomes more difficult for them to intercept in some way or other the unfavourable consequences which are not at all or only partly predictable. Consequently, they will have to make additional decisions at the moment when disturbances occur. These disturbances can be dealt with only at the moment when they occur or are perceived. These circumstances require the presence of flexibility in the organization. According to Krijnen, 'a flexible firm has the ability to change itself in such a way that it remains *viable*' (1979: 64). In this context, change stands for:

- flexible *adaptation* to circumstances, events taking place in the environment which were by no means predictable or foreseeable;
- altering the organization by taking into account developments in the environment which are likely to occur. That is, the firm *anticipates* these changes by means of planning;
- developing activities in order to *influence* the environment so that the firm does not have to adapt itself.

In accordance with Ansoff and Brandenburg (1971), Krijnen argued that changes may appear to be necessary at *three levels of the decision-making process*. First, changes may be essential at the *strategic level*, that is, the level of strategic policy at which the economic and basic social goals, the strategy, and the product market combinations (PMCs) of the firm are fixed. At this level, there is a great deal of strategic flexibility when the firm is able to change easily the composition of all the PMCs by renewal of products, by switching to new markets or different technologies, by the acquisition of other firms, and via divestment of unviable business units. Secondly, the *organizational level*, consisting of the organizational structure, and the decision-making and communication processes, may be subject to change. There is structural flexibility when the firm has the possibility of easily changing the existing structure itself when doing so proves to be necessary. Finally, the organization may have to adapt regularly at the *operational level*. A firm shows a great deal of operational flexibility when it is able to react efficiently to changes in the production volume as a consequence of temporary fluctuations in demand for products. For Krijnen, an organization is flexible when it is able to implement the necessary changes adequately at these three levels.

Weick   In *Weick's* (1982) treatment of loosely coupled systems, organizational flexibility stands for *adaptability* to exploit future opportunities. These opportunities may appear suddenly when the environment changes and may require a repertoire of responses that have been neglected because of their irrelevance to present demands. In these situations, flexibility is required to modify current practices so that non-transient changes in the environment can be adapted to. Thus, the organization must detect changes and retain a sufficient pool of novel responses to accommodate to them. According to Weick, flexibility is the opposite of *stability*, which provides an economical means for handling regularities by using an organization's memory and its capacity for repetition. Weick argues that both total flexibility and chronic stability have disruptive effects on the organization (see also Sect. 3.3). Total flexibility makes it impossible for the organization to retain a sense of identity and continuity, while chronic stability, as represented by past wisdom, disregards more economical ways of responding and neglects new environmental features.

Weick conjectured that tight coupling improves adaptation to a well-known environment, whereas loose coupling stimulates flexibility. According to him, the ways in which loose coupling preserves flexibility are straightforward.

Loose coupling . . . encourages opportunistic adaptation to local circumstances, and it allows simultaneous adaptation to conflicting demands. Should problems develop with one departmental unit, it can be more easily sealed off or severed from the rest of the system. Moreover, adjustment by individual departments to environmental perturbances allows the rest of the system to function with greater *stability*. Finally, allowing local units to adapt to local conditions without requiring changes in the larger system reduces coordination costs for the system as a whole. (Weick, 1982: 387)

Weick's discussion of loosely coupled systems clearly illustrates that an organization can reconcile the need for flexibility with the need for stability, thus contradicting his initial assertion that flexibility is the opposite of stability.

Quinn   As a part of *Quinn*'s (1980, 1985) incrementalism, flexibility means keeping *options* open by specifying broad performance goals and allowing different technical approaches to compete for as long as possible; intermediate steps are not developed in detail (see also Sect. 3.1). Quinn's research illustrates that these free options have to be consciously developed: 'Logic dictated that managers purposely design needed flexibilities into their organizations and have reserve resources ready to deploy incrementally as events demanded' (Quinn, 1980: 122).

Three activities are essential in achieving designed flexibility: (1) establishing a *horizon scanning activity* to identify the general nature and extent of the most likely opportunities and threats the organization might encounter, (2) creating sufficient *resource buffers*—or 'slacks'—to respond effectively as events actually unfurl, and (3) developing and positioning *activists* with a psychological commitment to move opportunistically and flexibly at the right moment.

The essence of the first activity is not in estimating which events will occur and planning for them in detail, but in anticipating what types and levels of resource buffers and organizational flexibility are needed to exploit likely futures effectively. Designed flexibility requires quick access to resources to cushion the sudden impact of forceful random events (notice the similarities with Ansoff's definition), to offset opponents' sudden attacks, or to build rapid

momentum for new strategic shifts. Quinn's sample shows that in order to utilize such flexibilities more entrepreneurial companies develop 'credible activists'
whose role is to press proactively for movement as opportunities or threats
develop around specific strategic initiatives.

Aaker and Mascarenhas (1984) considered organizational flexibility as a *strategic
option*. When environmental changes become increasingly undefined, fast moving, and numerous, it is risky to rely upon conventional strategic management
approaches. Another approach is to exercise the strategic option of developing
organizational flexibility. In this context, flexibility is defined as 'the ability of the
organization to adapt to substantial, uncertain, and fast-occurring (relative to
required reaction time) environmental changes that have a meaningful impact
on the organization's performance' (1984: 74). The focus is upon environmental
changes that are substantial enough to impose severe long-time constraints
and/or to create a need for strategic adaptation.

In considering this option, Aaker and Mascarenhas illustrated that flexibility
can be achieved in a variety of ways: (1) by *diversification*, which can be defensive
or offensive (e.g. participating in multiple product markets, using multiple distribution channels, or producing from multiple plants in different locations), (2)
by investment in *underused assets* (e.g. increasing the liquidity of assets, using
general-purpose facilities and equipment, maintaining extra R&D capability or
using inventories as a buffering mechanism), or (3) by *reducing specialized commitments* (e.g. reducing specialized facilities, cutting down R&D investments in
very specific technologies, using multiple suppliers, subcontracting work, or
avoiding vertical integration in order to decrease exit and entry barriers).

As part of its strategic thinking, a firm should consider whether it is necessary
to increase its flexibility and, if so, which approach is the most appropriate and
effective. According to Aaker and Mascarenhas, this *flexibility-decision* involves a
series of steps:

- *identifying external changes*: this step involves careful focusing on the potential environmental changes facing the firm;
- *evaluating these changes*: this step involves consideration of the size of the
  impact of the environmental change upon the organization, the probability
  that the environmental change will occur, and the lead time needed to
  adapt to the environmental change; and
- *considering the flexibility option*: the final judgement about the need for flexibility and the most appropriate approach rests upon an analysis of the
  potential environmental changes and upon an evaluation of alternatives,
  such as insurance, control, avoidance, prediction, and contingency planning.

More recently, there is an increased interest in strategic flexibility in high-tech
industries (e.g. personal computer, consumer electronics), not as a strategic

option but as a strategic necessity. Strategic flexibility is widely used by strategy researchers to denote the firm's deliberate or emerging *capabilities* to manoeuvre defensively or offensively (Evans, 1991) in *dynamic competitive environments* (Boynton and Victor, 1991; Sanchez, 1995) or *hypercompetitive environments* (D'Aveni, 1994). According to *Sanchez* (1995), strategic flexibility depends jointly on the inherent flexibilities of the resources available to the firm (e.g. range of alternative uses, costs of switching, and time required to switch) and the firm's coordinative capabilities in applying those resources to alternative courses of action. One might think of a modular organization of development and production processes, 'quick-connect' electronic interfaces (computer-assisted design and development, computer-integrated manufacturing) to coordinate product development and production processes, or concurrent product creation processes that greatly reduce the total time required to develop and manufacture a new product. These coordinative capabilities enable a firm to take advantage of a greater number of possible future outcomes in a dynamic environment. Similarly, *D'Aveni* (1994) argues that in hypercompetitive environments, where only temporary advantages can be achieved, consistency and commitment undermine the firm's ability to shift from one advantage to another. Rather, a firm has to develop flexible capabilities for speed and surprise. These capabilities derive from broad knowledge-bases, generalizable resources, and core competencies that can be applied in various ways. For instance, Corning, one of the world's largest manufacturers of fibre optics, is converting and expanding its process manufacturing capabilities from single-product capacity to a flexible manufacturing platform capable of building customized fibre products to order.

4.2 Dimensions of Dynamic Control

Although the above review of definitions of organizational flexibility is not comprehensive, it clearly illustrates the variety of definitions and the ambivalence with respect to the terminology used. This ambivalence is manifested by the use of opposing terms by scholars to denote the same phenomenon. For example, while Eppink (1978) associated internal flexibility with his active component of flexibility, Ackoff (1971) and Reichwald and Behrbohm (1983) referred to it as a passive component of flexibility.

We will focus on the rough similarities and differences between these definitions to draw a clearer picture. In this evaluation, we will also refer to comparable definitions not presented above. Using these comparisons, we can construct several underlying dimensions for an overall definition of organizational flexibility (see Table 4.1). To begin with, the review of definitions reveals that flexibility can be considered as a new way to achieve some form of control in

Flexibility: A Multidimensional Concept

TABLE 4.1. Flexibility in terms of dimensions of dynamic
control

Essential dimensions
• adaptive capacity
• response time
• change and stability
• internal/external flexibility
• unforeseen/foreseen change
• level of responsiveness
• potential flexibility
• strategic perseverance

extremely turbulent environments. As is demonstrated in the definitions of Aaker and Mascarenhas (1984), D'Aveni (1994), and Krijnen (1979), flexibility facilitates a higher order of control in changing environments. While bureaucratic forms based on hierarchy and commitment provide some form of static control in stable environments, new, changing environments require flexible modes to achieve *dynamic control*. This need implies that a flexible organization must observe events which can have important consequences for its functioning. It has continuously to translate and interpret these events with respect to their domain and their degree of intensity, and try to influence them in a positive manner. If that is not possible, the organization has to adapt itself efficiently and effectively, and in a socially acceptable manner. All the definitions considered above provide certain dimensions of dynamic control.

An adaptive capacity Nearly all definitions of organizational flexibility emphasize the adaptive capacity of management in terms of an ability (Aaker and Mascarenhas, 1984; Frazelle, 1986; Kieser, 1969; Scott, 1965; Zelenovic, 1982), a repertoire (Weick, 1982), a degree of freedom (Sanchez, 1993; Thompson, 1967), or free options (Quinn, 1985; Sanchez, 1995) to initiate or adapt to competitive change. This capacity may consist of a quantitative capacity which can be used only once, such as creating large inventories as buffering mechanisms, and a qualitative capacity which is not restricted in its use, such as developing multipurpose machinery or training multiskilled personnel.

Response time Many of these definitions suggest that not only the capacity to respond, but also the reaction time required are important. In other words, the speed with which an organization can run through the various control cycles is crucial (Aaker and Mascarenhas, 1984; D'Aveni, 1994; Frazelle, 1986; Sanchez, 1995). Regarding this aspect, Reichwald and Behrbohm (1983) discuss two variables, namely the warning time and the retardation time. The former term refers to the time which elapses between the moment when a possible change is signalled and the moment the change actually happens. The retardation time covers the period between the actual change and the moment when adequate action is taken. Figure 4.1a illustrates that an organization can increase the warning time and reduce the retardation time in a situation of continuous change (the retardation time may even become negative). However, in situations of unforeseen change, there is no warning time (that is to say, there is only a negative one, as can be seen in Fig. 4.1b). Therefore, Ansoff *et al.* (1975) argued that in confronting this discontinuity, management may act decisively or prudently. Management may act decisively in the sense that it immediately decides to take measures to respond to change. It can also act prudently in that it waits until the impact has reached a certain threshold level, and only then decide to take action. Thus, with respect to the reaction time, we may conclude that both the speed of observing new events and the acceleration of the process of change are important aspects.[1] The latter factor describes whether the process of implementing proceeds slowly and continuously over a long period or in short series with intermittent periods of no change.

Change and stability   While most definitions oppose flexibility to stability, only a few emphasize that flexibility must be combined with stability if it is to have

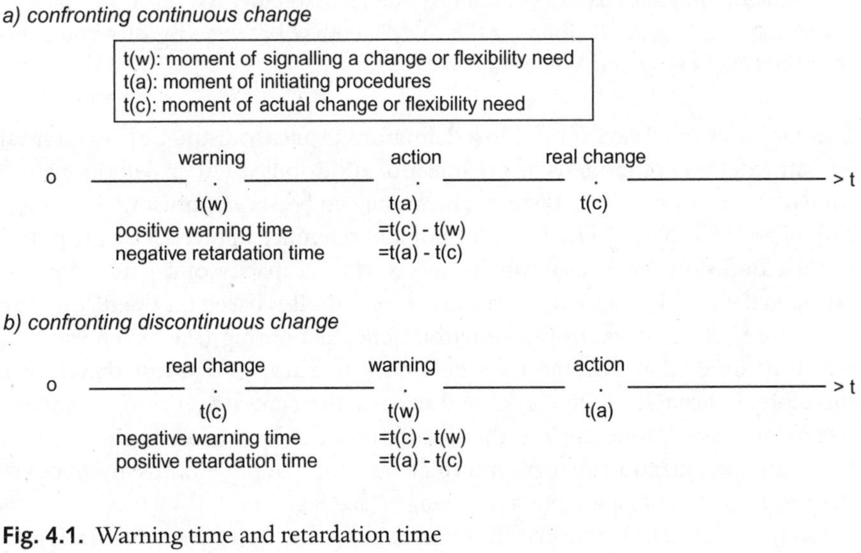

a) confronting continuous change

| t(w): moment of signalling a change or flexibility need |
| t(a): moment of initiating procedures |
| t(c): moment of actual change or flexibility need |

	warning	action	real change	
o				> t
	t(w)	t(a)	t(c)	
	positive warning time	=t(c) - t(w)		
	negative retardation time	=t(a) - t(c)		

b) confronting discontinuous change

	real change	warning	action	
o				> t
	t(c)	t(w)	t(a)	
	negative warning time	=t(c) - t(w)		
	positive retardation time	=t(a) - t(c)		

Fig. 4.1. Warning time and retardation time

Flexibility: A Multidimensional Concept

value. Not surprisingly, in reaction to the problems of overbureaucratized organizations, most scholars stress only one side of the paradox of change and stability. They define flexibility as the organization's ability to change and the speed at which it can change. In clarifying their bias towards change, however, many scholars are confronted with the limits of flexibility due to requirements of stability. For instance, Scott (1965) observed that creating too great a capacity to respond by deliberate postponement of decisions resulted in a lack of decisiveness, progressively increasing costs, and a continual revision of plans. Too great a reaction capacity or too short a reaction time may lead to overreaction, excessive information search, and wasted resources. Weick (1982) concluded that total flexibility makes it impossible for the organization to retain a sense of identity and continuity; in other words, flexibility without stability results in chaos. More recently, Van Ham *et al.* (1987) stressed the stability component of flexibility as necessary to preserve the identity and maintain the controllability of the organization. Similarly, Adler (1988) claimed that flexibility is advantageous or a meaningful concept only against a backdrop of stability. On the basis of a field study of thirty-seven high-technology firms in California's Silicon Valley, Bahrami (1992) found that emerging flexible firms were structured and yet chaotic.

Their organization systems were by no means chaotic, but neither were they in total control. They were not frugal although a cost-conscious mentality pervaded their style. The management teams were not mavericks, yet an entrepreneurial zeal and anti-bureaucratic sentiments were frequently observed. They focused on generating short-term results but did not lose sight of their long-term mission. (Bahrami, 1992: 45)

A flexible organization is thus inherently stable. Instability is a result of a lack or excess of flexibility, so flexibility is the middle course between rigidity and over-reaction (De Leeuw and Volberda, 1996).

Internal and external flexibility   Most definitions explicitly distinguish an internal and an external component of organizational flexibility. Other definitions use similar terms for the same distinction, which can be very confusing. However, as depicted in Table 4.2, clarifying the point of reference may reduce a great deal of this confusion. Internal flexibility refers to the capacity of organizations to quickly adapt to the demands of the environment. It is based on a deterministic conception of the organization–environment relationship (see also Sect. 3.2), which assumes that adaptation is necessary to survive. In most definitions, therefore, internal flexibility is defined as a reactive capacity resulting in corrective manoeuvres. None the less, this does not have to be the case in situations in which the organization changes internally as a kind of pre-emptive manoeuvre (Evans, 1991) to anticipate possible changes (see Fig. 4.2).

On the other hand, external flexibility is the capacity of the organization to

TABLE 4.2. Similar terms for internal and external flexibility

Internal flexibility	External flexibility	Point of reference
active (change)	passive (limiting change)	organization (Eppink, 1978; Kieser, 1969; Scott, 1965)
passive (reactive)	active (proactive)	environment (Ansoff, 1965; Evans, 1991)
'eigen' (inside)	'fremd' (outside)	organization (Reichwald and Behrbohm, 1983)
self-adaptation	other adaptation	organization (Ackoff, 1971)

actively influence the environment, thereby reducing the vulnerability of the organization. It is based on a more voluntaristic approach, which assumes that there is 'slack' for strategic choice and that different organizational configurations are possible (Ansoff, 1978; Child, 1972). Ansoff (1965) asserted that external flexibility can result either in protective (defensive) or exploitive (offensive) manoeuvres (see Fig. 4.2).

Unforeseen/foreseen change   A number of definitions relate flexibility distinctly to unforeseen change, while other definitions do not specify the type of change at all. In his *Managing the unforeseen*, Eppink separated flexibility from adaptiveness by relating the latter to foreseen change. None the less, he did not elaborate

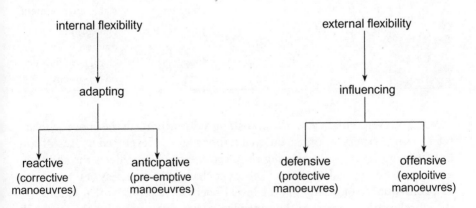

Fig. 4.2. A further distinction of internal and external flexibility

further the difference between flexibility and adaptiveness and even suggested that they may overlap. In addition, as a part of his typology, he discussed flexibility in relation to predictable and regular changes. Moreover, some researchers argued that even the most unforeseen changes are to some extent predictable (cf. Evans, 1991). Therefore, unforeseen change is not an adequate determinant for the concept of flexibility in general. However, it seems to be an important factor for the distinction of different types of flexibility. In other words, it is likely that unforeseen change requires a different type of flexibility than foreseen change.

Level of responsiveness This review clearly illustrates that different types of flexibility can be distinguished in relation to different levels of the decision-making process in an organization (e.g. operational, organizational, strategic (Krijnen, 1979)), to the time frame (e.g. short term, medium term, or long term (Evans, 1991)) or to the nature of change in the environment (e.g. stable environment, changes in the direct environment, changes in the indirect environment (Eppink, 1978)). Unfortunately, these criteria for classification result in multiple interpretations of different types of flexibility (see Table 4.3). For instance, it is possible that strategic flexibility may be found at the operational level of decision-making where it is applied in order to bring about changes in the direct environment. Similarly, strategic flexibility may have a short-term orientation.

TABLE 4.3. Criteria for classifying types of flexibility

	Criteria for classification		
	Level of decision-making process	Time frame	Nature of change
Types of flexibility	operational	short term	stable environment
	organizational	medium term	changes in direct environment
	strategic	long term	changes in indirect environment

It is, however, remarkable that in making a distinction, all the above scholars refer to three criteria of organizational responsiveness developed by Ansoff and Brandenburg (1971): (1) operating responsiveness, which reflects the ability of an organization to make quick and efficient changes in the levels of throughput as a consequence of changes in the level of demand or competitive actions, (2) structural responsiveness, or the capability of the organization to change itself, and (3) strategic responsiveness, which represents the firm's ability to respond to changes in nature (rather than volume) in its throughput, such as the obsolescence of products, changes in product technology, emergence of international markets, opportunities to enter new lines of business, and so on.

Potential flexibility Another distinction, which can be found in several definitions (Gerwin, 1993), is among the potential flexibility inherent in an existing organization, the actual flexibility allocated by management to a real flexibility need, and the required flexibility for that need. Potential flexibility indicates what can occur given the existing organization design, while the actual flexibility stems from the utilization of certain capabilities. When the required flexibility is larger than the actual flexibility but there is enough potential flexibility, management must simply utilize more capabilities. When the required flexibility is larger than the potential flexibility, however, the firm has to vary its potential by radically redesigning the organization (see Table 4.4). The boundary between this so-called static (existing potential) and dynamic flexibility (re-designing potential) depends on what Zelenovic (1982) labelled the design adequacy of the organization. The adequacy of organizational design is a measure of the probability that the organization will adapt to environmental conditions within the limits of their given design parameters. In order to vary their potential, organizations sometimes have to change these parameters. Recent efforts of business-process re-engineering in many large corporations are directed primarily at enlarging the flexibility potential of these organizations (Hammer and Champy, 1993).

TABLE 4.4. Similar distinctions for existing potential and designing new potential

Existing potential	Designing new potential
static flexibility	active flexibility (Mandelbaum, 1978)
adaptive flexibility	design flexibility (Zelenovic, 1982)
'Bestands-Flexibilität' (pool flexibility)	*'Entwicklungs-Flexibilität'* (development flexibility) (Reichwald and Behrbohm, 1983)

Strategic perseverance Finally, it is clear from the various definitions that organizational flexibility is related to certain strategies and commitments. Still, there remains some ambiguity regarding the perseverance with which these strategies are pursued. Some scholars assume that flexibility is required in order to reach certain a priori strategies. For instance, according to Reichwald and

Behrbohm (1983), organizations need flexibility to compensate for or take advantage of strategy-deviating and strategy-amplifying effects of possible events. Such flexibility may result in high-commitment, capability-oriented organizations that are able to develop new routines to adapt within the limits of a dominant strategy. By contrast, others assume that organizational flexibility also includes the redefinition of strategies (D'Aveni, 1994; Quinn, 1980). In a stable environment, the tendency of an organization to make investments in irreversible courses of action and to persist with a certain strategy is a key component in competitive success (Ghemawat, 1991; Porter, 1980). In turbulent environments, commitments are so rigid and consistent that they become easily understood, overcome, or imitated by competitors (D'Aveni, 1994: 240). In such environments, flexible firms have to redefine their strategy to create new strategic options (Sanchez, 1993). Highly flexible, options-oriented companies like Amstrad and Dell Computers have challenged more traditional, high-commitment, capability-oriented organizations such as Sony and Apple by fundamentally reducing commitments (Bartlett, 1993).

4.3 The Management and Organization Design Challenge: A Multidimensional Definition of Flexibility

On the basis of the comparison of theoretical contributions and the evaluation of integrated definitions, we can derive a more comprehensive definition of organizational flexibility. The theories discussed and the definitions reviewed provided the conditions for and essential dimensions of an appropriate definition.

As Table 4.5 shows, some of these conditions and dimensions overlap. Consonant with the formulated conditions, we can observe that different types of flexibility are distinguished and that some definitions include contradictory attributes of the paradox of change and preservation. Notwithstanding this overlap, we believe it is useful to conceptualize flexibility in such a way that its essential dimensions are integrated and systematized, while at the same time its conditions deduced from the various theoretical perspectives are fulfilled. In providing this conceptualization, insights from control theories are used (De Leeuw and Volberda, 1996).

The review showed that flexibility can be considered as a way to achieve some form of control in turbulent environments. The various definitions stress certain dimensions of dynamic control. A firm is 'under control' when there is a corresponding managerial capability and firm response for each competitive change. In stable environments, competitive change tends to be incremental and

TABLE 4.5. Comparison of conditions for and dimensions of a comprehensive definition of organizational flexibility

Comprehensive definition of organizational flexibility	
Conditions for selection	Essential dimensions
• possess contradictory attributes of the paradox of change and preservation • allow to deduce different types of flexibility • allow to distinguish effective trajectories for handling the paradox	• adaptive capacity • response time • change and stability • internal/external flexibility • unforeseen/foreseen change • level of responsiveness • potential flexibility • strategic perseverance

sufficiently infrequent that the development of specialized managerial routines is both feasible and desirable (see Fig. 4.3). Together with reduction mechanisms, such as standardization, formalization, and complex planning systems that decrease the perceptible variety in the environment, the responsiveness of the organization diminishes. In this perspective of static control,[2] competitive change is viewed as equilibrium-disturbing. Hence for an organization to remain stable, it is believed that fluctuations must be minimized. Consequently, firms have long been described as mechanisms by which to buffer uncertainty in order to minimize risk (cf. Cyert and March, 1963; Knight, 1921; Thompson, 1967).

In extremely turbulent environments, control does not derive from specialized routines but from adaptive capability. In contrast with the static control concept prevalent among Western firms, flexible capabilities are required to permit rapid responses to unpredictable changes. Competitive change cannot be predicted but only responded to more or less efficiently *ex post*. In this perspective of dynamic control,[3] competitive change is viewed as a major vehicle for creating order, not for destroying it. In hypercompetitive environments, in which competitive change is frequent and radical, organizations may easily become adrift because flexibility requires high organizational responsiveness (controllability) and sufficient managerial capabilities to exercise control (control capability of management). The flexibility of an organization is the outcome of an interaction between (1) the controllability or responsiveness of the organization and (2) the dynamic control capacity of management (see Fig. 4.4). This interaction is such that the elements must be in balance. More controllability does not compensate for less capacity. The system is only as effective as the

Flexibility: A Multidimensional Concept

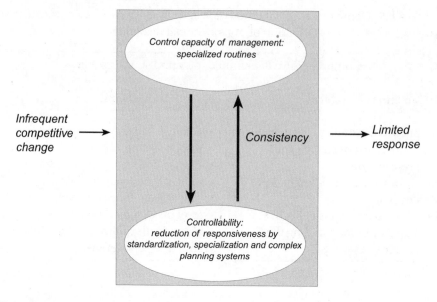

Fig. 4.3. Static control: consistency between specialized routines and limited responsiveness of the organization

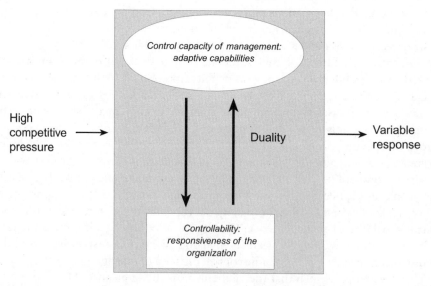

Fig. 4.4. Dynamic control: duality of control capacity and controllability

weakest dimension. Using the analogy of the car, the flexibility of a car–driver combination is the match between the steering capacities of the driver and the control properties of the car. If one outweighs the other, there is no gain. Hence, flexibility is a function of the interaction of two sets of variables.

We can see this duality in two separate tasks (see Fig. 4.5). First, flexibility is perceived to be a managerial task. Can managers respond at the right time in the right way? In this connection, the concern is with the managerial capabilities that endow the firm with flexibility; for example, manufacturing flexibility to expand the number of products the firm can profitably offer in the market or innovation flexibility to reduce the response time for bringing new products to

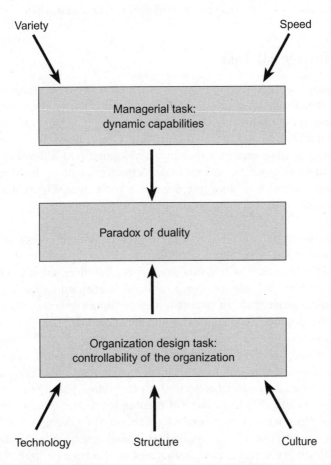

Fig. 4.5. Organizational flexibility and the associated managerial and organization design tasks

market. Secondly, flexibility is perceived to be an organization design task. Can the organization react at the right time in the directed way? The concern here is with the controllability or changeability of the organization, which depends on the creation of the right conditions to foster flexibility. For instance, manufacturing flexibility requires a technology with multipurpose machinery, universal equipment, and an extensive operational production repertoire (cf. Adler, 1988). Similarly, innovation flexibility requires a structure of multifunctional teams, few hierarchical levels, and few process regulations (cf. Quinn, 1985; Schroeder *et al.*, 1986). From these two tasks, we derive the following definition (Volberda, 1996*a*):

> Flexibility is the degree to which an organization has a variety of managerial capabilities and the speed at which they can be activated, to increase the control capacity of management and improve the controllability of the organization.

The Managerial Task

As a managerial task, flexibility involves the creation or promotion of capabilities for situations that generate unexpected disturbance. Yet, developing such capabilities is not exclusively the role of the manager. In principle, every organizational member participates in this process (Grant, 1996). Whereas authoritarian managers may restrict capability development to a limited number of people, more democratic and more participative forms of decision-making in organizations can result in a much wider involvement. Figure 4.5 shows two core dimensions of this managerial task, variety and speed.

Variety of managerial capabilities   Both the currently used arsenal of capabilities and the collection of potential flexibility-increasing capabilities that are not yet activated are important. Currently used capabilities have already been deployed for the purpose of flexibility (Reichwald and Behrbohm, 1983; Gerwin, 1993). The possible emergence of opportunities or threats requires management to have some potential capabilities as insurance against risk (see Scott, 1965). Ashby (1964) demonstrated that to be able to respond to all circumstances, a firm must have a variety of capabilities at least as great as the variety of disturbances in the environment. In a turbulent environment, management needs an extensive, multidimensional collection of capabilities. Variety can be in terms of either the quantity (the number) of capabilities or the quality of capabilities (such as temporary versus durable flexibility-increasing capabilities). For instance, the training of multiskilled personnel results in a durable improvement in flexibility, whereas the contracting out of certain peripheral activities or 'hire-and-fire' employment practices results in a temporary improvement in flexibility. Temporary flexibility-increasing capabilities lead to a reduction in the potential for use once allocated, but durable flexible capabilities are not restricted in use.

Speed Management may have the necessary capabilities, but may not be able to activate them in time (see Fig. 4.6). Flexibility is not a static condition, but a dynamic process. Speed is therefore an essential factor of organizational flexibility. Still, it should be emphasized that contrary to popular opinion (cf. Dumaine, 1989; Stalk, 1988) too short a reaction time may lead to overreaction and excessive information search and even result in chaos. Therefore management sometimes has to act prudently by either waiting until the impact has reached a certain threshold level (increase of retardation time) or slowly and continuously implementing change (increase of response time). In the case of prudent management, the mean acceleration of the process of change is reduced. Thus, speed of implementation is a function of the required time and the acceleration of the process of change.

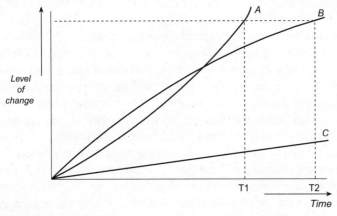

Fig. 4.6. Flexibility and speed

Note: The management of organizations A, B, and C possess the same collection of capabilities. Nevertheless, in the figure, organization A is able to activate these capabilities faster than B and C. The respective times of attainment of the desired level of change for organizations A and B are T1 and T2. Organization C is not able to accomplish the desired change within the time span depicted. In organization A the speed of change is increased by a positive acceleration, which may lead to overreaction. In organization B the speed is reduced by a negative acceleration. Organization C has a constant low speed of change without acceleration.

The Organization Design Task

The ability to initiate the repertoire of managerial capabilities also depends on the design adequacy of organizational conditions, such as the organization's technology, structure, and culture (Zelenovic, 1982). Those conditions determine the organization's controllability or responsiveness. Capabilities can be utilized efficiently only if the hierarchy of capabilities corresponds to the architecture of the firm (cf. Grant, 1996). If management tries to increase the flexibility repertoire beyond the limits of organizational conditions, the controllability of the organization will diminish.

Designing the appropriate organizational conditions requires identifying the type of technological, structural, or cultural changes necessary to ensure effective utilization of managerial capabilities. For many service and manufacturing organizations, recent developments in *technology* have created a range of programmable automation systems and general information systems that seem to afford much greater flexibility potential (Adler, 1988; Ittner and Kogut, 1995). In this connection, 'technology' refers to the hardware (such as machinery and equipment) and the software (knowledge) used in the transformation of inputs into outputs, as well as the configuration of the hardware and software. The design of technology can range from routine to nonroutine, corresponding to the opportunities for routine capabilities. Richardson's study (1996) of fashion apparel firms shows those firms that redesigned their technology by implementing new information technologies such as CAD / CAM equipment and EDI developed a much greater potential for operational flexibility.

Increases in controllability might also involve changes in *organizational structure*. Organizational structure comprises not only the actual distribution of responsibilities and authority among the organization's personnel (basic form), but also the planning and control systems and the process regulations of decision-making, coordination, and execution. The structural design of the organization can range from mechanistic to organic (Burns and Stalker, 1961), corresponding to the opportunities for adaptive capabilities.

Many large corporations are undertaking organizational restructuring to increase their responsiveness. For instance, Xerox was able to exploit its superior technological and market capabilities after fundamentally changing its organizational architecture by creating business divisions with self-organizing teams and developing new reward and recognition systems (Howard, 1992). Similarly, Smith and Zeithaml (1996) illustrated that the newly developed capabilities of two Regional Bell Operating Companies (RBOCs) could be successfully deployed after drastic restructuring and organizational redesign.

Not only structural changes, but also cultural changes may be necessary to increase the controllability of the firm. *Organizational culture* can be defined as the set of beliefs and assumptions held relatively commonly throughout the organization and taken for granted by its members (Bate, 1984). Essential features of such beliefs are that they are implicit in the minds of organization members and to some extent shared (Hofstede, 1980). These beliefs may constrain managerial capabilities by specifying broad, tacitly understood rules for appropriate action in unspecified contingencies (Camerer and Vepsalainen, 1988). The organizational culture can range from conservative to innovative, depending on the slack within the current norms and value systems for strategic capabilities.

The beliefs and assumptions of the organizational culture also play a central role in the interpretation of environmental stimuli and the configuration of organizationally relevant strategic responses (Johnson, 1987). Does the organization see new strategic options? Can it deviate from present patterns? The more innovative the culture, the greater the leeway for strategic flexibility within the organization. Hence, many large Western corporations such as GE, Philips, and ABB have not only restructured themselves, but also tried to change their corporate cultures. After downsizing and delayering, GE started its famous workout programme, best-practice sessions, and change-acceleration programme (Tichy and Sherman, 1994). In the same way, Philips's Centurion program started with an efficiency drive but was followed by a cultural revitalizing module initiated by the concern committee, Values and Behaviour (the Philips Way). An even more radical cultural change was attempted by ABB, which developed a twenty-one-page 'Mission, Values, and Policy' booklet referred to inside the company as the policy bible when it formed its global matrix structure. Moreover, Craig's (1996) study of two players in the Japanese beer industry reveals that cultural change is also an important issue in Japanese companies. Asahi initiated and Kirin responded to hypercompetition by not only working on their functional structure, but also reconsidering their intolerant culture. Both firms fundamentally changed their corporate culture by corporate identity and empowerment programmes.

The Paradox of Flexibility

Combining the managerial and organization design tasks involves a process of matching, typically called duality or resolving paradoxes (see Fig. 4.7). Increases in the control capacity of management might involve developing flexible manufacturing capabilities, JIT purchasing capabilities, multi-sourcing capabilities, quick-response capabilities, or product-development capabilities. Increases in the controllability of the firm might involve changes in technology (e.g. CAD/CAM, FMS), structure (e.g. delayering, autonomous groups), and culture (e.g. empowerment, corporate identity programmes). The challenge for management is to develop dynamic capabilities that enhance flexibility and to have an adequate organizational design to utilize those capabilities. In other words, a flexible organization must possess some capabilities which enhance its flexibility to avoid becoming rigid, but it must also be anchored in some way in order to avoid chaos. Rather than accepting the dichotomy of preservation and change, this paradox implies that organizational flexibility incorporates both change and preservation. Consequently, management has to deal with a constructive tension (Kanter, 1983) between developing capabilities and preserving organizational conditions. A tension, for example, between the need for

Flexibility: A Multidimensional Concept

managers to question and challenge versus the preservation of core values and organizational mission; between the need for new ideas and directions and the need for continuity and preservation of core technologies (Johnson, 1988). Or, as Ulrich and Lake (1990: 245) formulate it, the flexible organization asks for a willingness to shift, flex, and change and at the same time an unconditional commitment, concern, and loyalty to the organization.

If there is no balance between the two dimensions, flexibility efforts will fail (see Table 4.6). For instance, if management develops dynamic capabilities but the organization remains inert, the firm will experience chaos. Management will overreact to competitive change and the organization will be unable to respond. IBM managers tried to foster renewal, but their initiatives were stifled because the organization was inert. Conversely, if the responsiveness of the organization is increased but the managerial capabilities are limited, the new flexibility potential will be largely unrealized. For instance, many US firms invested heavily in flexible manufacturing systems (Jaikumar, 1986), yet, the management of these firms was unable to tap the flexibility potential that these new technologies made possible. They simply lacked certain managerial capabilities. They used the FMS the wrong way: for high-volume production of few parts rather than for high-variety production of many parts at a low cost per unit. Similarly, many firms have started with delayering, creating teams, and

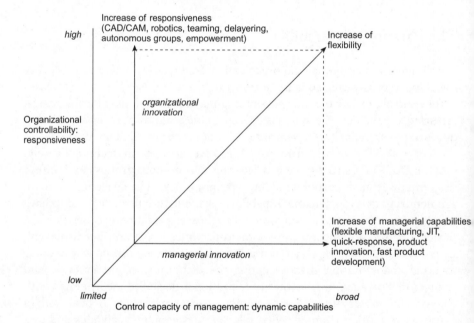

Fig. 4.7. The paradox of control capacity and controllability

104

empowering people while their management is unable to utilize the increased flexibility potential. In the following chapters, we will elaborate on the managerial and organization design tasks of flexibility. Doing so will help us to analyse more carefully the managerial repertoire of flexible capabilities and the responsiveness of the organization.

TABLE 4.6. Resolving the flexibility paradox: sources of adaptive failure

High responsiveness	Non-adaptive management: flexibility potential unrealized	Fully flexible: constructive friction between managerial capabilities and organizational responsiveness
Low responsiveness	Rigid: all-round failure	Inert organization: managerial initiatives stifled
	Specialized routines	Dynamic capabilities

Notes

1. Speed and acceleration of change were factors of the flexibility-scale in the original Aston studies (Pugh *et al.*, 1963).
2. The concept of static control is based on Cybernetics I, which has developed extensively through experience stemming from the study of man-made systems (such as engineering and computer systems), whereas the insights derived from natural systems have remained by and large much less formally developed. In Cybernetics I, organizations are viewed as open systems as a result of attempts to make sense of such systems from the standpoint of an external observer. These open systems are in constant interaction with their environment, transforming inputs into outputs as a means of creating the conditions necessary for survival (Morgan, 1986: 236).
3. The concept of dynamic control is derived from Cybernetics II. In particular, Maturana and Varela (1980) offered a new perspective for understanding the logic through which living systems change, which lays the foundation for Cybernetics II (Morgan, 1986: 236). In this theory, all living systems are organizationally autonomous systems of interaction that make reference only to themselves. Maturana and Varela have used the term autopoiesis to refer to this capacity for self-production through a closed system of relations. Nevertheless, they developed

105

their theory primarily as a new interpretation of biological phenomena, and they have strong reservations about applying it to the social world. Accordingly, the literature of Cybernetics II suggests that there is a difference between naturally occurring autopoietic structures and those of social entities. Varela therefore proposes to use 'autonomy' instead of 'autopoiesis' as the proper term for referring to the identity-preserving capability of 'social organizations'. The attention in Cybernetics II is drawn to system processes that try to maintain identity by ignoring or counteracting threatening fluctuations, and to the way variations can lead to the emergence of new modes of organization. Random changes can trigger circular interactions, the final consequences of which are determined by whether or not the current identity of the system will dampen the effects of the new disturbance through compensatory changes elsewhere, or whether a new configuration of relations will be allowed to emerge. In this context, fluctuation is viewed as a major vehicle for creating order, not for destroying it. For instance, the theory of dissipative structures founded by Prigogine (1976) suggested that near-equilibrium order is destroyed, whereas far-from-equilibrium order is maintained.

5 The Managerial Task: Creating Flexible Capabilities

> While product demands placed upon firms are changing in dramatic ways—product life cycles are shorter, demand for product choice and customization is swelling, pressures for globalization and technological innovation are overwhelming—the firm's need to respond to change with stable and long-term, yet flexible and responsive, process capabilities is greater than ever before.
>
> (Boynton and Victor, 1991: 53)

In the preceding chapter, we defined flexibility and its essential dimensions, and articulated the managerial and organization design tasks of flexibility. In this chapter, we further examine the managerial task of flexibility, which involves increasing the variety and speed of managerial capabilities. While the speed of change in today's turbulent environments weakens the sustainability of specialized routines, it increases the importance of the advantage provided by flexible dynamic capabilities, which remain valuable as long as competitive change persists. Firms still need specialized routines, but these routines have a dysfunctional flipside because rapidly changing environments make them obsolete (see Sect. 3.4). For instance, in the 1980s, US automobile producers found that a simple high-volume, standardized production repertoire (low variety, low speed of response) appeared to be insufficiently comprehensive to cope with the many challenges posed by the changing environment. Rather, these challenges required a willingness to invest heavily in extremely flexible capabilities (high variety, high speed), often far beyond what might be utilized at any given point in time. Successful Japanese companies have showed these capabilities offer far more than the ability to make multiple products simultaneously. They also offer the benefits of reduced changeover costs across product generations and the ability to adjust the product mix in the face of uncertain demands, even at low volumes.

These days it may seem impossible for any manager to ignore change in markets, products, and technologies. Yet the popular business press is full of successful companies that focused too much on past routines, such as DEC, Wang Computers, and Sears. In other companies such as IBM, Kodak, and Philips that are currently undergoing massive changes, existing or new managers are working on developing new flexible capabilities. But how can management create dynamic or flexible response capabilities? And what kind of flexible capabilities in terms of variety and speed of response? In our review of definitions, for instance, we noticed that flexibility is sometimes related to changes in routines, organizational structures, or even goals and associated strategies. Moreover, some definitions focused on internal changes, while other definitions emphasized the importance of bringing out changes in the environment.

In this chapter, we will focus on the comprehensive arsenal of flexible capabilities of management. First, we clearly delineate flexible capabilities from specialized routines and explicitly discuss specific managerial requirements of flexible capabilities (Sect. 5.1). Subsequently, we consider various managerial roles in creating capabilities, ranging from cross-hierarchical and cross-functional to cross-value capability development (Sect. 5.2). As a result of its activities, management may develop a certain repertoire of dynamic capabilities, which we shall call the flexibility mix. From this examination, we shall distinguish four types of flexibility: steady-state, operational, structural, and strategic (Sect. 5.3). Each type represents a simple combination of more/less variety of capabilities and fast/slow response. The more turbulent the environment, the more a firm will need a large flexibility mix.

5.1 Flexible Capabilities versus Specialized Routines

As a managerial task, flexibility involves the creation or promotion of dynamic capabilities. Dynamic or flexible response capabilities denote the managerial ability to respond reactively or proactively to various demands from changing competitive environments. They are based on dynamic models of competition that suggest the capacity to change is an important source of competitive advantage (cf. Teece et al., 1997). These capabilities permit rapid response (speed) to a variety of unpredictable contingencies and demand changes (Ittner and Kogut, 1995). Many of them are developed in functional areas like flexible manufacturing, flexible supplier relationships, or flexible human resource management. However, the more complex ones are more broadly based (Stalk et al., 1992), encompassing the entire value chain such as short product development capabilities or fast product and process innovation capabilities.

Dynamic capabilities must be clearly distinguished from specialized routines (see Table 5.1).

Dynamic competition Specialized or static routines in terms of managerial directions, policies, or procedures embody management's capacity to replicate previously performed tasks (Teece et al., 1997). These routines are perfectly

TABLE 5.1. Managerial requirements of dynamic capabilities

Specialized routines	Dynamic capabilities
• static control	• dynamic control
• limited expertise	• broad and deep knowledge-base
• low absorptive capacity	• high absorptive capacity
• fixed managerial mindsets and no experimentation	• broad managerial mindsets and much experimentation
• lower-level learning	• higher-level learning

illustrated by McDonald's operating manuals or KLM's directives, policies, and procedures for aircraft maintenance. In contrast with dynamic capabilities, specialized routines are based on static control and static models of competition, which do not view the capacity to change as an essential feature of sustained success. For certain competitive changes, a standard or preprogrammed behaviour is prescribed. The primary virtue of specialized routines is that they eliminate the need for further communication and coordination among subunits and positions. Consequently, they provide a memory for handling routine situations.

Our description of specialized routines clearly illustrates that they are limited to those competitive changes which can be anticipated and to which an appropriate response can be identified. In non-routine situations, exceptions to programmes are more frequently encountered. Of course, some programming is still necessary in these situations in order to make interaction predictable and to save time. One might think of safety instructions in case of emergencies or instructions for communication in the army during a battle. None the less, when they occur, it is impossible to programme how to solve a problem because routines inhibit the utilization of new expertise. Instead, routines reward management's strict compliance with inadequate programmes. Over time, limited attention to specific programmes kills managers' initiative to search for adequate solutions.

Broad knowledge-base / variety of managerial expertise Instead of limited expertise, flexible capabilities require a broad and deep knowledge-base (technological, market, product, distribution knowledge) and a variety of managerial expertise in order to devise appropriate responses. For instance, new products today are more likely than not to emerge through innovation at the interface of different specialties (Grant, 1996). The managerial ability to combine knowledge-bases housed in different core technologies often distinguishes flexible and innovative companies. For example, when 3M consumer research showed that customers complained about rusting steelwool pads, experts from 3M's adhesives, abrasives, coatings, and non-woven technologies divisions got together to create Never Rust plastic soap pads (Leonard-Barton, 1995: 67). Similarly, Corning views its knowledge about glass and ceramic processes as a strategic resource and continuously invests in its enhancement. By managing a broad knowledge-base emerging from a variety of expertise, Corning is able to develop dynamic capabilities such as rapid product innovation and customization in order to exploit rapid, unpredictable product opportunities (Boynton and Victor, 1991). Finally, the credit card industry discovered how an outsider firm's broad knowledge-base can result in a formidable new competitor when AT&T used its marketing and distribution knowledge to enter the credit card market. These examples illustrate that the depth of a knowledge-base is necessary to solve complex problems, but that the breadth of knowledge-base is especially important for creating new dynamic capabilities.

Absorptive capacity   Related to a broad knowledge-base, dynamic capabilities require a high absorptive capacity of management (Cohen and Levinthal, 1990) for recognizing the need to change. Successfully absorbing signals beyond the periphery of the firm is essential for developing capabilities. The ability of management to recognize the value of new, external information, assimilate, and apply it to commercial ends is critical to its dynamic capabilities. Absorptive capacity requires porous boundaries, scanning broadly for new soft information, and identifying and effectively using those employees who serve as gatekeepers and boundary spanners (Leonard-Barton, 1995). Liebeskind *et al.* (1996) show that successful new biotechnology firms were able to develop flexible capabilities in new product development because their management developed high levels of absorptive capacity through social networks and boundary spanning. This absorptive capacity helped them to quickly source new knowledge from various universities and research institutes.

On the other hand, the absorptive capacity of specialized routines is limited. Rather, the suppression of choice is a condition for the efficient exploitation of routines. We already observed that firms like GM, IBM, and DEC have become prisoners of their deeply ingrained routines and irreversible, fixed assets, turning their competences (big cars, mainframe computers, minicomputers) into new problems to be resolved (see Sect. 3.4).

Managerial experimentation and broad managerial mindsets   Management must have an ability to identify and support new ideas rather than to exploit existing routines to the maximum extent. Experimentation is limited when knowledge extension is based on routines which work like well-worn grooves to channel managerial activities. By relying on these routines, management concentrates on its own specialized areas and avoids the need to construct its notion of the whole for new activities. As a consequence, routines exacerbate the separation of functional areas, impede learning processes, and further restrict the development of new capabilities by imposing old understandings. However, experimentation and broad mindsets can contribute to an increasing variety of dynamic capabilities.

In this connection, the experiences of firms such as NCR and GM are illustrative. Because of their reluctance to experiment and continued focus on established lines of business (respectively electromechanical cash registers and big-car business) these firms were temporarily outperformed by others. Likewise, Sharp was able to develop dynamic capabilities in the electronic calculator industry while TI was not because of TI's limited managerial mindsets that were narrowly focused on the semiconductor market. Also, Honda's success in the US motorcycle market was based primarily on managerial latitude for experimentation and complementary managerial mindsets. While Sochiro Honda, the inventive founder of the company with a large ego and mercurial temperament, had a strong bias towards motor technology, his partner Takeo Fujisawa's primary focus was on market, distribution, and financial knowledge.

Development time and higher-order learning Dynamic capabilities like flexible manufacturing or fast product development cannot be purchased off the shelf but require strategic vision, development time, and sustained investment (Amit and Schoemaker, 1993). They take time to identify, nurture, and leverage and tend not to be the kind of assets that management can turn on or off with the exercise of an option. Firms simply lack the capacity to develop new capabilities quickly (Teece *et al.*, 1997). That is, dynamic capabilities cannot be easily bought, but they must be built; skill acquisition and learning become fundamental issues. While routines also require learning and take time to develop, they can often be built on an extrapolation of trends, imitation of others, or past experience. These modes of single-loop learning are all based on repetitive reinforcement in which no cognitive change takes place in the organization. By contrast, dynamic capabilities require higher-order learning such as double-loop learning, which hinges on the ability to fundamentally challenge operating assumptions (see Sect. 3.3).

To conclude, the development of dynamic capabilities requires

- managers' absorptive capacity to recognize quickly the need to change;
- managers' knowledge-base, expertise, or ability to devise appropriate responses;
- managerial experimentation and broad mindsets to increase the variety of dynamic capabilities;
- higher-order managerial learning abilities to sustain an adequate repertoire of dynamic capabilities.

5.2 Managerial Roles in Capability Development: Vertical, Horizontal, and Ideological Management

Of course, we have to realize that developing dynamic capabilities is not exclusively the role of the manager. While in many situations managers do indeed dominate this process, in principle every organization member participates in it. That is to say, capabilities grow through the actions of employees at all organizational levels (Leonard-Barton, 1995: 28).

Vertical Management: Cross-Hierarchical Capabilities

Traditionally, identifying and building capabilities are viewed as a hierarchical process with the CEO and top management playing a central role (cf. Chandler, 1962; Schumpeter, 1934). In particular, capability development is considered a *top-down, deliberate managerial process*, where the exploration of capabilities created by heuristics, skill development, and fundamentally new insights takes place at the corporate management level, while the exploitation of these capabilities takes place at the business-unit or lower levels. This perspective was recently supported by Prahalad and Hamel (1990) and Stalk *et al.* (1992), who argued that the development of adequate capabilities depends on the strategic intent (Hamel and Prahalad, 1989) of the CEO or corporate management based on superior industry foresight.

Examples of such predominantly top-down capability development processes include GE's corporate revitalization guided by its CEO Jack Welch and Philips's corporate change initiated by Jan Timmer and further accelerated by its new CEO Cor Boonstra. What is unique about these companies is the fact that their CEOs drove the entire process of capability development, starting by introducing new concepts, communicating them in an understandable manner through the use of metaphors and analogies, and reiterating them repeatedly. Consequently, new capabilities such as speed, simplicity, and market responsiveness were passed down the organization almost as an order or instruction to be followed (cf. Nonaka and Takeuchi, 1995). However, not every firm can simply copy this top-down approach, given the fact that strategy in large complex firms is often less centralized in top management, more multifaceted, and generally less integrated.

In contrast, building on Bower's work (1970) on the management of the resource allocation process, a rich body of literature has suggested that perhaps the most effective process of capability development is through originating, developing, and promoting strategic initiatives from the front-line managers (cf. Kimberly, 1979; Burgelman, 1983; Quinn, 1985). This research finds that capabilities typically emerge from the autonomous strategic behaviour of individuals or small groups in lower levels of the organization. Front-line managers typically have the most current knowledge and expertise and are closer to the sources of information critical to new capabilities.

Within the *reactive bottom-up, emergent perspective*, the role of top management is described as retroactive legitimizer (Burgelman, 1983) or judge and arbiter (Angle and Van de Ven, 1989) and that of middle management as supporter and intermediary of lower-level initiatives. Exploration of new capabilities takes place at the lowest level by double-loop learning or generative learning (Senge, 1990); the interactions with the market and demanding clients spur front-line managers to call into question their norms, objectives, and basic policies. At the upper managerial levels, the exploitation of already developed capabilities takes place by single-loop or adaptive learning, which helps the firm to exploit previous experiences, to detect causalities, and extrapolate to the future. It permits top corporate management to persist in its set policies and achieve its formulated objectives. An example of a more reactive bottom-up process of capability development can be found in 3M. In this highly innovative firm, the role of top management is limited to sponsor, coach or mentor; flexible capabilities, like innovation and speed of innovation, clearly derive from initiatives at the bottom. Not surprisingly, the names of successive CEOs at 3M are relatively unknown, while the inventors and intrapreneurs of the lower levels of the company have received the most attention (e.g. Scotch tape invented by Dick Drew or post-it notes by Art Fry).

By contrast, in the *proactive bottom-up, emergent perspective*, the role of top management is considered to be more than retroactive sense-making of bottom-up initiatives; it is the creator of purpose and challenger of the status quo of the firm (Bartlett and Ghoshal, 1993). This creative tension (Senge, 1990) at the level of corporate management forces the firm to balance exploitation of capabilities with the cost of adaptability to new capability development. One could argue that in the proactive bottom-up, emergent perspective, top management is involved in single-loop and double-loop learning at the same time, sometimes called deutero-learning (cf. Bateson, 1936; Argyris and Schön, 1978). In other words, top management's exploration of unknown futures and its exploitation of known pasts balance each other (Hedberg and Jönsson, 1978: 50). ABB can be considered as a firm in which capabilities are developed in a proactive, bottom-up fashion. New capabilities derive from front-line managers, but the direction is partly inspired by Percy Barnevick's very ambitious, future-oriented sense of mission.

Given these divergent views on vertical or cross-hierarchical capability development, it is impossible to give an integrated perspective on the managerial roles of different hierarchical levels. Vertical capability development can arise from lower as well as middle and upper levels. Essential for both top-down and bottom-up cross-hierarchy perspectives on capability development is that management must guarantee that in the end all levels are involved. If not, the firm will not be able to create corporate-wide flexible capabilities but will instead suffer from the tyranny of the business unit or the tyranny of top management and the resulting fragmentation of capabilities.

Horizontal Management: Cross-Functional Capabilities

In contrast with vertical capability development, horizontal capability development refers to more democratic and more participative forms of capability development in organizations, which may be explicitly designed (e.g. teams, projects, or task forces) but may also emerge out of a process of interaction. As an illustration of the difference between horizontal and vertical capability development, one could argue that the Taylorist principles of incentives and staff organization are cross-hierarchical capabilities for accomplishing standardized production at lower costs. On the other hand, we could classify Toyota's principles of decentralized authority and lateral communication across functions, buyers, and suppliers as cross-functional capabilities to generate speed and flexibility.

In many contemporary firms, the role of management has shifted from vertical coordination through a hierarchical command and control structure to providing appropriate organizational support for horizontal exchange of knowledge. In all such firms, horizontal or self-coordination among experts is more efficient than vertical coordination by managers. However, self-coordination across functional and organizational boundaries cannot take place without managerial permission or active managerial support (Liebeskind et al., 1996). None the less, horizontal or cross-functional capability development is in many cases disrupted by managerial meddling (Weick, 1979: 8). Management intervenes in the mistaken belief that single individuals develop capabilities, denying that capabilities may be developed implicitly in causal circuits and interpersonal influence processes. Failure to acknowledge these forms of self-control, coupled with interventions that actively disrupt these self-regulating activities, are the occasions for much mismanagement in organizations.

Ideological Management: Cross-Value Capabilities

In addition to vertical capability development by means of hierarchy and horizontal capability development by means of teams, we can distinguish an ideological type of capability development. A shared ideology may facilitate capability development among various parts or subcultures of the company by specifying broad, tacitly understood rules for appropriate action under unspecified contingencies (De Leeuw and Volberda, 1996; Camerer and Vepsalainen, 1988). These cross-value capabilities refer to the ability of the firm to produce a shared ideology that offers members an attractive identity as well as convincing interpretations of reality. The infusion of beliefs and values into an organization takes place over time, and produces a distinct identity for its participants, colouring as it does all aspects of organizational life, and giving it a social integration that goes far beyond the vertical cross-hierarchical and horizontal cross-functional capabilities discussed above. These cross-value capabilities determine what kinds of knowledge are sought and nurtured, and what kind of capability-building activities are tolerated and encouraged. They serve as capability-screening and control mechanisms. Japanese companies like Canon and Honda try to enhance cross-value capabilities by facilitating dialogue, camp sessions, or brainstorming seminars held outside the workplace, and even drinking sessions (Nonaka and Takeuchi, 1995).

Mintzberg connected cross-value capabilities to his concept of the missionary form and the ideological strategy (cf. Mintzberg, 1979; Mintzberg and Waters, 1985). In addition, Ouchi's (1980) concept of clan control shows that shared norms and values facilitate exchange of tacit knowledge without resort to market pricing, contracts, or managerial authority. In a similar vein, Bradach and Eccles (1989) defined trust as the alternative mode of knowledge exchange, where trust is engendered by shared norms. Furthermore, a recent study by Liebeskind et al. (1996) on new biotechnology firms illustrates that the sourcing of tacit external knowledge is possible only through shared social norms.

Ideological capability development rests in firms with a core identity, in which one can find a coherent set of beliefs, shared values, and common language. Through it, every member identifies strongly with, and professes loyalty to, the goal of preserving, extending, or perfecting the organization's mission, and so can be trusted to make decisions in the organization's interests. Hewlett-Packard's corporate values like trust and respect for individuals, uncompromising integrity, and teamwork (the HP Way) or 3M's eleventh commandment of 'Thou shalt not kill ideas for new products', tolerance for failure, and bias for action culture help these firms easily to develop flexible capabilities.

Of course, capability development can take place vertically, horizontally, and ideologically sequentially or even at the same time (see Fig. 5.1). For instance, Leonard-Barton (1995) discussed T-shaped capabilities, which are cross-functional as well as cross-hierarchical and essential for successful innovations. These capabilities imply deep know-how and expertise within a functional area (the stem) completed with more superficial knowledge about the interaction with other functional areas (the crossbar). Moreover, Nonaka (1994) describes middle-up-down management in Japanese firms such as Honda, Canon, and Toyota in which all members of the organization work together horizontally

Creating Flexible Capabilities

Vertical	Horizontal	Ideological
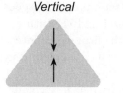	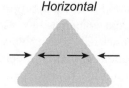	

- cross-hierarchy: top-down/bottom-up
- command-and-control structure / flat hierarchy
- extrinsic management: enforcing capability development by distinct leadership tasks at various levels varying from Executive Champion, Product Champion, or Intrapreneur

- cross-function: teaming
- self-control
- intrinsic management: supporting capability development by horizontal linking

- cross-value: core culture
- ideological control
- intrinsic management: facilitating capability development by creating a vision, shared ideology, or identity

Fig. 5.1. Various managerial roles in flexible capability development

and vertically. Teams play a central role in this kind of dual organization, with middle managers serving as team leaders who are at the intersection of the vertical and horizontal flows of information. Non-hierarchical, self-organizing activities of teams are indispensable for generating new capabilities through intensive, focused research. On the other hand, hierarchy is more efficient and effective for exploitation of capabilities (Romme, 1996).

Finally, we wish to note that horizontal or ideological capability development is not necessarily superior to vertical capability development. To take an organizational example of horizontal management which can be judged negatively, one can imagine a situation in which organizational members are all prisoners of the bundle of relations that tie them together. In the same way, ideological management can also create a mental prison if the culture hampers the ability to see important changes in the market. Powerfully strong cultures usually suffer from xenophobia (Ouchi, 1981), that is, they resist deviance, retard attempts at change, and tend to foster inbreeding.

5.3 The Flexibility Mix: Types of Flexibility

As a result of the various managerial activities in dynamic capability development (cross-hierarchical, cross-functional, and cross-value), management may develop a certain repertoire of dynamic capabilities over time. Those dynamic capabilities that endow the firm with flexibility are manifested in the 'flexibility mix'. Considering the variety and speed of dynamic capabilities, we can distinguish four types of flexibility (see Table 5.2): steady-state, operational, structural, and strategic (Ansoff and Brandenburg, 1971; Volberda, 1992). Each type represents a simple combination of more/less variety of capabilities and fast/slow response.

TABLE 5.2. Types of flexibility

	High	Structural	Strategic
Variety			
	Low	Steady-state	Operational

Low   High

Speed

Steady-state flexibility (low variety, low speed) consists of static procedures to optimize the firm's performance when the levels of throughput and the nature of throughput remain relatively stable over time. It hardly seems to be a real type of flexibility because under steady-state conditions there is only minor change and a relatively low premium on speed of response to external conditions.

For the other three types of flexibility, a distinction can be made between internal and external flexibility (Ansoff, 1965). Internal flexibility is defined as management's capability to adapt to the demands of the environment. External flexibility is defined as management's capability to influence the environment so that the firm becomes less vulnerable to environmental changes (see also Sect. 4.2). Examples of these types of flexibility are provided in Table 5.3. The table shows that the variety and speed of managerial capabilities may result in various levels of managerial manoeuvring capacity and can be both internal and external.

Operational flexibility (low variety, high speed) consists of routine capabilities that are based on present structures or goals of the organization. It is the most common type of flexibility and relates to the volume and mix of activities rather than the kinds of activities undertaken within the firm. The routines used are directed primarily at the operational activities and are reactive. Operational flexibility provides rapid response to changes that are familiar. Such changes typically lead to temporary, short-term fluctuations in the firm's level of activity. Although the variety in the environment may be high, the combinations of conditions are sufficiently predictable for management to develop routine capabilities to reduce uncertainty.

Operational flexibility can be internal or external. Examples of internal operational flexibility are the variation of production volume, the building up of

Creating Flexible Capabilities

TABLE 5.3. Examples of internal and external types of flexibility

	Internal	External
Routine manoeuvring capacity	*Internal operational flexibility* • variation of production volume • building up of inventories • use of crash teams	*External operational flexibility* • use of temporary labour • multi-sourcing • reserving of capacity with suppliers
Adaptive manoeuvring capacity	*Internal structural flexibility* • creating multifunctional teams • changing managerial roles • alterations in control systems	*External structural flexibility* • purchasing of components from suppliers with a short delivery time (JIT) • purchasing of subassemblies from suppliers (co-makership) • developing of subcomponents together with suppliers (co-design)
Strategic manoeuvring capacity	*Internal strategic flexibility* • dismantling of current strategy • applying new technologies • fundamentally renewing products	*External strategic flexibility* • creating new product-market combinations • using market power to deter entry and control competitors • engaging in political activities to counteract trade regulations

inventories, and the maintenance of excess capacity. For instance, vertically integrated fashion apparel firms like Benetton or The Limited have developed 'quick-response' capabilities aimed at shortening the manufacturing cycle, reducing inventory levels, and enabling manufacture in response to sales during the season (Richardson, 1996). These routine capabilities in rapid learning, communication, and coordination supplant traditional core competencies in design and fashion sense. Rather than bet on a few designs from the most savvy designers, these firms try out many designs, quickly imitate others, and continue to produce what sells. Though product innovations and demand changes are rapid and somewhat unpredictable, introducing new products and responding to changing demands are routine manoeuvring in fashion apparel. New styles and designs do not usually require new types of inputs or process technologies. The object of this kind of internal operational flexibility is a more efficient, less risky operation in a volatile end-market. In addition to these internal types, external operational flexibility can be achieved by contracting out certain peripheral activities, using temporary labour to adjust the size of the workforce to shifts in product demand, or obtaining resources from more than one supplier.

Such capabilities enhance management's capacity to adapt to or influence input and output fluctuations in the environment. By developing a greater number of these capabilities, management tries to reduce uncertainty to a minimum, which enables the firm to operate as efficiently as possible. Routine capabilities are often the result of cross-hierarchical managerial activities. They strengthen and reinforce existing commitments, such as the products produced or markets served. As a result, management becomes very concerned with 'doing things right'. Its growing concern is to achieve stability and equilibrium. The risk of the preponderant emphasis by management on achieving operational flexibility is that it can lead to organizational inertia. Routine capabilities like these first have to be unlearned before an organization can change (Starbuck, 1983).

Structural flexibility (high variety, low speed) consists of managerial capabilities for adapting the organization structure, and its decision and communication processes, to suit changing conditions in an evolutionary way (Krijnen, 1979). When faced with revolutionary changes, management needs great internal structural flexibility or intraorganizational leeway to facilitate the renewal or transformation of current structures and processes. Examples of internal structural flexibility are horizontal or vertical job enlargement; the creation of small production units or work cells within a production line; changes in organizational responsibilities; alterations in control systems; the use of project teams; and the transformation from a functional grouping to a market-oriented grouping with interchangeable personnel and equipment.

Structural flexibility can also be external in terms of interorganizational leeway in supporting and sheltering new technologies or developing new products or markets. Examples include various forms of JIT purchasing, co-makership, co-design, or even joint ventures and other co-alignments. By increasing structural relations with outsiders, the organization can engage more easily in new developments. This type of flexibility is perfectly illustrated by Nordvest Forum, a group of forty-six small- and medium-sized firms in and around the city of Alesund on the north-west coast of Norway (Hanssen-Bauer and Snow, 1996). In order to cope with hypercompetitive environments, these regional firms developed network relationships that expedite the learning process and help the member firms to upgrade their adaptive capacity so that they can compete more effectively in both the national and international marketplaces. More extreme examples of superior external structural flexibility include large dominating firms or strategic centres such as Nike, Nintendo, Sun Microsystems, and Toyota (Lorenzoni and Baden-Fuller, 1995). These firms responded to increasing competition by forming tight network organizations in which they perform only a few unique functions along the value chain and outsource the remaining functions to specialist partners. Such relationships can be temporary, as in the case of a past alliance between IBM, Intel, and Microsoft in the computer industry, or it can endure, as in the long-standing relationships between Nike and its production partners in the athletic footwear and apparel industry. From the focal firm's standpoint, external structural flexibility raises interesting questions about the relative efficacy of internal versus external avenues towards new products, technologies, and knowledge (cf. Pennings and Harianto, 1992). When management retains the opportunity to modify the structural relationship and leave a relationship that no longer meets its needs (external structural flexibility), external avenues can be very attractive. If not, internal avenues by means of internal structural flexibility are more appropriate. For both internal and external structural flexibility, a combination of cross-hierarchical and cross-functional managerial roles is required.

Strategic flexibility (high variety, high speed) consists of managerial capabilities related to the goals of the organization or the environment (Aaker and Mascarenhas, 1984). This most radical type of flexibility is much more qualitative and involves changes in the nature of organizational activities. It is necessary when the organization faces unfamiliar changes that have far-reaching consequences and needs to respond quickly. The issues and difficulties relating to strategic flexibility are by definition unstructured and non-routine. The signals and feedback received from the environment tend to be indirect and open to multiple interpretations, 'soft' and 'fuzzy'. Because the organization usually has no specific experience and no routine answer for coping with the changes, management may have to change its game plans, dismantle its current strategies (Harrigan, 1985), apply new technologies, or fundamentally renew its products. Its response may also be external, for example influencing consumers through advertising and promotions (Mascarenhas, 1982), creating new product-market combinations (Krijnen, 1979), using market power to deter entry and control competitors (Porter, 1980), or engaging in political activities to counteract trade regulations. Besides cross-hierarchical and cross-functional managerial roles, strategic flexibility requires intensive ideological management and cross-value capability development. New values and norms are necessary and past experience may not provide any advantage (Newman *et al.*, 1972). The creation of new activities in new situations may be very important. For instance, regional Bell operating companies (RBOCs) that were spun off from AT&T developed strategic flexibility from international expansion activities because the international managers in the unregulated side of the business questioned past practices, raised new assumptions about the organization, and promoted significant changes in strategy. The transfer of strategic capabilities from international operations to domestic network operations was helpful in awakening wireline operations to the realities of coming competition and the need for employees to be flexible, strategic thinkers (Smith and Zeithaml, 1996).

To recapitulate, in this chapter we investigated the managerial task of flexibility. First, we defined flexible capabilities and considered specific managerial roles in creating them. Subsequently, on the basis of the variety of dynamic capabilities and speed of response, we systematically distinguished four types of flexibility. Management's flexibility mix may be composed of steady-state, operational, structural, or strategic flexibility or of some combination of them. In the next chapter, we will consider the appropriate organization design for utilizing these capabilities.

6   The Organization Design Task: Reducing Organizational Barriers

> Firms have long been described as designing mechanisms by which to buffer uncertainty in order to minimize risk. Yet the development of flexible capabilities implies a contradiction of this learning. The value of flexibility lies in increasing an organization's ability to respond to changing and uncertain environments. Designing an organization that does not shield itself from this uncertainty requires fundamental organizational changes ... With no buffers to shield the fragile system from uncertainty, flexible capabilities are required to permit rapid responses to unpredictable production contingencies and demand changes. These capabilities are embedded not only in hardware such as flexible manufacturing systems, but also in the organization's employees, or what they call the 'humanware'.
>
> (Ittner and Kogut, 1995: 155–6)

So far, we have considered the management challenge of flexibility, which is manifested in the managerial repertoire of flexible capabilities. We have seen that increasing the variety and speed of managerial capabilities is a challenging goal. Without an appropriate organization design, however, the firm is unable to utilize those flexible capabilities. In this chapter, we will therefore explore further the organization design challenge of flexibility, which involves designing the appropriate organizational conditions necessary to effectively exploit the flexibility mix. In this connection, the existing organization design determines the organization's potential for flexibility. As regards this challenge, therefore, two settings can be distinguished. When the potential for flexibility or leeway within the organizational conditions is adequate for activating a sufficient flexibility mix, no redesign of organizational conditions is necessary. When the potential within the organizational conditions is inadequate for activating a sufficient flexibility mix, however, redesign of organizational conditions will be necessary. In this chapter, we will analyse various organizational barriers to flexibility.

It should be noticed that 'organization (re)design' in this context is not restricted to developing new technologies or transforming structures, but also includes intervening in organizational cultures. Clearly, technology is part of the answer, but technology by itself will not create flexibility. Investments in advanced manufacturing technology without commensurate changes in the firm's structure and organizational culture are unlikely to maximize the full range of potential flexibility inherent in these new technologies (Lei *et al.*, 1996). It is therefore not surprising that concepts such as business process reengineering have received growing attention; engineers involved in designing flexible technologies have realized that information technology alone is insufficient for creating flexibility. In the same way, structure can stand in the way of flexibility, or conversely be an important catalyst for it. However, structural change is seldom sufficient to achieve truly effective flexibility. As Xerox's CEO Paul Allaire argued, flexibility efforts will certainly fail if we change the structure but still try to run the company the way we used to do (Howard, 1992). Xerox's new architecture was thus based on changes in the hardware of the company (structure and reward systems) along with changes in the software of the company (leadership, workpractices, and values).

In the integrated design approach applied in this chapter, technology, structure, and culture are considered as separate partsystems of an organization. In other words, each partsystem may evolve according to its own internally derived logic and needs, quite independently of the others. However, there are various relations between these partsystems: for example, autonomous changes in culture will exert pressure on the organization's structure and technology.[1] None the less, the exact relations between these partsystems for creating a flexible organization design is still a major area of theoretical debate. For instance, some scholars, frequently referred to as technological determinists, view technology as the primary determinant of an organization's structure and culture (Woodward, 1965; Thompson, 1967; Perrow, 1967). Their assumptions are based largely on a technological imperative. Others recognize the existence of a mutual interdependence between technology, structure, and culture (Daft and Lewin, 1993). They maintain that each partsystem can both influence and be influenced by the other partsystems.

Taking into account the above arguments, we shall successively analyse the most relevant technological, structural, and cultural design variables that affect the firm's potential for flexibility. In particular, we shall consider how much they enhance or inhibit a firm's flexibility potential. From this analysis, we shall describe the organization design challenge by using the variables of technology, structure, and culture to 'locate' an organization. Different organizations are likely to show different characteristics or designs of technology, structure, and culture corresponding to variations in their organizational potential for flexibility. Of course, this potential does not say anything about the actual flexibility activated by management.

6.1 Technological Barriers

There is little consensus as to the exact meaning of organizational technology. The term technology is employed in almost as many different senses as there are writers on the subject. This confusion reflects both the diversity of orientations in the study of organizations and the divergent approaches that have been developed to measure it.[2] An approach to technology that has gained at least some measure of general acceptance within organization theory conceives of technology as the means by which, and the configuration in which, an organization transforms inputs into outputs (cf. Bedeian, 1980; Hunt, 1972). Building on this basis, our concept of technology refers to (1) the *hardware* (like machinery and equipment) and the *software* (knowledge, techniques, and skills) used in the transformation of material or informational inputs into various outputs (either goods or services), as well as (2) the *configuration* of the hardware and software. This conception of technology is applicable to all types and kinds of organizations, not just industrial or manufacturing. All organizations, whether production-oriented or service-oriented, are presumed to involve organizational participants in various kinds of activities resulting in the transformation of inputs (like requests, raw materials, students, data) into outputs. The fact that some of these activities deal with less tangible objects in no sense obviates the need to consider the hardware and software used.

On the basis of the above conceptualization of technology, we will consider to what extent certain technologies inhibit or facilitate flexibility. This exercise requires a *classification scheme* of various technologies with respect to their potential for flexibility. There is not, however, a single commonly accepted technological classification system. Most classifications consider only the form of technology, such as Woodward's (1965) well-known classification of unit, mass, and process production. Only a few classifications consider not only the form of technology, but also the amount of 'changefulness' within a form. For instance, a widely referenced classification system developed by Harvey (1968) employs a technology dimension ranging from 'specificity to technical diffuseness'. Technical specificity implies a firm in which only one or a small number of outputs are produced consistently. In contrast, a firm is considered to be technically diffuse when it utilizes a number of techniques, processes, and transformation means to produce a wide range of outputs that vary over time. Moreover, Perrow (1967) makes a distinction between extreme routine technologies, which can deal with only a few exceptions and analysable problems, and extreme non-routine technologies, which can deal with many exceptions and unanalysable problems.[3] In the same way, using Perrow's dimensions, Hage and Aiken (1969) classified technologies within health and welfare agencies on the basis of the degree of routinization. Similarly, Grimes and Klein (1973) categorized technology according to the degree of task variability or variation in personnel discretion.

On the basis of the above classifications, which take into account the degree of freedom within a chosen technology, technologies can be classified according to their potential for flexibility. In this connection, technology can range from *routine* to *non-routine*. That is to say, a routine technology restricts the potential for flexibility, and a more non-routine technology enhances the potential for flexibility. In this section, four technological design variables are derived which indicate possible barriers to flexibility (see Table 6.1).

TABLE 6.1. Classification scheme for flexibility potential of technology

Technology	routine _____ non-routine
	(low flexibility potential) (high flexibility potential)
mode of production	*process . . . . .mass . . . . .large batch . . . . .small batch . . . . .unit*
physical layout	*line . . . . .group . . . . . . .functional . . . . .workstation*
means of transformation	*specialized . . . . .multipurpose . . . . .universal*
operational production repertoire	*limited . . . . .extensive*

The Mode of Production: Process or Mass Production versus Flexible Job Shops

This technological design variable considers the choice of process (Hill, 1983: 24) or the typical modes of production available to an organization by which it is able to produce the goods or provide the services for its customers. The decision involves a selection from various volume or run-size alternatives in manufacturing systems or service alternatives in service systems (Chase and Aquilano, 1977). Important indicators with respect to the potential for flexibility of various modes of production are the throughput volume, the variability of production capacity, the range of raw materials and data used, and the range of products and services produced. On the basis of these indicators, a continuum can be developed ranging from process production to project, jobbing, one-off, and unit production (see Table 6.2).

This continuum is based largely on Woodward's (1965) original threefold classification of technology with numerous subgroups. In her influential classification, technical complexity was conceptualized as ranging from the

TABLE 6.2. Modes of production: indicators determining their flexibility potential

	low flexibility potential ——————— high flexibility potential
Mode of production	*process . . . mass . . . large batch . . . small batch . . . project, jobbing, one-off, unit*
Indicators	• throughput volume ($\leftarrow$) • variability of production capacity ($\rightarrow$) • range of raw materials and data ($\rightarrow$) • range of products and services ($\rightarrow$)

Note: ($\rightarrow$) = increasing from low to high   ($\leftarrow$) = decreasing from high to low

production of single units according to customer specifications through an intermediate category involving large-batch and mass production to continuous-flow process production.

Woodward's scale has been criticized by scholars in the field. For instance, Hunt (1970) and Harvey (1968) pointed out that unit production can sometimes be as complex as process production. After many reconsiderations and revisions, however, there seems to be some agreement upon Woodward's categorization as a scale of 'smoothness of production' from the ad hoc irregularity of unit production, and the regularity of discrete outputs of mass production, to the complete continuity of process production (Starbuck, 1965). According to this scale, unit production is the least regulating and sophisticated, large-batch and mass production are typically very regulating with more impersonal control, while process production is usually highly regulating, frequently to the point of complete automation (Mintzberg, 1979: 253).

The more regulating the mode of production, the less the potential for flexibility. Therefore the leeway for flexibility is the largest in *unit* and *small-batch* modes of production (on the right of our continuum). Here, the range of inputs is very large, while the products and services provided are 'tailor-made', based on specific operations. As a provider of non-standard items, the organization can offer a diverse range of products/services in order to meet differing customer requirements and can easily vary its production capacity. For this reason, the organization sells a set of capabilities rather than a product. One might think of the production of special-order machine tools or the creation of tailor-made management development programmes (Hill, 1983: 31).

If we move to the left on our continuum, the variety in the production capacity and product range is increasingly limited by technical constraints. In the case of *large-batch* and *mass* modes of production, a choice is made to provide high-volume, standard products which are often made-to-stock. The process is dedicated to the needs of a single or small range of major products or services. In mass production, the repetitive process is one in which the products or services are made, with each product/service passing through the same sequence of operation (Hill, 1983: 28). Examples of mass production include the production of cars or domestic appliances. Batch production refers to a mode of operation in which each entire production-lot passes through one stage of the production process before going to the next stage (Van Donk *et al.*, 1991). When the operations involved in a particular stage have been completed on all the products in a batch, the batch passes on. Thus, the capacity at each stage of production is used to meet the different requirements of different orders, as illustrated by the production of car components or the carrying out of certain clerical functions where the job is broken down into different operations, with each batch of work completed by one person and passed along to the next person. In the mass and large-batch modes of production, process times will tend to be short and plant utilization high (Hill, 1983), while 'learning by doing' and 'economies of scale' effects facilitate competition on price. None the less, the degree of freedom for flexible capabilities is severely limited. Little accommodation is provided in the process to meet product changes or variations in capacity. For instance, product variety and demand fluctuations resulted in decreasing 'economies of scale', fewer learning effects, and larger process times in a large-batch assembly unit of Philips Semiconductors.

At the *process* end of our continuum, the flow of work is highly programmed and many decisions about input and output are predetermined when facilities are built and complex monitoring devices are installed. In this case, the technical system becomes so regulating that it approaches the state of automation. As a result, the production capacity is determined largely by machines, and the variety in operations and number of setups depend on the machine design. In order to increase the controllability and predictability of such a work flow, the organization opts for a non-varying input and output. A basic material is processed through successive stages and refined into one or several products. Thus, the potential for flexibility is most limited in the process mode of production. High-volume, highly standardized, commodity products, such as petroleum products, chemicals, and pharmaceutical products are good examples of the outputs of process technology.

In short, the more we move to the left of our continuum, the more the potential for flexibility is limited due to technical constraints. None the less, some recent developments in programmable automation systems have challenged the underlying assumptions of this variable. These developments will be considered in the discussion of the third technological design variable, the specificity of the means of transformation.

The Physical Production Layout: Traditional Lines versus Flexible Workstations

Besides the mode of production, the physical layout determines the leeway for flexibility which technology permits. This second design variable describes the basic way in which the production means are located (Van Donk *et al.*, 1991) or the configuration of the hardware within the organization. It corresponds to some extent to Hickson's work-flow rigidity dimension (Hickson *et al.*, 1969). Important indicators with respect to the potential for flexibility of various layouts are:

- the *changeability of design and configuration*: according to Hill (1983: 95), it is necessary to include some slack in layout designs so as to reduce the need for the redesign of facilities. For instance, parallel work flows, the potential to switch over to other stations ('shunt flexibility'), or change the sequencing of operations ('routing flexibility') or machines, all contribute to a larger flexibility potential;
- the *stage of production* in which the products are differentiated: if this differentiation takes place in an early stage of production, the possibilities for modification are minimal;
- the *lead time*, especially processing times and waiting periods between various production stages: the configuration of the means of transformation is an important factor for variations in lead times;
- the *positioning of inventories* and types of inventories (raw materials, work-in-progress, or finished goods inventories): for instance, if inventories are moved upstream, they can be allocated to multiple products, but the completion time for them increases. Thus, both the reaction capacity and reaction time increase. On the other hand, if these inventories are moved downstream, the possibilities for both reallocation and the completion or reaction time decrease.

From these indicators a continuum can be derived in which basically four different layouts can be positioned: line, group, functional, and workstation (see Table 6.3).

In a *line layout*, the physical grouping is such that all the operations on a certain product or service are executed in the same strict sequence using different production means (Van Donk *et al.*, 1991). That is to say, operations are successively lined up in sequence (see Fig. 6.1*a*). The differentiation of the final products takes place very early in the process. This type of layout therefore scores very low with regard to the possibility of switching over to other products or of varying the complexity of existing products. Moreover, in the line layout, the cycle time per station or per machine is minimized. None the less, the balancing

TABLE 6.3. Physical layouts: indicators determining their flexibility potential

	low flexibility potential ——— high flexibility potential
Physical production layout	line . . . . group . . . . functional . . . . workstation
Indicators	• changeability layout ($\rightarrow$) • degree of product differentiation ($\leftarrow$) • lead time • position of inventories

Note: ($\rightarrow$) = increasing from low to high   ($\leftarrow$) = decreasing from high to low

of all these stations frequently results in process times that are often much longer than the cumulative cycle times per station. The sequential grouping increases the sensitivity to disturbances, which are manifested in long waiting periods between stages. For instance, the single line for the assembly of glass-bead diodes in a plant of Philips Semiconductors hampered the production of various product types as well as fluctuating volumes. The many interdependencies in the assembly process resulted in long lead times and made it very difficult to absorb disturbances.

In a *functional layout*, operations are grouped according to methods, techniques, and machines used instead of according to products (see Fig. 6.1b). In this layout, volume requirements do not justify a specialized process being dedicated to a small range of products or services. This layout therefore possesses a high potential for flexibility in terms of its possibilities for enlarging the product range and varying the complexity of products. None the less, the advantage of being able to route different orders through functionally based work areas is gained at the cost of increased complexity and time required in the movement of the product (Hill, 1983: 96). Consequently, the process time of this layout is much longer than the line layout.

A middle course might be the implementation of a *group layout* (see Fig. 6.1c), which attempts to gain for a functional layout some of the advantages, such as acceptable process times, inherent in the line layout (Hill, 1983). Hence, a typical functional layout is changed into a work-cell layout so that each work cell is dedicated to the production of a family of products in the form of mini-lines. This arrangement implies that machines have to be grouped together on the basis of the production of similar products. For instance, the single assembly line for the production of glass-bead diodes in a plant of Philips Semiconductors was subdivided into two parallel mini-lines, one for simple glass-bead diodes and one for the more complex ones.

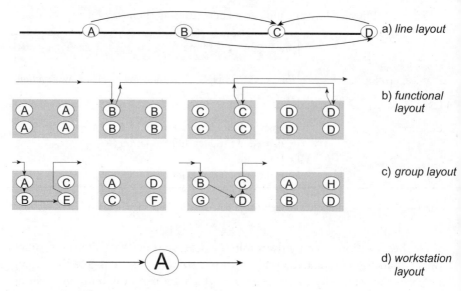

a) *line layout*

b) *functional layout*

c) *group layout*

d) *workstation layout*

Fig. 6.1. Four basic layout forms

Finally, in the case of a *workstation layout* we can hardly speak of a form of layout (see Fig. 6.1*d*) because there is only one workstation involved. Consequently, the potential for flexibility in a workstation layout is not limited by layout decisions. In many service organizations where individuals have considerable discretion, there is often only one workstation between input and output.

Of course, it must be emphasized that there are all kinds of intermediate variants of our four basic layout forms and that the description of this technological variable depends largely on the level of aggregation involved (Van Donk *et al.*, 1991). For example, a functional layout may contain some lines. Furthermore, there are many relationships between the mode of production and layout form, some of which are more realistic than others. In process and mass production we often find a line layout, while in unit and batch production a functional layout is more likely. Yet, new technological developments in production means, which are considered below, provide opportunities for other effective combinations.

The Means of Transformation: Highly Specialized versus Universal Equipment

This design variable describes the range of operations for which the transformation means such as machines, apparatus, tools, and information systems can be employed. This can range from *specialized equipment*, which is used exclusively for the production of one product or service, or *multipurpose machinery*, which can be applied to the production of a range of products, and to *universal equipment*, which can be used for the production of a very broad range of products and services. Major indicators determining the flexibility potential of the means of transformation are the applicability of machines, tools, and other equipment as well as the rapidity by which these machines, tools, and equipment can be reset to produce other products or services (setting times). Of course, the more universal that equipment, the larger the degree of freedom for flexibility (see Table 6.4).

TABLE 6.4. Transformation means: indicators determining their flexibility potential

	low flexibility potential ———— high flexibility potential
Transformation means	*specialized* . . . . *multi-purpose* . . . . *universal*
Indicators	• applicability of transformation means ($\rightarrow$) • rapidity by which transformation means can be adjusted ($\rightarrow$)

Note: ($\rightarrow$) = increasing from low to high   ($\leftarrow$) = decreasing from high to low

Recent developments in manufacturing technology and information systems have had a tremendous impact on this design variable because they have created a range of programmable automation systems and general information systems that seem to allow for much greater flexibility potential in manufacturing and service organizations (Adler, 1988). The associated widening of technological constraints has resulted in the blurring of clear distinctions between the classical unit and mass mode of production. Flexible automation has challenged the long-held belief that in general higher levels of automation are by nature less flexible. It now appears clear, for example, that Woodward's classical typology of technology which implies that one-of-a-kind products should be optimally produced in job shops, not in large-batch, mass, or process modes of production is valid only at a given level of technology. In several industries, new flexible technologies facilitate a shift from large-batch and mass production of highly standardized products to increasingly customized production or even mass customization; low-cost production of high-variety, even individually customized goods and services is now possible (Kotha, 1995; Pine, 1993). In a more dynamic perspective we therefore need to consider the implications of recent automation trends, which make it possible to envisage the production of less standardized products in a mass mode of production.

In the case of flexible production automation (FPA), the organization applies programmable microelectronics for controlling the production system (Boerlijst *et al.*, 1985). FPA may concern the design (CAD), the work preparation, the production control (CAM), or the production itself. In the latter case, one might think of NC machines, CNC machines, or even robotics.[4] By combining CNC machines with robotics, a flexible manufacturing system (FMS) can be developed. An FMS is capable of producing a range of discrete products with a minimum of manual intervention. Linking such systems to computer-aided design systems (CAD) by so-called computer-aided manufacturing (CAM) systems allows firms to run production processes directly from CAD product-design files (Sanchez, 1995). Furthermore, new computer-mediated communication technology such as electronic data interchange (EDI) enables firms to integrate their FMS with their suppliers' production system to assure timely delivery of parts and components. A growing number of firms such as Ford Motor, Motorola, and Boeing are using advanced CAD/CAM systems to accelerate design feasibility studies, testing, and prototyping. Motorola, for example, uses a CAD/CAM network that links the customized design and manufacture of new generations of cellular phones (Lei *et al.*, 1996).

The implications of FPA are profound. It undermines the prevailing belief in a negative corollary between *efficiency and flexibility* (cf. Woodward, 1965). On the one hand, FPA's potential implies that the flexibility of mass and large-batch production systems can be improved while their efficiency is maintained. On the other hand, the productivity or efficiency of unit and small-batch production systems can be increased without affecting their flexibility too much (Krabbendam and Boer, 1989).

Implementation of multipurpose machinery in a large-batch or mass mode of production facilitates the possibility of increasing the applicability of machines and of decreasing the setup times for switching to other products. The hallmark of these new flexible technologies is that they provide the firm with the opportunity to combine speed and greater product variety with increased productivity. For example, by introducing modern computerized ovens and robots in its glass-bead assembly line, Philips Semiconductors fundamentally increased its potential for operational flexibility. Moreover, implementation of FPA within a mass production system often leads to a shift from a line layout to a group layout; clusters of CNC machines produce similar products (family group).

However, the introduction of FPA within mass and large-batch production systems may also lead to *new rigidities*. In Section 2.1, we observed that FPA goes together with an enlargement of the control cycle. The more extensive the amount of integration within the production system, the more complexity is introduced in the control of production. Moreover, the integration necessary for implementing FPA exerts pressure on interfacing systems. For instance, if drastically shortened lead times are to occur with FPA, then interfacing systems must also be ready to use shortened lead times. This requirement can be a particularly difficult problem for external parties such as subcontractors and other vendors, unless they are warned in time and helped to prepare for the change (Meredith, 1988). Therefore flexible automation of mass and large-batch production systems can result in a large assortment, short delivery times, and small supplies only when combined with just-in-time (JIT) purchasing. Benetton, for example, not only developed a CAD/CAM production system to respond quickly, but at the same time designed a real-time retailer information system that enables fast communication between retailers, production, and subcontractors.

Since FPA requires a perfectly integrated production process, this mandate implies a drastic reorganization for unit and small-batch production. These modes of production are accustomed to rely a good deal on improvisation, which is precisely what FPA does not allow. Everything in FPA must be laid down and proceed according to a standard. In addition, the process knowledge has to be formalized and made available to all organizational participants. Thus, when FPA is used in unit and small-batch production, the potential for flexibility is often reduced.

In sum, the importance of FPA is that it facilitates the possibility of combining the efficiency of large-batch and mass production with the flexibility of unit and small-batch production. Consequently, the potential for flexibility of unit production decreases at the gain of some efficiency, while the flexibility potential of mass production increases (see Fig. 6.2). Thus, while increased sophistication of means of transformation in the form of mechanization has traditionally led to higher regulation and a decrease in flexibility potential, recent developments in the form of automation largely preserve the existing flexibility potential.

The Operational Production Repertoire: Narrow versus Broad Skills and Knowledge

The three technological design variables discussed above relate largely to the operations technology, which involves the equipping and sequencing of activities in the work flow. By contrast, the operational production repertoire refers to what Hickson et al. (1969) called the knowledge technology, that is, the knowledge used in the work flow. This variable can range from a limited to a very extensive repertoire of methods of working, procedures, skills, and software. The more extensive the repertoire, the larger the possibilities for

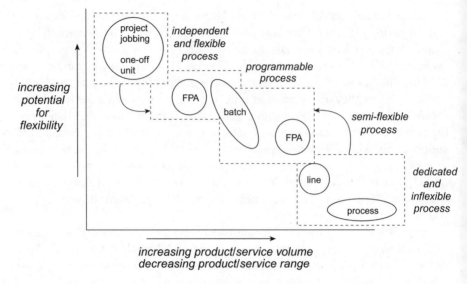

Fig. 6.2. The impact of FPA on the flexibility potential of various modes of production

Source: based on Hill (1983: 42)

flexibility. Major indicators determining the potential for the flexibility of this variable are:

- *variability in operations*, tasks, materials requirements, and setups: the more well defined these operations are, the less the potential for flexibility is;
- the *explicitness of control*: for instance, if quality control is designed in the production process as a separate stage (extrinsic), the control capacity or production repertoire is strongly reduced. When the quality control is not well defined, but rather based on informal spot checks or self-control (intrinsic), then the degree of freedom for flexibility is much larger;
- the *level of skills*, crafts, arts and know-how: the higher this level, the more slack there is for flexibility.

These indicators of the operational production repertoire provide a continuum of increasing flexibility potential (see Table 6.5). In analysing technological barriers to flexibility, most managers focus on the hardware of technology and tend to ignore the skill and knowledge variables. In the Dutch Postbank for instance, the most important barrier was not so much the technological hardware but the limited skill repertoire of workers owing to fixed production tasks, rigid work instructions, and tight production norms.

TABLE 6.5. Operational production repertoire: indicators determining the flexibility potential

	low flexibility potential ——— high flexibility potential
Operational production repertoire	*limited* . . . . *extensive*
Indicators	• variability of operations ($\rightarrow$) • explicitness of control ($\leftarrow$) • level of skills ($\rightarrow$)

Note: ($\rightarrow$) = increasing from low to high   ($\leftarrow$) = decreasing from high to low

Routine versus Non-Routine Technology

To summarize, in this section we explored how to reduce technological barriers to flexibility. In this connection, 'technology' refers to the hardware (such as machinery and equipment) and the software (knowledge) used in the transformation of inputs into outputs, as well as the configuration of the hardware and software. The design of technology can range from routine to non-routine, corresponding to the opportunities for routine capabilities (see Table 6.1). Routine technology is often characterized by mass or process modes of production, a typical line layout, specialized equipment dedicated to specific products, and a limited production repertoire. It is focused on volume to create learning by doing or economies of scale. Consequently, its potential for flexibility is minimal. Non-routine technology is characterized by small-batch or unit modes of production combined with a group layout. In addition, the means of transformation are often multipurpose and the operational production repertoire is large. This redeployable technology gives leeway for search processes because the potential for flexibility is not restricted by technological constraints. Of course, various intermediate technological designs also are possible. On the basis of this classification of technology, various technologies can be assessed in terms of their potential for flexibility. From this classification scheme, it is clear that the existing technology determines the *potential for operational flexibility* within the organization.

6.2 Structural Barriers

Just like technology, organizational structure is defined in many different ways. Nearly all scholars define structure as the ways in which labour is divided into distinct tasks and coordination is achieved among them. Yet a further examination reveals that most definitions of structure are rather limited in nature.

First, many definitions emphasize only the formal side of structure. Khandwalla (1977: 482), for instance, defines structure as the network of durable and formally sanctioned organizational arrangements and relationships. Human relations theorists,[5] however, have made us aware of the informal structure or the unofficial relationships within the organization which do not correspond with the formal structure. Such relationships arise spontaneously in organizations over and above those sanctioned by the organizational hierarchy. In an even more comprehensive view of structure, Crozier (1964) showed that in bureaucratic structures the formal structure impinges on, and is in turn affected by, the informal structure. This finding led Mintzberg (1979: 11) to conclude that formal and informal structure are intertwined and often indistinguishable. We will therefore refer to structure as the *actual structure* of an organization, which may often deviate from the officially sanctioned or prescribed arrangements and relationships. In this connection, the actual structure includes only those relationships which really exist within the organization. The informal structure is that part of the actual structure which is not present in the formal structure.

In addition to their focus on formal relationships, most definitions of structure accentuate the highly visible part of structure, or the boxes and lines, while they neglect the less visible processes within the organization. Taking into account the above shortcomings, we shall apply a much broader concept of structure which contains the visible as well as the less visible elements of structure.

First, structure reflects the actual distribution of responsibilities and authority among the organization's personnel. This distribution results in the construction of a *basic organizational form* made up of various parts, such as functions, units, and divisions. These stable elements have to be flexible so that they can be easily and adequately modified in other mutual relationships, when necessary, at low cost and little resistance, and without losing their efficiency and effectiveness. Whether it is possible to use the potential flexibility of the basic organizational form optimally depends on the planning and control systems and the procedures used within the organization.

The *planning and control systems* are developed for dealing with various aspects within the organization, such as the allocation of budgets (budgeting systems), the rewarding of employees (reward systems), the selection, training and development, promotion, and transfer of employees (human resources development and management development systems), and the gathering of information (information systems). For each of these aspects, the planning and control systems may include the establishing of priorities, the internal programming of these priorities (degree to which priorities are translated into programmes), and the progress control and evaluation of results (degree to which the organization controls and evaluates the progress and results with respect to these priorities).

Besides the basic organizational form and the planning and control systems, the actual structure reflects the less visible processes of decision-making, coordination, and execution within the organization. These *process regulations* are often neglected, but if we want to understand the functioning of the parts and how they are joined together, we need to further analyse the flows of authority, information, and decision-making.

On the basis of this conceptualization of organizational structure, a classification scheme of various structures with respect to their potential for flexibility can be developed. This scheme is presented in Table 6.6. In accordance with Burns and Stalker's typology, the structure can range from *mechanistic* to *organic*. In a mechanistic structure, the potential for flexibility is severely limited by the configuration of stable elements, the elaborate planning and control systems, and the extensive process regulations. In an organic structure, the basic organizational form, the rudimentary planning and control systems, and the limited process regulations do not restrict the potential for flexibility. In this section, we will consider the design variable(s) concerning the basic organizational form, the planning and control systems, and the process regulation, and explain the extent to which these design variables inhibit or enhance the flexibility potential of the actual structure.

The Basic Organizational Form: Traditional Forms versus Dynamic Forms

A basic organizational form is viewed as an organizational infrastructure which enables the process of capability development. The different organizational forms can be roughly determined by analysing the way of grouping, the number of hierarchical levels, and the degree of functionalization of management tasks, which is commonly depicted by the organization chart (See Table 6.7).

Grouping describes the various ways of successive clustering of individual positions, units, and so on until the entire organization is contained in the final cluster (Mintzberg, 1979). It has been described by others (Hrebiniak and Joyce, 1984; Khandwalla, 1977) as a choice of departmentalization involving the ways personnel is allocated to departments, divisions or sections. With respect to the potential for flexibility, three essential ways of grouping can be distinguished:

TABLE 6.6. Classification scheme for flexibility potential of structure

Actual structure	mechanistic _____ organic
	(low flexibility potential) (high flexibility potential)
basic organizational form	functional . . . . .division . . . . .matrix
• grouping	function . . . . .product/service . . . . .target market
• hierarchical levels	many . . . . .few
	(tall) (flat)
• functionalization	high . . . . .low
planning and control systems	elaborate . . . . .rudimentary
process regulations	high . . . . .low
• specialization	high . . . . .low
• scope of task	narrow . . . . .broad
• depth of task	simple . . . . .complex
• interchangeability	low . . . . .high
• standardization	high . . . .: . . . . .low
• formalization	high . . . . .low
• training and education	low . . . . .high
	(routine) (professional) (craft)
• liaison devices	high . . . . .low
	(influence form) (group) (natural form)
• horizontal decentralization	low . . . . .high
	(tightly coupled) (loosely coupled)
• delegation	low . . . . .high
• participation	low . . . . .high
	(exclusive) (participative)

functional grouping, comprising the bases of knowledge and skill, work process, and function, *product/service grouping*, and *target market grouping*, comprising the bases of client and place. The flexibility potential for a functional grouping is minimal. When unforeseen contingencies or exigencies crop up, the need for coordination between interfacing units becomes urgent (Khandwalla, 1977). Because functional grouping lacks a built-in mechanism for coordinating the work flow, it obstructs quick reactions to change. Consequently, slowness of response is characteristic of functional grouping. The large number of interdependent functional departments increases the response time needed to activate flexible capabilities, especially the more complex ones encompassing the entire value chain such as innovation frequency and fast delivery of customer orders.

The flexibility potential for a product/service grouping is derived from the fact that units are relatively self-sufficient. Due to this self-sufficiency, each unit

Table 6.7. Design variables of the basic organizational forms and their flexibility potential

Basic organizational form	low flexibility potential ———— high flexibility potential
ways of grouping	*functional* . . . .*product / service* . . . .*target market*
hierarchical levels	*tall* . . . .*flat*
degree of functionalization	*high* . . . .*low*
	(matrix) *(functional)* *(line / staff)* *(line)*

has a relatively high degree of autonomy. Compared to a functional grouping, each unit can do more tasks and change tasks more easily (Mintzberg, 1979). The self-containment of units shortens lines of communication between interdependent personnel, makes planning and coordination easier, and facilitates quick adaptation to environmental changes (Khandwalla, 1977).

In the case of grouping by target market, the potential for flexibility is the largest. The increased self-containment of target market units, together with the numerous direct client contacts and boundary-spanning activities, facilitate quick adaptations to changes in specific customer demands or to demand changes in local areas. Being exposed face-to-face with demanding customers increases the likelihood that the action threshold of organizational participants will be triggered and will stimulate them into paying attention to changing environmental conditions or customer needs (Van de Ven, 1986: 596).

Occasionally, organizations may find that they require the advantages of more than one type of grouping. For very complex tasks, it may be necessary to use more than one type of grouping at the same level and at the same time. We will discuss this simultaneous grouping in our treatment of the matrix form. Furthermore, grouping may be stratified hierarchically. For instance, units may be grouped by product and each product unit can be grouped successively by function. This possibility brings us to the second design variable of the basic organizational form which determines the flexibility potential of the actual structure, namely the number of *hierarchical levels*.

Regarding the number of hierarchical levels of formal authority, two extreme positions can be distinguished, namely tall and flat structures, corresponding to low and high flexibility potentials (see Table 6.7). A *tall structure* is characterized by a long chain of authority with relatively small groups at each hierarchical level. As a consequence, information originating in the lower reaches of the organization has to travel through many levels before it reaches the appropriate level of authority. Not only is this process time consuming, but the information it carries is often distorted. The aggregation of information makes what finally reaches the higher levels so abstract and vague that it becomes of limited use in the making of specific decisions. Similarly, when information originating at upper management levels filters down the hierarchy, it is so larded with the selective perceptions of the intervening human filter that it is almost unrecognizable by the time it reaches the lower levels (Khandwalla, 1977: 514–18). Furthermore, as the number of new situations increases, the hierarchy easily becomes overloaded. Thus, the taller the structure, the slower and less accurate the two-way vertical flow of information. Consequently, the potential for flexibility in tall structures is severely limited by their slowness of response and inadequate information.

A *flat structure*, on the other hand, has few levels, with relatively large work groups at each level. It possesses quick, accurate information-handling characteristics due to a truncated hierarchical communication network. This structure thus shortens the reaction time of organizations (Quinn, 1985) and facilitates speedy cross-hierarchical capability development. Therefore flat structures are typically much more effective than tall structures in creating a flexibility potential.

Finally, the *functionalization* of management is an important design variable of the basic organizational form for clarifying variations in the flexibility potential of various structures. This design variable describes the extent to which management is subdivided into various functional areas (Hill *et al.*, 1974). High functionalization or partitioning of authority results in fragmented basic organizational forms, in which each manager is specialized in a specific aspect of management. When unexpected disturbances occur, supplementary coordination is required among the several management tasks. Splitting broad management tasks into several components narrows the variety of managerial capabilities and further increases coordination costs. In the Research Department of the Dutch Gas Company, for instance, the functionalization of authority resulted in many coordination problems because researchers had as many as five supervisors: a research director, a research area manager, an activity manager, a senior specialist, and a project manager. On the other hand, restricted functionalization guarantees integrated management tasks so that coordination problems are minimal and fast decision-making is possible, thus enhancing the potential for flexibility (see Table 6.7).

Flexible Organizational Forms

On the basis of these design variables regarding the configuration of stable elements of structure, four basic organizational forms can be distinguished: the functional, the divisional, the matrix, and the innovative organization (see Fig. 6.3). Various scholars (e.g. Ansoff and Brandenburg, 1971; Eppink, 1978; Krijnen, 1979) have tried to compare these basic organizational forms in terms of their potential for the various types of flexibility (such as steady-state, operational, structural, and strategic flexibility) and the environmental conditions in which they function most optimally.

✓ Functional Form

function 1 function 2

✓ Divisional Form

division 1   division 2   division3

✓ Matrix Form

projects

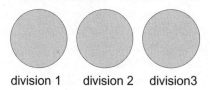

functions

✓ Innovative Form

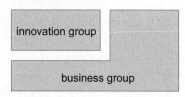

innovation group

business group

✓ Dynamic Forms

network
forms

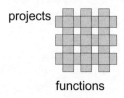

hybrid
forms

project

traditional
hierarchy

- virtual corporation
- hollow corporation
- dynamic network form

- hypertext form
- platform organization
- multidimensional organization
- alloplastic organization

Fig. 6.3. Basic organizational forms

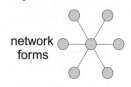

The Organization Design Task

The *functional form* is based on a functional grouping of similar activities under major functional managers, a hierarchy of authority consisting of many hierarchical levels with small spans of control, and a degree of functionalization of management which may range from low (no staff functions) to high (staff functions with formal authority). The principal advantage of the functional form is its efficiency or steady-state flexibility attained from economies of scale, overheads, and skills. This form, however, has rather limited operational flexibility. It might be appropriate only in stable and homogeneous environments where there are few product-market combinations (PMCs) with a relatively long life cycle (Krijnen, 1979). In more unstable conditions, conflicts of priorities occur, decisions and products begin to queue up, communication lines get longer, and time responsiveness to external conditions is degraded (Ansoff and Brandenburg, 1971). Consequently, the strategic as well as the structural flexibility is inherently poor in the functional form (see Table 6.8). Due to the functional grouping, operational decisions tend to pre-empt structural and strategic decisions. Moreover, structural and strategic decisions are referred upward in the hierarchy, further overloading top management.

TABLE 6.8. Basic organizational forms and their potential for different types of flexibility

Organizational form—flexibility potential matrix	functional form	divisional form	matrix form	innovative form
operational flexibility	+/−	+	+	+
structural flexibility	−	+/−	+	+
strategic flexibility	−	−	+	+
steady-state flexibility	+	−	−	+/−

Note:
   − = low
+/− = moderate
   + = high

The *divisional form* is based on grouping by product/service or target market, a limited hierarchy of authority consisting of few hierarchical levels with large spans of control, and a limited functionalization of management in the form of some central staff functions. Because of the autonomy of divisions in terms of operational decisions and their direct contacts with the environment, this form is characterized by a high potential for operational flexibility. None the less, economies of scale have to be sacrificed to this increase of operational flexibility. The structural and strategic flexibility of the divisional form is, on the whole, superior to that of the functional form. Compared to functional managers, divisional managers have more room to allocate attention to strategic and structural questions. Yet the structural flexibility of the divisional organization is still moderate, while its strategic flexibility is restricted (see Table 6.8). The divisional form represents only a limited improvement in structural and strategic flexibility. According to Krijnen (1979), structural adaptations of the divisional form as a whole are not easily realized as divisions will often resist change of a strategic nature. Furthermore, the 'loose coupling' among divisions facilitates local changes in the short-term goals of divisions, but suppresses changes in the shared long-term goals of the whole organization (Weick, 1982). Therefore a divisional form is most appropriate in a dynamic environment with a large number of different groups of PMCs that have few characteristics in common and in which the life cycle is relatively long (Krijnen, 1979: 70).

The *matrix form* is based on a dual grouping of activities, a dual hierarchy of authority consisting of few hierarchical levels, and a high degree of functionalization of management tasks. The matrix combines the principles of specialized functional departments and self-sufficient, more or less autonomous units or divisions, in situations where a number of (temporary) divisions or autonomous units need to be created. According to Eppink (1978) and Krijnen (1979), the matrix is flexible in all ways (see Table 6.8). Its operational flexibility is high because in case of fluctuations in the level of operations (e.g. delay or speeding up of projects taken up), persons and means can be switched from one project to another quite easily. Moreover, the ability of each unit to seek the organizational form most appropriate to the project it is handling facilitates structural flexibility since it can quickly change shape and form (Khandwalla, 1977: 497). Finally, the fact that available means and persons can be allocated to various projects guarantees a reasonable strategic flexibility. On account of its high potential for flexibility, this form is appropriate for organizations that function in environments with many new PMCs with relatively short life cycles. None the less, the increased flexibility of the matrix form is detrimental to its steady-state flexibility. Economies of scale will be rather small because different functions, experts, and tools will be needed in different simultaneously executed projects, which results in only partly occupied resources.

Eppink, Krijnen, and Khandwalla have neglected, however, the many problems of coordination originating from the high degree of functionalization in the matrix form. In a matrix organization, the organization sets up a dual authority structure corresponding to its two bases of grouping. An additional lateral line of communication is created which constitutes a supplementary hierarchy that overlays the traditional line of authority. The matrix structure is therefore the optimum of functionalization. For instance, in a matrix structure, project managers and functional managers are equally and jointly responsible for the same decisions and therefore forced to reconcile between themselves the differences that arise. As a consequence, such an organization has to resolve its conflicts through informal negotiation among equals rather than resorting to formal authority, such as the formal power of superiors over subordinates or line over staff (Mintzberg, 1979: 170). Notwithstanding the matrix structure's potential for flexibility, its high degree of functionalization creates some major obstacles for developing flexibility (Hrebiniak and Joyce, 1984). First, a balance of power between the hierarchical and lateral dimension is very difficult to maintain. Not surprisingly, interpersonal conflict occurs frequently in matrix and project structures. Secondly, a perfect balance without cooperation between managers of the vertical and lateral hierarchies can lead to so many disputes going up for arbitration that both hierarchies become overloaded. Further, in contrast with limited functionalization of management, highly functionalized structures require many more managers. Moreover, much more communicating has to be done, because more information has to get to more managers (Knight, 1976: 126). We conjecture that the potential for flexibility of the matrix form can be activated only if a perfect balance of power is maintained.

Ansoff and Brandenburg (1971) suggested the *innovative form*, which negates some of the disadvantages of the matrix. The matrix is not applicable in a large majority of manufacturing firms in which economies of scale are important, assets and competences are relatively inflexible, and products have long lives. The underlying principle of the innovative form is therefore to gather currently profitable, established product markets into a current business group and to place development of new product-market positions into an innovation group.

New product-market entries are conceived, planned, and implemented by the innovation group on a project basis. The group remains responsible for the project until its commercial feasibility has been established . . . At the point of feasibility, the project is transferred into the current business group where it may become a part of an existing division or forms the nucleus of a new division. (Ansoff and Brandenburg, 1971: B-725)

Thus, the innovation group functions on a project basis, while the current business group can be structured either divisionally or functionally, depending on which of the two types of grouping is more appropriate. As depicted in Table 6.8, the innovative organizational form possesses a high potential for operational, structural, and strategic flexibility. The degree of steady-state flexibility depends on the scale at which operations take place and on whether the new PMCs are transferred to a new or an existing division (Krijnen, 1979: 72).

While the innovative form seems to be most appropriate in terms of its potential for flexibility, we must keep in mind that Ansoff and Brandenburg's work is more conceptual than empirical. However, in the 1980s and 1990s many large corporations developed such innovative structures by separating new business development from operating business by means of skunk works (Peters and Waterman, 1982), corporate ventures (Burgelman, 1983; Roberts, 1980), or complete new venture departments (Fast, 1979). Firms like 3M, HP, and Motorola have decentralized decision-making regarding new business development at the divisional level and encourage spin-off projects. For instance, 3M's New Business Development Division is charged with the responsibility for evolving, nurturing, and maintaining diverse business activities at the various stages of development. When new products are big enough to be self-sustaining, it spins them off into the organization as part of an existing division or a new product line division.

The assumptions regarding the flexibility potential of the basic organizational forms are summarized in Table 6.8. None the less, we have to look at this classification in perspective. A functional structure, for instance, can be made reasonably flexible by the creation of temporary task forces, standing committees, project teams, or various other liaison devices that overlay the functional structure (Galbraith, 1973; Mintzberg, 1979). In this connection, Nonaka and Takeuchi (1995) proposed the hypertext form, which combines the steady-state flexibility of the functional form with the strategic flexibility of a flat, crossfunctional task force (see Fig. 6.3). For instance, Sharp's R&D operations have a traditional functional structure, but when it comes to new product development the company easily utilizes the task-force organization, which is a completely independent, parallel structure. The hypertext organization differs from the matrix organization in that its members report to only one boss (business or project manager) at one point in time. Of course, there are many other hybrid forms. Therefore we might ask ourselves if thinking in terms of basic forms does not lead to a limitation of our conception of flexibility.

As was indicated in our integrated definition, flexibility is not a static concept, but a process. As such, it is not the basic structure that enlarges the potential for flexibility, but the opportunity to continuously rearrange the structure throughout the process. In his advocacy of flexible organizations, Ackoff (1977) asserted that the basic organizational form serves more as a draft than as a detailed blueprint. Consequently, costly and disruptive reorganizations involving a regrouping of activities, refunctionalization of management tasks, and the like can be avoided. New organizational forms such as the multidimensional organization in which units can be easily added or subtracted (Ackoff, 1977), the platform or shapeless organization that keeps generating new forms through frequent recombination (Ciborra, 1996), the network or flexible cluster of firms or specialized units coordinated by market mechanisms instead of a vertical chain of command (Miles and Snow, 1986), or the hollow corporation or virtual corporation (Davidow and Malone, 1992) are all based on a more dynamic perspective of organizational structure. The most distinctive quality of these *dynamic forms* is their potential to move and transform structures. They facilitate crosshierarchical, cross-functional, as well as cross-value capability development. We believe, however, that most of these new forms are modifications or hybrids of the four basic organizational forms discussed above. For instance, the stable network form proposed by Miles and Snow (1992) is essentially a dominant functional form that creates market-related linkages to a limited set of upstream or downstream parties. In the same way, their internal network form comes close to the matrix form in that both forms try to gain competitive advantage through shared utilization of scarce resources and the continuing development and exchange of managerial and technological know-how. Moreover, the hypertext or parallel structure seems to be a hybrid of the matrix and innovative form.

To conclude, in order to maintain the potential for flexibility of the actual structure, overstructuring of the organization is quite unacceptable. The objective is to provide sufficient structure to create a basic order, but to prevent structure from getting in the way of capabilities which quickly respond to environmental change. From our flexibility studies within Philips, the Dutch Postbank, Ericsson, KLM Cargo, and Van Ommeren Tank Storage, we found that all these firms have flattened their hierarchies by delayering levels of management, creating larger management tasks, and clustering departments according to product/service or target market. Whether it is possible to use the flexibility potential inherent in a more organic organizational form depends on the organization's planning and control systems and process regulations.

Planning and Control Systems: Comprehensive versus Rudimentary Systems

The basic organizational form divides the organization into groups, hierarchical levels, and various management tasks. Planning and control systems and process regulations are developed to solve the residual interdependencies. In essence, planning and control systems regulate various aspects of structure, such as the allocating of resources, the training and development of personnel, and the gathering of information. In this connection, planning systems identify the issues that become candidates for managerial scrutiny, while control systems specify the times for review and discussion of progress against objectives.

Planning and control systems are often added to the basic organizational form to provide a stimulus for action and to ensure the appropriateness of these actions. They can be *rudimentary* or *elaborate*. In our discussion of various planning strategies (Sect. 3.1), we concluded that comprehensive planning is adequate only in a stable environment, where there is less need for flexibility. Elaborate planning and control systems focus efforts in prescribed areas and limit the self-control of organizational units and participants (Van de Ven, 1986). Usually, such systems are oriented to specifying activities that will take place in the form of programmes, schedules, and operating plans. However, by implementing comprehensive planning and control systems, the actual structure may lose its potential for flexibility. Should an unforeseen change require a redirection of the firm's strategy, it may be very difficult in terms of costs and required time to change the firm's course since the planning and control systems have been set firmly in support of the current strategy (Bourgeois and Brodwin, 1984). In this situation, existing planning and control systems only stimulate repetitive use of procedures which may have little to do with future success (Starbuck, 1983). This repertoire creates superstitious learning, discouraging any options for flexibility. For instance, we found that the time devoted to creative thought in the Research Department of the Dutch Gas Company was inevitably reduced owing to the organization's very elaborate planning rituals (strategic plan, three-year plan, budget proposal). In contrast to such elaborate systems, non-comprehensive planning systems encourage self-initiative and allow fast, low-cost actions in order to offset threats or take advantage of new opportunities. While elaborate systems are either concerned with input or means-oriented, rough planning and control systems are more focused on overall performance. Instead of seeking to regulate specific actions, they leave some space for ambiguous information and necessary experimentation and intuition. This freedom facilitates the creation of original solutions for new problems.

Some major indicators of the flexibility potential of planning and control systems are:

- regulation of goal and priority setting; in the case of top-down planning focused on short-term, quantitative goals, the potential for flexibility is seriously limited. Top-down decision-making ignores the contributions of lower levels that are not in line with higher-level goals. In addition, the focus on hard quantifiable data of elaborate planning and control systems leads to disjointed and fragmented insights. Consequently, long-term, soft, qualitative information, which cannot be sliced into small pieces, is ignored. Therefore increased quantification of planning and control harms flexibility potential (Lenz and Lyles, 1985);
- internal programming of planning and control; loose planning systems, which are open to a wide spectrum of information, encourage fresh insights into emerging problems. Frequently, this looseness is regarded as inefficient and steps are taken to improve the administrative efficiency of the system by making the process more routine and predictable (Lenz and Lyles, 1985). One might think of standardized data inputs, rigid formats of planning documents, or timetables for data preparation. Owing to this increased structuring, the time devoted to creative thought is inevitably reduced. Consequently, the flexibility potential diminishes;
- progress control and evaluation of results: such controls track performance against the desired ends and provide the feedback necessary to gauge and evaluate results and take accurate actions, if needed. They can be very useful. However, the models and techniques used may become the dominant framework for defining and evaluating planning and control issues. Thus,

emerging, ill-defined issues that often prove important may not be detected because they either do not correspond to variables in the model or fall outside the scope of the analytical tool. Such deterministic thinking obstructs the flexibility potential of the actual structure.

On the basis of these indicators, Table 6.9 presents a continuum of increasing flexibility potential with respect to planning and control systems.

TABLE 6.9. Planning and control systems: indicators determining their potential for flexibility

	low flexibility potential ——— high flexibility potential
Planning and control systems	*elaborate* .... *rudimentary*
Indicators	• regulation of goal and priority setting (←) • internal programming of planning and control (←) • progress control and evaluation of results (←)

Note: (←) = decreasing from high to low

Process Regulations: Limited versus Extensive

In order to assess the potential for flexibility of the actual structure, not only the basic organizational form and the planning and control systems, but also the processes of decision-making, coordination, and execution have to be considered. The design variables of these processes are complementary instruments for reducing the residual interdependencies and uncertainties of the basic organizational form and the planning and control systems (Khandwalla, 1977: 502). From our flexibility audits in large corporations, we found that many firms are working on their basic organizational form and planning and control systems, but that they often leave their tacit process regulations intact. Failure to acknowledge these tacit regulations creates the opportunity for there to be many hidden rigidities in the actual structure. Basically, organizations can regulate their processes in four ways, namely:

- regulation of tasks by task specialization;
- regulation of behaviour by direct or indirect programming;
- regulation of mutual adjustment or horizontal decision-making;
- regulation of vertical decision-making

This order of presentation assumes that firms start with regulation of tasks, for residual interdependencies with regulation of behaviour, and end with regulation of vertical decision-making. However, more often than not this sequential design logic of complex organizations results in a vicious circle that leads to overregulated firms (see Fig. 6.4). We will therefore consider various design variables of process regulation and the extent to which they inhibit or facilitate flexibility.

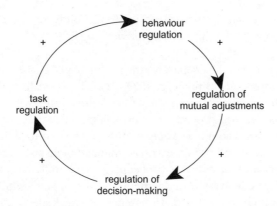

Fig. 6.4. A vicious circle of process regulations

Regulation of Tasks

The first basic organizing decision concerning the regulation of the process is the degree of *task specialization* or division of labour. That is, should each person carry out a 'whole' task from beginning to end, or should the work be specialized, with each person doing only a small portion of the task? Regarding this division of labour, we can distinguish a horizontal component concerned with the breadth and scope of work, and a vertical component concerned with the 'depth' or the degree of control over the work.

Horizontal specialization This is the predominant form of division of labour, dividing the work into many specialized tasks, in which often only a few basic operations have to be performed. Indicators determining the potential for the flexibility of horizontal specialization are the cycle time or time required for a worker to complete a set of elementary operations as well as the variety of basic elementary operations a worker has to perform. Work consisting of few basic operations together with short cycle times results in a narrow scope of tasks which increases the repetition of work, thereby facilitating learning by doing, development of specialized equipment and tools, and savings in time which was otherwise lost in switching tasks (Mintzberg, 1979: 72). However, this often creates more problems than it solves. First, it results in increasing interdependence, which requires extra coordination and communication. Not surprisingly, reaction times increase when there is high horizontal specialization. Moreover, these narrow tasks suppress self-initiative, which often goes together with decreasing motivation. Horizontal specialization therefore limits the flexibility potential of the actual structure in terms of variety and speed of response. Job enlargement, when workers engage in a wider variety of tasks or perform broader tasks, enhances the potential for flexibility of the actual structure. Above all, it may increase the quality of working life.

Vertical specialization This separates the performance of the work from its control or administration (Mintzberg, 1979: 71). The control is often passed to a manager with the overview necessary to coordinate the work, or the control is laid down in rules and procedures. Vertical specialization eliminates intrinsic self-control within tasks and replaces it with extrinsic control. It results in a separation of thinking and doing; extrinsic management tasks are created in the form of supervisors or rules or procedures, while only simple tasks remain. Consequently, the leeway for judgement and the opportunities for setting priorities are strongly diminished. In essence, vertical specialization leads to a reduction of flexibility potential in terms of reaction capacity. By vertical job enrichment, workers may gain more control over their tasks, which enlarges their circle of responsibility and authority. For instance, in the glass-bead assembly unit of Philips Semiconductors, the far-reaching specialization (limited scope and depth) led to single-skilled personnel, few learning opportunities, and no self-regulation of work teams. As a part of a flexibility redesign project, workers could decide how the work would be shared and carried out, and were even given responsibility for the production of a complete product or subpart within autonomous working groups. Within Philips Semiconductors as well as the Dutch Postbank, we found that vertical job enlargement or empowerment by concepts of self-control and self-responsibility improved workers' problem-solving capacity and self-initiative.

To conclude, high degrees of horizontal and vertical specialization impede change and renewal processes, thereby limiting any potential for flexibility. By contrast, redundancies in functions (Trist, 1981) create an understanding of the essential considerations and constraints of all aspects of change and renewal in addition to those immediately needed to perform the individual task. It means 'think globally, while acting locally' (Van de Ven, 1986). Redundancies in functions therefore reflect a potential for flexibility within the organization.

Interchangeability Besides the scope and depth of tasks, the interchangeability of the workforce is an important design variable for determining the flexibility potential. Interchangeability of work is evidenced by the ability to transfer employees to other work within the firm (Mascarenhas, 1982). When specialization is high (narrow and simple tasks) and there is no interchange between tasks, the potential for flexibility is extremely low. In this case, workers can neither be replaced in case of illness nor switched to other parts of the organization when demand patterns change. This vulnerability can be reduced when workers periodically interchange tasks with colleagues. Consequently, the variety of the workers' tasks increases together with the quality of working life. Of course, it must be kept in mind that there are limits to the degree of horizontal and vertical task enlargement and the interchange of tasks owing to the specific knowledge and experience required. It pays only to the extent that the gains from increased potential for flexibility offset the losses from less than optimal technical specialization.

Table 6.10 presents a continuum of increasing flexibility potential with respect to specialization on the basis of the scope, depth, and interchangeability of tasks and their indicators.

TABLE 6.10. Design variables of task specialization: indicators determining their flexibility potential

Task specialization	low flexibility potential ——— high flexibility potential
horizontal: scope of task indicators	*narrow* . . . .*broad* • cycle time ($\rightarrow$) • variety of basic operations ($\rightarrow$)
vertical: depth of task indicator	*simple* . . . .*complex* • work autonomy ($\rightarrow$)
interchangeability indicator	*low* . . . .*high* • transfer of employees to other work ($\rightarrow$)

Note: ($\rightarrow$) = increasing from low to high

Regulation of Behaviour

The behaviour of organizational participants may be more or less standardized. This process regulator describes the degree to which behaviours are programmed in advance of their execution (Galbraith, 1973: 10; Khandwalla, 1977: 512).

Standardization In terms of theories of control, standardization is a form of 'open-loop steering'. For certain regularly occurring events, preprogrammed behaviour is prescribed. Consequently, the behaviour of participants is predictable:

workers know what to do, and they can react very quickly. Indicators determining the flexibility potential of standardization are

- the degree to which the contents of the work are specified or programmed. Mintzberg (1979) calls this standardization of process. This mode of standardization leaves nearly no room for organizational participants to manoeuvre;
- the degree to which results of the work, such as products or performance, are specified. This is what Mintzberg (1979) called standardization of output. Output standardization means interfaces among tasks are determined. Compared to standardization of process, it leaves some more room to manoeuvre: only the result is specified, but not how the result must be achieved.

These indicators contribute to a continuum of increasing flexibility potential for standardization (see Table 6.11). Standardization facilitates the development of specialized routines but inhibits the creation of dynamic capabilities. In the case of both process and output standardization, the potential for flexibility is therefore extremely low.

Formalization For some structures, standardization goes together with formalization of behaviour. This variable describes the extent to which programmed

TABLE 6.11. Structural design variables of behaviour: indicators determining the flexibility potential

Behavioural regulations	low flexibility potential ——— high flexibility potential
standardization	*high* . . . .*low*
	standardization *standardization*
indicators	• specification of contents of the work (←)
	• specification of results of the work (←)
formalization	*high* . . . .*low*
	formalization *formalization*
indicators	• job descriptions (←)
	• work instructions (←)
	• general rules (←)
training and education	*low* . . . .*high*
	(routine) *(professional)* *(craft)*
indicators	• number of professionals (→)
	• number of internal development programmes (→)

Note: (→) = increasing from low to high   (←) = decreasing from high to low behaviour is described and prescribed. It reflects the degree to which rules, procedures, instructions, and communications are laid down in written documents (Pugh *et al.*, 1963; Khandwalla, 1977: 512). For instance, are contracts of employment with the organization in writing? Is there an official organizational chart? Are there written job descriptions? Are there memo forms? Are there work assessment records? All these written rules, procedures, and clearly specified job descriptions reduce the need for coordination within the organization.

Frequently, standardization and formalization are mistaken for each other. There is, however, a sharp distinction between the two. Not everything that is standardized in the organization is based on written documents. Often, standardization is derived from certain unwritten habits and traditions. In these situations, a high degree of standardization goes together with a low degree of formalization. Thus, formalization always requires standardization, but standardization does not have to result in formalization (De Leeuw, 1986).

Formalization is used especially when tasks require precise, usefully predetermined coordination. Moreover, it is often used to ensure fairness to clients and to abandon favouritism. For instance, government agencies must treat everyone equally and many rules are therefore instituted to protect clients. Organizations which rely purely on formalization to achieve coordination are generally referred to as bureaucracies. Crozier (1964) described how these formalized structures result in paralysed organizations. In these structures, organizational participants comply with rules as a purposeful action. If such organizations are confronted with non-routine change, the dominance of rules forces participants to adopt risk-averse behaviour in which they hide behind so-called object rules and procedures. In addition, Crozier showed that formalization leads to communication rigidities as a result of peer-group pressures within each hierarchical level. Consequently, deviant impulses are sanctioned, with the effect that each level or unit is focused on its own goals at the expense of the broader goals of the organization.

Just like standardization, formalization limits flexibility potential (see Table 6.11). It strongly reduces the perceptible variety of stimuli in the environment (Beer, 1985), thereby reducing the viability of the system. Under it, every member of the organization is totally deprived of initiative and completely controlled by rules imposed from the outside. Major indicators of the flexibility potential with respect to formalization are:

- specifications related to the job itself in the form of formal job descriptions. De Leeuw (1986: 258) points out that in highly formalized structures, these job descriptions primarily describe the tasks in terms of activities to be performed (means) instead of their function in terms of the contribution to the organizational goals (results);
- specifications attached to the work itself in the form of instructions which regulate the work flow;

- specification of rules which apply to all situations, all jobs, all work flows, and all workers. These rules are most common in bureaucratic organizations in the form of: 'Thou shalt work in jacket and tie'.

Education and Training   When jobs entail a body of knowledge and a set of skills that are both complex and non-rationalized, direct process regulation through formalization in terms of rules and procedures is no longer adequate. While standardization and some formalization were appropriate for regulating tasks for the Dutch Postbank, these design variables were inadequate for the highly complex activities within the Research Department of the Dutch Gas Company. An organization can achieve indirect process regulation, however, by hiring educated professionals who can be further trained in the organization. Education and training are appropriate design variables for professional as well as craft work.[6] In this connection, education refers to the process by which job-related skills and knowledge are taught by some kind of professional associations (universities or polytechnics). On the other hand, training refers to the process by which job-related skills are taught and developed within the organization itself.

For both education and training, the intention of the organization is to ensure that job holders are programmed with the necessary standard skills and an associated body of knowledge. Since professional education programmes can seldom impart all the skills and knowledge necessary for the proper performance of a job, they are generally followed by some kind of on-the-job training. According to Mintzberg (1979), education and training are forms of standardization of inputs or skills that achieve indirectly the control and coordination of work that standardization of work processes or of work outputs achieves directly. On the job, professional or craft workers appear to be acting autonomously, but they are in fact guided by trained skills and acquired knowledge. None the less, no matter how effective the training programme, the inherent complexity of the work ensures that considerably more discretion is left in it than in unskilled jobs. Many important judgements must be made regarding which skills to apply in each situation. Furthermore, broad training and education can give organizational participants a better idea of the functioning of the whole organization. We conjecture therefore that the more education and training, the higher the potential for flexibility (see Table 6.11). When participants have low levels of education and training, their autonomy is limited and tasks are relatively routine and unskilled. If workers have high levels of education and a reasonable amount of training, their work is professional and their autonomy is standardized to some extent by skills and knowledge. In the case of high training with or without high education, craft work with much room to set priorities and make self-judgements is used. For instance, to become a manager one must first acquire managerial skills and knowledge in a business school setting. Subsequently, these skills must be practised on the job. Therefore, a junior manager usually assumes the role of apprentice under a senior manager who himself learned the job in the same way.

The design variables considered so far are often insufficient to regulate the coordination process. Important interdependencies may remain after the tasks are specified, behaviour is standardized, work processes and outputs are formalized, education is specified, and skills are developed (see Fig. 6.5).

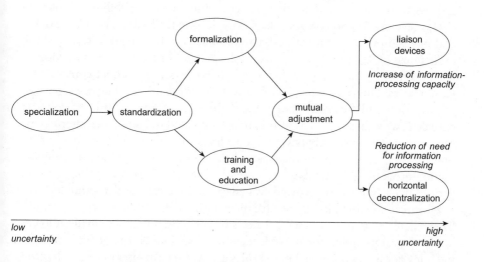

Fig. 6.5. Design variables of process regulation: a rough continuum of increasing uncertainty

Regulation of Mutual Adjustment

As more uncertainty is involved, the favoured means of process regulation seem to shift. In a stable environment, specialization may be sufficient. When there is more uncertainty, some programming is necessary, which can be partly achieved by formalization. In situations of even higher uncertainty, further formalization in the form of rules and procedures leads to a decrease in the flexibility potential below the required response. In addition, outputs cannot usually be specified in advance in such situations. Therefore, training and education may be more adequate for coordination. They broaden the scope and improve the quality of cross-hierarchical capability development. None the less, in a very turbulent environment, mutual adjustment becomes the favoured means of coordination.

Liaison devices   There are several liaison devices as separate design variables for regulating mutual adjustments between individuals or units. They result in lateral forms of communications and joint decision-making processes that cut across lines of authority. Instead of referring a problem upward in the hierarchy, managers solve the problem at their own level, contacting and cooperating with peers in those units affected by new information. Thus, liaison devices move the level of decision-making down to where the information exists rather than bringing it up to the points of decision. Consequently, they decentralize decisions without creating self-contained units, thus increasing the capacity to process information and to develop cross-functional capabilities. Galbraith (1973) developed various types of liaison devices on the basis of the degree of lateral inclusion in decision-making. Lateral inclusion is defined in terms of the explicitness of the horizontal decision role and authority in decision-making.

The simplest, most natural forms of liaison devices are direct contacts and liaison roles. Direct contacts avoid upward referrals to another manager and remove overload from the hierarchy. If there is a large volume of contacts between two subtasks, a liaison role may be created to handle the interdepartmental contacts and to bypass the long lines of communication involved in upward referral. Group approaches to liaison devices are utilized when information-processing demands exceed the capabilities of a single liaison role and various departments are involved. Managers of these various departments form a task force or team to jointly resolve the issues. Finally, influence approaches to liaison devices are used when more decisions of consequence are made at lower levels by groups and problems of leadership arise. In this connection, integrating roles or even managerial linking roles are created. An integrator is delegated formal influence to coordinate the process, but not to participate in the work. Unlike the integrator, the linking manager can decide for the group. His role is more like that of a normal manager.

According to Mintzberg (1979: 178), liaison devices are primarily tools of organic structures. They are flexible mechanisms to encourage loose informal relationships. Moreover, Lawrence and Lorsch (1967) demonstrated that the plastic industry (organic), which had the highest uncertainty score, used the most developed liaison devices, while the food industry with reasonable environmental uncertainty used less-developed devices, and the container industry (mechanistic), operating in a rather certain environment, had no liaison personnel at all. None the less, Eppink (1978) argued that this study was oriented mainly towards operational and competitive change and that it did not consider strategic change. In addition, Mintzberg (1979: 180) admitted that even the flexible liaison devices are simply too structured. Therefore we suppose lateral relations are adequate only for creating potential for operational flexibility. In this connection, liaison devices are mechanisms of the organization to increase its capacity to handle more information. Faced with strategic changes, however, extrinsic liaison devices may lead to very long and overloaded horizontal communication lines which inhibit quick reactions to unanticipated events. The long horizontal chains within a product line of Philips Semiconductors are illustrative. The many formal and informal liaison devices limited the autonomy of the management team and further destroyed the development of self-contained task groups. The increased integration boosted the line's vulnerability to disturbances and harmed its stability; disturbances in one part were reproduced throughout the whole organization. Therefore, to develop strategic flexibility for coping with fundamental uncertainty, a reduction in the need for information processing is required. Thus, the more well-developed and extrinsic the liaison devices (e.g. formal peer relationships, committees, teams, or task forces), the less the potential for flexibility (see Table 6.12).

TABLE 6.12. Design variables of mutual adjustment: indicators determining their flexibility potential

Regulation of mutual adjustment	low flexibility potential ——————— high flexibility potential		
liaison devices	linking role	team	liaison role
	integrating role	task force	direct contact
	(influence form)	(group form)	(natural form)
indicators	• formal peer relationship (←)		
	• committees (←)		
horizontal decentralization indicators	tightly . . . . loosely		
	coupled		coupled
	• pooled interdependencies (→)		
	• sequential interdependencies (←)		
	• reciprocal interdependencies (←)		

Note: (→) = increasing from low to high   (→) = decreasing from high to low

Horizontal decentralization Confronted with fundamental uncertainty, an organization can reduce its need for information processing by creating self-contained units (Galbraith, 1973). The reduced need for information processing increases the horizontal decentralization of units. This design variable describes the degree of horizontal autonomy of various units within an organization. When there is a high degree of horizontal decentralization, units do not need each other to accomplish their tasks. It allows units to self-organize and to choose courses of action to solve their problems within an overall mission and set of constraints prescribed for the units by the higher levels.

The principle of autonomous work units based on horizontal decentralization has been developed largely by Trist (1981) and is consistent with

The Organization Design Task

Thompson's (1967) logical design[7] principle of placing reciprocally and sequentially interdependent activities closely together in a common unit in order to minimize coordination costs. Only pooled interdependencies remain between units. Such highly horizontal decentralized structures possess unique properties of multistability; relatively loosely coupled units are able to create new stabilities in new situations without influencing the other units. In other words, in organizations designed according to these principles, disturbances are likely to be localized in their effects. Allowing local units to adapt to local conditions without changes in the larger system reduces coordination costs and information needs for the system as a whole.

Table 6.12 represents the indicators determining the flexibility potential of various degrees of horizontal decentralization. As demonstrated in this table, tightly coupled systems based on limited horizontal decentralization possess a rather small potential for flexibility. They increase the information-processing capacity of the organization, thereby facilitating adaptation to exploit present opportunities. Limited horizontal decentralization is therefore adequate for improving operational flexibility.

In situations of fundamental uncertainty, however, information about all changes, spurious as well as serious, flows through a tightly coupled system and overloads channels of communication (Weick, 1982). To cope with this overload, tightly coupled systems ignore signals of environmental change and therefore miss the necessity for organizational change. Because they also have to undertake a more significant retooling to adapt to what may prove to be a spurious event, lags persist and escalation of current commitments is likely. For instance, the many sequential dependencies between the business units, cargo operations, sales, and customer service in KLM Cargo inhibited the business units from easily adapting to changes in the cargo market. On the other hand, loosely coupled systems based on extensive horizontal decentralization possess a large potential for flexibility to accommodate to unexpected changes. They reduce the need for information processing and increase the organization's adaptability so that it can exploit future opportunities. Horizontal decentralization is therefore most adequate for improving strategic flexibility.

Regulation of Decision-Making

The autonomous self-organizing units considered above can develop their potential for flexibility only if authority is delegated to them.

Delegation In this context, delegation is a design variable which describes the degree to which decision-making power is transferred down the chain of authority to subordinates (Hill *et al.*, 1974). Lawrence and Lorsch (1967) found that decision-making power tends to rest at the level where the relevant information can best be accumulated. In situations of relatively few uncertainties, decisions tend to be made at higher levels because the appropriate information can easily be accumulated there. Thus, a low degree of delegation seems most appropriate for improving the potential for operational flexibility. In situations of many uncertainties, which require decision-making based on specific and detailed information, it is difficult to transfer information up the hierarchy. Hence decision-making power is transferred to the lower hierarchical levels. Such delegation enables the organization to respond more rapidly to local contingencies. In addition, it is a powerful motivator of subordinates because it satisfies their higher-order needs for autonomy and more meaningful and responsible work. Above all, it frees top management from the drudgery of relatively routine decisions so that it can devote attention to strategic, non-recurring, novel problems. Thus, a high degree of delegation enhances the organization's potential for strategic flexibility. Table 6.13 shows a continuum of increasing flexibility potential with respect to delegation.

TABLE 6.13. Design variables of decision-making; indicators determining the potential for flexibility

Regulation of decision-making	low flexibility potential ——————— high flexibility potential
delegation indicator	*low* . . . . *high* • decision-making power transferred to lower levels ($\rightarrow$)
participation indicators	*exclusive* . . . . *participative* • individualistic decision-making ($\leftarrow$) • consensus-seeking decision-making ($\rightarrow$) • sharing of information ($\rightarrow$)

Note: ($\rightarrow$) = increasing from low to high   ($\leftarrow$) = decreasing from high to low

Besides this potential for strategic flexibility, however, delegation exposes the organization to the risk of a lack of coordination among the activities of managers. Too many vested interests in the lower hierarchical levels breeds resistance to organization-wide changes and therefore makes the organization vulnerable in a crisis. In this context, top management faces the delicate task of controlling lower-level units without restricting their autonomy unduly. Some authors (e.g. Ansoff, 1974; Burton and Damon, 1975; Eppink, 1978; Mintzberg, 1979: 281) suggest that the degree of delegation in crisis situations of extreme hostility has to be temporarily reduced in order to facilitate strategic flexibility in terms of quick decision-making (see Fig. 6.6).

The Organization Design Task

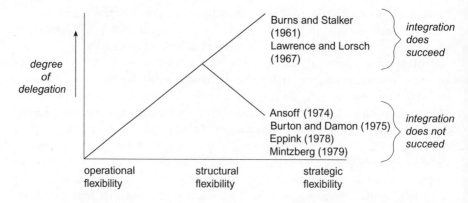

Fig. 6.6. The relationship between the degree of delegation and the potential for various types of flexibility

While we conjecture on the basis of the Lawrence and Lorsch study that the more unpredictable and uncertain the parts of the environment, the more authority has to be delegated to lower levels, such delegation facilitates the potential for strategic flexibility only if it goes together with higher levels of integration. Therefore, in situations of extreme hostility when integration is hard to attain and the organization cannot respond quickly, it may turn to its leader for direction. It may centralize power and survive for a time, but once its slack resources are used up, it simply expires.

Participation   In situations in which delegation is a necessity, participation in decision-making can supply the integration to offset the differentiation that delegation causes (Khandwalla, 1977). Participation describes the extent to which subordinates take part in the decision-making of superiors (see Table 6.13). Thus, subordinates can give their opinions, make suggestions, and present arguments, but the superior always makes the final decision. This design variable can be utilized to ensure proper coordination among lower levels that have considerable discretionary authority. In addition, it enhances the self-initiative and responsibility of lower levels. Low levels of participation therefore result in poor decision-making because there is little sharing of information; such a segmentalistic approach is inadequate for non-routine problem solving, which requires multiple perspectives. In this context, a lack of participation deprives lower levels of their flexibility potential. A high degree of participation results in more global, richer, more integrated decisions, based on various contributions of lower levels. Moreover, participation helps the lower levels of the organization to develop a capacity to think globally; they are aware not only of their specific

160

function, but also of the broader organizational goals. Consequently, the participants' commitment in the implementation of decisions is enhanced.

On the other hand, when participation is not tied up with some delegation of authority, it can be frustrating for lower levels and result in feelings of powerlessness (Perrow, 1974: 35). Many empowerment projects within large corporations seem to fail because of such situations. As an illustration, middle line managers at Philips Semiconductors complained about the lack of participation of workers in decisions, but at the same time refused to delegate authority. High levels of participation facilitate the potential for flexibility only if there is a certain degree of delegation.

Mechanistic versus Organic Structures

To sum up, in this section we explored structural barriers to flexibility. We showed that organizational structure comprises not only the actual distribution of responsibilities and authority among the organization's personnel (basic form), but also the planning and control systems and the process regulations of decision-making, coordination, and execution. The structural design of the organization can range from mechanistic to organic (Burns and Stalker, 1961), corresponding to the opportunities for adaptive capabilities. On the basis of this classification, various structures can be assessed in terms of their potential for flexibility (see Table 6.6). A functional type of organizing with many hierarchical levels is characteristic of a mechanistic structure. Processes may be highly regulated through elaborate planning and control systems, specialization of tasks, and high degrees of standardization and formalization. Training and education and horizontal decentralization are very restricted, while the few liaison devices are highly formalized. As a result, the levels of participation and delegation are low. Only minor incremental changes are possible in such a highly formalized and centralized structure (Cohn and Turyn, 1984).

In contrast, an organic structure can exist as a divisionalized form, or a project or matrix form consisting of few hierarchical levels. Essential for both the divisional and matrix forms are planning and control systems that are predominantly performance-oriented instead of means-oriented and allow for ambiguous information and necessary experimentation and intuition. Moreover, direct process regulation in the form of specialization and formalization is extremely low, whereas indirect process regulation by training and education is well developed. Furthermore, liaison devices in the form of lateral relations between units are minimized, but intensified within horizontal, decentralized units. Delegation of authority to these units encourages their participation in higher-level decision processes. The preceding principles of organic structure are basic guidelines. Because of the 'equifinality' of the various structural design variables, different configurations of those variables can constitute the organic structure. Such organic structures provide great leeway for structural flexibility.

Finally, we want to emphasize that the actual structure determines the potential for structural flexibility within the organization. In our treatment of the various design variables, however, we have seen that the organizational structure indirectly determines the potential for operational and strategic flexibility. That is, when only operational flexibility is required, the need for structural flexibility is minimal. Operational flexibility can therefore be found in a mechanistic structure with a low potential for flexibility. On the other hand, strategic flexibility can be found only when there is structural flexibility, and it can therefore be developed only in an organic structure with a large potential for structural flexibility.

6.3. Cultural Barriers

So far, we have analysed technology and structure in terms of dimensions which may explain the variation in flexibility potential between organizations. More recently, the concept of organizational culture has proved useful in shifting attention in organizational analysis from too much concern with variables of technology and structure towards a concern with the underlying beliefs and values of participants and their effect on the flexibility potential. For instance, on the basis of his study of the reactions of three companies to the oil crisis in 1973, Eppink (1978) concluded that organizational structure in the sense of the basic organizational form did not seem to be very important, but that the 'shared values' and people's tolerance for ambiguity were important factors that influenced the reaction process. Also, in their study in predicting changes in the work programmes of sixteen public welfare organizations, Hage and Dewar (1973) found that the elite values of the dominant coalition contributed more to the change potential of these organizations, than did structural characteristics like centralization, formalization, and specialization. Moreover, Meyer's (1982) longitudinal observations from nineteen hospitals dealing with a crisis showed that ideologies exert strong forces guiding organizational responses to external threats, whereas structures exert only weak constraints.

Of course, the above cultural phenomena have always been within the mainstream of the organization literature. Yet popular management theorists such as Ouchi (1981), Pascale and Athos (1981), Deal and Kennedy (1982), and Peters and Waterman (1982) can be said to have constituted the 'first wave' of the corporate culture boom. Despite their vagueness concerning the concept of culture, these authors were united in espousing a 'new management gospel', which advocated an increased focus on soft aspects of the organization such as values, norms, and beliefs, and a move away from the hard aspects of technology and structure. From our perspective, this new-found respect for organizational culture, based largely on the apparent success of companies with strong cultures, raises an interesting question: 'What is a strong culture and does such a culture enhance or inhibit the potential for flexibility?' Though a plethora of theory and research is currently appearing in the organization literature under the general rubric of organizational culture, this work is extremely diffuse and is based on different, often competing assumptions. Furthermore, while a number of studies on organizational culture have investigated its relationship to other organizational key variables, such as strategy (e.g. Weick, 1985), control (e.g. Ouchi, 1979), efficiency (e.g. Camerer and Vepsalainen, 1988), or performance (e.g. Barney, 1986), none of them explicitly dealt with culture and its potential for flexibility. In this paragraph, we first provide a clear definition of organizational culture. Subsequently, we will develop several cultural variables that indicate a culture's potential for flexibility.

On the basis of concepts from anthropology, Allaire and Firsirotu (1984) distinguished between management theorists who view organizational culture as meshed into the social system and those who conceive of it as a conceptually separate, ideational system. The former apply an adaptationist view, which concentrates on behaviour or action, while the latter apply an ideational view, which concentrates on ideas (Johnson, 1987: 223). In the adaptationist view, culture is considered as an aspect of structures and technologies within organizations. That is, all partsystems within the organization have a cultural dimension: technological and structural characteristics are imbued with values and norms. For instance, Starbuck (1982: 9) even argued that organizational structures and technologies are largely superficial facades. None the less, in this approach, the possible tensions between an organization's affective, symbolic dimensions and its structural and technological dimensions are ignored. The notion of organizational culture as an ideational system forces consideration of this issue. Although culture cannot be 'factored out' of behavioural products, it can nevertheless be considered as a separate, conceptual realm that may develop in ways that are not consonant with an organization's technology and structure. This distinction leads to a conceptualization of culture as a system of ideas, or as 'inferred ideational codes lying behind the realm of observable events' (Keesing, 1974, quoted in Allaire and Firsirotu, 1984: 197). In this approach, culture is considered as a partsystem which can be distinguished analytically from the other partsystems of the organization, and which can be described separately in its specific existence (Pennings and Gresov, 1986). That is, organizational culture is another critical lever or key by which managers can influence or direct the course of their organization (Smircich, 1983: 346).

The conception of culture as a set of beliefs and assumptions held commonly throughout the organization, and taken for granted by its members, is supported by many theorists (Bate, 1984; Johnson, 1987, 1988; Meyer, 1982; Schein,

1985). These idea systems are *implicit* in the minds of organization members and to some extent *shared* (Bate, 1984; Hofstede, 1980). The former feature refers to the fact that the system of ideas is not something that is 'out there' with a separate existence of its own; neither is it directly observable. The latter feature refers to the fact that people hold these ideas, meanings, and values commonly and collectively subscribe to them. While not denying the differences between individual beliefs, this concept of culture tends to focus on the commonalities which give an organization shared perspectives and thus constitute the social glue holding the company together.

We admit that the above conception of organizational culture is somewhat narrow compared to the catch-all concepts of culture, in that our conception focuses only on beliefs and assumptions rather than activities and systems (Johnson, 1987; Pennings and Gresov, 1986). Since this set of beliefs and assumptions is taken for granted by organizational participants and is not problematic for them, it may be difficult to state these idea coherently and explicitly. However, Schein (1985) recognizes that other organizational artifacts may be of value in so far as they help signify what is important in the belief systems of members of the organization. For instance, Johnson (1988: 85) remarks that these idea systems are preserved and legitimized in a cultural web of organizational activities in terms of myths, rituals, and symbols which support and provide relevance to core beliefs. Similarly, Meyer (1982: 45) argues that organizational ideologies are manifested and sustained by beliefs, stories, language, and ceremonial acts. Hofstede *et al.* (1990) refer to the latter as cultural practices.

Thus, culture expresses the values or social ideas and the beliefs that organizational members come to share. These values or patterns of beliefs are manifested by symbolic devices such as myths, rituals, stories, legends, and specialized language (Smircich, 1983: 344). Our concept of culture, however, contains not only the idea systems as expressed in the symbolic field which creates the organization's *identity*. It also includes the cultural mechanisms developed to maintain and change these idea systems, namely *leadership, unwritten rules*, and the *external orientation*. Leadership is critical for creating an ideology to support the founding ideals. Unwritten rules strengthen beliefs about the right way to behave in the organization, while the external orientation guides the very broad beliefs about the relationship of the organization to its environment.

On the basis of the above conceptualization of culture as a set of ideas which is developed and maintained by the organization's identity, leadership, unwritten rules, and external orientation, we will consider to what extent certain cultures inhibit or facilitate potential for flexibility. A classification scheme of various cultures with respect to their potential for flexibility is presented in Table 6.14. The culture can range from *conservative* to *innovative*. In a conservative culture, the existing idea system severely restricts the potential for flexibility, while in an innovative culture the existing idea system enhances the potential for flexibility. In this section, we will consider the cultural variables concerning the organization's identity, leadership, unwritten rules, and external orientation and explain the extent to which they inhibit or enhance the flexibility potential of culture.

TABLE 6.14. Classification scheme for flexibility potential of culture

Organizational culture	conservative ——————————— innovative
	(low flexibility potential) (high flexibility potential)
identity formation	
• communality	*strong. . . . . weak*
• scope	*narrow . . . . broad*
• homogeneity	*homogeneous. . . . . heterogeneous*
leadership	
• leadership style	*instructive . . . .consultative . . .participative . . . .delegative*
• planning approach	*blueprint . . . . . . .mixed-scanning . . . . . .muddling through*
• management attitude	*routine . . . . .heuristic . . . . .improvisation*
unwritten rules	
• discipline dominance	*strong. . . . . weak*
• socialization	*strong. . . . . weak*
• attitude formal-actual	*unequivocal . . . . equivocal*
• tolerance for ambiguity	*low . . . . high*
external orientation	
• focus	*strong . . . . .medium term . . . . .long term*
• openness	*narrow . . . . open*
• planning attitude	*homogeneous . . . . .inactive . . . . .proactive . . . . .interactive*

Identity Formation: Tight versus Loose Identities

A firm's identity is a commonly shared understanding of what the organization is all about and how it should operate (Berg, 1986: 296). It is manifested in values and cultural practices. According to Hofstede *et al.*, cultural practices consist of symbols, heroes, and rituals, and are the more superficial expressions of identity, while values are at the deepest level of identity formation. In particular, 'Symbols, heroes, and rituals can be subsumed under the term "practices", because they are visible to an observer although their cultural meaning lies in the way they are perceived by insiders' (Hofstede *et al.*, 1990: 291). At the surface level, *symbols* are words, gestures, pictures, or objects that carry a particular meaning within a culture. To create a durable and potent identity, claims of uniqueness need corroboration from these symbols (Clark, 1972; Meyer, 1982). At a deeper level, *heroes* or champions are persons, alive or dead, real or imaginary, who possess characteristics highly prized in the culture and who serve as models for behaviour. At an even deeper level, *rituals* and ceremonial behaviours are collective activities that are technically superfluous but socially essential within a culture.

In contrast with the above cultural practices, the core *values* of a firm's identity are 'feelings that are often unconscious and rarely discussable that cannot be observed as such but are manifested in alternatives of behavior' (Hofstede *et al.*, 1990: 291). These core values are shaped largely by the organization's history and its mission, which can in turn be studied to discover these values (Sanders and Neuijen, 1987: 17). The organization's mission consists of some broad ideas that prevail in the organization and which everybody understands and can identify with concerning the relation of the organization to its wider environment. This is concerned with such questions as 'What were the ideals of the founder?' and 'How did the organization react to critical events?' Organizational stories, legends, and anecdotes contain ideological parables that express, enhance, and codify values, and provide rationales for repeating and embellishing these stories (Meyer, 1982). Consequently, they perpetuate the organization's identity by anchoring the present in the past and lending meaning to the future. They intermix historical facts, retrospective justifications, and wishful thinking.

Three cultural variables can be distinguished regarding the flexibility potential of the organization's identity: its communality of identity, its scope, and its degree of homogeneity. These variables can be roughly determined by analysing the cultural manifestations of identity (symbols, heroes, rituals, and values) and the organization's history and mission.

Communality Communality of identity describes the extent to which the identity is shared by and unique to a given organization (Schein, 1985; Smircich, 1983). In an organization with a strong identity, one can find a coherent set of beliefs, highly shared values, a common language, and strongly agreed-upon kinds of appropriate behaviour. In such organizations, culture is an integrating mechanism which leaves almost no room for deviant interpretations. On the other hand, there is no consensus concerning the core values in organizations with a weak identity, as the organizational identity is composed of a collection of values and cultural practices, some of which may be contradicting. For instance, values may be inconsistent with cultural practices (Meyer and Rowan, 1977), or else there is no common language because the same words carry contrasting meanings in different contexts (Meyerson and Martin, 1987).

It is often believed that organizations with strong identities are better performers than organizations with relatively weak identities. Peters and

Waterman (1982: 75) remarked in their 'search of excellence' that the 'domi-nance and coherence of culture proved to be an essential quality of the excellent companies'. Indeed, in companies like 3M and HP, strong cultures place signifi-cant conformity pressures on members, who collectively conform to one another without knowing it. Yet Peters and Waterman also noted that poorer-performing companies often have strong, but dysfunctional identities. Also, Camerer and Vepsalainen (1988) observed that many firms have cultures which are consistent and thick, but are inappropriate to their business. Large self-con-fident companies like GM, IBM, and Philips realized far too late that their iden-tities were so strong that they had become blind to dramatic environmental change. As we stated in Section 3.1, organizations with extremely strong cul-tures usually suffer from xenophobia (Ouchi, 1981); independent thinking and the proposal of original alternatives may be discouraged in such organizations, with rather dangerous effects on their flexibility potential. To conclude, organi-zations with strong cultures tend to engage in discriminatory practices and often exhibit a potentially fatal lack of flexibility potential.

Scope   The scope of the organization's identity reflects the extent to which it con-tains a rich assortment of values and beliefs. In organizations with a focused iden-tity, this assortment is limited. In organizations with a robust identity, there is a variety of values and beliefs. In similar terms, Brunsson (1982) discussed narrow and precise versus broad ideologies, Camerer and Vepsalainen (1988) thin versus thick cultures, and Meyerson and Martin (1987) local versus organization-wide cultures. Organizations with too narrow an identity obstruct valuable strategic initiatives from rising from the front line. Such focused identities rule out changes which are too radical. By contrast, broad identities facilitate a high potential for flexibility. The scope of an organization's identity is specifically manifested in the organization's mission and goals. In this context, Quinn argued that 'Broad goals can create identity and elan . . . . They enable people to develop an identity larger than themselves, to participate in greater challenges, and to have influence or seek rewards they could not achieve alone' (Quinn, 1980: 74).

For instance, the broad mission of KLM Cargo to rank among the top three customer-driven suppliers of high-quality transport, distribution, and informa-tion services creates more potential for flexibility than a narrowly focused mis-sion on air transport.

Homogeneity   Besides the communality and the scope of the organization's identity, the homogeneity of the identity significantly determines the potential for flexibility. Most conceptions of culture consider it as a master blueprint with uniform interpretations. More recently, however, some culture theorists have argued that the organization may conceivably play host to, or provide a milieu for, one or more identities that may be either 'nested' or 'overlapping' (Gresov,

1984; Louis, 1983; Martin and Siehl, 1983; Rose, 1988). This metalevel conception of culture is at once more complex and more fertile in terms of cultural options for flexibility, as it admits the possibility of cultural heterogeneity as well as homogeneity.

Organizations with a homogeneous identity consist of a single, monolithic culture. According to Feldman (1988), organizations with a homogeneous identity are antithetical to flexibility and innovation because they limit the sources of change and creativity to top decision-makers. Burgelman (1983) argued that homogeneity around the organization's identity is essential for the preservation of order, but not for the ability of the organization to change. Similarly, Friedlander (1983: 220) pointed out that a homogeneous identity involves investment, commitment, and rigidity. All these characteristics preclude learning because their existence depends on limiting knowledge to that which will reinforce investment in the established mission. On the other hand, Carrol (1967), March and Simon (1958), and Meyer (1982) asserted that diversity in subcultures stimulates the potential for flexibility.

TABLE 6.15. Cultural variables of the organization's identity: indicators determining their flexibility potential

Identity formation	low flexibility potential ———————— high flexibility potential
communality	strong . . . . weak
scope	narrow . . . . broad
	(focused) (robust)
homogeneity	homogeneous . . . . heterogeneous
indicators	• history: stories, legends, anecdotes, critical events
	• mission: mission statements
	• symbols: language, special terms
	• heroes: meaningful persons
	• rituals: celebrations, funerals
	• values: broad, non-specific feelings concerning good/evil, normal/abnormal, rational/irrational, beautiful/ugly

Table 6.15 presents the variables of the organization's identity and their indicators for determining variations in the potential for flexibility. Many scholars and practitioners would argue that a strong identity is always homogeneous, and a weak identity always heterogeneous. If this were the case, communality and homogeneity could be reduced to one variable. However, an organization with a heterogeneous identity may be composed of a diverse set of subcultures that may or may not share some integrating elements of a dominant culture (Meyerson and Martin, 1987). These integrating elements refer to an array of

distinct subcultures that exist in relation to a core or umbrella culture. Sub-cultures may, for example, consist of pockets or enclaves of individuals within a dominant broader culture whose core values are widely shared and are endorsed by top management. Such an identity is relatively strong and hetero-geneous and facilitates cross-value capability development among the various subcultures. For example, there were many subcultures related to the different operations in the KLM Cargo division (the cargo factory, sales, customer service, and the various business units) but the strong collective pride in the division ('everything is possible here') created the glue for overcoming a segmented culture. The KLM Cargo culture contains diversity and values it.

On the other hand, an organization with a loose constellation of unique cultures not connected to an overriding core culture can be said to have a weak and heterogeneous culture. These organizations possess an 'unlimited' potential for flexibility, but they might easily be transformed into a chaotic state because they do not preserve a core culture (see Sect. 3.5). For instance, the Research Department of the Dutch Gas Company had a relatively weak identity in the sense that it had no consensus concerning its mission and core values. In fact, the department had a dual identity varying from 'long-term research and development' to 'short-term problem solving'. This duality resulted in a very heterogeneous culture that generated tremendous potential. This potential could not be allocated, however, due to many internal frictions (uncontrolled flexibility potential). Many theorists argue that organizations at the same time require not only belief and value systems with which their participants can strongly identify (strong identity), but also a 'creative tension' in which differences of approaches, of attitudes, of beliefs, and of actions can maintain sensitivity to a changing environment and the motivation for change (heterogeneous identity). Thus, organizations with core belief sets of a relatively high order along with rather heterogeneous sets of beliefs at the other levels are the really excellent organizations in that they develop sufficient flexibility potential without destroying their identity (controlled flexibility potential).

Leadership: Traditional versus Institutional Leadership

Within the organization, leadership is crucial for creating a culture or set of ideas that foster a potential for flexibility. An unsupportive culture can easily undermine the flexibility potential of a non-routine technology and an organic structure. In this context, leaders appear to be the creators and transmitters of culture; founders and leaders bring with them a set of assumptions, values, perspectives, and artifacts to the organization and impose them on their employees (Dyer Jr., 1986). Their essential function is the management of meaning in organizations, which is often called institutional leadership. The institutional leader is primarily an expert in the promotion and protection of values (Selznick, 1957). In other popular studies on excellent organizations, such leaders are called 'charismatic leaders' (Tichy, 1983), 'heroes' (Deal and Kennedy, 1982), 'change masters' (Kanter, 1983), or 'purposing leaders' (Vaill, 1982).

It is often thought that an organization loses its potential for flexibility when institutional leadership sets in. However, institutional leadership is needed for developing flexibility, particularly in situations where the organization is open to alternative ways of doing things or forced to consider them. During these periods, Selznick (1957) emphasized that the central and distinctive responsibility of institutionalized leadership is the creation of the organization's culture. Specifically, the challenge that leaders face is one of creating an organizational culture that is conducive to flexibility: a culture which encourages creativity and innovation, and values experimentation. If leaders default in performing these tasks, a set of values and guiding principles may emerge in the organization that are counterproductive to flexibility. For instance, the lack of institutional leadership in the Research Department of the Dutch Gas Company in terms of support and feedback stimulated fun-research and resulted in a lack of commitment.

The ability of leaders to develop a supportive culture depends on their style of leadership, their planning approach, and management attitude. These are the cultural variables with respect to leadership that determine the flexibility potential of culture (see Table 6.16).

Leadership style   The leadership style usually consists of a combination of directing and collaborating behaviour. Directing or task-oriented behaviour is characterized by an emphasis on task performance, one-way communication, and control. By contrast, collaborating or relation-oriented behaviour is characterized by an emphasis on mutual relationships, two-way communication, and the involvement of employees in decision-making. Consequently, four leadership styles can be roughly distinguished (see Table 6.16), namely:

- much direction and little collaboration, or an instructive leadership style; step by step specifying of what must be done and accurately controlling the task performance;
- much direction and much collaboration, or a consultative leadership style; asking for contributions from employees in decision-making and closely following their task performances;
- little direction and much collaboration, or a participative leadership style; joint decision-making with employees and direct support in task execution;
- little direction and little collaboration, or a delegative leadership style; leaving decisions about tasks as well as the responsibility for these decisions to employees.

The most appropriate leadership style depends largely on the type of task to be performed (routine or improvisation), and the capacity and motivation of the employee. Hence, Hersey and Blanchard (1982) argue that leaders must be able to perform various leadership styles. Yet, it is clear that an instructive leadership style limits an organization's flexibility potential and results in a monotonous organizational culture in which task obedience is reinforced and self-initiative and deviations are forbidden. Of course, authoritarian leaders with a certain charisma may provide the organization with a clear vision and stability, but these traits are considered to be highly negative from the perspective of freedom, self-responsibility, and ethics. In contrast, a more delegative leadership style facilitates the potential for flexibility and leads to a culture in which creativity, innovation, and trial and error are highly valued (Kanter, 1983). This leadership style, however, requires highly capable and motivated employees. Without them, a lack of direction from leaders may transform the organization into a chaotic state. Harrison therefore proposes 'stewardship' as a leadership style which might be an adequate alternative to a directive or a delegative style.

He or she is more open and non-defensive . . . and less likely to use fear, domination, or militant charisma than heretofore. The picture is one of a personally secure and mature individual who can articulate the values and high principles which give organizational life meaning, but who is more humble and receptive than we normally expect visionary leaders to be. (Harrison, 1984: 103).

TABLE 6.16. Cultural variables of leadership: indicators determining their flexibility potential

Leadership	low flexibility potential ——————— high flexibility potential
leadership style indicators	*instructive* . . . . . *consultative* . . . . . *participative* . . . . . . *delegative* • degree of direction (←) • degree of collaboration (∩)
planning approach indicators	*blueprint* . . . .*mixed scanning* . . . .*muddling through* • top-down decision-making (←) • fixed goals; instrumental planning (←) • quantification of goals (←) • comprehensiveness of goals (←)
management attitude indicators	*routine* . . . .*heuristic* . . . .*improvisation* • specified procedures and activities; routines (←) • procedures of urgency, priority rules; heuristics (∩) • ad hoc activities; improvisation (→)

Note: (→) = increasing from low to high
(←) = decreasing from high to low
(∩) = reversed u-form relationship

The Organization Design Task

Planning approach   Besides the leadership style, the planning approach is an essential dimension of leadership which generates variations in flexibility potential. This dimension describes the extent to which leaders think developments in the organization can be planned. Three approaches to planning can be distinguished.

The most extreme approach to planning is blueprint or synoptic planning, which is concerned with establishing stable goals and developing integrated plans or blueprints to achieve them. This approach assumes that the uncertainty in the environment can be reduced to an acceptable level. Consequently, choices are predetermined by the blueprint and all other options are cut off. However, blueprint planning has a number of shortcomings which contribute to over-complexity and inflexibility (Peters and Waterman, 1982; Levy and Merry, 1986: 51), namely:

- an obsession with cost and quantitative elements, not with qualitative elements or values;
- a bias towards abstract heartless philosophies;
- an abhorrence of mistakes and ignorance of experimentation.

If the future turns out to be different from what was laid down in the blueprint, the organization may go adrift.

In contrast with this analytical approach, Lindblom (1959) suggests a 'muddling through' approach which emphasizes the iterative nature of planning and the resultant need to make and remake planning (see Sect. 3.1). In this highly incremental approach, all options are kept open. Notwithstanding the tremendous flexibility potential of this approach, this strategy of extreme flexibility can also lead to serious difficulties if not disaster. Etzioni (1968: 282–309) proposes a mid-position, namely a mixed-scanning approach towards planning. Leaders develop a long-term broad vision (fundamental decision) and proceed step by step from this vision into the short term (incremental decision). Thus, this approach is not just 'muddling through', but 'muddling through' with a global vision. It worked extremely well for the Research Department of the Dutch Gas Company, where researchers originally had a high aversion to planning.

Table 6.16 depicts the three planning approaches and the indicators determining their flexibility potential. It is important to understand that the appropriate planning approach depends on the type of flexibility required within the organization. In Section 3.1, we have already pointed out that the more uncertainty involved, the more an organization needs room for flexibility as a complement to planning. When only operational flexibility is required, the level of uncertainty is reasonably low because the signals and feedback from the environment are very clear and direct (see Sect. 5.3). Consequently, a blueprint planning approach will suffice. This instrumental approach is based upon existing goals and structures.

On the other hand, when strategic flexibility is the dominant mode, the level of uncertainty is much higher. Signals received from the environment are very ambivalent and the lead time is very long. Strategic flexibility therefore requires a 'mixed-scanning' or even 'muddling through' approach, in which leaders create open and adaptive idea systems with a high degree of freedom.

Management attitude   Finally, the management attitude of leaders is a crucial cultural variable for determining variations in flexibility potential. It describes the extent to which leaders consider managing as routinization or improvisation. Consequently, this variable can vary from the routine and heuristic to improvisation (see Table 6.16). When leaders think about managing as routinization of work, all their attention is focused on the specification of procedures and activities. The resulting proliferation of routines limits the flexibility potential, but this potential may still be sufficient for steady-state and operational flexibility. Operational flexibility is largely routine and generates well-structured problems that can be solved on the basis of experience, imitation, or extrapolation and other optimizing techniques of operation research (e.g. problems concerning scheduling, routing, or the production volume). Although operational flexibility may involve the development of new routine capabilities, these are based largely on extensions or refinements and not radically different from previously followed ones. None the less, a routine management attitude inhibits structural and strategic flexibility. Philips Semiconductors' management attitude towards routine proliferation is illustrative: for every possible change they tried to develop a sophisticated routine. This attitude, however, was highly insufficient for the strategic changes they were confronted with, such as the introduction of high-quality plastic diodes, new crystal types, and radical demand fluctuations.

For dealing with structural flexibility, a heuristic management attitude may be fitting. This attitude towards managing recognizes that it is not possible to specify everything in advance, but that some priorities can be set on the basis of quasi-analytical tools. Such priority rules are adequate for ill-defined problems.

Regarding strategic flexibility, even a heuristic management attitude does not suffice because problems relating to strategic flexibility are by definition unstructured and non-routine. Usually, the future is no longer an extension of the past, but can show trend breaks and discontinuities. Extrapolation or other conventional management tools are not useful in this context. Routines may even prove to be a handicap, as they may lead to blocks in creativity. Rather, such problems require a management attitude directed towards new values and norms or improvisation.

To sum up, a directive leadership style together with a blueprint planning approach and a routine management attitude restricts the potential for flexibility and results in a conservative culture. On the other hand, a delegative leadership style with a 'muddling through' planning approach and a management attitude that favours improvisation enhances the potential for flexibility and results in an innovative culture.

Unwritten Rules: Restrictive versus Supportive

Besides identity formation and leadership, the unwritten rules determine the potential for flexibility or innovativeness of culture. These rules are the broad, tacitly understood rules which tell employees what to do under a wide variety of unimaginable circumstances (Camerer and Vepsalainen, 1988). Organizational participants are required to acknowledge, and, to some extent, conform to these unwritten rules, which may stretch far back into the organization's history. Not surprisingly, over time these rules may become inappropriate in that they do not fit the strategic needs of an organization. Inappropriate cultural rules can prevent meaningful interaction and induce a condition of 'learned helplessness', 'a psychological state in which people are unable to conceptualize their problems in such a way as to be able to resolve them' (Bate, 1984: 44). These rules thus narrow the potential for flexibility. Hence, investigating an organization's unwritten rules may be very helpful in clarifying variations in flexibility potential. The content and volume of unwritten rules in the organizational culture are shaped by the discipline dominance among organization members, processes of socialization, the organization members' formal-actual attitude, and their tolerance for ambiguity.

Discipline dominance   The discipline dominance describes the extent to which the unwritten rules within the organization are dominated by the values and practices of a certain discipline or profession (see Table 6.17). In their recent empirical study on organizational cultures, Hofstede *et al.* (1990) concluded that value differences between organizational units within the same country are dependent primarily on demographics like education and age, and only secondarily on membership in the organization as such. Thus, occupational cultures have an enormous effect on the organization's values. Entering an occupational field means the acquisition of both values and practices, which takes place at school or the university, between childhood and beginning work. Also, after education the occupational values and practices are reinforced by meetings, courses, and social events of occupational associations. It is remarkable that such occupational cultures have received considerably less attention in the literature than have national or organizational cultures (Hofstede *et al.*, 1990: 311–12).

A strong occupational culture or a strong discipline dominance within the organization, such as an organization made up predominantly of engineers, lawyers, or scientists, largely shapes the unwritten rules. Consequently, these rules may become extremely rigid, stagnant, limited in scope, and cause 'learned

TABLE 6.17. Variables of the organization's unwritten rules: indicators determining their flexibility potential

Unwritten rules	low flexibility potential ———— high flexibility potential
Discipline dominance	*strong* .... *weak* *discipline* *discipline*
Indicators	• the percentage of employees with the same education (←) • the percentage of employees with the same experience (←) • the percentage of employees of the same age level (←)
Socialization	*high* .... *low* *socialization* *socialization*
Indicators	• indoctrination of 'new arrivals' (←) • HRM systems; career policy, MD systems, reward and sanction systems, recruitment policy (←) • programmes and training which reinforce unwritten rules (←)
Attitude formal-actual	*unequivocal* .... *equivocal* *(enhancing)* *(orthogonal)* *(overlapping)* *(counter)*
Indicators	• formal rules • unwritten rules
Tolerance for ambiguity	*low* .... *high* *tolerance* *tolerance*
Indicators	• new ideas, opinions (→) • deviant behaviour (→) • predictability of relationship (→)

Note: (→) = increasing from low to high   (←) = decreasing from high to low

helplessness' or even 'occupational helplessness'. For example, for a product line of Philips Semiconductors that primarily employed managers and workers with a technical education, problems were often framed in technical terms while the more social problems were ignored. Similarly, lawyers are focused only on formal rules laid down in written contracts and do not value informal rules. Of course, the above descriptions of occupational cultures are only rough stereotypes which are seldom adequate, but it can none the less be said that a strong discipline dominance severely limits the potential for flexibility. Especially with respect to strategic flexibility, strong occupational cultures obstruct the development of new values and norms. For instance, Leonard-Barton (1992) found that at Kodak, the chemical engineers were more dominant than the mechanical and manufacturing engineers. The lower status of non-dominant disciplines was manifested in

175

pervasive but subtle negatively reinforcing cycles that constrained Kodak's potential for new product development and limited the cross-integration so necessary to innovation. Similarly, the discipline dominance of design engineering at DEC and HP enabled these companies to grow very strong in design, but their marketing and manufacturing capabilities suffered. The pervasive perception that manufacturing people and their concerns were relatively less important became a significant problem at both companies (Leonard-Barton *et al.*, 1994: 127).

Socialization   Unwritten rules are transmitted by a process of socialization. This variable describes the extent to which unwritten rules are thoroughly explained and maintained within the organization. These rules can be incorporated by:

- indoctrination of new arrivals; one can think of introduction programmes in the attempt to ensure that new arrivals 'fit in', through 'initiation rites' designed to show new managers that they have things to learn, to intimidation rituals of isolation and defamation (Johnson, 1987: 214);
- HRM systems; the unwritten rules can be formally expressed in the career policies, the reward and sanction systems, and the criteria that are applied for the recruitment of personnel.[8] Furthermore, management development programmes may stimulate job rotation in such a way that organization members incorporate many unwritten rules;
- by special programmes and training: the primary intention of these programmes is continuously to reinforce the unwritten rules.

A high degree of socialization results in a thick culture with many unwritten rules. Such cultures encourage an orthodoxy of beliefs and a non-confrontational stance. Hence, the flexibility potential for deviant behaviour and new ideas is minimal (Kanter, 1988: 176). On the other hand, low degrees of socialization, in which there is much room to manoeuvre, enhance the potential for flexibility (see Table 6.17).

Attitude formal/actual   Besides discipline dominance and the socialization process, the number and content of unwritten rules is determined by the organization members' attitude on formal versus actual. This cultural variable reflects the extent to which organization members value differences between the formal and actual organization. Accordingly, it helps us understand the attitude of organization members towards formal rules and procedures. Can they make exceptions, violating the formal rules? Or do they try to continuously reduce the gap between formality and actuality by stressing formal rules?

Four positions can be distinguished from this variable (cf. De Leeuw, 1989):

- the actual organization is a part of the formal organization (see Fig. 6.7a): in this situation, members adhere even more fervently to the formal rules than is required. There are no unwritten rules outside the area defined by the formal rules. In fact, the unwritten rules are even stricter and more limiting than the formal rules. The fear of violating formal rules results in even more formality than is required. Such an enhancing culture concerning formal rules is devastating for any possible potential for flexibility (Rose, 1988: 163);

- the formal organization is a part of the actual organization (see Fig. 6.7*b*): members adhere to the formal rules, but have also developed an unconflicting set of unwritten rules unique to themselves (Martin and Siehl, 1983). In such orthogonal cultures, formal rules cannot specify all contingencies. Hence, unwritten rules are developed for appropriate action under unspecified contingencies (Camerer and Vepsalainen, 1988);
- formal and actual organization overlap (see Fig. 6.7*c*): in this overlapping culture, some formal rules are confirmed by unwritten rules, while other formal rules are laid down only on paper. There are also unwritten rules which deviate from these formal rules. This situation guarantees some potential for flexibility;
- formal and actual organization do not overlap: in this situation, all the formal rules conflict with the unwritten rules of the organizational culture (see Fig. 6.7*d*). In this counterculture, the organization has two faces since the unwritten rules are totally different from the formal rules.

In Table 6.17, these four positions are placed in a continuum ranging from unequivocal to equivocal concerning the attitude towards the formal-actual.

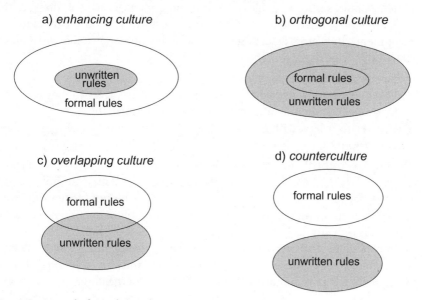

Fig. 6.7. Attitude formal-actual

The Organization Design Task

The more unequivocal, the more members try to reduce the gap between formal and actual by stressing formal rules, and the more limited the potential for flexibility. On the other hand, in a counterculture like that of the Research Department of the Dutch Gas Company, rules are violated by definition. This circumstance guarantees a large potential for flexibility, but often leads to a chaotic organization. The schizophrenia of this research department resulted in distorted information that managers could not use to make appropriate decisions. Consequently, the environment (i.e. board, internal clients) was able to control the department by forcing it in a certain direction.

Tolerance for ambiguity   Finally, the tolerance for ambiguity of the organization members describes the extent to which the unwritten rules themselves leave some room to manoeuvre. These rules define the limits of the organization's ability to deal with environmental change. When there is a low tolerance for ambiguity, organization members prefer well-defined, stable, and unchanging rules in the work situation. This stability may be adequate for operational flexibility, which is largely predictable and straightforward. Signals are very tangible and not easy to ignore. Not reacting to them or ignoring them will have clear consequences for the short-term success of the organization. By contrast, in situations where there is high tolerance for ambiguity, the unwritten rules allow a high degree of freedom for the members' own interpretations. Such tolerance is required for strategic flexibility, through which the organization can interpret unfamiliar signals from the environment. This action cannot be accomplished on the basis of rigid rules or experience, but calls for new ideas, values, and organizational solutions. In this context, tolerance of ambiguity prevents members from becoming blind to new developments. Indicators determining the flexibility potential of this variable (see Table 6.17) may be the way members think about:

- new ideas or different opinions;
- deviant behaviour (e.g. when members dress differently than they normally do, or when someone puts up a tremendous performance);
- their relationships with colleagues: are they largely predictable or is there some room for surprise?

In the Dutch Postbank, for instance, the tolerance for ambiguity was very low; most participants of the Corporate Accounts Department were non-creative and conservative. Deviating opinions or new ideas were not brought forward, and their chances of success were low. To exemplify this, one employee's splendid idea was only implemented after six years.

To recapitulate, a strong discipline dominance, strong processes of socialization, an unequivocal attitude towards formal-actual, and a low tolerance of ambiguity contribute to a minimal potential for flexibility of the unwritten rules.

Based

External Orientation: Narrow versus Broad-Minded

Finally, the external orientation of the idea systems which make up the organizational culture determines the potential for flexibility. It reflects the beliefs about the relationship of the organization to its total environment. The potential for flexibility which the external orientation permits depends on the organization members' focus, their openness, and their planning attitude towards the environment.

Focus The focus describes the members' shared ideas of the future and the time frame they apply to the future. This variable can range from a short-term to a long-term focus. When members have a short-term focus, the potential for flexibility is limited because they are interested only in short-term developments with direct feedback. A long-term focus requires the scanning of weak and indirect signals. A short-term focus might therefore be appropriate for operational flexibility, while strategic flexibility requires a long-term focus. Table 6.18 represents a continuum of increasing flexibility potential regarding the focus towards the future.

Openness The openness dimension of the external orientation describes the extent to which organization members consider their organization as sensitive to external developments. This variable can vary from closed to open.

In a closed external orientation, the organization is considered to be insensitive to market developments, industry changes, changes in government regulations, and so on. The organization is regarded as an instrument designed for the

TABLE 6.18. Variables of the organization's external orientation: indicators determining its flexibility potential

External orientation	low flexibility potential ———— high flexibility potential
Focus Indicators	*short term* . . . .*medium term* . . . .*long term* • idea of future • time frame ($\rightarrow$)
Openness Indicators	*closed* . . . .*open* • sensitivity to external developments ($\rightarrow$) • means oriented ($\leftarrow$)/product oriented ($\rightarrow$) • technology driven ($\leftarrow$)/market driven ($\rightarrow$) • interactions with outsiders ($\rightarrow$)
Planning attitude Indicator	*reactive* . . . . *inactive* . . . . *proactive* . . . . *interactive* • idealization of future ($\rightarrow$)

Note: ($\rightarrow$) = increasing from low to high   ($\leftarrow$) = decreasing from high to low pursuit of clearly specified goals. Consequently, these organizations perceive their task towards the outside world as the implementation of inviolable rules. Signals which can threaten their external orientation are ignored. Extreme examples of such organizations are monasteries, revolutionary parties and groups, and other strongly ideological organizations. Because their goals are stable, such organizations try to optimize processes, while possible changes are technology-driven. In addition, their members have minimal interactions with people outside the organization. This closed-system thinking does not allow much leeway for flexibility because only a minimal amount of operational flexibility on the basis of existing goals can be accomplished.

In an open external orientation, the organization is considered to be highly sensitive to external developments. The organization is seen as a mechanism which must be continuously adapted in order for it to survive. The resistance to signals which can threaten the existing idea system towards the environment is low, and results in the adapting of the idea system. As a result, such organizations focus their attention on the product instead of the process, and changes in the product are market-driven. Moreover, members have frequent interactions with people outside the organization: face-to-face interactions with customers trigger adaptations of the external orientation. In Peters and Waterman's (1982) terminology, such organizations 'stay close to the customer'. In the Research Department of the Dutch Gas Company, this stronger client orientation resulted in a breakthrough in the one-way traffic from Research towards Clients, an increase in the face-to-face interactions with internal and external clients, and a higher involvement by clients in the research process. This orientation permits an enormous potential for flexibility, and may be adequate for the development of strategic flexibility (see Table 6.18).

Planning attitude Besides the focus and openness of the external orientation, the planning attitude describes the members' beliefs about the extent to which the organization can control its environment or is subject to its forces. Regarding this attitude, we can distinguish four positions (Ackoff, 1974):

- reactive: the organization tries to maintain existing achievements (market share, customers, products). In other words, planning is considered as a conservative activity directed towards the preservation of previous achievements. Hence, the external vision is based on the past;
- inactive: the environment is considered to be uncontrollable, so the organization does not undertake any actions. In this passive approach, planning is considered useless. The external vision is based on the present;
- proactive: the organization tries to predict future developments on the basis of extrapolation of trends. Planning is seen as a means for anticipating likely developments. The external orientation is based on a likely future;
- interactive: the organization designs an idealized future without taking into account the past. In other words, planning is considered as a continu-

ous activity directed towards creating an idealized future. Consequently, the external orientation is based on a desired future.

We have already pointed out that flexibility is a complement to planning. The reactive and inactive planning attitudes, however, destroy any potential for flexibility (see Table 6.18). In the Dutch Postbank, the external orientation of the Corporate Accounts Department was focused on the short term and not very open to new market developments. According to the management team, environmental changes influenced only the work volume and required size of the workforce, but not the kind of activities performed. Most of them thought that they could not control the environment and were subject to its forces. According to Beer (1985), 'the lethal variety attenuator is sheer ignorance'; such attitudes ignore the variety within the environment and do not develop an adequate external vision for dealing with this variety. Over time, failure to do this may threaten the organization's survival.

When a proactive planning attitude dominates, the organization tries to adapt to a likely future. None the less, when the future turns out to be different from that predicted, the leeway for adaptations is minimal. A strong commitment to a likely future therefore reduces the organization's flexibility potential. On the other hand, continuously changing the likely future that is adapted to may lead to overreactions.

In the interactive planning approach, the potential for flexibility is based on a long-term vision and an idealized picture of the future. The organization knows that this idealization can never be accomplished, but tries to reach it as much as possible. Interactive planning encourages the organization not only to adapt as in the proactive approach, but also to control its environment in order to achieve a desired future.

Thus, with respect to the external orientation of the organizational culture, we may conclude that a short-term focus, a closed external orientation, and a reactive planning attitude inhibit the potential for flexibility, whereas a long-term focus, an open external orientation, and an interactive planning attitude facilitate the potential for flexibility.

Conservative versus Innovative Cultures

In this section, we have explored cultural barriers to flexibility. Organizational culture was defined as the set of commonly held norms and values throughout the organization and taken for granted by its members. It can range from conservative to innovative, depending on the slack within the current norms and value systems for strategic capabilities. On the basis of this classification, various cultures can be assessed in terms of their potential for flexibility (see again Table 6.14).

The Organization Design Task

A conservative culture consists of a strong and homogeneous identity with a narrow scope. Leaders apply a directive leadership style. There are large repositories of unwritten rules as a result of a strong discipline dominance, socialization processes, and a low tolerance of ambiguity. Moreover, a conservative culture has a closed external orientation, which is mainly short term and reactive. Cross-value capability development is very limited in a conservative culture.

In contrast, an innovative culture has a weak and heterogeneous identity with a broad scope. Leaders apply a delegative leadership style and are biased toward improvisation. There are only a few unwritten rules as a consequence of a low discipline dominance (free exchange of knowledge and information between the various disciplines), weak socialization processes, and a high tolerance of ambiguity. Exceptions involving violations of the formal rules are possible. The external orientation is very open and focused on the long term. An innovative culture facilitates cross-value capability development.

The beliefs and assumptions of the organizational culture play a central role in the interpretation of environmental stimuli and the configuration of organizationally relevant strategic responses (Johnson, 1987). Does the organization see new strategic options? Can it deviate from present patterns? A conservative culture generates enough potential for operational flexibility, in which no change of fundamental norms and values is necessary. In contrast, strategic flexibility requires changes in fundamental norms and values, which can be accomplished only by broad and easily changeable idea systems. Strategic flexibility generated by an innovative culture often requires a large degree of the structural flexibility generated by an organic structure (see Sect. 6.2).

To conclude, in this chapter we explored the organization design challenge of flexibility. Designing the appropriate organizational conditions requires identifying the type of technological, structural, or cultural changes necessary to ensure effective utilization of flexible capabilities. We provided categorizations of technology, structure, and culture which help the manager to analyse and reduce organizational barriers to flexibility. Several questions, however, remain: how much flexibility potential in design is adequate and what repertoire of flexible capabilities is sufficient? Do all firms require extremely flexible adaptive capabilities together with flexible organization designs? In the next chapter, we will consider ways to match the managerial and organization design challenges under various levels of competition.

Notes

1. Besides an external fit between contingency factors and design variables, many contingency theorists have argued that there must be an internal consistency among technological, structural, and cultural design variables within the organization as well. Mintzberg (1979: 219) refers to the latter as the configuration hypothesis.
2. Gillespie and Mileti (1977) conclude in an overview and appraisal of technology and the study of organizations that the concept of technology 'has been elusively defined, refined, treated solely as an independent variable, applied holistically to organizations, confused with structure, crudely measured, and studied mainly in manufacturing organizations'.
3. In Perrow's classification scheme, craft industries (few exceptions, but unanalysable problems) and engineering (analysable problems, but many exceptions) represent midpositions.
4. A numerical control (NC) machine refers to the operation of machine tools from numerical data stored on paper or magnetic tape, tabulating cards, computer storage, or direct information. Computer numerical control (CNC) systems, on the other hand, use a minicomputer to perform NC operations which are stored in a computer memory. Robotics are machines which can perform human-type operations (Hill, 1983: 93, 94).
5. e.g. Likert (1961), or Roethlisberger and Dickson (1939) who carried out a series of experiments on workers at the Western Electric Hawthorne plant. For a discussion of the various schools of management we refer to Section 2.2.
6. Professional work is complex and non-rationalized work, but the body of knowledge has been recorded to some extent and the required skills have in part been specified. If not, such work is generally referred to as craft (Mintzberg, 1979: 95–103).
7. Thompson (1967) discussed three basic kinds of interdependence: pooled, involving only the sharing of resources; sequential, where the work is fed from one task to the next; and reciprocal, where the work is passed back and forth between tasks.
8. According to Hofstede et al. (1990), socialization has its largest effect on cultural practices (symbols, heroes, and rituals). Such cultural practices are learned at the workplace, which we usually enter as adults, with the bulk of our values firmly in place. New cultural values can enter the organization only by the recruitment of new personnel.

7   Resolving the Paradox: Flexibility under Various Levels of Competition

> Static models of strategy describe competition at one point in time. This is effective in an environment in which changes are slow and sustaining advantage is the goal. But in hypercompetition, where change is rapid and the goal is disruption, effective strategy has to have a more dynamic focus. Strategy requires a theory that pays attention to the sequential moves and countermoves of competitors over long periods of time. As competition has heated up, this dynamic interaction among competitors has become the key to competitive success. Success depends not on how the firm positions itself at a certain point in time, but on how it acts over long periods of time. So the shift from static thinking to dynamic focus is crucial to understanding strategy in the long run.
>
> (D'Aveni, 1994: 17)

In the previous chapters, we worked out the most important building blocks of our strategic framework of flexibility, namely the managerial and organization design tasks. Doing so helped us to analyse the managerial repertoire of flexible capabilities (flexibility mix) and the responsiveness of the organization. In this chapter, we will apply a more dynamic perspective and consider how firms put the two building blocks together. What repertoire of flexible capabilities is sufficient and how much flexibility potential in design is adequate? To be more specific, when can management combine operational flexibility with tight organizational conditions and when must it combine structural or even strategic flexibility with looser organizational conditions?

The answers to these questions require a more detailed consideration of the third building block of our strategic framework of flexibility, namely changing competitive forces (see Fig. 7.1). We will argue that this building block determines the sufficiency of the flexibility mix and the design adequacy of the organizational conditions. First, we will analyse the competitive forces which may generate environmental turbulence (Sect. 7.1). Secondly, we will examine the competitive dynamics that contribute to increasing competition and environmental turbulence (Sect. 7.2). In particular, the more dynamic (frequency and intensity of environmental changes), complex (number and relatedness of environmental

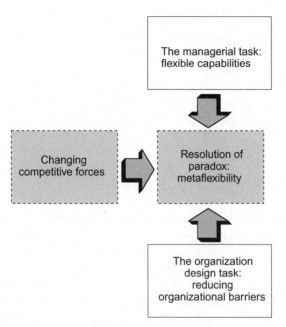

Fig. 7.1. The building blocks of flexibility

changes), and unpredictable the competitive forces (extent to which cause-effect relationships are incomplete), the higher the level of competition and environmental turbulence the firm is confronted with. Consequently, the more difficult it is to handle the managerial and organization design tasks of flexibility.

Combining the managerial and organization design tasks under various levels of competition involves a process of matching, typically called duality or resolving paradoxes. The managerial task is to provide dynamic capabilities for change, whereas the organization design task is to configure technology, structure, and culture for preservation and control. Consequently, management must cope with a constructive tension (Kanter, 1983) between developing capabilities and preserving organizational conditions. This process of matching represents *metaflexibility* (Sect. 7.3). There has been relatively little focus on the specifics of how firms develop flexible capabilities and how they renew them to respond to shifts in the business environment. None the less, the superiority of flexible capabilities cannot be taken for granted. For effective flexibility, management must reconfigure the flexibility mix and redesign the organizational conditions in line with future competitive changes (see Fig. 7.1). This metaflexibility requires higher-order learning capabilities to monitor the environment, shift between flexible capabilities or create new capabilities, and redesign the organization.

Resolving the Paradox

The discussion of metaflexibility helps us to consider various ways of resolving the flexibility paradox. This paradox can be portrayed in a more sophisticated version of our framework that relates competitive environments, certain types of flexibility, and organizational conditions. In particular, the framework explains in which competitive environments certain types of flexibility and organizational designs are effective (Sect. 7.4). Therefore, we can obtain several alternative flexible forms from this framework, each of which reflects a particular way of coping with the flexibility paradox of change and preservation.

7.1 Analysing Competitive Forces

Our strategic framework suggests that heightened environmental turbulence highlights the need for extremely flexible capabilities together with loose organizational designs. But what exactly is environmental turbulence and how can firms develop a proper notion of the level of turbulence they face? Organizations' environments have been analysed in a bewildering variety of ways and with respect to a number of potentially important dimensions (Khandwalla, 1977: 332). By contrast, there is a great lack of clarity and virtually no agreement as to the exact meaning of environmental turbulence.

In our discussion of organization–environment theories (Sect. 3.2) and their conceptions of environment, we showed that static contingency theory and population-ecology theory view organizations' environments as real, material, and separate (deterministic approach). They do not question the pivotal notion of environments as independent, external, and tangible entities. In reaction to these assumptions, the dynamic contingency theory argues that environments can, to some extent, be understood as socially constructed phenomena (voluntaristic approach). In other words, organizations can construct or redefine the objective features of an environment, thereby purposively creating their own measures of reality and delimiting their own decisions (Child, 1972; Weick, 1979). None the less, there are still discernible features of the actual environment, such as the number of PMCs, suppliers, distribution channels, or various niches that clearly exist, which might be intractable to control by individuals and their organizations (Hrebiniak and Joyce, 1985). At times the effects of these discernible features are peremptory, while at other times they can be easily controlled or manipulated.

In our conceptualization of environmental turbulence, we will therefore rely as much as possible on the discernible features of the environment to which the organization might respond. Although we admit that perceptual measures are more appropriate for explaining managerial behaviour than objective environmental measures (Bourgeois, 1980), these perceptions of the environment may strongly deviate from the real environment. Many organizations perceive their environment as highly turbulent, while in fact they are confronted with a great number of small changes which are largely predictable. For instance, the Corporate Accounts Department of the Dutch Postbank perceived fluctuations in the demand of services as highly turbulent. None the less, it appeared that this turbulence was not fundamental, but a result of ignorance of relevant data. The fluctuations were caused by promotion activities for certain special services undertaken by district offices and the introduction of new services by the Corporate Banking Division. By formalized consultations with the Corporate Banking Division and a better interchange of plans with the division manager, the management discovered that the environment was not turbulent at all. In assessing the sufficiency of management's flexibility mix we have to determine the real features of the environment.[1]

To keep the discussion of environmental turbulence within certain limits, we shall focus attention on the characteristics of environmental turbulence and identify the competitive forces that cause the environment to be perceived as turbulent. By considering various levels of aggregation, we will decompose the environment into forces which may conceivably generate turbulence. After this identification of competitive forces, we will examine which of their characteristics contribute to environmental turbulence (Sect. 7.2).

Competitive Forces at Different Levels of Aggregation

The level of competition and environmental turbulence a firm has to cope with are rooted in various competitive forces that go well beyond the established combatants in the particular firm's industry. The real environment of an organization can be examined at different levels of aggregation (Castrogiovanni, 1991: 545). At the lowest environmental level, the organization takes the raw materials, resources, and knowledge needed for its operations from the environment, and exports to the environment the products and services needed by the environment (see Fig. 7.2). At this *micro-environment level*, the focus is therefore on the concrete inputs and outputs of the primary process of the organizational unit. Most researchers from engineering and operations research focus on this level.

At the *task-environment level*, the organization unit engages in exchanges with external elements or constituents—suppliers, potential employees, financiers, distribution intermediaries, and customers—to attain the raw materials or necessary inputs and to dispose of its outputs. Note that if the unit of analysis is not autonomous but an embedded organization, that is, a department or division of a larger organization, the parent organization may function as supplier, financier, distribution intermediary, or customer. Contingency theorists consider the task environment as most important. This concept was first used by

Resolving the Paradox

Dill (1958) and later by Thompson (1967: 27–8) to denote those forces of the environment which are 'relevant' or 'potentially relevant' to goal setting and goal attainment. These authors argued that task environments could be composed of four major forces, namely (1) customers, distributors, and users; (2) suppliers of materials, labour, capital, equipment, and work space; (3) competitors for both markets and resources; and (4) regulating groups, including governmental agencies, unions, and interfirm associations.

According to Castrogiovanni's multi-level analysis (1991), however, the latter two competitive forces belong to higher environmental levels. In this connection, the *aggregation environment level* or industry level is composed of associations, interest groups, constituencies, and other sanctioning groups that influence a focal set of organizations or industry as a whole. These groups (Kotler, 1972), including competitors, customer markets, unions, and trade associations, may restrict or regulate both inputs and outputs. For example, researchers within industrial organization economics focused on industry structure and its effect on the level of competition within a given industry (Bain, 1968; Porter, 1980).[2]

At an even higher level, we can identify the *macro-environment level*, which consists of the larger societal forces that affect all the actors in the organizational unit's task and aggregation environment, namely the demographic, economic, physical, technological, political/legal, and socio/cultural forces (Kotler, 1988: 136). In the population-ecology theory, these forces receive most attention.

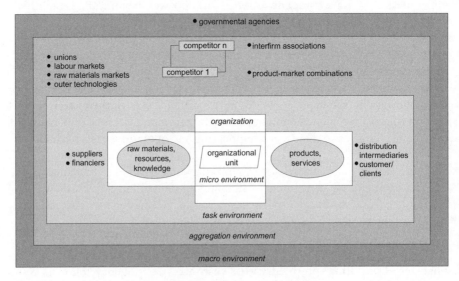

Fig. 7.2. A multi-level decomposition of the environment

Considering the above levels of aggregation, we have to select the environmental levels most important for the managerial and organization design tasks of flexibility. In our framework, we try to explain variations in the flexibility mix and the organization design of firms operating in different environments. An understanding of the level of environmental turbulence that firms face is therefore best facilitated by studying the task and micro environments. From the point of view of the firm, the core of its environment is its network of business relationships, which comprises transactions with suppliers and customers. It is advisable, however, to examine other levels in order to add richness to findings concerning the task and micro environment (Castrogiovanni, 1991). For instance, environmental forces at higher levels (macro and aggregation environment) can have transitive influences on organizations through their effects on lower-level forces (task and micro environment). On the basis of a multi-level environmental analysis, we will therefore decompose the organization's environment into competitive forces (cf. Duncan, 1972; Porter, 1980), each of which may generate environmental turbulence directly or indirectly (see Fig. 7.2).

On the input side, we can distinguish six major competitive forces:

- raw materials, resources, knowledge;
- suppliers of raw materials, labour, and know-how;
- financiers;
- labour markets;
- raw materials markets; and
- outer technologies.

In this interpretation of technology as an outer aspect (Walker, 1962),[3] technology is considered as a competitive force consisting of external know-how and concrete things which may change and influence the organization (e.g. substitute technologies, and process or product innovations).

On the output side we can distinguish four competitive forces:

- products/services;
- distribution intermediaries (middlemen or physical distribution firms);
- customers/clients groups (consumer, industrial, government and non-profit, or international); and
- product-market combinations.

Finally, there are two competitive forces which may influence inputs and outputs, namely:

- competitors (for both resources and markets); and
- regulating groups (government agencies, unions, or interfirm associations).

This decomposition of the environment into competitive forces is much more delimited in scope than the residual term 'environment', which refers to 'everything else' (Thompson, 1967: 27). With appropriate modifications of the specific forces (e.g. substituting clients for customers, services for products, and omitting distribution intermediaries), we have a useful conception of possible competitive forces a firm is confronted with. Moreover, the specific competitive forces to which the organization must respond vary from one organization to the other, and do not fit neatly with any of the typical distinctions among organizations. For instance, one organization may have to deal with turbulence generated by process innovations (outer technology), rivalry among existing competitors, and new entrants (competitors), while another is confronted with turbulence originating from scarcity of resources (raw materials), shifts in the number of suppliers (suppliers), or the introduction of substitute markets (PMCs). Knowledge of these underlying sources of competitive pressure provides the groundwork for assessing the level of environmental turbulence the firm faces.

7.2 Analysing Competitive Dynamics: Dimensions of Environmental Turbulence

Most environmental analyses end by summing up the competitive forces that determine the nature and intensity of competition and which determine profitability (Porter, 1980). They assume that the structure of competitive forces is stable and non-changing. However, a key feature of the competitive process is that competitive forces are continuously being changed, both consciously by a firm's strategic decisions and as an outcome of the competitive interaction between firms. In other words, it is not merely the competitive forces that are a reliable guide to the level of competition and environmental turbulence, but the degree of change in these competitive forces.

On the basis of the above identification of competitive forces, we will consider which characteristics of these forces contribute to turbulence. According to Khandwalla (1977: 333), a turbulent environment is a dynamic, unpredictable, expanding, fluctuating environment; it is an environment in which the competitive forces are marked by change. Emery and Trist (1965) suggested the turbulent environment had both a high degree of interconnectedness with the organization and a high degree of change itself. Babüroglu (1988) supports this view of increased complexity, relevant uncertainty, and dynamic and unexpected directionality of occurrences, but he especially accentuates the transitional state of turbulent environments. Likewise, the notion of continuous transition was proposed by Schön (1971), who coined the term 'the loss of the stable state'. More recently, D'Aveni (1994) introduced the concept of hypercompetition, which is an environment characterized by intense and rapid competitive moves, in which competitors must move quickly to build advantages and erode the advantages of their rivals.

This discussion of environmental turbulence concepts clearly illustrates that turbulence is a complex aggregate of various dimensions related to change, and that some dimensions are more important than others. In particular, task environments have been investigated with respect to a number of potentially important dimensions. For our purposes, the dimensions dealing with the static-dynamic, simple-complex, and predictable-unpredictable nature of competitive forces seem most useful. At this point of theory development, these three dimensions appear to be crucial with respect to environmental turbulence and they have the important advantage that they can be applied to all types of environments. Figure 7.3 represents all possible configurations of these dimensions regarding environmental turbulence. Although these dimensions affect environmental turbulence simultaneously, we will first consider them independently. Subsequently, we will consider their joint effects in order to develop a classification scheme for assessing the degree of environmental turbulence.

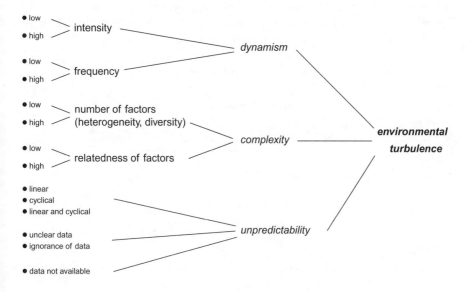

Fig. 7.3. Dimensions and variables of environmental turbulence

Dynamism

Many researchers have focused on dynamism or change as a key environmental dimension, arguing that the more variable the competitive force, the more flexibility is needed within the organization (Burns and Stalker, 1961; Dill, 1958; Duncan, 1972; Thompson, 1967). This dimension describes the degree to which competitive forces remain basically *static* over time or are in a continual process of *dynamic* change (cf. Duncan, 1972: 311). For instance, in a dynamic environment we may find changes in technologies, variations in customer preferences, fluctuations in product demand and supply of raw materials, and a continuous withdrawal or entrance of competitors. None the less, while many investigators have considered environmental dynamism, most of them have not distinguished between the rate of environmental change (frequency) and the intensity of the changes and have therefore implicitly equated the two. Burns and Stalker (1961), for example, focused only on the rate of change in the commercial and technical conditions that the firms investigated had to cope with. Similarly, Dill (1958) emphasized only the rapidity of shifts in the environment. It is, however, possible to have fast-occurring changes in the environment with a low intensity (e.g. day-to-day fluctuations in demand), or substantial changes with a low frequency (e.g. a slow decrease in demand). Accordingly, we can distinguish four configurations with respect to environmental dynamism (see Table 7.1). In ranking these configurations of environmental dynamism, we assume that frequent changes with a low intensity and infrequent changes with a high intensity result in the same scores with respect to environmental dynamism.

TABLE 7.1. Ranking configurations of environmental dynamism

Environmental dynamism

Frequency	Intensity	Score
−	−	1
+	−	2
−	+	2
+	+	3

Note: + = high − = low

Complexity

In addition to dynamism, theorists (Dill, 1958; Duncan, 1972; Lawrence and Lorsch, 1967; Thompson, 1967) have stressed the complexity of the environment. Once again, however, their studies are somewhat confusing. Most of them have considered only the numbers of factors involved concerning a particular competitive force. The larger the number of factors involved, the more complex the environment. It seems correct to state that this subdimension of complexity corresponds to the diversity dimension mentioned by Lawrence and Lorsch (1967), Khandwalla (1977), and Mintzberg (1979), and the heterogeneity dimension mentioned by Thompson (1967) and Dill (1958). An organization which offers a broad range of special products and services, which is confronted with a broad range of clients, which is active in a variety of quite distinct markets and geographic areas, and which also has to deal with many suppliers and multiple technologies clearly functions in a heterogeneous or diverse environment. For each competitive force (as exemplified above for suppliers, technologies, products/services, clients, and markets), such an organization has to consider many factors.

None the less, we agree with Lawrence (1981), in his evaluation of the Harvard Organization and Environment Program, that not only the number of factors but the interdependencies of these factors contribute to environmental complexity. When there are few interdependencies between the many factors of a competitive force, they can be easily divided into homogeneous segments. This principle is in line with Thompson's proposition (1967: 70) that organizations focusing on heterogeneous task environments seek to identify homogeneous segments. For instance, when a firm has to deal with many unrelated products or services, it can segment them into product groups, or when a firm faces different clients (industrial, consumer, governmental) it can segment them into different client groups. In these situations, there is little complexity. However, when there are strong relations between the many factors, segmentation is not possible anymore. In this situation, the environment is very complex. When a firm has many markets together with large substitution effects between them, the complexity regarding product-market combinations is high. Promoting product market A may have negative consequences for product market B. This second subdimension of environmental complexity—the relatedness of factors within competitive forces—is very similar to Perrow's (1970) dimension of analysability.

To sum up, the complexity of the environment depends on the number of factors within a competitive force and their relatedness, and can range from *simple* to *complex*. There are thus four possible configurations regarding environmental complexity (see Table 7.2). In our ranking of these configurations of complexity, we assume that competitive forces with many factors but weak interdependencies are less complex than competitive forces with few factors but strong relations. The former allows decomposition into simple segments, while the latter does not.

Unpredictability

Finally, the unpredictability dimension has received by far the most attention in research on organizational environments and the consequent need for

TABLE 7.2. Ranking configurations of environmental complexity

Environmental complexity

Number of factors	Relatedness of factors	Score
−	−	1
+	−	2
−	+	3
+	+	4

Note: + = high − = low

flexibility (cf. Eppink, 1978; Krijnen, 1979). None the less, unpredictability, uncertainty, or unfamiliarity are usually considered as a single ultimate dimension which includes the above-mentioned dimensions of dynamism and complexity (cf. Duncan, 1972; Lawrence and Lorsch, 1967). It is, however, possible to have highly dynamic and complex environments which are largely predictable. This is, for instance, an adequate characterization of the environment of Hak, a Dutch cannery of fruit and vegetables which produces a variety of products for many related markets and faces frequent, intensive, but regular changes in supply and demand. Under such circumstances, the organization does not actually confront uncertainty, as managers feel reasonably confident about the sort of environmental conditions they will face in the future. In our conceptualization of environmental turbulence, unpredictability is therefore a separate dimension which reflects the extent to which cause-effect relationships concerning competitive forces are incomplete (Thompson, 1967: 85). In unpredictable environments, developments within competitive forces have multiple effects with ramifications in different directions and at varying distances into the future.

The unpredictability dimension can range from *predictable* to *unpredictable*. When transitions (of factors) within competitive forces are linear, or cyclical, or both linear and cyclical, management can extrapolate past developments. In such environments, in which cause-effect relationships are specified, management can anticipate future developments. For example, the seasonal demand patterns of the Dutch cannery Hak are predictable, and the need for structural and strategic flexibility is therefore minimal.

Nevertheless, there is a lack of clarity of information in many environments (Lawrence and Lorsch, 1967: 27); data concerning future developments are unclear. For example, the future might show trend breaks or discontinuities, but it is unknown when and in which direction these will occur. Similarly, data

regarding product-life cycles or the introduction of new products are ambiguous and the time span for definite feedback is very long. On the other hand,
because of limitations of scope, management may ignore certain relevant data
(Lawrence, 1981: 216). In both these situations, the environment is relatively
unpredictable. To compensate, the organization might increase its capacity to
process information which has a rather high degree of inaccuracy and uncertainty (Eppink, 1978: 58; Galbraith, 1973). For the remaining unpredictability, it
will need some flexibility.

Finally, some organizations function in competitive environments in which
data are simply unavailable. In fundamentally unpredictable environments such
as the computer and software industry, management has to develop a high
degree of flexibility.

The possible configurations of unpredictability and their ranking with respect
to the degree of unpredictability are presented in Table 7.3. When transitions
within environmental forces are linear, or cyclical, or both linear and cyclical,
environments will have low levels of unpredictability. When data concerning
future developments are unclear, or when management ignores certain relevant
data because of limitations of scope, there will be a medium level of environmental unpredictability. Finally, when data are simply unavailable, the result will
be the highest level of environmental unpredictability.

TABLE 7.3. Ranking configurations of environmental unpredictability

Environmental unpredictability

Predictable		Unpredictable			Score
linear	cyclical	data unclear	ignorance of data	data unavailable	
+	−				1
−	+				1
+	+				1
		+	−	−	2
		−	+	−	2
		−	−	+	3

Note: + = high   − = low

Assessing environmental turbulence

So far, we have considered the three dimensions of environmental turbulence separately. Yet, in examining environmental turbulence and the resulting need for flexibility, all the dimensions must be considered simultaneously. The environment is not merely relatively static or dynamic, but also relatively simple or complex, predictable or unpredictable. Hence, the degree of environmental turbulence which an organization faces is a particular configuration of the specific degrees of each of these dimensions. Moreover, while it is convenient to discuss an organization's environment as a uniform, single entity, we explained that every organization faces multiple competitive forces. Consequently, the turbulence may be high with respect to outer technologies, suppliers, and raw materials, while it may be low with respect to customers and markets. In order to determine the degree of environmental turbulence, we therefore have to cumulate scores of environmental dynamism, complexity, and unpredictability for each of the competitive forces discussed earlier.

However, not every dimension causes a similar increase of environmental turbulence. In other words, an increase of dynamism, complexity, or unpredictability certainly leads to a higher level of environmental turbulence, but not to the same extent. We claim that, for assessing environmental turbulence, the unpredictability dimensions outweigh the other dimensions. In particular, we propose that the unpredictability dimension of the environment is a more important contributor to turbulence than the dynamism dimension, while the dynamism dimension is a more important contributor to turbulence than the complexity dimension.

The latter assumption is partly validated by Duncan's empirical research (1972) into characteristics of organizational environments and their perceived environmental uncertainty. He showed that organizational decision units functioning in a dynamic-simple environment perceive more uncertainty than units functioning in a static-complex environment. However, his dynamism dimension did not distinguish predictable from unpredictable changes. In addition, Duncan did not relate these environmental characteristics to environmental turbulence, although we may assume that higher levels of uncertainty are a result of increasing turbulence.

With respect to the dominance of the unpredictability dimension, we argue that organizations functioning in a dynamic, complex environment which is largely predictable face less turbulence than organizations in a highly unpredictable environment. In a dynamic, complex, but predictable environment, there are frequent, intensive changes in many related factors. Of course, organizations in such environments are confronted with a relatively high degree of environmental turbulence, but the numerous complex, substantial changes are to some extent predictable. In response, the organization may increase its capacity for processing information (Galbraith, 1973) and develop many sophisticated routines to deal with these complex changes. Thus, organizations in dynamic, complex, but predictable environments face acceptable levels of environmental turbulence that allow them to develop operational flexibility.

In unpredictable environments, the organization is confronted with highly unfamiliar changes. When responding to these changes, the organization has no specific experience and therefore no routine answer to tackle them. The organization thus has to reduce the need for information processing and has to develop strategic and structural flexibility to facilitate radical changes in highly turbulent environments.

In order to validate the consistency of the above assumptions regarding the degree of dynamism, complexity, and unpredictability and to determine their weight for assessing environmental turbulence, we conducted a scaling experiment between two experts and a survey among strategists within Dutch firms (see Volberda and Van Bruggen, 1997). The results indicate that our conceptualization of environmental turbulence is fairly consistent. In addition, they show that our categories with respect to dynamism, complexity, and unpredictability can be reduced to the ones presented in the Tables 7.1, 7.2, and 7.3. On the basis of these empirical tests, we were able to assign cumulative turbulence scores to competitive forces, consisting of dynamism, complexity, and unpredictability scores. The above conceptualization of environmental turbulence in competitive forces and their turbulence scores permits meaningful comparisons of different kinds of competitive environments and is accurate enough to be analytically useful.

7.3 The Metaflexibility: A Managerial Process of Matching

The more turbulent the environment, the more difficult it is to handle the managerial and organization design tasks of flexibility. It is not just fast-moving, high-tech industries, such as computers, or industries shaken by deregulation, such as airlines and telecommunication, that are facing increasing environmental turbulence. For instance, D'Aveni (1994) argues that intense turbulence or hypercompetition is widespread, even in what once seemed the most sedate industries. Revolutionary technology, globalization, new business methods, radically new communication and information-processing techniques, and low-cost foreign labour are all conspiring to heat up competition everywhere in the world. The boldness and aggressiveness of dynamic movement by various competitive forces accelerates to create a condition of constant disequilibrium and

Resolving the Paradox

change. How does management succeed in matching a sufficient repertoire of flexible capabilities with an appropriate organization design in such environments?

Evidence shows that large successful European firms of the 1980s (DAF, Philips, Daimler-Benz, ICI) had great difficulty with radical competitive change (e.g. technological discontinuities, changing customer expectations, excess capacity, global competition) and that their management was unable to foresee or even understand these changes. US-based (IBM, GM, Caterpillar, Xerox, Sears, and DEC) and Japanese (NEC, Fujitsu, Matsushita, and Komatsu) firms face the same problems of inflexible designs and lack of capabilities to respond to the new competitive landscape (Hamel and Prahalad, 1994). Why did these changes in competitive forces escape systematic and persistent attention from managers?

To answer these questions regarding the managerial process of putting the building blocks of flexibility together in turbulent environments, we have to consider the fourth block of our strategic framework: metaflexibility, which is a managerial ability to resolve paradoxes. Even in turbulent environments, organizations still need operational flexibility to accomplish some of their primary functions (Ansoff, 1978). For instance, when demand increases, production levels must be raised. Otherwise, if the firm is exposed to risks associated with its dependence on a few resources, it may decide on flexible sourcing from existing suppliers or stockpiling of these essential inputs. On the other hand, organizational norms and rules and organizational designs are never perfect or complete and thus require continual monitoring and evaluation with respect to the environment. In other words, management needs structural and strategic flexibility to meet new challenges from the changing competitive forces.

These paradoxical requirements imply that there are balances to be struck if the firm wants to remain competitive. An excess of operational flexibility or totally crediting existing norms and values may finally result in a rigid organization (Weick, 1979; 1982). By contrast, a surplus of strategic and structural flexibility or totally discrediting norms, values, and associated structures may create a chaotic organization. At a higher level of the organization there must therefore be a reflective capacity to effectuate an appropriate composition of the flexibility mix and design of the organization. This so-called metaflexibility can be viewed as management's supporting monitoring system or learning system, which engages in deutero-learning (see Sect. 3.3). On the basis of reflections on the composition of the flexibility mix and design of the organization, it may help the management to develop operational flexibility for exploiting previous experiences and in order to detect causalities as well as to develop structural and strategic flexibility so that the organization can do away with obsolete structures and invalid norms and values.[4]

Static Routines, Dynamic Capabilities, and Meta-Capabilities

Instead of specialized routines or dynamic capabilities, metaflexibility builds on creative or meta-capabilities (see Table 7.4). It involves the creation, integration, and application of flexible capabilities in a flexible way by focusing on 'the flexibility of the flexibility'. It implies developing new flexible capabilities, integrating existing ones (Henderson and Cockburn, 1994), and improving or even destroying old ones in the flexibility mix. In Philips Semiconductors, for instance, management's metaflexibility resulted in a shift from operational flexibility in terms of fast changes in the volume and mix of a limited range of diodes to strategic flexibility in terms of increased product variety and fast introduction of new product types (faster higher-voltage diodes, new crystal types). Similarly, on the basis of its reflections on the division's existing repertoire of flexible capabilities, the management of the R&D division of the Dutch Gas Company decided to develop strategic flexibility in terms of programme flexibility; while the division could easily change the operational capacity between projects and form new project teams within programmes, it had severe problems initiating new programmes within the existing research and development package.

Compared with operational, structural, and strategic flexibility, metaflexibility requires higher-order learning capabilities that monitor and adapt the flexibility mix and the organization design. Such meta-capabilities are the basis of deutero-learning so vital to organizations (Bartlett, 1993; Collis, 1994). These might include the flexibility to shift between capabilities more efficiently or faster than competitors (Hayes and Pisano, 1994) or the ability to respond to or initiate radical changes so that under changing competitive forces a firm always focuses on the capability which is most relevant at a point in time (D'Aveni, 1994).

Considering the managerial requirements of dynamic capabilities as discussed in Section 5.1, metaflexibility appeals particularly to management's absorptive capacity and higher-order learning ability (see Table 7.4): the ability to access new knowledge from outside the boundaries of the firm, environmental scanning of possible technological changes or shifts in market preferences in the industry environment, and the evaluation of the implications for the organization. The results may challenge the appropriateness and durability of management's strategic schemas (Sanchez and Heene, 1996). In fact, unlearning and relearning may be one of the most important outcomes. As an illustration, the scanning of new business opportunities and the willingness of management to unlearn in KLM Cargo resulted in new managerial mindsets and a reconsideration of its dominant strategic frame. Instead of framing themselves as an airline operator of transport and distribution services, they now

TABLE 7.4. Managerial capabilities and requirements of metaflexibility compared with other flexibility types

Type of flexibility	Flexibility repertoire	Managerial requirements	Outcome
steady-state flexibility	specialized routines	• static control • limited expertise • low absorptive capacity • fixed managerial mindsets/ no experimentation • single-loop learning	increasing efficiency of response
operational, structural, and strategic flexibility	dynamic capabilities	• dynamic control • broad and deep knowledge-base • medium absorptive capacity • broad managerial mindsets/ much experimentation • double-loop learning	increasing variety and speed of response
metaflexibility	meta-capabilities	• high absorptive capacity • deutero-learning	facilitating unlearning and relearning, developing industry foresight

perceived themselves to be a provider of integrated logistics. This new strategic schema brought along a totally different perspective of competitive forces: other logistic providers such as Fedex, United Parcel Service (UPS), or Nedloyd, not the traditional airlines, became their new competitors. This unlearning of their old strategic schema and relearning of a new one required them to invest heavily in new flexible capabilities to provide a variety of customized added-value services. Furthermore, they had to fundamentally redesign their organization.

Especially in hypercompetitive environments, in which change is frequent and disruptive, metaflexibility requires the development of a supporting monitoring or learning system, particularly the intelligence-gathering and information-processing functions of management. Such a system may contribute to the firm's vision of where the next advantage will be discovered, where the company should focus its disruption, and which capabilities it does or does not need. D'Aveni (1994: 246) calls this visioning process 'strategic soothsaying', which is concerned with understanding the future evolution of markets and technology that will proactively create new opportunities to serve current or new customers. In a similar way, Hamel and Prahalad (1994) use the word 'industry foresight', meaning an ability to synthesize the collective impact of competitive forces that involves imagining the future and developing sufficient flexible capabilities and an adequate organization design.

The Process of Metaflexibility: Absorptive Capacity and Deutero Learning

To achieve metaflexibility, what matters are not only the repertoire of flexible capabilities but the absorptive capacity and deutero-learning abilities by which management accumulates and dissipates flexible capabilities. These meta-capabilities determine how flexible capabilities are expanded, developed, and redeployed. Figure 7.4 represents the phasing of the process of metaflexibility in a diagram form. In this representation, the signalling of alterations in competitive forces is of crucial importance (T0). This signalling must occur as soon as possible and is dependent on the absorptive-capacity of the management (T1). In Section 4.2 we concluded that this so-called 'warning time' is mostly negative in case of discontinuous change. When management perceives a gap between flexible capabilities and competitive forces, it should initiate adequate capabilities (acting decisively). In this connection, management must decide whether a new capability must be created or if it can limit its search to the existing capabilities of the flexibility mix. In addition, management may decide to wait until the impact has reached a certain threshold level (acting prudently). This learning process in which management reflects on its repertoire of capabilities (deutero-learning) is often very time-consuming (T2). After this process, the new capability can be activated or the chosen capability of the flexibility mix can be applied (T3). In this context, the reaction or implementation time of these capabilities is a factor which management has to take into account. The organizational barriers in technology, structure, and culture discussed in Chapter 6 can influence this implementation time. General Motors's efforts to develop flexible manufacturing capabilities based on Toyota's system of lean production is illustrative. Implementation was a slow and painful process because much of the underlying knowledge was tacit and deeply rooted in Toyota's history and culture (Grant, 1996). Finally, if other competitive forces can be isolated, management may be able to assess the effects of the capabilities activated (T4).

Besides the implementation time, Figure 7.4 clearly illustrates that the success of metaflexibility depends largely on the time which elapses between confronting the discontinuity (T0) and responding to discontinuity (T3) (Ansoff et al., 1975; Eppink, 1978). Factors related to management's absorptive capacity and deutero-learning ability may cause this retardation time (Section 4.2), namely:

Resolving the Paradox

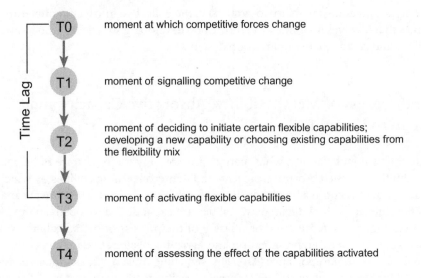

Fig. 7.4. Phases of the process of metaflexibility

- systems delay, or the time required for observing, interpreting, and transmitting the information to responsible managers;
- verification delay, or the time consumed by management for assessing the intensity, frequency, and permanence of these changing competitive forces;
- political delay, or the time required for neutralizing opposing actions of organizational participants for whom these changes might have negative consequences in terms of reputation and status;
- unfamiliarity rejection delay, or the time required for changes which do not correspond to the management's dominant frame of reference.

On the basis of metaflexibility, an adequate volume (number of capabilities) and composition (steady-state, operational, structural, strategic) of the flexibility mix can be determined. Many strategy scholars applying an evolutionary perspective (Grant, 1996; Kogut and Zander, 1992; Nelson and Winter, 1982) argue that metaflexibility is limited to deploying and extending existing flexible capabilities rather than constantly recreating new capabilities. However, firms such as Microsoft, McDonald's, Honda, and Benetton were able to continuously recreate new flexible capabilities in various competitive rounds resulting from their management's extensive absorptive capacity and learning ability. Consequently, they developed superior industry foresight and knew which flexible capabilities they did and did not need. For example, CEO Bill Gates argues that sheer size is not all positive but rather cleverness is vital in Microsoft's extremely turbulent environment (*Business Week*, 1993). Cleverness implies that when a firm has missed a business opportunity such as the Internet, it has the learning ability to readapt its strategic schema.

Alternatively, in the case of a large flexibility mix, we may presuppose that the need for metaflexibility is less relevant. For example, large resourceful firms that are confronted with deregulation and increasing competition often start with developing flexible capabilities without a clear sense which capabilities they need. Smith and Zeithaml (1996), for instance, showed that after their divestiture from AT&T, regional Bell operating companies (RBOCs) randomly developed many flexible capabilities in the unregulated side of their business without a clear strategic focus. Within British Telecom (BT), this lack of focus resulted in wasteful foreign acquisitions. In 1990, for example, BT sold its stake in Mitel, the loss-making Canadian telecom equipment manufacturer, for a quarter of the original price. Moreover, the privatized Dutch PTT Telecom developed flexible capabilities in various markets (e.g. Sport Channel 7, Unisource, and Planet Internet) that appeared to be unprofitable (Hulsink, 1996). Due to their lack of absorptive capacity and learning ability, these firms created an overkill of costly flexible capabilities to offset possible environmental disturbances. Ansoff (1980) refers to the strategy of a surplus of flexible capabilities as 'surprise management'.

Most organizations lie in between these two extremes. In many situations, their absorptive capacity and reflective learning ability is insufficient for composing an appropriate flexibility mix. In addition, the flexibility mix itself is often inadequate in proportion to the disturbances in the environment. Even in situations when the flexibility mix is more than sufficient, management has to know whether it must adapt to change or influence change. In short, every process of increasing flexibility starts with metaflexibility.

7.4 A Strategic Framework of Flexibility

In this chapter, we have further elaborated on how management can resolve the paradox of flexibility under various levels of competition. We argued that the more dynamic, complex, and unpredictable the environment, the more difficult it is to handle the management and organization design challenges. In the introduction to this chapter, we showed that this two-dimensional conception of flexibility together with the turbulence characteristics of the competitive environment can be portrayed in a basic framework of flexibility. On the basis of our detailed treatment in the preceding sections of changing competitive forces and metaflexibility, we will now present a more sophisticated version of our strategic framework of flexibility (see Fig. 7.5). This framework relates the composition of the flexibility mix and the design of organizational conditions to the degree of environmental turbulence. However, the causal connection between

Resolving the Paradox

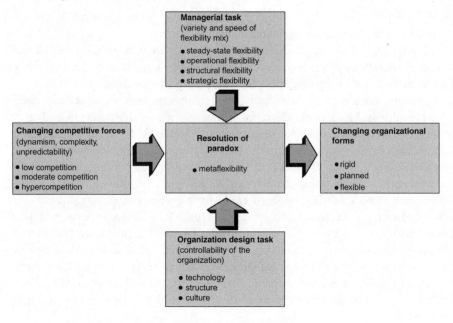

Fig. 7.5. An advanced strategic framework of flexibility

the environment and the firm is not assumed to be one way. Firms may influence their environment and vice versa. The basic assumptions of the framework are that:

1. management's flexibility mix must match the degree of environmental turbulence (*sufficiency of the flexibility mix*);
2. to activate a sufficient flexibility mix, the design of the organizational conditions must provide adequate potential for flexibility (*design adequacy of the organizational conditions*); and
3. the sufficiency of the flexibility mix and the design adequacy of the organizational conditions must be continuously matched with the degree of environmental turbulence.

The first assumption reflects the managerial task of flexibility, the second reflects the design task of flexibility, and the third indicates the difficulty of matching the two tasks in a dynamic context. From this framework we can obtain three optimal organizational forms, each of which reflects a particular way of coping with the flexibility paradox of change and preservation.

The Rigid Form under Low Competition

In a static, simple, and predictable (non-competitive) environment, the optimal organizational form employs a limited flexibility mix and has a routine technology, a mechanistic structure, and a conservative culture. In addition, the intelligence-gathering and information-processing aspects of metaflexibility are very elementary (see Fig. 7.6). This organizational form is very straightforward. In non-competitive environments, firms have established positions that enable them to develop absolute sustainable competitive advantages and generate excessive profit potential. In such environments, there is little need for managers to expend effort on a flexibility mix or for the organizational conditions to generate potential for flexibility. Too much flexibility is a nuisance. Consequently, intelligence gathering and information processing can be restricted to the primary functions of the organization.

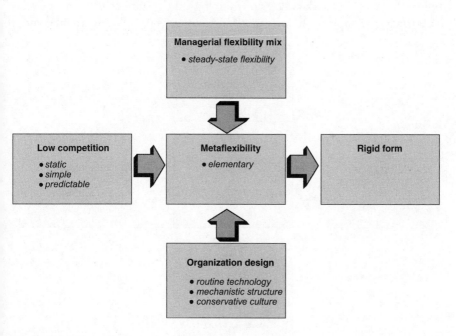

Fig. 7.6. The rigid form

The Planned Form under Moderate Competition

In a dynamic and/or complex but largely predictable (moderately competitive) environment, the optimal form employs a more comprehensive flexibility mix dominated by operational flexibility and has a less routine technology, a relatively mechanistic structure, and a conservative culture. In addition, intelligence-gathering and information-processing capacity is very extensive and directed towards the proliferation of routines (see Fig. 7.7). For survival in a dynamic and complex but largely predictable environment, managers must activate many sophisticated routines to cope with complex changes. They need a potential for operational flexibility originating from a non-routine technology. In such moderately competitive environments, firms seek to establish stable 'oligopolies' by implicit collusion or developing sustainable competitive advantages (D'Aveni, 1994: 224). The creation of strong entry and mobility barriers can reduce intra-industry rivalry. Competition may be characterized by relatively long periods of incremental, competence-enhancing changes (Tushman and Anderson, 1986). In Clark's (1985) terminology, the result of this competition is a narrowing of approach instead of the emergence of new management

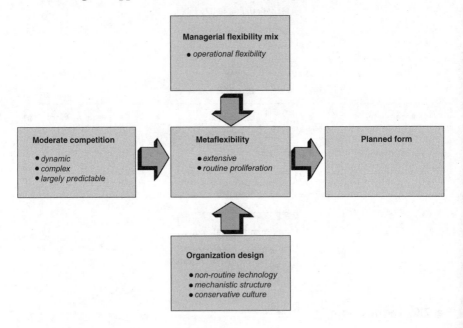

Fig. 7.7. The planned form

approaches. Although competitive changes can be very dynamic and complex, they may be predictable to a large extent and various routines (ranging from simple to sophisticated) can be developed. Management therefore needs an extensive information-processing capacity to anticipate complex changes and to facilitate the development of routines.

The Flexible Form under Hypercompetition

In a fundamentally unpredictable environment, which may also be dynamic and complex (hypercompetitive), the optimal form employs a broad flexibility mix dominated by structural and strategic flexibility and has a non-routine technology, an organic structure, and an innovative culture. The intelligence-gathering and information-processing aspects of metaflexibility are directed towards enhancing the receptiveness to new environments (see Fig. 7.8). This third organizational form suggests that, in hypercompetitive environments, management must activate both strategic flexibility and structural flexibility, which originate from innovative culture and organic structure. The escalating degree of competition results in short periods of advantage punctuated by frequent disruptions, which are associated with departures from current approaches that reduce the

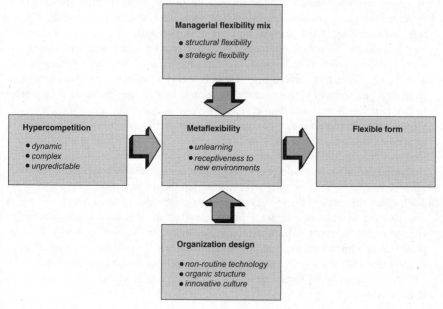

Fig. 7.8. The flexible form

Resolving the Paradox

value of established commitments and competence and require fundamentally new capabilities. The liability-of-newness problem plagues new firms confronting moderate competition within well-established markets, whereas the liability of age and tradition constrains established successful firms confronting hypercompetition (Stinchcombe, 1965; Tushman and Anderson, 1986).

Hypercompetition is facilitated by the disequilibrium-creating activities of firms that are capable of breaking new ground, pioneering new fields, promoting radical innovation, and partially or completely transforming the organization in the process. Instead of building on current routines as a part of their operational flexibility, such firms develop high levels of structural and strategic flexibility.

Notes

1. In our model, the perceived environment is manifested in the external orientation as a part of the idea system or culture of the organization. The breadth of the external orientation gives us an impression of the potential for flexibility within the organization (see Sect. 6.3).
2. The theoretical framework that developed out of this effort became known as the structure-conduct-performance model. The term 'structure' refers to industry structure, measured by factors such as number of buyers and sellers in an industry, the level of product differentiation, barriers to entry, cost structure, and vertical integration. 'Conduct' refers to firm-specific actions in an industry, including pricing behaviour, product strategy, advertising, research and development, and investment in plants and equipment. 'Performance' is related to firm performance and performance of the economy as a whole.
3. On the other hand, technology as an inner aspect (firm level) refers to the hardware (machines, equipment) and software (skills, techniques) used within the organization for transforming materials or informational inputs into outputs. In Section 6.1 we explained that inner technology is an important organizational condition which may inhibit or facilitate the flexibility potential within the organization.
4. Notice that operational flexibility, in this context, leads to monostability. As long as disturbances are not too large, a position is restored. Whenever circumstances change radically, structural and strategic flexibility are required to reach different points of equilibrium. The latter equilibrium stands for a higher level of stability, namely ultrastability. Finally, metaflexibility results in multistability, which stands for a reflective ability of management to adapt in an ultrastable way to simultaneous and different changes.

8   Towards the Flexible Form

The trouble with total flexibility is that the organization can't over time retain a sense of identity or continuity. Any social unit is defined in part by its history, by what it has done and by what it has chosen repeatedly. Chronic flexibility destroys identity. Stability provides an economical means to handle new contingencies, since there are regularities in the world that any organization can exploit if it has a memory and the capacity for repetition. However, chronic stability is dysfunctional because more economical ways of responding might never be discovered; this in turn would mean that new environmental features would never be noticed.

(Weick, 1979: 215)

Much has been written about the breathtaking changes that are redefining the competitive environment and are forcing companies in almost every sector to re-examine their flexible capabilities and organization designs. Both gigantic corporations and small firms are undertaking transformations with the intention of replacing their old bureaucratic and hierarchical structures by new, untested flexible forms. Since there are no theories of the new organizational forms and as yet no ideal-type description of the flexible form, however, managers of contemporary firms are engaged in organizational experiments without the guidance and benefits of theories and models (Daft and Lewin, 1993). For instance, do all firms have to become flexible? Is there such a thing as a permanently flexible form?

A well-established stream of research in contingency theory has examined organic forms adapted to highly complex and dynamic environments (Burns and Stalker, 1961; Duncan, 1972; Lawrence and Lorsch, 1967; Thompson, 1967). None the less, the defining characteristic of the hypercompetitive environments of today is that firms, in their struggle for control, continuously have to identify and develop new advantages, thereby creating temporary disequilibria. This dynamic process requires new organizational forms that are able to explore new opportunities effectively *and* exploit them efficiently, to change their strategic focus easily *and* develop some strategic direction, and to alter their dominating norms and values *and* correct deviations from essential norms and values. These paradoxical requirements imply that firms must strike balances if organizational forms are to remain vital. Yet doing so means that firms must reconcile the conflicting forces of change and preservation.

In the previous chapter, we developed a strategic framework that distinguishes the building blocks needed to analyse and discover new flexible forms. From this framework, we derived three optimal organizational forms that connect different types of competitive environments with effective types of flexibility and organization designs. In essence, the strategic framework clarifies the various types of flexibility held by an organization, as well as its organization design. None the less, this instrumental model ignores both the *process* of variation in the composition of the flexibility mix and the design of the organization *over time*. In other words, how does management cope with change? Our assumptions about optimal organizational forms for coping with various competitive environments (Sect. 7.4) raise serious doubts as to whether or not an organization can be permanently flexible. Shifts may occur in the level of competition, and the composition of the flexibility mix and the design variables of the organizational conditions must vary correspondingly. An ongoing process of variation in the flexibility mix and related organizational conditions is needed. In this process of change, the organization has to prevent itself from overshooting and becoming extremely rigid or chaotic (Weick, 1979; 1982).

Recently, several dynamic approaches have been suggested for coping with this paradox, such as the virtual corporation (Davidow and Malone, 1992), the dynamic network form (Miles and Snow, 1986), the hypertext organization (Nonaka and Takeuchi, 1995), the platform organization (Ciborra, 1996), and the shamrock organization (Handy, 1995). All of these approaches seem to reinforce models of flexible, fluid, and continually evolving organizations. As argued before (see Sect. 1.2), however, most of these research efforts are concerned with justifying and rationalizing the success of a particular flexible firm (e.g. Sun Microsystems, Dell computers, Sharp, Olivetti), rather than discovering new flexible forms in general. In this chapter, we will consider more systematically how organizations deal with the flexibility paradox over time. To begin this task, we use the strategic framework developed in Chapter 7 to discover various alternative flexible forms that enable firms to initiate or respond successfully to different kinds of competition (Sect. 8.1).

From this rich typology of organizational forms, trajectories of organizational 'success and failure' in meeting various levels of competition are obtained. In the old mode of competition in which firms' attention is directed towards reducing the level of competition, a natural trajectory of routinization is most likely (Sect. 8.2). This transition from a chaotic state towards a rigid organization may be regarded as a 'life cycle'. Recently established entrepreneurial firms that are steadfast in pursuing the evolution of their processes and products may find that they have achieved the benefits of high productivity and specialized routines only at the cost of decreased flexibility and innovative capacity. As a consequence, they become extremely bureaucratic firms that must face competition from innovative, flexible organizations.

In the new mode of rapid, escalating hypercompetition, a trajectory of revitalization is more likely to be successful (Sect. 8.3). Firms in hypercompetitive situations must continuously increase the variety and speed of their flexible capabilities as well as their organizational responsiveness. Many theorists doubt, however, that large, established firms can self-consciously change themselves very much or very often, or that conscious initiatives by management are likely to succeed. Others, like Kanter (1994) and Baden-Fuller and Stopford (1994), have demonstrated that mature firms can become flexible enough to balance corporate discipline with entrepreneurial creativity. In fact, there are many routes mature corporations might take to effect this goal (Volberda, 1997). On the basis of our organizational typology, we will provide a more systematic analysis of alternative trajectories directed towards the 'revitalization' of mature or declining organizations. Such trajectories are most likely to be effective in extremely turbulent environments.

8.1 A Typology of Alternative Flexible Forms

Our strategic framework shows that the managerial task and the organization design task have to be matched with various levels of competition to achieve effective flexibility (see Sects. 4.3 and 7.4). On the basis of these two central building blocks of our framework—the extensiveness of the flexibility mix and the controllability of the organizational conditions—many organizational forms are possible for coping with changing levels of competition. In addition to the three ideal types,[1] *rigid*, *planned*, and *flexible*, there is at least one other, the *chaotic* form (see Fig. 8.1). Each type represents a particular way of addressing the flexibility paradox of change versus preservation, and some types are more effective than others.

The *rigid form* has a very restricted flexibility mix and the controllability or responsiveness of the organization is low. Its flexibility mix is dominated by simple procedures (steady-state flexibility). In addition, its choice and variation possibilities are limited; improvisation is forbidden in the organization. The mature technology (routine), the functionalized and centralized structure with many hierarchical layers (mechanistic), and the monotonous and narrow-minded culture (conservative) do not allow potential for flexibility and result in a fragile and vulnerable organization. The rigid form resembles what is commonly understood to be a bureaucratic organization—that is, a large, inefficient, role-bound organization, constrained by 'red tape' and fixed procedures. It is very different from the bureaucracy form conceived by Max Weber.

The *planned form* also has a narrow flexibility mix, but its variety of routines

Towards the Flexible Form

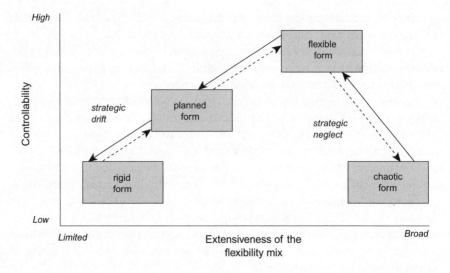

Fig. 8.1. A typology of alternative flexible forms for coping with hypercompetition

Note: ───── = natural trajectory of routinization.
- - - - - = reverse trajectory of revitalization.

and organizational responsiveness are less limited than in the rigid organization. The flexibility mix consists mainly of specific rules and detailed procedures, which are sophisticated and complex and require an extensive information-processing capacity. Moreover, for every possible change, management has developed a certain routine capability (superior operational flexibility). The rigidity of this organizational form is not a result of the technology or the basic organizational structure, but of strong process regulations such as standardization, formalization, and specialization, and very detailed planning and control systems. Moreover, the shared cultural beliefs and assumptions of its members give very little leeway for deviant interpretations of the environment, and dissonance is potentially threatening to the organization's integrity. This form resembles the 'ideal-type' bureaucracy of Weber (Perrow, 1986). As long as the organization encounters no unexpected changes, its controllability is high. However, if changes occur that are not anticipated in the planning repertoire and are threatening to the idea system shared by its members, the result is a situation known as *'strategic drift'* in which consciously managed incremental changes do not necessarily keep pace with environmental changes[2] (Johnson, 1988: 88). The incremental changes result only in further attempts by the firm to perfect its process regulations and basic beliefs and assumptions. These attempts increase organizational inertia, and rigidity sets in.

212

Examples of the planned form include the successful vertically integrated firms in the fashion apparel industry such as Giordano, The Gap, and The Limited (Richardson, 1996). By tight coupling, these firms lose some of their structural flexibility and become integrated firms that have control over manufacturing and retailing (cf. Clark, 1985; Utterback and Abernathy, 1975). Such firms are very similar to the planned form in our typology. They have operational flexibility mainly in terms of managerial routines to respond quickly, based on a non-routine technology (CAD/CAM equipment, EDI).[3] By linking design and production closely to retailing, these firms are superior at exploiting current opportunities through technological innovations known as 'quick response'.[4] None the less, their structural and strategic flexibility for developing new opportunities is low. Richardson's study (1996) shows that the exploitation of time and response opportunities requires further integration and may lead to new rigidities. Planned firms thus run the risk of being outperformed by flexible de-integrated firms that have more structural and strategic flexibility.

The *flexible form* has an extensive flexibility mix dominated by strategic and structural flexibility. In addition, its ability to change its organizational conditions is reasonably high. It adapts effectively to disturbances without the organization losing its distinctiveness. Resistance to signals of threat to the idea system is low; the firm can constructively incorporate new perspectives. It implements change easily through adaptations within the current (non-routine) technology and (organic) structure. At the same time, it develops some dominance over its environment to preserve its identity, and effects a balance between change and preservation.

The social network firm (Liebeskind *et al.*, 1996; Powell, 1990) and the cluster organization (Hanssen-Bauer and Snow, 1996) closely resemble the flexible form. Liebeskind and her co-authors argued that the social network is an appropriate organizational mode for sourcing scientific knowledge in the biotechnology industry. This form differs from hierarchy and market-exchange forms in the sense that it has a high degree of structural and strategic flexibility. It is characterized by a redeployable technology and an organic structure, but has strong ties between actors as a result of a strong professional culture. New biotechnology firms in a social network have much room to manoeuvre, but also preserve some commonly shared social norms. In other words, the network requires its members to have both a willingness to change and to renew and at the same time an unconditional commitment, concern, and loyalty to the social norms. The regional cluster organization, such as Norvest Forum Inc. in Norway (Hanssen-Bauer and Snow, 1996), might also be considered a flexible form. This cluster of forty-six small and medium-sized firms provides much strategic leeway for participating regional firms, while preserving both the social norms and structural relationships between them.

Finally, the *chaotic form* has a very extensive flexibility mix dominated by strategic flexibility, but is totally uncontrollable. In organizations with this form, the possibilities for variation are unlimited because there is no anchorage within a set of basic organizational conditions. The innumerable initiatives for change are impossible to implement. Chaotic organizations have no distinct technology, stable administrative structure, or basic shared values stemming from their organizational culture. Consequently, the environment can push a chaotic organization in any direction. In other words, the organization is controlled by the environment. A chaotic organization's lack of administrative stability is caused by *strategic neglect*, which denotes the deliberate tendency of managers not to pay attention to the administrative structure of the organization (Burgelman, 1983: 234–7). Strategic neglect can lead to severe and disruptive administrative problems. In his study of new internal corporate ventures, Burgelman concluded that the inherent administrative instability of these ventures is often exacerbated by the lack of strong strategic orientation that can address opportunistic behaviour by participants in the ventures. The range of possible capabilities that a chaotic form can develop is so large that making a choice is very difficult and managers' decision-making capacity is greatly reduced (Eppink, 1978; Scott, 1965).

The term 'chaotic form' generally has a negative connotation, but Smith and Zeithaml (1996) showed that it can help firms that are facing advancing hyper-competitive conditions to explore new opportunities. By examining how two regional Bell operating companies created new capabilities in their telecommunication service industry, they argued that resource-rich firms can use chaotic forms to develop new capabilities in their unregulated business. In their research, the chaotic forms were characterized by no clear agreement on outcomes, uncrystallized or problematic relations between means and ends, and a lack of focused strategy (cf. Hrebiniak and Joyce, 1985).

Of course, other combinations of levels of managerial flexibility and controllability beyond the four forms considered here are possible. One might think of the hollow corporation in the left upper corner in the typology; that form is highly controllable but the managerial flexibility repertoire of participating firms is restricted. The applied logic of discovery, however, can never be as comprehensive as reality. None the less, the four-cell typology of organizational forms is important for understanding the process of variation in the composition of the flexibility mix and the design of the organization over time. No such system of categorization related to flexibility has been proposed in the study of organizations. Forms are currently identified through typologies such as mechanistic-organic and bureaucratic-professional, or through empirically developed typologies. Although these fragmentary typologies contribute rich insights into flexible technologies, structures, and cultures, they are often not complex enough or sufficiently developed to permit a very comprehensive analysis of organizational flexibility. Consequently, the difference between the planned form (in which operational flexibility dominates) and the flexible form (in which structural and strategic flexibility dominate) is frequently unclear or confusing. For instance, the vertically integrated firm is perfectly able to exploit quick-response routines. Its superior operational flexibility enables it to identify mistakes and take corrective actions quickly. None the less, its structural and strategic flexibility diminishes because of its increased commitment to irreversible resources. In contrast, the social network firm has high levels of structural and strategic flexibility that enable it to engage more easily in radical new developments. Both the integrated firm and the social network are flexible, but in totally different ways.

8.2 Routinization of Entrepreneurial Firms: Decreasing Levels of Competition

The typology illustrates that none of the forms is a permanent solution to the flexibility paradox of change versus preservation. In both the rigid and the planned forms, there is a lack of structural and strategic flexibility caused by a preference for preservation rather than change. In the flexible and the chaotic forms, the dominance of structural and strategic flexibility indicates a competency for change. Yet the typology gives trajectories for coping with competitive change. Table 8.1 provides some examples of these trajectories of transformations based on empirical studies in two RBOCs (Smith and Zeithaml, 1996), vertically integrated firms in the fashion apparel industry (Richardson, 1996), two firms, Asahi and Kirin, in the Japanese beer industry (Craig, 1996), and flexibility audits in Philips Semiconductors, the Dutch Postbank, and the Dutch National Gas Corporation (Volberda, 1997).

The most likely trajectory firms go through is a transition from a chaotic state to flexible, planned, and rigid forms (see Fig. 8.2). During this process of decreasing levels of competition, management's increased capacity to process information (metaflexibility) facilitates the proliferation of routines, thus creating natural trajectories. These trajectories correspond with those in Nelson and Winter's evolutionary theory (1982), which holds that radical change becomes less possible as the organization ages (Rumelt, 1987: 151).

The natural trajectory of routinization suggests that new entrepreneurial firms and new ventures operate chaotically in order to develop new capabilities. In this earliest stage of perfect competition, superior organizations have to develop strategic flexibility in their flexibility mix to become more sensitive to the possibilities for creating 'new combinations'. In this 'fluid' period of development, performance criteria for new products are not well defined and market needs or process difficulties are approached through a variety of different product or equipment designs. In addition, the production process is often

TABLE 8.1. Trajectories for coping with competitive change

	Rigid-planned	Planned-flexible	Flexible-chaotic
Routinization (←)	*Strategic drift*	*Maturation* • exploitation of time and response opportunities in the fashion apparel industry resulting in further integration of firms	*Strategic focus* • identification of capabilities created within unregulated businesses of two RBOCs forced by top management intervention
Revitalization (→)	*Professional revitalization* • RBOCs becoming more market-driven in their core activities after divestiture • the Dutch National Postbank's movement from standardized to customized services	*Entrepreneurial revitalization* • ability of two firms in the Japanese beer industry to create new capabilities and to carry out radical internal change • transition of Philips Semiconductors from a bureaucratic and conservative to an innovative and responsive company	*Strategic neglect* • lack of administrative structures and a shared culture within the R&D Department of Dutch National Gas Corporation

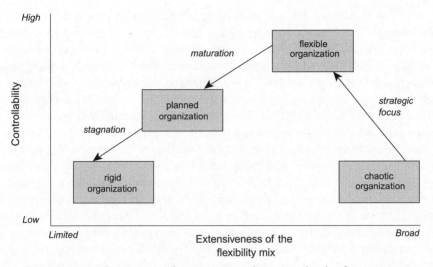

Fig. 8.2. The natural trajectory of routinization: decreasing levels of competition

highly flexible, relatively labour intensive, and somewhat erratic in work flow. In this uncoordinated state, innovation is relatively rapid and fundamental. Furthermore, the information-processing capacity of the organization is very inchoate and driven by obscure market needs or new opportunities.

Smith and Zeithaml's (1996) study on the international expansion of two RBOCs illustrates these points (see Table 8.1). These RBOCs were ill prepared for competition after divestiture, but their top managers allowed chaotic forms in the unregulated side of their business. This state of loose and unsettled relationships is organic and responds easily to environmental change, but necessarily has slack and is inefficient (Utterback and Abernathy, 1975: 641). To 'get off the ground', this form must be sufficiently well organized to change from a chaotic state of random, disconnected, and uncoordinated impulses. This transition requires a capacity for achieving some degree of *strategic focus*. Smith and Zeithaml's (1996) study showed how strategic flexibility was created from the firms' chaotic international expansion activities. Yet the new capabilities could not be utilized at either firm because these companies did not have the technology, administrative structures, and shared values required to implement this flexibility. The new strategic capabilities of the RBOCs could be deployed only through top management's *focus* on certain types of telecom services, project types, and countries and through drastic changes in organizational design. The chaotic forms are moving towards more flexible forms in which prior experiences with the chaotic forms can be maximally exploited.

As the level of competition decreases, the flexible organization faces a crisis.

Towards the Flexible Form

It must become more efficient in its operations to extract greater benefit from the changes that it introduced previously, and to exploit its existing knowledge and opportunities. These change efforts are particularly important if the organization is to stay ahead of its imitators and other competitors,[5] which are busy enhancing their competencies. The organization must now focus on creating a greater degree of internal 'balance', stability, and focus than is possible in the 'flexible' mode of organization. The transition from a flexible form towards a planned form can be portrayed as a process of *maturation* (Miller and Friesen, 1980: 285), which creates a greater need for the firm to professionalize and institutionalize its intelligence-gathering and information-processing functions, and to integrate the efforts of its decision-makers by formal means (process regulations). Whereas managers in the flexible form may have gathered information quite informally on their own (rudimentary metaflexibility), the firm must now set up systems and departments to gather certain types of information routinely and to disseminate this information to appropriate decision-makers (extensive metaflexibility). At this stage, the organization therefore needs to be able to codify its metaflexibility appropriately, so as to improve its capacity to plan, monitor, and control its environment, and to implement decisions and procedures which can help it reduce the level of environmental turbulence.

Thus, the 'planned' organization is able to alertly exploit existing knowledge and opportunities because it has the appropriate (conservative) culture, (mechanistic) structure (in terms of many process regulations and detailed planning and control systems), and a high level of operational flexibility which has been adapted to match the needs of the situation. In addition, it has a moderately high degree of controllability, which permits it to pursue the opportunities still emanating from the moderate level of competition by undertaking further adaptations in its technology, organizational structure, and culture. This trajectory of maturation can be seen in Richardson's (1996) study, where the vertically integrated firm gained more competitive advantage from current technological opportunities (CAD/CAM, EDI) than the more flexible de-integrated firms (see Table 8.1). However, in the process of adapting and refining the organizational conditions to efficiently exploit time and response opportunities, the planned organization runs the risk of losing its strategic and structural flexibility as it concentrates increasingly on accumulating and optimizing a large number of operational procedures and routines (operational flexibility). In such circumstances, it may become progressively more rigid.

In this progression towards *stagnation* (Miller and Friesen, 1980: 283–4), the routinization and systematization of organizational conditions bring bureaucratic momentum, traditions, and resistance to change. These all play an important role in boosting conservatism. As a result, the rigid form is characterized by a reduced emphasis on product-market innovation, risk-taking, and proactiveness. In addition, its information-processing capacity is restricted (elementary metaflexibility), and it rarely scans the environment. The rigid form has pursued the development of specialized routines at the cost of decreased flexibility and innovative capacity.

8.3 Revitalization of Large Established Firms: Escalating Levels of Competition

It is important to note that, in the natural trajectory of routinization, transitions from one stage to the next are smooth or evolutionary. Incremental changes and developments, rather than jumps and discontinuities, are typical of the process.[6] For many organizations, the transition from a chaotic state towards a rigid organization can be regarded as a natural trajectory. A transition in the reverse direction can also be perceived as a trajectory, though it may not be as easy to achieve or seem as 'natural' as the former process (see Fig. 8.3). Such trajectories of revitalization, initiated for creating temporary disequilibria, are most likely to be effective under situations of hypercompetition. Some examples are again provided in Table 8.1.

On the basis of our organizational typology, we will provide a conceptual foundation in this section for management efforts directed towards 'revitalization' and the 'turnaround' of mature or declining organizations. The dangers for

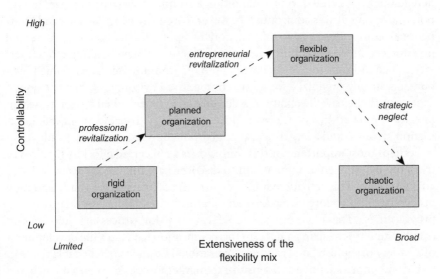

Fig. 8.3. The reverse trajectory of revitalization: escalating levels of competition

Towards the Flexible Form

rigid organizations in non-competitive environments stem from their increasing vulnerability to the occurrence of major change in their environments, and from the exhaustion of profitable opportunities obtainable in these niches. As these organizations are confronted by low and diminishing returns from established product lines and rapidly escalating competition from numerous rivals in the same field, they must seek to exploit opportunities flowing from more unstable environments, or attempt to generate major innovations. Confronted with escalating levels of competition, they face the task of shifting back towards the flexibility mix and the organizational conditions of the planned organization. This transition, or *professional revitalization*, involves the comprehensive and often dramatic movement away from traditions, conservatism, and rigidity and towards adaptiveness, vigilance, and diversification (Miller and Friesen, 1980: 281).

Smith and Zeithaml's (1996) description of the transformation within the core activities (local telephone service activities) of the RBOCs after divestiture seems to expand this trajectory (see Table 8.1). During their hundred-year history in AT&T, the rigid forms had functioned in the context of a monopoly. In 1982, however, the seven RBOCs were jolted from their rigid existence in AT&T. After divestiture, their core activities seemed to be moving towards the planned form. The same trajectory was evident within the Administrative Department of the Dutch National Postbank (see Table 8.1), which was recently privatized (Volberda, 1992). In the past, its main line of business had been retail banking because of restrictions imposed by the Dutch government. It provided mostly standardized services to more than six million account holders. After it was deregulated, it intended to provide more customized services as a part of corporate banking. It was confronted, however, with increasing national and international competition, new information technologies in banking, increased pressure on interest margins, and the introduction of new banking-related services. The Administrative Department of Corporate Accounts, which was bureaucratically organized for a non-competitive environment, had to adopt a more comprehensive flexibility mix dominated by operational flexibility, which in turn originated from a more adaptive technology (broadly applicable information systems) and a larger operational production repertoire by employees.

Perhaps most important for this transition is a concerted effort by the firm to track the external environment and to discover new market forces in order to adapt to them. This activity requires the firm to codify its limited basic scanning procedures into a more formalized set of information-gathering and processing programmes. The resulting increased capacity for processing information (metaflexibility) the firm gains from this codification facilitates the development of a variety of sophisticated routines (operational flexibility) that enable the firm to become more adaptive and sensitive to market forces. As a consequence, the organization offers a broader, more diverse product line with a shorter life cycle, and it becomes more aggressive and innovative in dealing with competitors and more imaginative in meeting the needs of customers. This non-routinization of technology increases the administrative complexity of the task of running the firm, however, thus requiring highly developed intelligence systems and more structural process regulations (formalization, standardization, specialization). Ad hoc committees become standing committees, and performance appraisals become routine and systematized. In addition, the firm's activities usually call for a higher level of expertise than was available within the rigid form, and so the level of professionalization within the firm increases.

When professional revitalization proves inadequate, the planned organization must transform itself further into a more flexible form. The planned form faces some constraints stemming from the combined effects of its surplus operational flexibility, mechanistic structure, and its relatively conservative culture. Although planned forms have developed a great number of complex routine capabilities, they are seriously handicapped when confronted with hypercompetition. Increasing the number of routine capabilities merely results in a suppression of choice. Moreover, the form's strong process regulations and tight planning and control systems serve to focus attention. Thus, the planned organization has to enhance its receptiveness to change by reducing its number of routines. In doing so, the organization should try to create greater structural and strategic flexibility. Strategic flexibility encourages the exploration of new opportunities or new ideas, while structural flexibility facilitates the restructuring of the organization in line with these new opportunities or ideas.

This change in the composition of the flexibility mix can be realized only if the organization moves towards even more flexible or multipurpose technologies, develops a more organic structure, and adopts a more heterogeneous, open, and externally oriented culture. Such efforts help to promote asymmetry within the previous organizational form while propelling the organization towards the creation of new temporary advantages better suited to hypercompetitive environments. This process of *entrepreneurial revitalization* is promoted by such changes as new leadership composed of visionary entrepreneurs, reduction of process regulations (specialization, formalization), loose basic organizational forms (grouping by target market, flat structure, and broad management tasks), a more open external orientation, and a high tolerance for ambiguity.

This kind of transition is perfectly described in Craig's (1996) study on hypercompetition in the Japanese beer industry (see Table 8.1). For a long time, this industry was a stable oligopoly in which competition was limited to well-understood non-price dimensions (moderate competition). The hypercompetitive behaviour of one firm with declining market share (Asahi), however, escalated the level of competition at the industry level. The only firms that could respond were those that could revitalize their cultures (e.g. through corporate identity campaigns, empowerment) and structures (redrawing organizational boundaries between marketing and production, shifting from functional to product-division structure, new evaluation and reward systems).

A similar transition occurred within Philips Semiconductors (Volberda, 1992; 1996b). The rapidly escalating competition in cost and quality (price erosion and unforeseen volume developments) and in timing and know-how (introduction of plastic diodes, release of higher voltages version, new crystal types, and the advance of integrated circuits in the application markets) forced the firm to increase its structural and strategic flexibility to more easily exploit unknown opportunities in those hypercompetitive areas. It effected this entrepreneurial revitalization by radically transforming itself from a bureaucratic, conservative company into an innovative and responsive one (see Table 8.1). Managers initiated autonomous task groups, created interdisciplinary marketing-production-development teams, used less formal planning and control systems, developed a unique logo for the plant, and organized social events, special training, and a news bulletin for employees. The combination of these efforts made the transformation possible.

These transitions from 'planned' to 'flexible' organizations significantly alter existing cultures and structures, and violate the established operational capabilities and specialized routines in an organization. For that reason, much resistance to efforts to transform the organization can be expected. If the resistance is successful, it will lead to organizational failure when there is hypercompetition. However, if the organization successfully transforms itself, it faces the opposite danger of overshooting its target and becoming chaotic. For example, the R&D Department of the Dutch National Gas Corporation had unlimited potential for flexibility, but managers could not capitalize on it (Volberda, 1992). In other words, the department was too flexible (see Table 8.1). The department had many initiatives for new research, but it could not implement them because it had no clear administrative structures or shared values stemming from its culture. Nor did it have adequate information about man-hours, costs, or technical progress per project. The schizophrenia of the department resulted in distorted information that managers could not use to make appropriate decisions. Consequently, various environmental forces (board, internal clients) could force the department in any direction. This *strategic neglect* resulted in a lack of decisiveness about research priorities, a fragmented structure, and a loose constellation of subcultures. As Kanter (1988: 195) pointed out, creating change requires some stability. Organizational structures and cultures must allow continuity and preserve the organization in the midst of change. In particular, Kanter proposed that strong social ties and strong beliefs in fundamental values create stability for the organization. If successful revitalization is not anchored in stability, it runs the danger of provoking chaos. On the basis of the typology and trajectories considered in this chapter, we provide a systematic method in Chapter 9 that helps managers revitalize their corporation.

Notes

1. In this typology, an ideal type is an intellectual construct for studying the variety and change of real organizations in terms of their flexibility mix and organizational conditions. Obviously, an 'ideal' type of organization in this sense is not necessarily 'ideal' in the eyes of those who manage organizations or those who are managed by organizations (Lammers, 1987: 5). The positive or negative connotations of terms like 'rigid' and 'flexible' are misleading in so far as they suggest desirability or lack thereof.

2. On the basis of three longitudinal case studies, Johnson (1988: 88) demonstrated that the phenomenon of 'strategic drift' can be accounted for as follows:
   - the sensing of external stimuli is muted because the stimuli are not in line with the organization's dominant idea system;
   - managers believe they are adapting to a changing environment while they are in fact adapting to signals which coincide with their idea system;
   - there is likely to be resistance to 'deviant' interpretations of the environment if they threaten the idea system. This resistance results in political pressure for conformity or marginal adjustment of strategy;
   - strategic drift is not easily discerned by managers. However, in the event of its detection, remedial action is likely to take the form of solutions constructed within the bounds of the existing idea system;
   - moreover, these adjustments may be enough to demonstrate the efficacy of the action to the satisfaction of the stakeholders since, given the application of the familiar, there is a good chance that there will be some signs of performance improvement, at least in the short term.

3. CAD/CAM equipment facilitates the design process as well as the transfer of designs to the manufacturer where programmable cutting and, to some extent, sewing machines are used. EDI links enable electronic transfer of information between separate facilities and companies involved in the production process. Orders and POS (point of sale) data can be transmitted electronically from the retailer to the manufacturer.

4. The use of vertically integrated forms in order to exploit quick response capabilities (operational flexibility) is not unique to fashion apparel and can be found in many other industries, such as the car industry (e.g. Chrysler) or the retail industry (e.g. Wal-Mart).

5. In Section 3.4, we pointed out that the originators of new opportunities (transition from chaotic to flexible) can be referred to as Schumpeterian entrepreneurship, while the exploitation of these available opportunities in a moderately competitive environment (transition from flexible to planned) is undertaken by Austrian entrepreneurs. For a more elaborate discussion of the various organizational forms with respect to flexibility and their modes of entrepreneurship, see Volberda and Cheah (1993).

6. This incremental view of change has been discussed in Section 3.3 (single-loop learning) and Section 3.4 (incremental innovations).

9   How to Improve the Firm's Flexibility: Tools and Techniques

> [J]udgements about flexibility options tend to be subjective and informal.
> Flexibility levels are rarely monitored or even measured
>
> (Aaker and Mascarenhas, 1984: 75)
>
> The various approaches to achieve flexibility should be systematically
> explored. A flexibility audit can illuminate areas of risk and stimulate strate-
> gic action. The monitoring of the flexibility associated with a key area of the
> firm's operations can be worthwhile. In any case, the measurement task
> needs to be addressed.
>
> (Ibid. 81)

So far, we have developed a strategic framework of flexibility that highlights the
building blocks necessary for creating flexible firms. From this framework, we
constructed a rich typology of alternative flexible forms. Using this typology, we
explored different trajectories of organizational development over time, especially those relating to revitalization. These trajectories gave us insight into both
methods for building flexible firms, and how to transform these organizations
so that they can deal with the tensions of flexibility over time.

In this chapter, we focus more on the process of diagnosing and improving
flexibility, and the organization of this process of change. Using the strategic
framework and the typology we have developed, we provide tools and techniques for supporting management efforts directed towards 'revitalizing'
mature or declining organizations and 'routinizing' chaotic organizations. In
particular, we describe flexibility audit and redesign (FAR), a method for diagnosing organizational flexibility and guiding the transition process. This method
uses the building blocks of the strategic framework and related data-gathering
and data-analysis instruments to assess an organization's actual flexibility and, if
necessary, to find ways to increase its flexibility. In this process, the actual flexibility mix and the flexibility potential within the client organization are compared to the required flexibility mix, which is derived from an assessment of the
turbulence in the environment. The FAR method thus pinpoints how an organization should create new flexible capabilities (managerial task) and reconfig-

ure itself to reduce certain technological, structural, or cultural barriers (organization design task).

Below, we shall explicitly describe the empirical claims of the FAR method and explain the constraints of the method in terms of its organizational reach and the required qualifications of the user (Sect. 9.1). After that, we shall develop the instructions for using the FAR method in the various phases of the process of flexibility improvement: orientation (Sect. 9.2), diagnosis (Sect. 9.3), and transition (Sect. 9.4). We present the relevant observation and analysis instruments for each phase. We then give a concise presentation of FARSYS, an advice support system, which helps the consultant to apply the FAR method (Sect. 9.5). In the final section (Sect. 9.6), we discuss an applied test of the FAR method and related support system, FARSYS, in a longitudinal study of three firms that were confronted with changing competitive environments, and show the diagnostic findings of the application of the FAR method in these corporations.

9.1 The Flexibility Audit and Redesign Method

Thus far, we have developed a theoretical basis for the paradox of flexibility (Chs. 2 and 3), a strategic framework for building flexible organizations (Chs. 4, 5, 6, and 7), and an organizational typology for transforming flexible firms (Ch. 8). In this section, we integrate the underlying theory, framework, and typology in a process model of flexibility improvement (see Fig. 9.1). This process model, along with the observation and analysis instruments, forms the basis of a method for diagnosing organizational flexibility and guiding the transition process.[1]

The FAR method provides the practitioner with instructions for systematically describing, analysing, and assessing the organization's actual flexibility relative to its desired flexibility. Moreover, this method helps the consultant derive recommendations for changing management's flexibility mix and redesigning the organization. In the various phases of improving flexibility, the FAR method poses the following questions.

Orientation

What is the point of departure of the organization (category of organization; stakeholder analysis; adequacy of flexibility label; boundary decisions; history)?

How to Improve the Firm's Flexibility

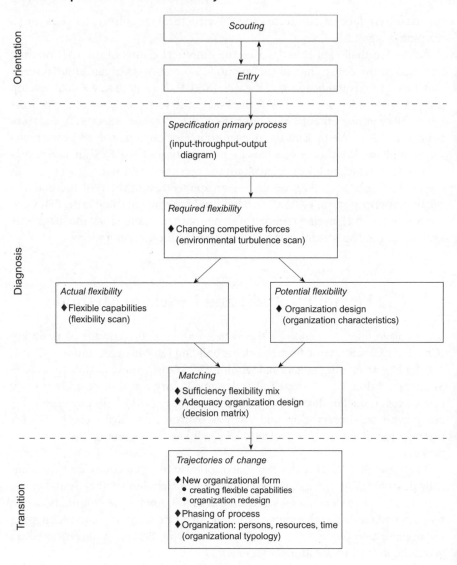

Fig. 9.1. The process model of the FAR method

Analysis

How does the firm put the building blocks of flexibility together?

- What are the inputs, throughputs, and outputs of the organization and which external elements or constituents are important for attaining these inputs and disposing of the outputs (specification of primary process)?

- How flexible does the organization have to be (desired state depending on the degree of environmental turbulence)?
- How flexible is the organization at the moment (current state based on the actual flexibility mix)?
- What is the organization's flexibility potential (flexibility potential within the organizational conditions)?

Assessment

Are there gaps between the required flexibility, the actual flexibility, and the potential flexibility (discrepancy analysis)?

- Is management's flexibility mix sufficient (required versus actual flexibility)?
- Is the organization design adequate (required versus potential flexibility)?
- What information activities are insufficient (metaflexibility)?

Transition

How should a more flexible organization be created?

- What are the relevant flexibility types for improving management's flexibility mix (operational, structural, strategic, and metaflexibility)?
- What are possible design variables for varying the flexibility potential of the organization (technological, structural, and/or cultural design variables)?
- What steps have to be taken (trajectories of change)?
- What persons and resources should be involved and at what time (management of change)?

Before discussing the instructions for using the FAR method and presenting the related data-gathering and data-analysis instruments, we shall consider the method's empirical claims and constraints in terms of its organizational reach and the required qualifications of the user.

The Empirical Claim

The flexibility audit and redesign method supports the manager or consultant in:

- generating a diagnosis of actual flexibility from a perspective of effectiveness;
- specifying areas of attention for management in order to improve management's flexibility mix;
- providing recommendations for organizational redesign in order to accomplish this improvement.

How to Improve the Firm's Flexibility

First, the application of the FAR method results in an assessment of the sufficiency of the flexibility mix (managerial task) and the design adequacy of the organizational conditions (organization design task). These assessments are founded on the basic assumptions of our strategic framework as specified in Section 7.4. This assessment has four possible diagnoses.

1. The flexibility mix may be sufficient and the flexibility potential adequate (flexible form). In this ideal situation, no management or redesign actions have to be taken.
2. The actual flexibility mix may be insufficient while the flexibility potential inherent in the organizational conditions is adequate. In this situation, flexibility improvement is a managerial task, requiring management to activate flexible capabilities.
3. The flexibility mix may be insufficient and the flexibility potential inadequate (rigid form). In this case, flexibility improvement is both a managerial and an organization design challenge. To increase its repertoire of flexible capabilities, management must enlarge the flexibility potential of the organization by loosening the organizational conditions, that is, creating a less routine technology, a more organic structure, and innovative culture.
4. The flexibility mix may be sufficient, while the flexibility potential may be far too large (chaotic state). In this exceptional case, flexibility improvement is an organization design challenge which involves the tightening of organizational conditions, that is, creating a more routine technology, mechanistic structure, and conservative culture.

Our second claim implies that the FAR method informs management of relevant flexibility aspects (e.g. suppliers, labour markets, production, personnel), types of flexibility, and information activities for flexibility improvement. Our third claim is that by locating organizations on the various dimensions of technology, structure, and culture, the FAR method supports management in selecting the appropriate design variables for varying the firm's flexibility potential and thus achieving flexibility improvement.

Constraints

These claims can be guaranteed only if the unit of analysis meets the following conditions, which act as constraints on the *organizational reach* of the FAR method:

- the unit of analysis must be an independent organization, or an organizational partsystem that is relatively autonomous.

In this context, relative autonomy means that the unit of analysis must generate a clear product or service through its own specific activities. This requirement means the unit of analysis can be distinguished from its environment, including other organizational units. Otherwise, the FAR method cannot be used because the organizational unit has no control over all the elements of its primary activity. For instance, a flexibility audit of a new Value-Added Services (VAS) department within PTT Telecom indicated the flexibility of this department was severely limited because it was highly dependent on other departments that provided knowledge and resources. A useful audit required a higher level of analysis in which these other departments were also included. Thus, the boundaries of attention must be defined carefully.

Besides constraints in terms of the organizational reach of the FAR method, there are also constraints concerning the *required qualifications of the user*:

- the users of the FAR method, who may be competent managers or qualified consultants, have to possess at least a professional quality orientation and apply a mixed expert/process approach.

We found that consultants with a strongly client-oriented quality orientation together with an exclusive process approach do not apply specific analytical frameworks or typologies (Volberda, 1992). In their view of flexibility improvement, both the process and product have to be defined by the client. Consequently, the contribution of the process consultant is not content-related; he or she coaches and monitors the process and generates optimal support and willingness for change. By contrast, the FAR method relies on expertise in analysis and transition; it is a standardized problem-oriented method for flexibility improvement with a strongly theoretical, conceptual, process-oriented, and instrumental basis. During the diagnosis, the FAR method provides an assessment of actual flexibility, while in the transition phase it facilitates the selection of appropriate types of flexibility, adequate design variables, and successful trajectories of change.

Taking into account these claims and constraints, we shall formulate the instructions for use of the FAR method and present the data-gathering and data-analysis instruments in the various phases of flexibility improvement. Consonant with our process model in Figure 9.1, we shall consider successively the orientation (Sect. 9.2), the diagnosis (Sect. 9.3), and the transition phase (Sect. 9.4) of the FAR method.

9.2 Orientation: How to Start

The starting point of every process of consultation on flexibility improvement is the stage at which the consultant is confronted with a client's subjective dissatisfaction with the actual organizational flexibility and the wish to do something about it. In this orientation phase, consisting of a scouting and an entry, the

How to Improve the Firm's Flexibility

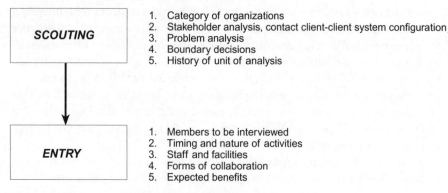

Fig. 9.2. The orientation phase of the FAR method

consultant tries to classify the situation into one or more core problems (see Fig. 9.2).

Scouting

In the scouting phase, the consultant tries to explicate the client's problems and the constraints that bind the features of their solutions. His approach is as yet unstructured and open-minded (Blank and Turner, 1987: 112). The FAR method requires the consultant to at least form an impression of the following items.

(1) The category to which the organization belongs We can roughly distinguish three major categories:

- profit organizations: organizations with a clear profit motive and in which a lack of flexibility leads directly to diminishing returns and profits. These organizations often have well-defined markets, and flexibility is necessary for their survival;
- semi-governmental organizations: these are governmental organizations which have either been privatized recently, or which have lost their monopolies received from the government. Well-known examples include the Dutch National Postbank; the UK Girobank; the UK Post Office; British Telecom; France Télécom; and the US RBOCs. These organizations must increase their flexibility to compete successfully in a more open market;
- institutional or non-profit organizations: organizations without a profit motive. In these organizations, flexibility may result in an increase in the quality of services provided and the quality of working life. One may think of rest homes, hospitals, nursing homes, or urban district councils.

(2) Stakeholders, contact client, client system In a stakeholder analysis, the consultant must try to identify the stakeholders and their problems or complaints. The consultant must also separate the contact client who commissioned him/her from the client system that is the focus of the project. Regarding the links between client and focal client system, there are three distinct consulting arrangements (cf. Ritsema van Eck, 1984: 8):

- the contact client is not involved in the focal client system: for instance, the contact client is the parent company, a financier, or the supervisory board. In these situations, the client system is often not convinced that it needs to improve its flexibility. Thus, the client system must be made aware that its flexibility mix is insufficient and its flexibility potential is inadequate;
- the contact client is part of the focal client system: for instance, the contact client is the management team, the works council, or a staff organ of the unit of analysis. This arrangement is the most common in consulting. Again, the focal client system is often not convinced that it needs to improve its flexibility. In such situations, the contact client plays an important role in making the focal client system aware of a lack or surplus of flexibility;
- the contact client is the focal client system: in this exceptional case, the client system unanimously decides to embark upon a process of flexibility improvement.

(3) Adequacy of the flexibility label In a problem analysis, the consultant has to check if the problem is really one of flexibility, or if it is a problem of biased perceptions or unreal goals. It is important to start with such an analysis as early as possible. When both the consultant and the client system believe the solution to the problem entails a process of flexibility improvement, we can speak of a *reality problem* (De Leeuw, 1986: 213–16). In many situations, however, the call for flexibility is primarily a *perception* or *goal problem*. In these situations, the consultant must influence existing perceptions (e.g. a misperception of the actual flexibility of the organization, an incorrect assessment of the market), or try to change the goals of management. For instance, organizations may strive towards higher levels of flexibility as a response to prevailing trends in management practice even when they have no clear need to achieve this goal; while there may be some environmental turbulence, it often can be neutralized. Of course, it is only after the diagnosis that valid assessments can be done concerning the type of problem, but it is important to consider the possibilities in advance.

(4) Boundary of unit of analysis The consultant has to decide which part of the organization (business unit, division, department, and so on) will be studied in the diagnosis, and which level(s) of analysis will be examined. These boundary

decisions determine what will be considered as environment, management, and organizational conditions. For instance, if the consultant decides to focus his attention on a certain department or division of a larger organization, the parent organization is a part of that unit's environment, the internal organization of that unit determines the organizational conditions, and all the members of that unit who exert control are labelled as management. In Section 1.1 we argued that the process of flexibility improvement is never restricted to a certain aspect, area, or level of organization. Rather, it requires an integrated approach. Hence, it is wise to choose the boundaries of the unit of analysis so that (cf. De Leeuw, 1986: 96):

- the unit of analysis is relatively autonomous. In other words, there are many intra-relations between the unit's elements but few interrelations of the unit with its environmental components, including other organizational units;
- the unit of analysis generates defined products/service that makes the unit distinctive;
- the problem of flexibility can be solved within these boundaries.

(5) History of the unit of analysis   A quick scan of the history of the changes the organizational unit has gone through may reveal:

- if there is readiness for change within this unit (Beckhard and Harris, 1977; Harrison, 1987: 42): for example, is the organizational unit faced with mounting signs of ineffectiveness such as declining sales, poor quality, eroding budget support, labour unrest, or high absence through illness rates? Has the organizational unit been confronted with dramatic change such as new technologies, new products, or large shifts in supply and demand?
- how members and external stakeholders will react to possible interventions: by tracking the organizational unit's history, the consultant should try to determine whether key decision-makers or other powerful groups are likely to support particular interventions and provide the backing and resources needed to implement them successfully. Consequently, in the scouting phase the consultant may find whether possible interventions are likely to encounter resistance or not.

The insights gained from unstructured observation and informal conversation in the scouting phase will enable the consultant to decide whether the FAR method is appropriate or not.

Entry

Sometimes the initial work may lead to a decision not to apply the FAR method. If, however, the consultant concludes that the unit of analysis satisfies the specified conditions and the constraints of the FAR method, he or she should develop an action plan to gain permission to conduct subsequent structured phases of the FAR method. In the entry phase, this tentative plan is usually formalized in a contract specifying:

1. the organization members to be interviewed;
2. the timing and nature of the consultant's activities;
3. staff and facilities to be supplied by both parties;
4. forms of collaboration; and
5. the expected benefits to all participants in the project (Harrison, 1987: 5).

This contract, in which the initially vague problems are represented in various ways and refined in such a way that they can be investigated by the FAR method, forms the basis of the diagnosis phase.

9.3 Diagnosis: Searching for Flexibility Gaps

In the diagnosis, the preliminary problem description of the orientation phase is used for a more detailed analysis and assessment in terms of the building blocks of our strategic framework: changing competitive forces, flexible capabilities, and organization design (see Fig. 9.3).

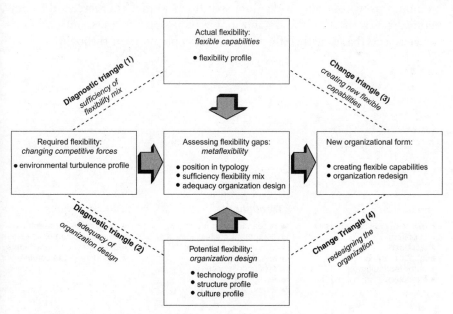

Fig. 9.3. The diagnostic framework of the FAR method

How to Improve the Firm's Flexibility

In the analysis, the consultant first specifies the primary process of the organizational unit. On the basis of these insights, he or she measures the level of environmental turbulence the unit is confronted with, the composition of the management's flexibility mix and information activities performed, and classifies the flexibility potential available within the organizational conditions.

In the assessment, the consultant compares these building blocks with each other to judge the sufficiency of the flexibility mix and the adequacy of the organization design.

Analysing the Building Blocks of Flexibility

Using the diagnostic framework as provided in Figure 9.3, the consultant describes the building blocks of flexibility. By analysing the changing competitive forces, he gains a sense of the required flexibility. In scanning management's flexible capabilities, he can delineate the actual flexibility of the firm. Moreover, his characterization of the organization design shows the potential for flexibility in the firm. The analysis should, however, always start with a *specification of the primary process* of the unit of analysis. The consultant must identify the inputs, throughputs, and outputs of the organizational unit and determine the unit's relevant external elements or constituents for attaining these inputs and disposing of the outputs. As a consequence, the primary process can be presented as an input-throughput-output diagram (see Fig. 9.4) that enumerates the competitive forces affecting the organizational inputs and outputs, and the functional aspects that directly influence the unit's operations or throughput.

Input	*Throughput*	*Output*
• raw materials/components	• production system; machines, equipment, tools	• distribution intermediaries
• suppliers	• information systems	• internal customers/clients
• workload	• inventories	• external customers/clients
• labour markets	• products/services	• product-market combination
• outer technologies	• personnel	
• financiers	• financial resources	

Fig. 9.4. Input-throughput-output diagram representing a primary process

Required flexibility: changing competitive forces   By dividing the firm's competitive environment into competitive forces on its input and output sides, the consultant lays the foundation of the *environmental turbulence scan*. This multi-level decomposition of the environment into competitive forces was thoroughly explained in Section 7.1. On the basis of structured interviews with organization members who perform boundary functions within the firm (e.g. marketing managers, purchase managers, or general managers), the consultant scans each competitive force on three dimensions, namely dynamism of changes (frequency and intensity), complexity of changes (the number of elements and their relatedness), and the unpredictability of these changes (unknown causes/effects). An elaborate treatment for analysing these dimensions can be found in Section 7.2. The result of this scan is presented in a turbulence profile, which indicates the minimum level of required flexibility (see Fig. 9.5). The standardized questionnaire of environmental turbulence can be found in Appendix I.

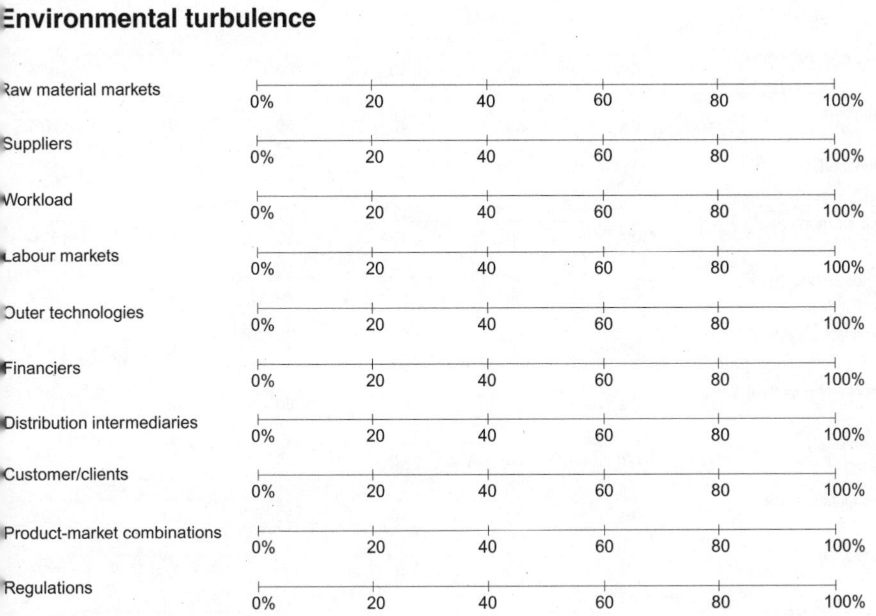

Environmental turbulence

Fig. 9.5. Environmental turbulence profile

Actual flexibility: flexible capabilities   Subsequently, the management team of the organization is asked to complete the *flexibility scan*, which is a systematic enumeration of all possible flexibility capabilities and information activities with respect to the aspects of the primary process (see Appendix I). In addition, management has to explicate the type of flexibility most often applied at the time at which they are filling out the survey (operational, structural, and/or strategic flexibility). From the scores of this quick survey, a flexibility profile can be derived that reflects management's actual flexibility mix: it is the repertoire of flexible capabilities activated by management in order to adjust the organization (internal flexibility) or shape the competitive forces (external flexibility). Each flexibility score in this profile indicates the percentage of flexible capabilities activated by management in relation to the total number of flexible capabilities (see Fig. 9.6). Therefore, by accumulating the scores concerning the competitive forces and functional aspects, the consultant can develop a measure for external and internal flexibility.[2] Moreover, management's score concerning the information activities it performs indicates the extensiveness of its metaflexibility.

Flexibility profile

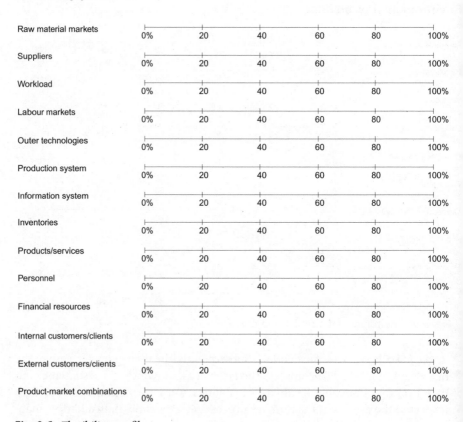

Fig. 9.6. Flexibility profile

Potential flexibility: organization design   Management's ability to increase the flexibility mix is demarcated by the organizational conditions. In the final stage of the analysis the consultant therefore has to *classify the flexibility potential available within the firm* by locating the organization on the various dimensions of technology, structure, and culture. On the basis of a series of standardized questionnaires, in which the dimensions are operationalized in the indicators as discussed in Chapter 6, the consultant is able to develop a technology, a structure, and a culture characteristic (see Tables 6.1, 6.6, and 6.14). These organization characteristics show the potential for flexible capabilities that can be activated when they are needed. The standardized questionnaires of technology, structure, and culture can be found in Appendix I.

Assessing Flexibility Gaps: Going through Diagnostic Triangles

At this stage, we compare the building blocks in order to assess the sufficiency of the flexibility mix and the adequacy of the organization design. To do so, we have to complete the two diagnostic triangles on the upper and lower left-hand side of our diagnostic framework (see Fig. 9.3).

The sufficiency of the flexibility mix: required versus actual flexibility   In this diagnostic triangle, the environmental turbulence profile and flexibility profile are compared in order to accurately assess the sufficiency of the flexibility mix. The environmental turbulence profile indicates the changing competitive forces to which management must either quickly adapt the firm by activating flexible capabilities (internal flexibility) or influence so that the organization becomes less vulnerable to changes in them (external flexibility). The flexibility profile and information coefficient indicate the composition and extensiveness of the actual flexibility mix and metaflexibility.

To support the consultant or client system in comparing the required and the actual flexibility, the turbulence profile and flexibility profile are combined in a decision matrix in the FAR method (see Fig. 9.7). Each cell of this matrix is a crossing point that relates a competitive force with a flexibility aspect.

The identification of gaps between the required and the actual flexibility can be done by the consultant or the client system. Identification by consultants exemplifies an *expert approach*, while the latter is often called a process or *group approach*. In the group approach, which is usually organized in the form of a management conference, the consultant facilitates and guides the discussion, records and summarizes it, and gives feedback without dictating the content of the assessment. In both situations, the diagnosis results in instrumental assessments of the sufficiency of the flexibility mix in terms of a flexibility deficit or

How to Improve the Firm's Flexibility

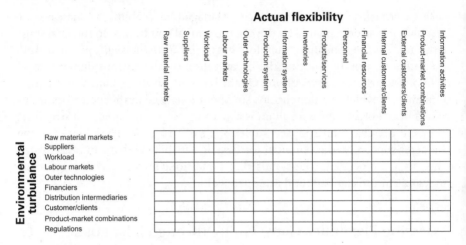

Fig. 9.7. The decision matrix

flexibility surplus. These assessments must be related to functional criteria of effectiveness in terms of empirical findings. Thus, the assessor, who may be a consultant or manager, must ask: 'Why is a deficit or surplus of flexibility problematic for the functioning of the organization?' We have shown that from a perspective of viability a deficit of flexible capabilities ends in organizational rigidity, while a surplus leads to a chaotic state. Nevertheless, a small surplus of flexible capabilities may be beneficial. For instance, a surplus may increase the quality of working life of organizational participants in routine organizations. It is therefore important to consider the criteria of effectiveness in the assessment.

On the basis of this functional assessment of the flexibility gap, the consultant must specify:

1. on what *aspects* the flexibility mix is insufficient, or excessive, in relation to the degree of environmental turbulence; the flexibility scan provides possible capabilities that can be activated or omitted for flexibility improvement;
2. the relevant *type(s) of flexibility* needed to overcome rigidity or chaos (operational, structural, or strategic flexibility);
3. the important *information activities* that have to be performed by management (metaflexibility).

Adequacy of organization design: required versus potential flexibility In this second diagnostic triangle, the consultant examines the organizational barriers (technological, structural, and cultural) to evaluate how feasible it is to implement the specified flexibility aspects and types of flexibility. When the organizational characteristics indicate that the potential flexibility within the organization is much smaller than the required flexibility mix, a redesign process is required in which the organizational conditions are loosened. Similarly, a redesign process is necessary when the flexibility potential within the organization is much larger than the required flexibility mix; in such an organization, redesign is concerned with the tightening of organizational conditions.

9.4 Transition: Orchestrating Trajectories of Change

Using the diagnosis triangles, the consultant has gained insights into how the firm puts the building blocks of flexibility together. From this knowledge, he can position the firm in the typology of alternative flexible forms. Besides diagnosing the actual form, however, the FAR method guides the transition process. It structures both the selection of flexible capabilities and design variables required to transform the firm. The change triangles on the upper and lower right-hand side of the diagnostic framework (Fig. 9.3) may help the consultant effect these changes. In addition, the FAR method assists in the phasing and the organization of the transition process.

Flexible Capabilities and Design Variables: Going through Change Triangles

If diagnosis reveals a flexibility gap, management must try to reduce this gap. For creating appropriate flexible capabilities (managerial task) and reducing organizational barriers to flexibility, the consultant can use the change triangles of the diagnostic framework.

Creating flexible capabilities In deciding which capabilities the organization should develop or unlearn, the consultant or the management has to compare the flexibility mix of the new flexible form with that of the actual form. The upper right-hand change triangle helps the assessor determine how to reduce the flexibility gap. First, management must try to reduce this gap by performing *additional information activities*. When management is ignoring relevant environmental data, increasing its capacity for information processing (metaflexibility) may reduce the level of environmental turbulence the firm is confronted with (see Fig. 9.8). Consequently, management knows which flexibility capabilities it needs. For instance, it may perform a scenario analysis, a vulnerability analysis, and other information activities which trigger information-gathering

How to Improve the Firm's Flexibility

about influences that can have tremendous consequences. As a result of these more extensive sensing and information-processing capacities, a smaller flexibility mix will suffice.

Subsequently, management has to vary its flexibility mix for the remaining environmental turbulence. First, it should develop *external flexibility* in order to neutralize a part of this turbulence (see Fig. 9.8). By actively influencing the competitive forces on the input and output side, the firm may become less vulnerable to changes (e.g. by increasing the number of suppliers, distribution intermediaries, and product-market combinations; switching to other components temporarily; contracting out activities in the form of co-makership or co-design; or influencing customers through advertising and promotions).

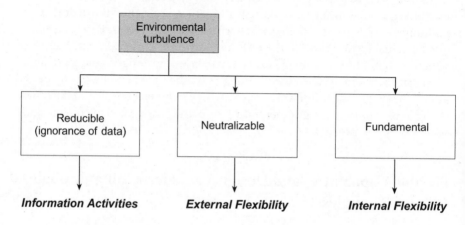

Fig. 9.8. Reducible, neutralizable, and fundamental environmental turbulence

To cope with the residual, fundamental turbulence, the firm has to adapt itself continuously by developing *internal flexibility* (e.g. multiskilled personnel; safety inventories; variable delivery times; variable production capacity; tailor-made products and services; or multipurpose machinery).

Organization redesign The triangle on the lower right-hand side of Figure 9.3 supports the management or consultant in selecting adequate design variables for altering the flexibility potential of the organization. Organization redesign in this context is not restricted to developing new technologies or transforming structures, but also includes intervening in organizational cultures. In the redesign phase of the FAR method, the consultant therefore has to use an integrated perspective in which he considers technological, structural, and cultural design variables (see Ch. 6).

In the case of a rigid form (flexibility deficit), closer scrutiny of the technological, structural, and cultural characteristics may reveal design variables that severely restrict the potential for flexibility. Some of these variables can be changed by management, others must be considered as constraints. In the same vein, when confronted with a chaotic organization (flexibility surplus), the consultant's investigation may result in design variables through which the organization is able to better control its flexibility potential.

Furthermore, in choosing the relevant design variables, the consultant is guided by the design of the desired organizational form. For instance, in a complex and dynamic but largely predictable competitive environment, management must activate numerous sophisticated routine capabilities. These capabilities require a potential for operational flexibility, which can be accomplished only by loosening the organizational technology (less routine). On the other hand, in a fundamentally unpredictable environment, the potential for structural and strategic flexibility can be accomplished only by loosening the organizational structure (more organic) and culture (more innovative).

Phasing of the Process: Engineering versus Development Approach

Besides creating flexible capabilities and selecting design variables for redesign, the consultant must decide what steps should be taken to improve flexibility. In our organizational typology, we distinguished various effective and ineffective trajectories of change (see Figs. 8.2 and 8.3). From this typology, the consultant can easily select an effective trajectory. For each of these, we pointed out that flexibility improvement must involve more than a once-and-for-all change; flexibility improvement has to facilitate ongoing processes of variation in the flexibility mix and related organizational conditions in order to overcome routinization and chaos. This requirement means that the consultant using the FAR method cannot employ merely a 'pure engineering approach', in which he draws a desired flexible form based on an organizational typology. He must also apply a development approach, in which he generates and reinforces certain higher-order flexible capabilities of the management team and the organization members.

While the engineering approach is concerned with the more static design variables (hardware) and easily transferable flexible capabilities, the development approach focuses on the tacit and intangible flexible capabilities and those design variables that facilitate learning processes and new developments (software) for continuous flexibility improvement (see Table 9.1). The appropriate mixture of the engineering and development approaches depends on the specific trajectory of change. For natural trajectories of routinization (e.g. a

TABLE 9.1. Design variables of engineering and development approach

Organizational design variables

Technology	Structure	Culture
mode of production	basic organizational form	identity formation
physical layout		leadership
transformation means	planning and control systems	unwritten rules
operational production repertoire	process regulations	external orientation

▒ = engineering approach
▓ = development approach

trajectory of maturation from a flexible towards a planned form), an engineering approach may be sufficient. Such transitions strengthen and reinforce existing commitments, and are therefore easily accepted.

By contrast, a reverse trajectory of revitalization (e.g. a trajectory of entrepreneurial revitalization from a planned towards a flexible form) requires something closer to a development approach. In this case, past practices need to be questioned, new assumptions about the organization have to be raised, and significant changes in strategy have to be considered. In other words, totally new values and norms are required and past experience may not provide any advantage. The creation of new activities in new situations is important. For this reason, much resistance can be expected against efforts to revitalize organizations. Hence, a development approach is more adequate.

Organization of the Process of Flexibility Improvement

Finally, the FAR method provides some general instructions concerning the organization of the transition process both in the form of persons and resources to be involved in this process and in its timing.

In contrast with the diagnosis phase, the consultant takes on a facilitative, reflective role in the transition process. In order to reduce resistance, he encourages the client organization to validate the functional assessment of the flexibility mix and the organizational conditions, and to participate in the change process. The organization's validation of the functional assessment may help him to *identify and elicit dissatisfaction with the current state*. Organization members have to express their complaints with the current state if they are to lose their inertia. In this connection, the discrepancy between the required and the actual flexibility can be used to create dissatisfaction. As a result, the diagnosis profiles can be important tools for initiating a process of flexibility improvement. Furthermore, engagement or *participation* of the client system in the change and redesign process tends to reduce resistance, builds ownership of the redesign, and motivates people to make the redesign work (Nadler, 1981: 201). This involvement can vary from case to case, ranging from transition group sessions, in which the client conducts interventions on the basis of the diagnosis, to diagnostic and transition sessions, in which the consultant merely supports the process. Finally, people need to be provided with the *time and opportunity to disengage from the present state* (Nadler, 1981). That is to say, the management of flexibility improvement is also a process of transitioning people, programmes, and investments from commitments in the past towards the future. For such processes to succeed, transitional rituals such as funerals or celebrations must be organized in order to commemorate the ideas, programmes, and commitments that have become obsolete and to create opportunities for ushering in those that must gain good currency for flexibility improvement (Albert, 1984; Van de Ven, 1986).

Additionally, the transition process must be supported by the *key decision-makers* or power groups within or outside the organization unit. Therefore the consultant must analyse who the actual key decision-makers are, particularly because these individuals may not be the formal decision-makers. In addition, the consultant must identify their *sponsors*. Moreover, he must *stimulate leaders to enhance the transition efforts* in various ways, such as explaining the need for flexibility, articulating the desired flexible form, modelling behaviour consistent with this form, and rewarding those who support the process.

If the resistance is successfully reduced and there is political power for the change and redesign process, in the transition state the consultant has to do the following:

(1) Develop and communicate a clear image of the desired flexible form   In the absence of a clear image of the future, individual expectations are formed on the basis of information that is often erroneous: rumours develop and people create their own scenarios. Therefore the clearest possible image of the future state needs to be written down to serve as a guideline, or target. For example, the flexibility improvement project in the Dutch Postbank nearly failed because the management refused to show employees a clear picture of the new organization. Even though nobody would be fired and employees would receive higher wages in exchange for a higher functional interchangeability, there was much resistance from the works council. Employees did not have enough information to compare the new with the old situation. Only after a description of what the future state would look like, how the transition would come about, why the change

was being implemented, and how individuals would be affected by the change did the works council actively support the change.

(2) Explicitly consider organizational arrangements for the transition state   The issue of developing structures to manage transitions has been discussed in depth elsewhere (Beckhard and Harris, 1977; De Leeuw, 1986; Nadler, 1981). In particular, decisions must be made concerning the persons who have to be included in the project team or transition team, the transition management structure, the resources for the transition, and the relation of the transition organization with the current organization. The radical change in Xerox from a functional organization that bred passivity towards a flexible one that combined speed and creativity with economies of scale was made possible largely by transition teams. In 1990, Xerox's new CEO, Paul Allaire, appointed a team of six young Xerox managers to think about the future architecture of the company (Howard, 1992). The members of this so-called 'Futuretecture' were selected for their outspoken ideas about what was wrong and right with Xerox. Their most extreme scenario to develop global business divisions was worked out, one year later, by an Organizational Transition Board (OTB), consisting of fifteen senior managers. It is not surprising that many of the managers who served on the Futuretecture team and the OTB received key leadership positions in Xerox's new organization.

(3) Integrate with the common symbols—gestures, pictures, or objects that carry a particular meaning within the unit—and language of the organization unit   By providing a language to describe the change, it is possible to define an ambiguous reality. Symbolic acts such as recognizing contributions in public and giving projects or positions particular names are examples of this. The flexibility improvement in Philips Semiconductors is illuminative. As a result of an integral change programme focused on flexibility improvement, the Assembly Department Glass-Bead Diodes had successfully undergone a revival. This was very surprising, since in 1980 the product manager of the product group Diodes and Transistors intended gradually to close down this assembly department. The product group's business plan showed glass-bead diodes being rapidly superseded by implosion diodes. By framing the flexibility improvement project in terms that associate with the revival spirit, however, management made the radical change possible. In particular, management developed a unique logo for the assembly unit, started special mailings that reinforced the spirit of revival, and initiated ongoing information rounds regarding the development of the flexibility programme.

(4) Build in stability   Too much emphasis on change may create dysfunctional effects; people may begin to panic, engage in extreme defensive behaviour, and

244

become irrationally resistant to any new change proposed. As we have argued in Section 4.2, organizations and individuals can stand only so much uncertainty and turbulence. Consonant with Nadler, one way of offsetting this reaction is: 'to provide some sources of stability to serve as "anchors" for people to hold onto and to provide a means for definition of the self in the midst of turbulence' (Nadler, 1981: 205). Thus, those design variables that will not change during a transition period need to be identified and communicated to organization members. In addition, design variables such as identity formation or unwritten rules need to be considered: they may create stability without restricting management's flexibility mix.

9.5 FARSYS: Automation of the Flexibility Audit

The application of the FAR method is very time-consuming for the consultant, and therefore very expensive for the organization. Hence, we developed a system that supports consultants in the application of the FAR method (Bouma *et al.*, 1994). This tool, called FARSYS,[3] supports the data-gathering (FARSYS I) as well as the decision-making process of the consultant (FARSYS II). The advice support system offers the following functions to the users:

- the automation of the information-gathering process;
- a user interface for the explication and elaboration of solutions;
- a knowledge bank to support the consultant in choosing and evaluating his solution;
- a utility function to measure the effect of the solutions chosen by the consultant.

Because the tool had to be flexible (the unstructured part of the FAR method asked for a design that was easy to change and easy to adapt) and robust (it was going to be used by people with minimal computer knowledge), the main part of the tool was built in an object-oriented environment (Visual Works).

FARSYS I is now operational. It provides the following functions:

- the creation and specification of questionnaires,
- the use of the questionnaires to obtain organizational data, and
- the processing and analysis of these data.

By applying FARSYS I, the consultant creates a database of organizational data that facilitates the diagnosis phase through graphical representations of organizational flexibility: a turbulence profile, a flexibility profile, and characteristics of the organizational conditions. A great advantage of the automation of the information-gathering is the possibility of statistical analyses on the collected data.

FARSYS II is still in development. It will support the consultant in

- the consultation of the database,
- the consultation of expert knowledge, and
- the combination of database and expert knowledge into suitable advice.

The consultant can use the profiles of FARSYS I, together with the knowledge base offered by FARSYS II, in order to derive recommendations for the transition process.

9.6 Diagnostic Findings: Testing the FAR method in Three Large Corporations

In order to justify the FAR method empirically, we started with a longitudinal study in which we undertook flexibility efforts within real organizations by using the FAR method. This study was achieved through research/practitioner partnerships based on mutual understanding of the benefits to be derived from research, with flexibility improvement within real organizations as its focal point (cf. Lewin and Minton, 1986: 526).

We were able to study only a very small number of cases using this approach. The application of the FAR method in two or three organizations demonstrates the usability of the method, but indicates nothing about the validity of our strategic framework and typology. To address this latter issue, the longitudinal study was designed so that these cases differed in terms of the building blocks of flexibility. In particular, we selected three extreme cases that were polar opposite 'ideal types' in our typology[4] (Eisenhardt, 1989; Yin, 1989). This sampling of cases was a particularly effective means of testing the empirical claims of the FAR method.

On the basis of interviews, documents, and unstructured observations, we selected three different organization units operating in different, changing competitive environments: an administrative unit X of the Dutch Postbank, a production unit Y of Philips Semiconductors, and an R&D unit Z of the Dutch Gas Company. In each of these cases, there was a clear need for flexibility due to a shift in the level of environmental turbulence:

- the relatively young administrative unit X for corporate accounts was confronted with mounting signs of ineffectiveness (e.g. high absenteeism, demoralization, high staff turnover). In the past, the bank organization operated in a static, simple, and predictable environment, with hardly any need for flexibility. The new administrative unit for registration activities of corporate accounts had to vary its production capacity in order to provide more custom-made services for corporate account holders;
- as a part of an Integrated Organization Renewal (IOR) programme, the assembly unit Y was a pilot case of a Redesign Production Systems (RPS)

project, in which the total plant tried, among other things, to increase its production flexibility. Instead of rigid central planning, production units were now responsible for reacting to variations in demand. This unit used to operate in a dynamic, complex, but largely predictable environment. Now it had to cope with a fluctuating workload, an increase in the volume of specialties, changes in the quality requirements of key customers, new competitors from the Far East and Eastern Europe, and a varying composition of its product mix;

- the R&D unit Z had to function more autonomously (budget centre). While the kind of research activities it had to perform were always difficult to predict, it now had to react more quickly to special as well as routine research questions from internal clients.

Besides these shifts to hypercompetitive environments, each organization unit selected had fewer than one hundred organization members and distinguished three or less formal hierarchical levels. Moreover, while these three units were each partsystems of larger corporations, the products and services they provided guaranteed they could be studied as distinct units.

In each case, we conducted pre-measurements of the level of environmental turbulence, the flexibility potential within the organizational conditions, and the composition of the flexibility mix. The data collected by means of the standardized questionnaires and quick survey were analysed with the FARSYS I computer program and generated the diagnostic profiles presented in Appendix II. These pre-measurements allowed us to generate advice concerning effective strategic trajectories of revitalization. After one year, we conducted a post-measurement in order to validate the recommendations of the FAR method. Table 9.2 shows the summary results of the longitudinal case studies conducted in the period between 1989 and 1992.

The Dutch Postbank: Professional Revitalization of Department X

Entry The Dutch National Postbank was recently privatized. In the past, its main line of business was retail banking because of restrictions imposed by the Dutch government. It provided mainly standardized services to more than six million account holders. After it was deregulated, it intended to provide more customized services as a part of its corporate banking efforts. In order to provide these special services for corporate account holders, organizational flexibility was one of the basic goals in the strategic plan for 1988 until 1992. We were asked to improve the flexibility of the Corporate Accounts Department X, which had existed for just one year.

TABLE 9.2. Empirical results of longitudinal cases FAR project

Measurement		Case X		Case Y		Case Z	
		pre-	post-	pre-	post-	pre-	post-
Environmental shift	dynamism	−	+	+	++	+	++
	complexity	−	+	+	++	+	++
	unpredictability	−	−	−	+/−	+/−	+
Flexibility types	operational	−	+	+/−	+	+	+
	structural	−	−	−	−	+/−	++
	strategic	−	−	−	+/−	−	+
F scores	F internal	44	43.4	46.7	35.2	40.6	42.4
	F external	35.4	37.8	31.6	38.5	36.3	44.3
	F total	39.7	40.6	39.2	36.9	38.5	43.4
Metaflexibility	I score	40	36.7	47.9	34.0	33.3	46.5
Flexibility potential	technology	−	+	+/−	+	+	+
	structure	−	+/−	−	+/−	+/−	+
	culture	−	−	−	+	++	+
Organizational form		rigid	planned	rigid/ planned	planned/ flexible	chaotic	flexible
Trajectory		professional revitalization		entrepreneurial revitalization		strategic focusing	

Note:
− = low   +/− = moderate   + = high   ++ = extremely high

248

Analysis On the basis of results of the pre-measurement, we found that Administrative Department Corporate Accounts of the Dutch Postbank had a limited flexibility mix. The sections of Administrative Department X were in a continuous state of tension between satisfying the wishes of account holders (small firms, large corporations, foundations, associations) and internal clients (business units, the district offices), and meeting the bureaucratic procedures of the Client Registration division (see Appendix II).

Moreover, its potential for flexibility was limited. The department had a routine technology, a very mechanistic structure, and a somewhat conservative culture. Its batch mode of production with highly standardized services and simple, fixed operations together with the specialized information systems, which regularly broke down, provided little accommodation for operational flexibility. Furthermore, the operational production repertoire of workers was limited owing to fixed production tasks, rigid work instructions, and tight production norms. In addition, the department's multi-level hierarchical structure limited its structural flexibility. The work was highly specialized and standardized, consisting of narrow tasks with very little leeway for control. In addition, the department had many temporary and seasonal workers on the basis of a pooling arrangement due to its high workload. This arrangement resulted in a low consensus concerning core values among the permanent workforce (incoherent set of beliefs). Employees' tolerance for ambiguity was very low; most participants of department X were non-creative and conservative. Deviating opinions or new ideas were not brought forward, and their chances of success were low when they were.

Assessment Department X clearly corresponded to the rigid form in our typology. None the less, its environmental turbulence profile showed that its environment was no longer stable, but highly complex and dynamic, especially regarding the composition of the workload, developments in information technologies, and specific requirements of clients. However, most of these changes were predictable. According to our typology, this shift in environmental turbulence required a more comprehensive flexibility mix dominated by operational flexibility and a less routine technology. Management had to activate many sophisticated routines to deal with these dynamic and complex changes. To facilitate this activation, the management of department X needed a more extensive information-processing capacity to anticipate complex changes. This transition from a rigid to a more planned organizational form can be referred to as a process of *professional revitalization* (see Fig. 9.9). Such a comprehensive movement away from traditions, conservatism, and rigidity towards adaptiveness, vigilance, and diversification could stimulate department X to track the external environment and to discover new market forces. The transition we suggested could help the department become more adaptive and sensitive to

How to Improve the Firm's Flexibility

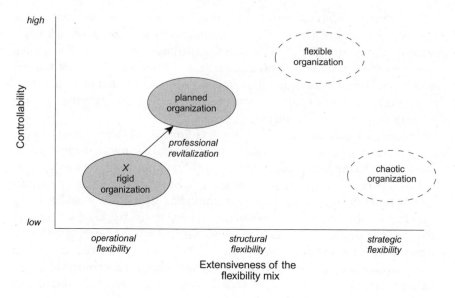

Fig. 9.9. Postbank: professional revitalization of Administrative Department *X*

market forces, to vary its product line and volume more easily, to become more aggressive and innovative in dealing with new services, and more imaginative in meeting the needs of external and internal clients.

Transition   In the management conference, in which we presented the results of the diagnosis, the management team of the department judged that operational flexibility in the form of short-term volume and mix flexibility was most important for its department. It had to vary quickly the volume and types of services provided according to the demands of internal and external clients.

Furthermore, by comparing the environmental turbulence profile with the flexibility profile, the management team decided that to reduce the gap between the required and the actual flexibility, it was necessary to improve the flexibility with respect to the workload, permanent workforce, and services provided. The flexibility with respect to the workload was extremely low. The department was not able to contract out certain standard registration activities to other departments within the division, to create back-up possibilities, or to curb the work volume during peak periods and to promote it during off-peak periods. This lack of flexible capabilities regarding the workload made it impossible for department *X* to process all orders in one day and resulted in large inventories of registration activities in progress and long processing times.

The flexibility of the personnel consisted predominantly of numerical labour flexibility for adjusting the size of the workforce to shifts in demand in the form of flexible working times (flexible duty roster), flexible employment contracts, or overtime arrangements. In extreme situations, the department contracted temporary workers on the basis of pooling arrangements or call-contracts (labour-market flexibility). The functional labour flexibility for transferring workers to various tasks within the department, however, was restricted. This type of personnel flexibility, requiring multiskilled personnel together with significant task variety, was very important for reducing the department's vulnerability so that custom-made services could be provided and special projects undertaken.

The flexibility regarding the services provided was reasonably high. Yet it had to be increased if more special projects for large account holders were to be undertaken, or new services were to be provided more quickly and easily with changed registration tasks.

To realize a process of professional revitalization as described above, a higher flexibility potential within the organizational conditions was required. Closer scrutiny of the technology characteristic revealed that the mode of production (large batch) and the physical layout could be influenced only marginally. However, the operational production repertoire—the number of methods of working and level of skills a worker can deal with—could be enlarged. As a part of the structural change, management intended to group the registration tasks according to target market. Unfortunately, the reorganization plan did not pay attention to strong process regulations like specialization, standardization, and formalization. By ignoring these requirements, the new structure of department X would get bogged down in a mechanistic structure again. Finally, in order to control the flexibility potential, management decided that some preservation was necessary in the department's culture in terms of a stronger identity for the whole department, more supportive and visible forms of leadership, socialization by means of an explicit career policy and personnel and management development systems, and a higher tolerance for ambiguity.

Post-measurement The post-measurement shows that a strategic trajectory of professional revitalization had resulted in a planned form. Administrative Department X, which was confronted with increasing environmental dynamism and complexity, was able to activate operational short-term volume and mix flexibility originating from a less routine technology with a less mechanistic organizational form. In particular, numerical labour flexibility was replaced with functional labour flexibility in order to reduce the vulnerability of special services and to increase the back-up possibilities. In addition, workers' ability to perform multiple tasks increased due to a weekly rotation system. Furthermore, the department could deal more easily with fluctuations in the workload.

None the less, as a consequence of a permanent workforce size that was too small, peak periods at the end of the year still caused major problems. Regarding the organizational conditions, the department's technology and structure facilitated a larger potential for flexibility. The enlargement of the workers' production repertoire and the extra equipment within the department had resulted in a less routine technology. Furthermore, the grouping according to target market, a flatter structure, and less functionalized management tasks had resulted in a less mechanistic structure. Moreover, the combination of the training programme with a job rotation system had increased the interchangeability of tasks. None the less, the lack of preservation within the department's culture still made it very difficult to allocate the increased potential within the technology and structure. The parochialism within the sections had decreased and the department's identity had become more homogeneous. Nevertheless, explicit and visible forms of leadership, which supported and directed employees in their work, were still limited. Furthermore, the transmission of appropriate core values by socialization was not sufficiently worked out by management. While there were now regular work progress discussions and annual performance assessments, there was not yet an introduction programme for new arrivals, a personnel and management development programme, or an explicit career policy. Also, the tolerance for ambiguity or innovativeness within the sections for standard registration activities was still low; workers were still not really involved in change processes. Therefore, we may conclude that the flexibility potential within the department's technology and structure had increased, but this increased potential could not be utilized optimally as a result of some process regulations in the department's structure (low participation, few lateral relations) and cultural design variables (no supporting leadership, limited socialization, lack of innovativeness).

Philips Semiconductors: Entrepreneurial Revitalization of Assembly Department Y

Entry This flexibility audit took place in a large plant of Philips Semiconductors. In the past, strong pressures from competitors (Far East and Eastern Europe) had forced Philips to close down one of the plant's production departments and to dismiss 400 employees. Yet the low competitiveness of the plant's major products, together with the depressing atmosphere throughout the whole plant, required a more radical change. In order to improve the plant's competitiveness in terms of market share, the management team of Philips Semiconductors organized an integrated change programme. As a part of this renewal programme, the Redesign Production Systems (RPS) project was initiated within the product line Medium Power Rectifiers and Stacks (MPRS). In line with this strategic reorientation and new philosophy, the product line had to redesign its product organization and equipment. The product line MPRS consisted of one diffusion department and three assembly departments, namely the Implosion Diode (ID) assembly, the Stack (S) assembly, and the Glass-Bead (GB) assembly.

Before the implementation of the RPS project, fluctuations in demand required the product line MPRS to rely on high buffer stocks between the various steps in production and assembly. In this traditional, stable, and high-volume manufacturing approach, errors in the planning forecast of the Central Planning Department (CPD) within the headquarters of the multinational resulted in large inventories and high costs. Moreover, these high volumes for various product types within a single line caused long waiting and lead times, many defects in the production process, very high percentages of rejected parts (sometimes as high as 50%), and a low quality of working life. With the introduction of the RPS project within the product line MPRS, production departments were now responsible for reacting to variations in demand. In other words, they had to offer a variety of diode types in smaller quantities within ever shorter delivery times. On the one hand, they had to cope with a more fluctuating workload, an increase in the number of specialties, higher quality requirements of key customers, and a varying product range. On the other hand, they had to handle low stock levels and high efficiency rates in production. In 1990, within the Assembly Department Glass-Bead (GB), the partial implementation of the RPS trajectory had resulted in a higher market share. Yet not all the changes suggested by the RPS had been implemented. Moreover, production workers felt little commitment to participate in the project. Management decided that the flexibility audit had to measure the progress of the RPS project in terms of flexibility within the Assembly Department and eventually facilitate the further implementation of the RPS trajectory through this focus.

Analysis Assembly Department Glass-Bead Diodes, which was professionally organized within the product line Medium Power Rectifiers and Stacks for a reasonably turbulent environment (dynamic, complex, but largely predictable), employed an extensive flexibility mix, dominated by operational flexibility, and possessed a less routine technology, a mechanistic structure, and a conservative culture. We also found highly developed intelligence systems that were part of the metaflexibility, as well as many structural process regulations meant to facilitate the development of routines. Management responded that the department adapted mainly through operational flexibility, specifically in terms of short-term volume and mix flexibility. By changing the capacity utilization within the installed capacity and by changing the production capacity between various product types, short-term fluctuations could be offset. None the less, due to the overload, the department operated with a maximum capacity utilization, which resulted in bottlenecks in the production line and high stress among the workforce. On the basis of the technology characteristic provided in Appendix II, we concluded that there was some potential for operational flexibility within the technology, but that the single assembly line, the many interdependencies in the assembly process, and the limited skill repertoire of workers hampered the production of various product types and fluctuating volumes.

Furthermore, the structure characteristic revealed that the potential for structural flexibility was seriously limited by the sophisticated planning and control systems and strong process regulations such as the far-reaching specialization and the many formal and informal liaison devices. These features led to single-skilled personnel, few learning opportunities, and no self-regulation of work teams. Finally, the culture characteristic indicated that the department had a relatively conservative culture emanating from a narrow and homogeneous identity and a management attitude directed towards routine proliferation: management tried to develop a sophisticated routine for every possible change. The department's many unwritten rules were shaped by the strong discipline dominance among the organization members. The department was made up predominantly of employees with technical backgrounds. Consequently, these personnel often framed problems in technical terms, while they ignored problems of a more social nature. In addition, supplementary unwritten rules were transmitted only on a limited scale by socialization processes.

Assessment Owing to the partial implementation of a large Technology Redesign Project, the technology was more routine as we had expected. Consequently, the department still had problems activating operational flexibility. The department did not totally correspond with the planned configuration, but was positioned somewhere between the rigid and planned form in our typology (see Fig. 9.10).

Moreover, the environmental turbulence profile showed that the environment of Assembly Department Y was no longer only complex and dynamic, but also unpredictable, especially regarding the developments in outer technologies (introduction of plastic diodes, release of higher-voltages versions, new crystal types, and the advance of integrated circuits in the application markets) and PMCs (price erosion and unforeseen volume developments). In this situation, pure anticipation in terms of routine proliferation was insufficient. A strong commitment to a likely future may have even reduced the assembly department's receptiveness to change. Instead of further increasing its information-processing capacity, management needed to reduce the need for information processing and develop structural and strategic flexibility. This transition from a merely planned form to a more flexible form is referred to as a trajectory of *entrepreneurial revitalization*.

The planned form is seriously handicapped when confronted with funda-

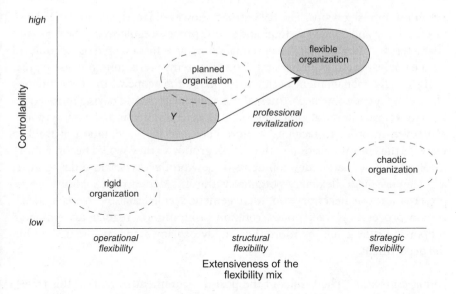

Fig. 9.10. Philips Semiconductors: entrepreneurial revitalization of Assembly Department *Y*

mentally unpredictable environments. A trajectory of entrepreneurial revitalization could help the Assembly Department to exploit unknown opportunities in technologies and PMCs more easily. In addition, the department still needed operational flexibility for short-term fluctuations in demand. Moreover, the sensor and information-processing capacity would have to be very rudimentary for strategic flexibility and be directed towards enhancing the receptiveness to new environments.

Transition Management decided to activate greater operational load flexibility and strategic capacity flexibility by means of a more variable production capacity, a multiskilled workforce, arrangements with regular clients, and faster incorporation of new technological developments. To facilitate these flexible capabilities, it had to reduce some organizational barriers. Regarding the department's technology, the shift towards a group layout and a small-batch mode of production would result in two homogeneous work flows with fewer dependencies. If these product flows were to operate as autonomous and flexible mini-lines, however, the skills repertoire of employees and the applicability of machines had to be increased. If not, the possibilities for operational flexibility would be seriously restricted. Furthermore, management intended to create autonomous task groups. The RPS project, however, largely ignored the elaborate planning and control systems and strong process regulations. The structure characteristic revealed that the potential of the new form would be neutralized by the sophisticated planning and control systems and strong process regulations. Finally, management decided to enlarge the scope of the department's identity by broadening departmental mission and goals and paying more attention to various cultural practices such as celebrations and shared symbols. Moreover, in order to facilitate a more open external orientation, it tried to increase the communication with the task groups so they would become more involved in new market developments or new product types. In order to guarantee an adequate flexibility potential within the department's culture, some preservation was necessary too. Management decided that by stronger socialization processes (career policy, rotation programmes, regular assessments), supporting rules could be more thoroughly explained and maintained within the department.

Post-measurement The results of the post-measurement show that this trajectory of entrepreneurial revitalization resulted in a hybrid of a planned/flexible form. Assembly Department *Y*, which was confronted with increasing unpredictability, was able to activate operational load flexibility and some strategic capacity flexibility originating from an increasingly non-routine technology, a moderately organic structure (organic form with strong process regulations), and a more innovative culture. The internal flexibility score, however, was temporarily curtailed because the replacement of the old solder and alloy ovens by modern computerized ovens caused many problems, while the expensive internal flexibility originating from large inventories significantly decreased. Moreover, because the department had not yet succeeded in creating mini-lines with autonomous task groups, the remaining interdependencies still hampered the activation of strategic flexibility. None the less, the smaller batch sizes, the larger skill repertoire, the extra production capacity, and improved switchability of machines and equipment facilitated a larger potential for operational flexibility. Although there were still no autonomous task groups, the larger shifts were more self-regulating than before. As a consequence of increased on-the-job training and the training in process control, the interchangeability within the shifts increased. Finally, the department's culture had become more innovative. By stimulating various cultural practices such as the celebration of the twelve-and-a-half-year existence of the department, the organization of an 'open house' of the assembly for the workers' relatives and other social events, the development of a unique logo for the department, and the start of special mailings for informing the shift workers about new market developments, management had succeeded in broadening the scope of the department's identity. Furthermore, by ongoing information rounds regarding the development of the change programme and the RPS project, special training for the assembly department's workers, and participation in the decision-making regarding the implementation of the RPS project, the openness and the tolerance for ambiguity increased within Assembly Department Y. Besides these communication channels, the MPRS product line had started with a news bulletin, directed by an editorial staff, informing the employees about the goals of the change programme.

The Dutch National Gas Company: Strategic Focusing of R&D Department Z

Entry The R&D Department Z is part of the Dutch Gas Corporation. The firm's main activities are the purchasing, transporting, and selling of natural gas in both The Netherlands and abroad. The corporation was founded in 1963 and had existed for twenty-five years when we conducted our flexibility audit. Fifty per cent of the shares were owned by two oil companies, 40 per cent by a state-owned chemical corporation, and 10 per cent were directly owned by the state. Although the firm had a monopoly and a fixed annual result of 80 million guilders, its top management wanted to create some artificial incentives to increase the competitiveness within the corporation. Consequently, it first started a management development programme based on job rotation throughout the whole corporation in order to break down walls and build in flexibility. In addition, it organized top one hundred lunches, in which the top executives of the corporation openly discussed the corporate mission. Later these lunches were replaced by open lectures given by famous professors.

Nevertheless, top management was convinced that a larger change programme was required to improve the communication of the mission and common values. In 1987, it instituted a Master Plan for changing the corporate mission, consisting of the projects 'culture and communication', 'structure', 'systems', and 'people'. As a part of this corporate change programme, it tried to create decentralized autonomous units with a strong client orientation and flexible use of resources and human assets. For those departments that provided well-defined products and services, this goal was relatively easy to achieve. It was more problematic, however, for the R&D Department, which provided intangible technical and scientific support services. To serve the firm's main activities (the purchase, transport, and sale of gas), the R&D Department was divided into three research areas: acquisition, transport, and market. In fulfilling these operations, the Service Department provided the equipment and facilities and specific support concerning mechanical engineering, electronics, and computer software. In addition, it conducted routine research activities like gas-flow measurements and gas calibrations.

How to Improve the Firm's Flexibility

As a result of the increased autonomy of the R&D Department (budget centre), the need for more adequate controls over the department's performance, and the increased competition from external research institutes, the department had decided to apply a more 'market-pull' approach. Consequently, clients became more involved in the research projects and determined the kind and volume of research activities. None the less, these tailor-made research projects and trouble-shooting activities for internal as well as external clients made the workload highly unpredictable. In addition, the department had some problems finding an adequate balance between routine research activities, trouble-shooting, applied research projects, and fundamental research. In our meeting with the management team, it was decided that an audit of the actual flexibility of the R&D Department could eventually help it to solve the above problems.

Analysis We found that the R&D Department functioned in an increasingly complex, dynamic, and unpredictable environment (see Appendix II). It was confronted with a high degree of unpredictability in the composition of the volume of services it provided, especially the volume of trouble-shooting activities. Furthermore, new priorities of internal clients resulted in radical shifts in the kind of research activities performed. Moreover, technological developments regarding gas transport (gas storage, gas mixing, capacity of transport system) and gas applications (apparatus development, apparatus research) were very unclear. Finally, the business developments of the research areas, 'transport' and 'market', were unclear. To what extent would research regarding the gas transport system become routinized and conducted by the internal clients (Operations and Engineering), and to what extent did the Commercial Sector want new applications (gas dryer, gas dishwasher)?

Furthermore, Department Z possessed a very non-routine technology and an extremely innovative culture. It applied a project-based mode of production in order to expedite the variety of projects it performed. Its versatile technology, with the exception of the more specialized equipment of Service and the skill repertoire of service workers, provided enough potential for flexibility. None the less, the lack of preservation in the culture of R&D Department Z hampered the allocation of the flexibility potential, especially the loose constellation of subcultures not connected to a core culture (weak and heterogeneous identity), the lack of institutional leadership, the prevailing corporate-wide socialization instead of departmental socialization, and the strong counterculture, in which rules are by definition violated.

Moreover, the department's structure was less organic than we had expected, owing to the division of management tasks, the many hierarchical levels, long horizontal chains, and elaborate planning rituals. Although the department had a matrix structure with a dominant grouping according to target market, there was much confusion about authorities and responsibilities. Research area managers interfered with the content and progress of research projects, while activity managers, project managers, and even senior specialists claimed line authority (selection, appraisal, rewarding of researchers). The toppling of the matrix towards a line organization resulted in at least six hierarchical levels and various enclaves, both of which impeded cross-sectional as well as cross-value capability development. Not surprisingly, the department's strategic flexibility was not as high as we had estimated. The initiation of new research programmes, which required cross-sectional projects, was especially problematic for the department. Also, the department's information-processing capacity was very rudimentary.

Assessment The R&D Department did not correspond to the flexible form; rather, it was better characterized as a chaotic form in our organizational typology (see Fig. 9.11). It had a substantial potential for flexibility, but management could not activate this potential owing to the lack of preservation in its culture. In other words, the department was too flexible. There were many initiatives for new research but they could not be implemented because there were no clear administrative structures or 'shared values' stemming from the department's culture. Nor did the department have adequate information regarding man-hours, costs, and technical progress per project. The schizophrenia of the department resulted in distorted information that management could not use to make appropriate decisions. This strategic neglect, or the dearth of both administrative structures and a shared culture, together with the opportunistic behaviour of individual researchers, resulted in a lack of decisiveness regarding research priorities, a fragmented structure, and a loose constellation of various subcultures.

Transition According to our organizational typology, a trajectory of *strategic focusing* was required (see Fig. 9.11) to lift this organization from a chaotic state of random, disconnected, and uncoordinated impulses, towards a more flexible form. This strategic focusing was manifested in preserving a higher-order core culture and establishing clearer administrative structures. Furthermore, management chose to increase the internal structural and strategic programme flexibility by influencing the research volume, establishing a multiskilled workforce, and facilitating the development of new innovative research programmes. To activate the appropriate flexible capabilities, management had to conduct more information-scanning to maintain metaflexibility.

Post-measurement Our post-measurement showed that the R&D Department was able to activate a broader flexibility mix dominated by structural flexibility and strategic programme flexibility originating from a clearer organic structure and a stronger preservation of the department's core culture. In order to

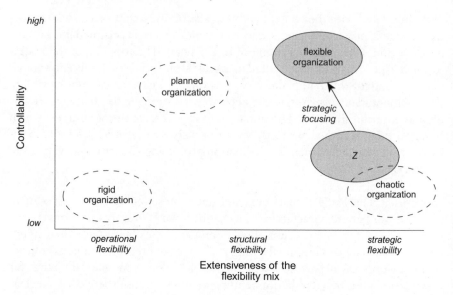

Fig. 9.11. The Dutch Gas Company: strategic focusing of R&D Department Z

preserve an adequate flexibility potential within the R&D Department Z, management had started various social events to create a higher-order core culture. Moreover, in order to strengthen some shared values and a common history, researchers had to stay in the research department for at least three years before they could move to a management position in the firm. In addition, managers gave more attention to their leadership style. They provided more direction and feedback (institutional leadership). By emphasizing a commonly shared management and organization philosophy, the distinction between the formal and actual organization was reduced. This overlapping culture enhanced the potential for flexibility, but also corrected opposing initiatives.

Evaluating the FAR Method

In each case, the FAR method produced assessments of the sufficiency of the flexibility mix and the design adequacy of the organizational conditions. In doing so, it supports our first claim for it, namely, that it generates a diagnosis of the actual flexibility from a perspective of effectiveness. In addition to generating a diagnosis, the FAR method supported management by specifying areas of attention for improving the flexibility mix. In each case, the FAR method provided relevant flexibility types, relevant flexibility aspects, and identified lacking or redundant information activities as a part of the metaflexibility. Increased attention from management for these areas resulted in changes in the compositions of the flexibility profile, thereby supporting our second claim.

Moreover, by locating the organization on the various dimensions of technology, structure, and culture, the FAR method provided management with clear design implications for varying the flexibility potential. A more balanced and integrated design perspective of this kind, in which management considered technological, structural, and cultural design variables, resulted in a greater capacity to orchestrate the transition process in all three cases. For instance, on the basis of the application of the FAR method in case X, the management not only employed a segmentalistic engineering approach focused on the basic organizational form, but also used a development approach that was directed towards enhancing the functional interchangeability of employees, the tolerance for innovations, and the preservation of a shared identity. In the same vein, as a part of the RPS project, in case Y, the FAR method supported the management's selection of technological and static structural design variables, but also generated design variables (process regulations of structure, cultural design variables) to complete the RPS project in order to develop and reinforce certain competences and organizational capacities. The fact that a development approach proved to be more effective in both of these revitalization processes supports our contention that an exclusively engineering approach is insufficient in trajectories of revitalization.

Finally, the acceptability of the results of the FAR method was very high. The validation of the assessments concerning the sufficiency of the flexibility mix and the adequacy of the organizational conditions made it possible to identify and bring to the surface dissatisfaction with the current state of affairs. In this connection, the diagnostic profiles were important tools for initiating a process of flexibility improvement. Furthermore, the participation of management in the redesign process fostered its receptiveness to feedback and commitment to actions. Besides the acceptability of the outcomes, the FAR method also proved to be reasonably efficient. In a period of three to four weeks, we succeeded in auditing the actual flexibility, the environmental turbulence, and the flexibility potential within the organizational conditions. In interviews with those managing cases X, Y, and Z, these managers argued that the FAR method gave a very complete picture of their organization's flexibility, as well as leading to clear recommendations for flexibility improvement that resulted in a redirection and acceleration of existing change programmes.

Notes

1. To develop a usable method for diagnosing and improving organizational flexibility, we used a clinical approach of acquiring knowledge by describing and classifying the

activities of skilled practitioners. On the basis of a global thinking model, we conducted twenty-two interviews with management consultants in which their consulting processes were examined. The consequent clinical understanding of the diagnosis, redesign, and change process, together with our strategic framework and organizational typology, was integrated in the Flexibility Audit and Redesign (FAR) method (Volberda, 1992).

2. A measure of internal flexibility is an accumulation of the scores with respect to the throughput aspects, that is Fintern = f(production system, information system, inventories, products/services, personnel, financial resources). In the same way, a measure of external flexibility is an accumulation of flexibility scores of the competitive forces on the input and output side of the organization: Fextern = f(raw materials markets, suppliers, workload, labour markets, outer technologies, financiers, distribution intermediaries, internal customers/clients, external customers/clients, product-market combinations). Finally, the information coefficient indicates the percentage of information activities performed by management in relation to the total possible number of information activities.

3. The FARSYS research project was made possible by a research grant of GITP Management Focus, Nijmegen, The Netherlands. Participants of the project were Ab Rutges (project leader), Frits Bouma and Geert-Jan Ringerwöle (programmers), three research assistants, and myself.

4. The logic underlying the selection of cases of theoretical interest is one of replication: each case was carefully selected in such a way that the use of the FAR method gave different but predictable results (in terms of types of flexibility, design variables, and trajectories of change). The goal of the longitudinal study was to expand and to generalize the empirical claims and underlying theory of the method, and not to enumerate frequencies of success of the method within a population of organizations (statistical generalization).

10 Discovering Flexible Corporations of the Future: Managerial and Theoretical Implications

> [T]he design of the organization itself has emerged as a new strategic variable . . . . Historically, managers designed and redesigned organizations by making modifications to traditional bureaucratic forms on the basis of intuition, past experience, imitation, and personal attitudes and preferences. The design of organizations that are flexible, that adapt and create change, that more fully use both human and technology resources, and that are global in scope, are perhaps the most significant variables of the new forms. Strategies for hypercompetitive environments can only be undertaken within the limits enabled by organization form. New organization forms open up new sources of sustained competitive advantage.
>
> (Daft and Lewin, 1993: ii)

Increasingly changing competitive forces have spawned experimentation with new and varied flexible organizational forms (cf. Ilinitch *et al.*, 1996). Managers and companies are coping as best they can. A few are experimenting with radical, ill-understood new organizational forms, largely without any guidance from research. Most managers, however, are thoughtlessly copying successful organizational forms with no clear ideas about changing competitive forces and their implications. What is needed is a new theoretical framework to manage and understand the new flexible forms of the future.

In this book, we considered alternative flexible forms that enable firms to initiate or respond successfully to different kinds of competition. On the basis of an elaboration of the flexibility paradox, a strategic framework was developed for building flexible organizations. The framework was used to construct a rich typology of organizational forms for coping with hypercompetitive environments. From the typology, trajectories of organizational success and failure in meeting various levels of competition were obtained. Finally, we developed the FAR method for supporting management efforts directed towards revitalizing mature and declining organizations and routinizing chaotic firms.

In this final chapter, we shall discuss the managerial and theoretical implications of this framework and typology. The empirical studies in this book provided examples of superior organizational forms for use with particular kinds of competition. In addition, some likely trajectories were considered with examples based on flexibility audits in Philips Semiconductors, the Dutch Postbank, and the Dutch National Gas Corporation. Nevertheless, in reconciling the 'logic of discovery' presented here with the 'logic of justification' applied in the empirical studies, a few remarks are necessary.

First, the logic of discovery in this book is to some extent speculative, based on a limited number of observations. At the moment, the FAR method has been applied in a multi-client study on strategic renewal, including large corporations such as KLM Royal Airlines, the Dutch PTT, Van Ommeren Tank Storage, and Ericsson. These flexibility audits support our framework and typology, but also suggest that there is an alternative trajectory for speeding up the revitalization process (Sect. 10.1)

Secondly, besides being speculative, the logic of discovery can never be as comprehensive as reality. Perhaps there are forms that span the boxes because the typology is restricted to only one level of analysis. If multiple levels or multiple parts are considered, different configurations of rigid, planned, flexible, and chaotic forms can be found. Our typology and trajectories have profound implications for the design of the flexible multiunit corporation. We shall consider four ways to reconfigure the multibusiness corporation to improve its overall flexibility: the network, the dual, the oscillating, and the balanced corporation (Sect. 10.2). Furthermore, on the basis of corporate transformations in these multiunit corporations, we found dual trajectories of transformation within a single company (Sect. 10.3). These multiple flexible forms and trajectories illustrate that there is managerial choice in building flexible firms (Sect. 10.4). We shall provide a rough sketch of the new flexible landscape of the twenty-first century.

10.1 Speeding up the Revitalization Process: A Trajectory of Radical Transformation

The logic of discovery applied in this book is to a large extent based on investigating multiple ways of solving the paradoxical nature of flexibility (Chs. 2 and 3). The strategic framework and typology developed (Chs. 4, 5, 6, 7, and 8), however, might be a fallacious attempt to reduce complex phenomena to simple dimensions. For instance, some dimensions might not be included in the framework. In addition, the typology does not address the question of causality, or how much the firm affects the market and vice versa. None the less, exploratory interviews with management consultants and flexibility audits within Philips Semiconductors, the Dutch Postbank, and the Dutch National Gas Corporation suggest that the ideal types correspond to some extent with actual organizations and clearly have some empirical value (Volberda, 1992). Furthermore, the FAR method has been systematically applied in several other large corporations in various industries, like KLM Royal Airlines, the Dutch PTT, Van Ommeren Tank Storage, Ericsson, Ytong (building materials), blood banks, hospitals, and provincial states. Moreover, the method is applied by students of the Erasmus University in several small companies, and by consultants.

On the basis of these flexibility audits, we may conclude that in moderately competitive environments in which firms' attention is directed towards reducing the level of environmental turbulence, a natural trajectory of routinization is most likely. Contrary to this evolutionary approach, a trajectory of revitalization is more likely to be successful in extremely hypercompetitive environments in which firms are confronted with unpredictable changes.

Of course, we have to realize that both trajectories have their pitfalls. The risk of a trajectory of routinization is that it will transform the firm into a rigid form as a result of strategic drift. The surplus of operational flexibility, consisting of sophisticated routines, creates inertia in the form of a very mechanistic structure and a very narrowly focused culture. Growing resistance in an organization to 'deviant' interpretations of the environment reflects a tendency towards 'overbalance' of the rigid form. On the other hand, a trajectory of revitalization risks turning a firm into a 'chaotic form' as a result of 'strategic neglect'. The surplus of structural and strategic flexibility in this situation can lead to unfocused actions with dysfunctional results. The chaotic form's lack of administrative structures, sense of direction, shared beliefs, and institutional leadership is characteristic of a tendency towards 'underbalance' of the chaotic form.

Besides these sequential trajectories of routinization and revitalization, our data from a flexibility audit of KLM Cargo suggests a more radical way to transform the firm. This short cut from extreme rigidity towards a highly chaotic state proved to be adequate for firms under substantial time pressure (see Fig. 10.1).

Radical Transformation of KLM Cargo

KLM Cargo, a division of KLM Royal Dutch Airlines, is one of the world's leading air cargo carriers. It intends to rank among the top three customer-driven suppliers of high-quality transport, distribution, and information services worldwide. It has embarked on a radical change programme, turning itself inside out in the process, to fulfil this mission.

A major step in this endeavour occurred in 1989 with the development of the KLM corporate programme Vision '93, which led to the reconfirmation of the airline's core activities and the creation of two divisions: passenger and cargo. In 1994, KLM Cargo launched the 'Division in Transition' programme, which incorporated not only issues of strategy and structure but the determination to effect behavioural change throughout the organization. Until then, KLM's main cargo activities were made up of predominantly generic transport services, which are packaged and supplied to the end-user. The margin on these generic services has been slowly eroded: carriers can provide these services only if the highest priority is given to efficiency. Moreover, KLM Cargo did not know who its clients were, and their customers—the freight-forwarding agents—frequently turned out to be their competitors. KLM Cargo's new strategy was therefore based on end-customers that are prepared to pay extra for value-added products, the exact nature of which differs from client to client. This move towards an organization that will be able to offer yet more added value to clients required a shift from Air Network, which offers a distributed network with a central hub, to Air Logistics or even Full Logistics. Essentially, all providers of base commodities (airlines, hauliers, shipping lines) find that the further they move downstream towards the customer, the more their perspectives need to shift from mono-modal to multi-modal, and from basic transportation services to more complete logistics service options.

In realizing this fundamental change, the creation of an entirely different mindset was most important. KLM Cargo now had to perceive itself as provider

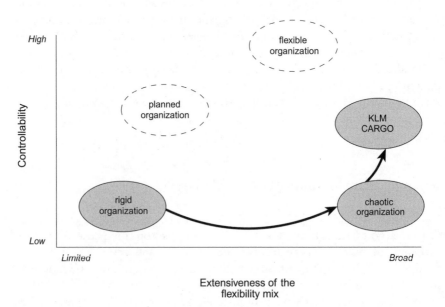

Fig. 10.1. KLM cargo: a trajectory of radical transformation

of integrated logistics instead of an airline operator with only transport and distribution services. This unlearning of its old strategic schema and relearning of a new one (metaflexibility) required it to invest heavily in flexible capabilities to provide a variety of customized added-value services. Furthermore, it decided to fundamentally redesign the organization. Thus, it flattened the organization and arranged its functions into three disciplines (Operations, Sales, and Customer Service), five business units (Cargo Service Centres, which perform handling activities; Mail; IT; Logistics; and a Special Cargo Unit, which is responsible for such cargoes as perishables, valuables, and live animals); and seven staff departments. The obvious reason for this structural change was to get closer to customers, cutting down the bureaucracy, and empowering people to act innovatively and swiftly.

In less than one year, KLM Cargo had managed to change its geographic hierarchical structure into a flat dual structure with central functional departments and autonomous business units. Everybody had to reapply for new management positions and managers often had to move from one continent to another. Furthermore, it created self-organizing teams in the factory. In order to facilitate these fundamental changes, management organized awareness courses, training seminars, and interactive workshops.

While this radical change from a rigid towards a chaotic state created momentum for change, however, it also caused some major problems. First, the applicability of both information systems and the skill repertoire of employees (rigidity of technology) to new services was very limited. Moreover, the splitting of the division into functional departments (Sales, Operations, and Customer Service) and five business units (Cargo Service Centre, Mail, IT, Logistics, and Special Cargo) resulted in large sequential interdependencies and fights about who owns the customer. Furthermore, there was much resistance from lower-level managers who were not involved in the change process (cultural values). In order to exploit its newly developed capabilities, management standardized the service portfolio (commodities, specialties, and customized) and developed a more transparent structure in which a new department 'business systems' was responsible for more efficient coordination. In addition, management tightened its strategic vision and developed a code of conduct for communicating the common cultural values in KLM Cargo. After the transformation, KLM Cargo could be positioned somewhere between the flexible and the chaotic mode (see Fig. 10.1).

One may ask when it is appropriate for management to choose a sequential revitalization from a rigid to a planned to a flexible mode, and when it should choose to radically transform the organization from a rigid to a chaotic to a flexible mode. Our data suggest that a radical transformation is less time-consuming, but more risky because the scope of change is large and the content of change is more difficult (Baden-Fuller and Volberda, 1997). It requires the organization to transform quickly and in a holistic manner, which carries severe dangers. There is a risk that the organization will disintegrate into chaos. Sequential revitalization will therefore be most effective when the firm is not concerned with speedy reaction. By contrast, radical transformation will be more effective when there is a pressing need for the organization to respond collectively.

10.2 Designing The Flexible Multiunit Corporation

So far, our framework and typology were applied to a division or business unit with only one line of business. But how do large multiunit firms reconcile the conflicting forces for change and stability? How do they promote order and control, while having to respond, renew, and learn? In terms of our typology, these organizations need properties of the flexible, planned, or even chaotic forms at the same time or in different portions of the corporation. Perhaps there are several corporate forms that span the boxes because the typology is restricted to only one level of analysis. Some examples of these meta-forms can be found in Section 3.4, which discusses various oscillating, balanced, and simultaneous modes of innovation as well in Section 6.2, which considers innovative and dynamic structures that seem to combine properties of both the planned and the flexible form. Building upon the ways of dealing with the flexibility paradox as discussed in Section 3.5 (Poole and Van de Ven, 1989), we distinguish in this section four corporate responses for combining in some way the elements of change and preservation (see Fig. 10.2): opposition (network corporations), spatial separation (dual corporations), temporal separation (oscillating corporations), and synthesis (balanced corporations).[1]

Opposition: The Network Corporation

Most corporations find it difficult to combine the discipline of a planned form with the openness of a flexible form. The network corporation accepts the tension between change and preservation, but believes that the opposition between exploitation of routines (planned mode) and exploration of new flexible capabilities (flexible mode) cannot be solved within the firm. Thus, it outsources the problem of change or preservation to others (Baden-Fuller and Volberda, 1997). It is essentially a broker of planned, flexible, or even chaotic organizational modes linked in a variety of complex ways (Miles and Snow, 1986). Resolving the paradox of change and preservation can take place in the network because there is no longer a clear distinction between competition outside the organization and cooperation inside. Rather, the partners in the network experience

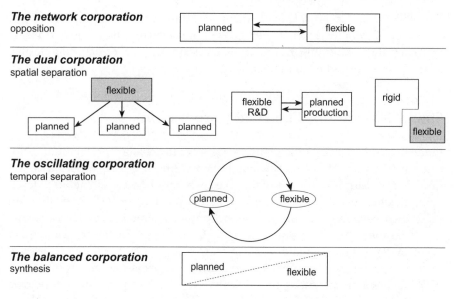

Fig. 10.2. The flexible corporation

both competition and cooperation. Competition is a driving force for change, but cooperation helps ensure resources and stability. This view was also espoused by Ouchi (1981) in his discussions of clans of organizations. The social pressures to aspire to higher achievement and the resources of the network provide industrial clans with powerful mechanisms for resolving the flexibility paradox of change and preservation. However, the same features which give these networks strength, especially the strong social bonds, can also slow radical change. In other words, corporate networks run the risk of becoming tight networks in which there is no real opposition or constructive tension between change and preservation.

Many will recognize this corporate network form as an approach that has been embraced by a small, but growing number of highly successful companies over the past decade. The UK-based Amstrad, which has battled successfully against much larger firms in the consumer electronics and computer industries, is illustrative. It has built market share for an expanding range of high-tech durables that are developed and manufactured with heavy dependence on outsourced components, subassemblies, and other inputs (Bartlett, 1993). Other examples include the Dutch computer firm, Tulip, or Nike, which has strategic flexibility in capabilities focused tightly on product design and marketing, and

269

externalizes almost all 'planned' manufacturing and distribution functions. To achieve flexibility in what they do without incurring high costs or losing efficiency, these central firms create alliances among smaller naturally flexible firms (Lorenzoni and Baden-Fuller, 1995).

Spatial Separation: The Dual Corporation

In the network, participating firms do not solve the change/preservation paradox but focus on one of its two components. Another way to deal with the flexibility paradox is to solve it within the corporation by simultaneously developing flexible and planned modes in different portions of the corporation. In these 'dual' corporations, one horn of the paradox operates at one level of analysis, while the other horn operates at a different level. Spatial separation can occur by level, function, and/or location (see Fig. 10.2). Level differences are related to hierarchy (e.g. top versus middle versus front-line managers), functional differences are caused by the distinctive functions performed, processes applied, or knowledge used (e.g. marketing, production, engineering), and location differences are influenced by geography or business unit. These ideas can be found in the literature on corporate restructuring (specific managerial roles for various hierarchical levels), learning theories (types of learning related to certain hierarchical levels), and internal corporate venturing (splitting up the company into an operating core and new business ventures). In this perspective, the dual corporation has to spell out and manage spatial relationships between flexible and more planned organizational modes.

An example of a *level* distinction (see Sect. 5.2 on vertical management) can be found in the traditional M-form, in which top management operates in a flexible mode and has a high absorptive capacity for exploring new business opportunities (Chandler, 1962). In this setting, the divisions operate best in the planned mode for maximally exploiting these business opportunities; they change only as a result of the strategic intent of top management. The new corporate form of GE emerging from Jack Welch's redesign efforts is a more sophisticated version of such a hierarchically divisionalized structure (Miles *et al.*, 1995). Yet, we can also think of corporations in which the strategic exploration of new opportunities takes place at the lowest level; interactions with the market and demanding clients cause front-line managers to call into question their norms, objectives, and basic policies. Corporate management operates in the planned mode, which permits it to persist in its set policies and achieve formulated objectives, which change as a result of the autonomous behaviour of front-line managers. This reversed hierarchy can be found in 3M.

Separation by *function* can be found in nearly all corporations. Usually, production departments operate in a rigid or planned mode for reasons of efficiency and scale, marketing departments operate in a more flexible mode since they are exposed to various customer demands, while R&D departments that are engaged in highly unpredictable research projects operate in a chaotic mode. More extreme examples of functional separation for solving the flexibility paradox can be found in Honda and KLM Cargo. In order to make functional tensions visible, Honda broke itself apart in a far more radical fashion than had ever occurred in its industry (Pascale, 1990). R&D and Engineering were split into two separate companies. While Honda Motor Company (with sales and manufacturing) is the parent, and primary customer, each of the three companies now has its distinct identity and specific organizational mode. The tensions between these companies, each highly independent, yet interdependent, are not suppressed, but serve as the engine of change and renewal.

Similarly, KLM Cargo decided to split its Cargo Factory (handling, warehouse management, and flight network control), in which volume and efficiency are most important, from the business units, in which service, market penetration, and the development of new logistic services dominate. The functional separation allows each business unit to respond to various well-defined markets, but still share in processes and technologies.

Yet dividing a corporation into its functional parts can result in dysfunctional tensions and a fragmented organization that has lost its synergies. In Section 3.5, we called this condition schismogenesis. To keep a divided company together, management has to develop strong cross-functional and cross-value capabilities. In Honda, these capabilities are strong enough to handle stress without tearing. In KLM Cargo, the lack of these capabilities increased the need for setting rules and guidelines on how to use shared assets. Management thus decided to create a new unit, Cargo Business Systems, which is responsible for coordination, systemization, and organization of the core processes.

A third way of spatial separation is by *location*. In almost every diversified firm, one sees asymmetry between high-growth businesses and older, mature operations. That is to say, mature divisions confronted with moderate competition operate in a planned mode, whereas some new divisions developed to create or counter hypercompetitive disruption may operate in a flexible or even chaotic mode (cf. Galunic and Eisenhardt, 1996).

Many scholars have tried to tackle the problem of creating flexible units within large established corporations. They question how new innovation-promoting flexible units should be organized, and what their relationship with the other parts of the organization should be. Van de Ven (1986) has drawn attention to 'the structural problem of managing part-whole relationships'. Drucker (1985: 161–3) expressed the view that flexible units should be organized separately, and should have substantial autonomy from the rest of the organization, in particular from the operational units. Galbraith (1982) stressed the importance of 'reservations', which are totally devoted to creating new ideas, while

Flexible Corporations of the Future

Peters and Waterman (1982) used the term 'skunk works' for this phenomenon. A refinement of their suggestion comes from Kanter (1988: 184–91) who distinguished between the 'generation' of an innovation which, in her view, requires frequent contact and closer integration with other parts of the organization, and the 'completion' or implementation of the innovation in flexible modes, for which segregation or isolation from the rest of the organization would be helpful.

Based on these perspectives, we can distinguish separation by location in different degrees, varying from the creation of skunk works (Peters and Waterman, 1982), to corporate ventures (Fast, 1979, Burgelman, 1983) to even completely new venture departments. At the simplest level, we can think of isolating a flexible unit from a rigid operating core. This principle was applied at IBM when the IBM PC was developed, as the mainframe logic was strongly preserved in IBM's culture and prevented entry into the new PC market. While at first IBM was very successful with this isolation strategy, it found that transferring these new capabilities from the flexible mode to the rigid operating core was very difficult. IBM could not exploit these capabilities in its operating core because it lacked communication channels and common mental frames. Similarly, Eastman Kodak, Philips, and Xerox have derived only modest success from their internal venturing and new business development programmes.

A more complicated form of separation involves the continuous splitting off of groups into separate organizations. Hewlett-Packard, Johnson & Johnson, and Origin are examples of corporations that have developed a system of small, semi-autonomous units, and encourage entrepreneurs to pursue their ideas in new separate divisions, while the older, more established divisions provide continuity and stability (Mintzberg and Westley, 1992). Overall, the organization appears to be in a perpetual stage of adaptation, never really rigid or planned as long as new units are being regularly spun off from the older ones. This process is best described as a regular cell fission, characterized by ongoing entrepreneurial revitalization. However, the downside to this cell structure is that such corporations may become overly divisionalized, and have problems with exploiting synergies across certain businesses. Because of continuous fission, these organizations lose their identity and become uncontrollable.

Approaches of spatial separation by location seem to assume that the parent organization can continue to operate in a planned fashion, while a flexible subunit of the organization is permitted to undertake pioneering (e.g. R&D) endeavours. None the less, to the extent that the relevant environment for the organization as a whole has been transformed from moderate competition towards hypercompetition, the crisis confronts the entire organization and requires a comprehensive response, not a partial one. Although the creation of a separate flexible unit accelerates progress in new areas of opportunity, it often leads to problems of morale, disruption, and re-assimilation (MacMillan, 1985).

Consequently, exploiting the new opportunities can be slow and frustrating (cf. Burgelman, 1983). Sometimes, a dramatic corporate-wide transformation may be necessary to temporarily explore new flexible capabilities. The limitations of spatial separation bring us to temporal separation as a way to deal with the flexibility paradox of change and preservation.

Temporal Separation: The Oscillating Corporation

Whereas opposition and spatial separation consider change and preservation occurring contemporaneously, temporal separation resolves the flexibility paradox over time (see Fig. 10.2). Periods of operational flexibility and tight organizational conditions (planned mode) are alternated with periods of strategic and structural flexibility and loose organizational conditions (flexible mode). In this perspective, the oscillating corporation is being sequentially manipulated into the flexible mode that stimulates the proposal of radical innovations and then back into the planned mode, which enhances adoption of incremental innovations.[2] In periods of change, there are radical transformations across the whole organization.

In making the distinction between the two different phases, almost all recognize that during periods of preservation, a firm can develop some new operational capabilities alongside the exploitation of the specialized routines. This process will be one of incremental development (Nelson and Winter, 1982). However, there will be moments where change and preservation cannot co-exist; these will occur when the trajectory becomes competence-destroying (Tushman and Anderson, 1986). At such moments, the organization cannot simultaneously exploit the old and develop the new, but has to 'choose' (perhaps unconsciously) between radical change and slow decline (Volberda and Baden-Fuller, 1996).

For small entrepreneurial firms, this dynamic alternation between flexible and planned organizational modes is part of their existence and competitive advantage. Their lack of tight commitments and relatively low sunk costs enable them to undertake radical change easily. For large corporations, complete transformations are much more complicated and nearly impossible. None the less, Kanter (1994) used case histories from companies such as Kodak and Apple Computer to argue that US corporate giants can learn to change. In addition, using examples of mature UK firms (Richardson, Edwards, and Hotpoint), Baden-Fuller and Stopford (1994) observed that although triggers for change may have to come from many quarters and may take time to gather speed, the state of the whole organization can change from rigidity to flexibility. Case histories of large capital-intensive corporations such as DSM Chemicals, Shell, and Unilever that operate in cyclical industries also give us examples of firms that have been successful in managing alternate cycles of convergence and divergence. However, the periods of change for these companies were infrequent and relatively short as compared to periods of preservation. In Unilever, for instance, over the last twelve years there have been three periods of sharp upheaval followed by periods of comparative stability (cf. Maljers *et al.*, 1996). By contrast, for corporations facing more hypercompetitive environments, the exploitation of capabilities becomes extremely difficult, while the periods of change are more frequent (cf. D'Aveni, 1994). Instead of long, stable periods in which corporations can achieve sustainable competitive advantage, hypercompetition is increasingly characterized by short periods of advantage punctuated by frequent disruptions. As an illustration, Microsoft initiates a corporate redesign every eight months in order to remain competitive because, in the software industry, the fully flexible company of today will be the rigid organization of tomorrow. In the process of frequent change, however, oscillating corporations have to prevent themselves from 'overshooting' and becoming extremely rigid or chaotic.

Synthesis: The Balanced Corporation

The corporate responses to the flexibility paradox of change and preservation considered so far leave each of the two extremes basically intact. We must ask whether there are corporate forms that make possible a synthesis of flexible and planned organizational modes at the same time and at the same level?

In Section 3.4, we discussed innovative forms that balance flexible with planned organizational modes. Applying these insights to our strategic framework of flexibility, a balanced corporation can choose to compensate for its mechanistic structure by encouraging and promoting cultural heterogeneity. Consequently, the firm will experience a constructive tension between strategic chance and structural preservation. If, on the other hand, an organization wants to compensate for the proven structural flexibility of its organic structure, it can seize upon the various devices used to solidify and extend a more homogeneous cultural pattern. Doing so will result in a tension between structural change and strategic preservation. Some large corporations such as 3M and Motorola have developed structures and cultures to achieve this balancing act (see Sect. 3.4). Weick (1982), however, noted that compromise responses might be detrimental to the total flexibility of the corporation because they usually dominate other alternatives since they are often acceptable to those with competing interests. Thus, such responses further reduce the variety of flexible capabilities. Should these corporations have to cope with a changed environment, they might not be able to develop the right responses since they have retained only composite alternatives.

Other corporate forms that come close to the balanced corporation are the hybrid forms discussed in Figure 6.3 of Section 6.2. For instance, Sharp's hypertext form combines the steady-state flexibility of the functional form with the strategic flexibility of a flat, cross-functional task force (Nonaka and Takeuchi, 1995). Even more complicated and diffuse is Olivetti's platform corporation in which there is the coexistence of a multiplicity of organizational forms (Ciborra, 1996): managers may operate within two or more organizational modes at the same time. The firm has much latitude for surprise and change, but retains the underlying bedrock of the collective cognitive schemas of participating managers.

10.3 Dual Trajectories of Transformation

The four ways of reconfiguring the corporation discussed here are not mutually exclusive. Many corporations apply some of these corporate forms sequentially or simultaneously. Furthermore, some evidence of corporate transformations in regulated companies suggests that if multiple levels or multiple parts are considered, dual trajectories of transformation for coping with hypercompetition can be found in a single company. We will consider these dual trajectories because they illustrate how large established firms can cope successfully with increasing competition.

Building on our typology, Smith and Zeithaml (1996) found two different

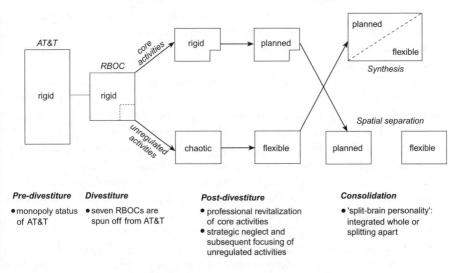

Fig. 10.3. A dual-trajectory model of organizational transformation within two RBOCs
Source: adapted from Smith and Zeithaml (1996)

trajectories within the same RBOC[3] (see Fig. 10.3). Before 1984, local telephone service activities were protected within the rigid organizational form and natural monopoly status of AT&T. After divestiture, the RBOCs shifted their core activities into more planned modes, but in their unregulated business they created more chaotic modes. In other words, the two distinct areas followed two different trajectories: professional revitalization of core telephone activities, and strategic neglect and subsequent focusing of early chaotic international activities.

The traditional wireline activities could be initially characterized as rigid because they still operated in highly regulated environments, had received a windfall local rate in 1984, and held a monopoly in local service. In the early 1990s the management efforts of two RBOCs resulted in a transition from extreme rigidity towards a more planned organizational form (reduction of domestic regulations, establishing incentive-based rate making) in the regulated side of the RBOCs' business. While managers in these two firms were trying to understand their new regulatory environment, they had neglected many of their more speculative unregulated activities, such as international expansion. Lack of supervision allowed chaotic forms, but top management intervention and focusing enabled international managers in these firms to develop some flexible modes with a high level of strategic flexibility: fast start-ups of new, international entrepreneurial ventures, flexibility in bidding on deals and partner selection, and learning about technologies such as a digital cellular and bypass operations. These 'marketing mavericks' and 'corporate renegades' led the development of new learning and new capability development from international activities. They determined that they could not continue to manage with their existing monopolistic mindset, in which they controlled all aspects of the business, and that they had to learn to react quickly to changes in international opportunities.

The fact that these two RBOCs now complain about their 'split brain' personality is not surprising given their two trajectories: one through chaos and another through a more planned mode. Within both RBOCs, the flexibility in international activities contrasted with the more planned nature of the rest of their activities. One RBOC solved this paradox by knitting the regulated and unregulated sides into an integrated whole (synthesis), whereas the other accepted the paradox by splitting the company in two (spatial separation) to increase both parts' chances for survival (Volberda, 1996a). In the integrated RBOC, the cross-fertilization was helpful in awakening the wireline operations to the realities of coming competition (Smith and Zeithaml, 1996: 395). The CEO of this organization tried to change the conservative culture under which the regular side of the business had operated for many years by integrating the learning, experiences, and capabilities of managers of unregulated activities into the regulated activities. The CEO of the other RBOC believed that its regulated and unregulated units would have better chances of developing appropriate types of flexibility by refocusing their activities rather than meshing them together (Smith and Zeithaml, 1996: 396). Recently, many large corporations (e.g. AT&T, Nedloyd, ITT, Unisys, Vendex) have split up into separate parts in order to separate well-developed planned core activities from new flexible growth activities. Other large established corporations have split off flexible parts of their rigid or planned core, such as EDS from GM, Eastman Chemical from Eastman Kodak, and Sprint Cellular from Sprint. Many other large established corporations will probably also divest because it seems that shareholders value extreme spatial separation of planned and flexible forms more than some kind of balanced corporation.

The dual-trajectory model of organizational transformation may be of value to other regulated companies, such as electronic utilities, railway, and post companies that must address dramatically changing competitive forces. In increasingly competitive environments (e.g. the introduction of competition in a nearly monopolistic industry), areas of chaos should perhaps be created or tolerated by

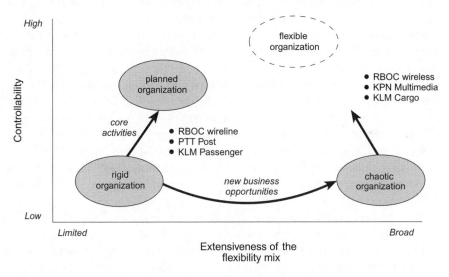

Fig. 10.4. A dual-trajectory revitalization of regulated firms facing extreme competition

top management, while core activities should move along a revitalization path. Similar trajectories were found in the Dutch PTT Post and KLM (see Fig. 10.4).

The Dutch PTT Post is one of the largest divisions of KPN and is made up of several business units (letters, parcel service, mediaservice, international, EMS, logistics, philately) and joint ventures (Post Offices, GD Express Worldwide,

Interpost Group of Companies). It is preparing itself for the transition from a highly regulated environment to a more competitive one. To revitalize its core activities and exploit new growth opportunities, it initiated several change projects such as Mail 2000, Tele-present, and New Formulas for the Post Office network. In the Mail 2000 project it worked together with A. T. Kearny on improving its competencies in physical transport and distribution of mail, still its core business. By automating the sorting process and reducing the number of sorting hubs, it increased the steady-state and operational flexibility of its primary process. In the Post Office project, it adopted a McDonald's formula to focus on the client. Despite this professional revitalization of its core activities, it realized, however, that the amount of mail it will deliver will further decrease due to other communication means, that its margins will diminish, and that wages and inflation will increase. To compensate for decreasing revenues and increasing costs in the traditional planned post organization, it needed new growth areas. To develop these areas, it started various chaotic projects such as the tele-present project with outside partners, VNU (a Dutch publishing firm) and RTL (a European mediaservice company). In this project it helped develop a new service: clients could give orders to send gifts, a kind of teleshopping. The service was located in a new developed business unit, namely mediaservice. It required the development of a call centre, a tele-present information system, warehousing (PTT Logistics), and distribution (Parcel Service). For PTT Post, this project formed an entry avenue into the electronic super-highway and the development of data distribution capabilities. In addition, this venture was the forerunner of a multi-mall project, in which clients could order products in a virtual store. None the less, in the consolidation of this project, the corporate management of KPN decided to position Tele-present in the KPN Multimedia Division, which is a 50–50 per cent joint venture of PTT Post and PTT Telecom. In order to develop data warehousing and distribution capabilities, PTT Post could learn much from the PTT Telecom Division, which had already coped with tough competition for several years.

This dual trajectory can also be found in less regulated companies such as KLM, which faces extreme competition. While KLM's Passenger Division is working on a trajectory of professional revitalization (continuously improving service levels, reducing overall costs, and increasing operational flexibility in terms of flight capacity and personnel), we showed in Section 10.1 that its Cargo Division had gone through a radical transformation from a rigid to an extremely chaotic organizational mode (offering an increased number of value-added services to customers, attracting new customers, and providing non-transport-related logistic services) and is now slowly shifting towards a more flexible mode (categorizing the service portfolio, a more transparent structure, tightening the strategic vision, and developing Cargo values and a code of conduct).

For these dual trajectories to succeed, top managers must be able to tolerate the presence of initially chaotic modes so that learning takes place. On the other hand, they should have some business intuition or metaflexibility of when to intervene, focus on certain activities, give additional resources, or terminate activities.

10.4 Building the Flexible Firm: Equifinality and Managerial Choice

To conclude, the most important contribution of this book is that it describes successful ways to achieve superior flexibility. As is clear from the empirical studies in this chapter, however, there will never be one best way to achieve flexibility in hypercompetitive environments. The trajectories discussed indicate that firms can arrive at the flexible form through strategic focusing of the chaotic mode or through entrepreneurial revitalization of the planned mode. In addition, the flexible form itself can be achieved in different ways, thus suggesting equifinality. There are several equally good ways to match high variety and speed of managerial capabilities with an adequate organization design in order to resolve the constructive tension between developing capabilities and preserving stability within the organizational conditions.

Finally, the train of thought in this book has been initiated in other areas, such as the work on strategy types (Miles and Snow, 1978; Mintzberg and Waters, 1985), archetypes of organizational transitions (Miller and Friesen, 1980; Nelson and Winter, 1982), and types of corporate entrepreneurship (Schumpeter, 1934; Stopford and Baden-Fuller, 1994). Although the logic of discovery was enriched by those works, the intention of this book is to develop theory and stimulate debate that goes beyond theory about traditional forms in stable competition. Since a dramatic and far-reaching shift has occurred in the nature of competition in most industries, bureaucracy is no longer the appropriate form of organization, and the emergence of new organizational forms can be expected (Lewin and Stephens, 1993). We should consider what forms might characterize organizations in the twenty-first century. What will these future flexible organizations that combine still higher levels of change and preservation look like?

Many (cf. Clegg, 1990, Kanter et al., 1992) have predicted that the future will be dominated by small flexible firms that will be predominantly service or information oriented and apply automated production and computer-based technology, informal and decentralized structures, and loose and tolerant cultures. Our framework and typology, however, suggest a much larger variety of effective flexible forms over which managers exercise some choice. Moreover, we think that planned or even rigid modes will still exist. They will, however, be viable only as long as they are part of network or dual corporations in which the forces

Flexible Corporations of the Future

of stability are counterbalanced by change. These units will be most effective when the organization needs to contain the risk of change and is not concerned with speedy reactions. None the less, our typology seems to suggest that successful firms will generally move along a diagonal of increasing variety and speed of managerial capabilities together with higher levels of organizational responsiveness (see Fig. 10.5). In this connection, the oscillating and the balanced corporations, which allow the whole organization to adjust to competitive change more holistically and quickly, seem to be more promising. Without constant adaptation, however, the fully flexible firm of today will become the rigid firm of tomorrow. Firms must continuously increase the variety and speed of their flexible capabilities as well as their organizational responsiveness. Doing

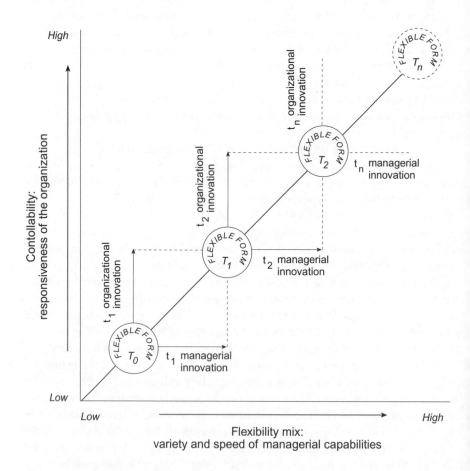

Fig. 10.5. The flexibility trajectory of successful firms of the twenty-first century

280

so requires innovation in managerial capabilities (flexible manufacturing, JIT, multi-sourcing, quick-response, product development capabilities) together with innovations in organization design (CAD/CAM, FMS, delayering, teaming, empowerment, corporate identity).

But how can firms reinvent themselves as they move along the flexibility trajectory? Unfortunately, most managers try only to copy existing successful forms rather than create new flexible forms. Consequently, their firms can at best be as good as their competitors, but never outperform them. The conceptual underpinnings of the viability of new flexible forms in situations of hypercompetition have not been discussed properly. Nevertheless, the strategic framework and typology of alternative flexible forms developed in this book may provide researchers with a useful guide for the discovery of effective organizational forms in the new world of hypercompetition. Moreover, managers and practitioners can use our framework and typology proactively in order to build the flexible firms of the future. These new forms may open up new sources of competitive advantage. The logic of discovery applied in this book has something to offer.

Notes

1. Many of the ideas of how to reconfigure the corporation for dealing with change and preservation that are worked out in this section are derived from the article 'Strategic Renewal from an Evolutionary Perspective: Four Dynamic Mechanisms' that I wrote with Charles Baden-Fuller (1996).

2. Mintzberg (1978), too, showed how organizations not only go through periods of strategy adjustment characterized by continuity, flux, or incremental change, but also require more global changes. In addition, Greiner (1972) charted periods of evolution and revolution in corporate development. Moreover, the tenor of this cyclical process is in line with Burns and Stalker (1961), who concluded that the organic form was temporary because the internal dynamics necessary for its success could not be sustained. Their speculations of an oscillating organizational mode are supported by many other scholars. Duncan (1976), for instance, referred to the bifurcated organization as the ambidextrous organization, while Shepard (1967) called it the two-state organization (see also Sect. 3.4).

3. The discussion of the trajectories within the two RBOCs is based largely on the fruitful discussions I had with Anne Smith while completing my paper on flexible forms for a special issue of *Organization Science* (1996) on 'Hypercompetition and New Organizational Forms'. Moreover, further details of these trajectories were enriched by Smith and Zeithaml's empirical paper on 'Garbage Cans and Advancing Hypercompetition' in this same special issue.

Appendix I

STANDARDIZED QUESTIONNAIRES OF THE FAR METHOD

On the basis of standardized questionnaires, the consultant collects data during interview sessions with organization participants. The topics contained in these questionnaires cover the three building blocks of our strategic framework of flexibility: the environment (Sect. A), the actual flexibility mix (Sect. B), and the flexibility potential available within the organizational conditions (Sects. C, D, and E).

To speed up the data-gathering process, the consultant can use the software system FARSYS I. With this system, the consultant can edit the questionnaire, ask respondents to put their answers on a floppy disk containing the questionnaire, and analyse the data with the FARSYS software. The application of FARSYS results in a database with organizational data and a graphical representation of this data in six diagrams: an environmental turbulence profile, an actual flexibility profile, a technology characteristic, a structure characteristic, a culture characteristic, and a decision support matrix.

A ENVIRONMENTAL TURBULENCE SCAN

1. Primary process

If we consider your unit/department as a productive system, what comes in (literally or figuratively) as 'assignments, tasks, or work orders/basic materials' on the one side and what goes out as 'products' on the other side?

Input	Transformation process	Output
• basic materials	• expertise	• products/services
• suppliers	• production means	• PMCs
• workorders/ assignments	• inventories	• internal clients
• internal suppliers	• products being manufactured, services provided	• external clients
• external suppliers	• personnel	
• labour market	• financial resources	
• provision of means	• information system	
• technology		
• financiers		

2. With regard to basic materials (input)

   a. What basic materials do you use?
- number
- related
- to manufacture the same product / to manufacture different products

   b. Do you buy these at different raw material markets?
- number
- dependent / complementary markets

   c. Have changes in the supply of raw materials or subcomponents occurred recently? If so, what changes?
- unavailability of raw materials / subcomponents
- more expensive or cheaper raw materials / subcomponents
- transportation problems of raw materials / subcomponents
- substitute raw materials

   d. What has been your organization's reaction to this?
- capable of temporarily or permanently switching to other raw materials
- consciously using various raw materials / restricting to one or some raw materials due to cost advantages
- safety stocks
- arrangements with suppliers

   e. To what extent do these changes occur, that is, what are their consequences (intensity), and how often do they occur (frequency)?

   f. Can (could) these changes be predicted?
- subject to trends / cyclical

   g. If not, what information did (do) you lack?
- kind of change
- extent of the change
- time of occurrence

   h. Do you expect changes in the future with regard to raw materials / subcomponents and how does your unit / department try to anticipate these changes?
- predictable / not predictable

3. Concerning products supplied / services provided

   a. Does your unit / department mainly manufacture standard products, that is, very simple mass products, or is the emphasis more on one-time products, that is, custom-made goods?

   b. How many products does your unit / department manufacture? Can you make a division of the products supplied, and orders or activities executed?
- complementary / substitute products or services
- consisting of similar components and / or activities / consisting of completely different components and / or activities

   c. Have changes occurred or can they be expected concerning the products supplied? If so, what changes?
- change in quantity and / or sales volume (quantitatively) of products

- change in kind of product (qualitatively), in connection with product demands of internal and external clients, and so on
- generation of substitute products or completely new products

d. How does your unit/department anticipate these changes?
  - several steering measures
  - quality of steering measures
  - speed of introducing these measures

e. Are these changes far-reaching or not (intensity) and how often do they occur (frequency)?
  - quick and frequent fluctuations in size of the products to be supplied
  - short life cycles of the products
  - quickly varying demands of internal and external clients

f. Is it possible to predict the changes with regard to the products supplied? If not, what information is lacking?
  - kind of change
  - extent of change
  - time of occurrence

Let us have a look at the unit/department in its environment.

4. Suppliers of raw materials/basic materials

a. Who are the suppliers (of raw materials and semimanufactures) of the department/unit?
  - diversification/no diversification

b. Is it easy to change suppliers?

c. Is the unit/department very dependent on these suppliers? If so, is the unit trying to reduce this dependence?

d. Can changes be expected or have there been changes in the network and/or supply of suppliers? If so, what changes?

e. To what extent do these changes occur (intensity) and how often do they occur (frequency)?

f. Can these changes be predicted?
  For instance, with regard to the supply of raw materials and semimanufactures, are there more or less predictable peaks that return regularly? For instance, is there an annual cycle?
  If not, what information is lacking?
  - kind of change with regard to suppliers
  - extent of change
  - time of occurrence

5. Customers and buyers

a. Who are your customers/buyers or groups of customers/buyers?
  - internal clients
  - external clients

b. Do you have any insight into and information about the needs and demands of these customers (groups)?

- special varying demands of customers (fluctuating quantities and types)/non-varying demands of customers

c. Is the uniqueness of your products related to delivery time or quality, or is it normally the price that is decisive?
  - delivery time/quality/price

d. Are there changes to be expected with respect to the groups of clients/buyers and their demands? If so, what changes?
  Are these changes far-reaching? How often do they occur?
  - far-reaching/not far-reaching
  - often/sometimes
  - not predictable/predictable

e. As for external clients, does this differ per market segment?

f. Are there more or less predictable work peaks that return regularly, with regard to the sale of products? Is there, for instance, an annual cycle? Is the demand of clients predictable?

6. Markets and competitors

a. What market segments (PMCs) can be distinguished?
  - spreading/concentration
  - not related/related
  - phase of the life cycle

b. Is there a certain interdependence between these markets?
  - related/not related
  - strengthening each other/weakening each other

c. What position does your organization take in the relative market(s) (market share)?
  - practically unthreatened position
  - rather competitive and/or critical environment
  - vitally threatened position

d. Who are the competitors of the unit/department?

e. Are there changes to be expected in the existing market segments? If so, what changes?
  - generation of new markets
  - collapse of existing markets

f. How does your department/unit anticipate this?

g. To what extent do these changes occur (intensity)? How often do they occur (frequency)?
  - intensity
  - frequency

h. Are the changes concerning the market segments predictable? If not, what information is lacking?
  - kind of change
  - extent of change
  - time of occurrence

i. Are the exit barriers of existing market segments high or low?

j. Are the entry barriers of new potential markets high or low (capital, increase in scales, distribution channels, product name)?

k. Are there new potential competitors expected?
- quick and regular entering and leaving of competitors
- predictable / not predictable

l. Do you have sufficient information about your competitors (assortment, and so on)?
- quick and cheap registration of the wishes of customers
- strength / weakness analysis of the market
- competition analysis.

7. Distribution channels

a. What distribution channels does the organization have?
b. Are the entry and exit barriers of these distribution channels large or small?
c. Are there changes expected in the distribution system (way of distributing)?
- far-reaching / not far-reaching changes
- often / sometimes
- not predictable / predictable.

8. Labour market

a. What is the position of your unit / department in the labour market, that is, what are the possibilities for permanent jobs and personnel?
- almost trouble-free recruitment of a sufficient number and quality of staff
- possibilities for permanent jobs rather limited
- quantitatively / qualitatively very restricted for permanent jobs

b. How much learning time, schooling, education, and training is required to be able to carry out the work?
- interchangeability of personnel
- horizontal and vertical job enlargement

c. Do you use temporary personnel?
If so, in what form (temporary employees, employees on call, seasonal employees, and so on)?

d. Do you have staggered working hours, flexible compensation plans, or personnel being lent in and out?

e. Do you have the impression that in the course of time changes have occurred within your unit / department concerning the quantity and quality of personnel and equipment (predictable / not predictable)? Has the organization anticipated such changes (personnel policy, manpower planning, and so on).

9. Provision of financial means

a. Does your unit have financial means, budgets or certain resources that have not yet been granted?

b. What maximum amount could you currently reserve for extra investments through internally available means or other means?

c. How do you assess the mobility of the assets, the budget, and so on?
- possibilities of restrictions on the planned outflow (personnel, production, budgets)

- possibilities to split large investments into smaller independent parts, depending on the available means
- average pay-back period on investments

d. What is the relationship between fixed and variable costs? Can changes be observed in that relationship?

e. What is the relationship between direct and indirect costs? Can changes be observed in that relationship?

f. Has the organizational unit concluded any long-term contracts, non-terminable before maturity, with any stakeholders? If so, which stakeholders? What are the interest and the term of the contract?

10. Know-how

a. Are there changes to be expected concerning the technology/expertise of the unit/department? If so, what changes?
- new technologies
- innovation of process/product
- substitution technologies

b. Are these technological changes:
- far-reaching/not far-reaching
- regular/irregular
- fast/slow

c. Do you have sufficient insight into and information about any new technologies to be applied? (predictable/not predictable)
If not, what information is lacking?
- kind of technological change
- extent of change
- time of occurrence

11. Restrictions by government, by statutory restrictions, or by internal organization

a. Do you have to deal with specific government stipulations, statutory restrictions, and/or restrictions laid down by controlling departments?

b. Are there changes to be expected concerning these restrictions? To what extent can these changes be influenced?

Considering the above: can the external climate under which the organization must function be characterized as hardly changeable or as very changeable?

unchangeable	hardly changeable	rather changeable	changeable	very changeable
............./	................/	.............../	............./	....

B THE FLEXIBILITY SCAN

> Several flexible capabilities will be presented in the following checklist, concerning the aspects of input, throughput, and output of the department. By this flexibility scan (a systematization of flexible capabilities), it is possible to determine the management's flexibility mix. The questions ask you to indicate for every capability (by circling the correct number) whether your department:
>
> 1. does not use it
> 2. hardly uses it
> 3. uses it regularly
> 4. uses it often
> 5. uses it very often.

1. Input

1.1 Subcomponents, Basic Materials

1/2/3/4/5 Buy various kinds of subcomponents and basic materials (enhancing ability to react)

1/2/3/4/5 Buy various kinds of basic materials and subcomponents to manufacture the same product

1/2/3/4/5 Temporarily or permanently switching to alternative basic materials and/or subcomponents (backup possibility)

1/2/3/4/5 Buy basic materials and subcomponents that can be used for the production of various kinds of end-products (alternative applicability of basic materials and subcomponents)

1/2/3/4/5 Make the product composition such that the necessary number of different subcomponents and basic materials is minimized (enhancing quickness of reaction)

1.2 Workload

1/2/3/4/5 Ensure a constant volume of supply (contracyclical supply policy); curb supply of work (orders) during peak periods and promote supply during off-peak periods

1/2/3/4/5 Tune the supply of work in advance to the capacity of machinery and work; determine in advance possible bottlenecks in production and the workforce in order to anticipate these adequately

1/2/3/4/5 Set priorities concerning weekly orders/work orders in case of lack of capacity: orders of key customers before orders of ordinary customers

1/2/3/4/5 Fill safety stocks of outlets and distribution channels in case of overcapacity

1/2/3/4/5 Be able to switch over temporarily or permanently to alternative activities; backup possibility in case of undermanning (e.g. training)

1/2/3/4/5 Contract supply of work to other organizations

1/2/3/4/5 Contract supply of work to other departments within your organization

Appendices

1/2/3/4/5 Make the product package so that the necessary number of different work orders is minimized (enhancing the quickness of reaction)

1.3 Suppliers

(suppliers of key components and basic materials needed for the production of end-products)

1/2/3/4/5 Purchase subcomponents (semimanufactures) and basic materials from different, non-related suppliers (multi-sourcing); have at least a second supplier

1/2/3/4/5 Purchase subcomponents and basic materials from suppliers with a very short delivery time (just-in-time purchasing)

1/2/3/4/5 Purchase subcomponents and basic materials that cannot be kept in stock from suppliers with a reliable delivery time that is as short as possible

1/2/3/4/5 Periodicity of orders. That is, grant the complete order to one supplier, but let the orders rotate within a fixed circle of suppliers. The advantages are:
- spread of risk
- reliable delivery time because of greater involvement

1/2/3/4/5 Manufacture a very small percentage of the subcomponents/semimanufactures yourself, and purchase the rest from suppliers

1/2/3/4/5 Make arrangements with regular (large) suppliers concerning the quantity to be purchased and its quality: specifically with suppliers of key components

1/2/3/4/5 Purchase subassemblies from suppliers (co-makership)

1/2/3/4/5 Develop subcomponents together with the supplier(s) (co-design)

1/2/3/4/5 Build up stocks of basic materials and/or subcomponents with the supplier(s). That is, shifting the buildup of stocks backward

1/2/3/4/5 Reserve capacity with suppliers

1/2/3/4/5 Reserve capacity with the stipulation that when no appeal is made to this capacity, the supplier may use it through moderately efficient work in order to prevent a machinery standstill; the difference between normal efficiency and moderate efficiency must be paid in addition

1/2/3/4/5 Contract non-core activities to suppliers (outsourcing)

1.4 Labour market

(temporary workforce)

1/2/3/4/5 Use temporary personnel

1/2/3/4/5 • employment contract for a certain period or a certain job

1/2/3/4/5 • on-call contract

1/2/3/4/5 • contract with vacation workers

1/2/3/4/5 • contract to perform some services

1/2/3/4/5 • freelance contract

1/2/3/4/5 • temporary employees

1/2/3/4/5 • outworkers

1/2/3/4/5 • trainee contract

1/2/3/4/5 • articles of apprenticeship/employment contract

1/2/3/4/5 Contract personnel

1/2/3/4/5 • pooling arrangements for temporary employees

1/2/3/4/5 • external pooling arrangements (with other companies)

1/2/3/4/5 Contract work out (subcontractors)

1/2/3/4/5 Lend in varied and multipurpose personnel

1/2/3/4/5 Use good procedures for deploying replacement personnel

1.5 Technology

(technological developments with regard to the production process and product development)

1/2/3/4/5 Use technologies of different natures in the fields of production and development

1/2/3/4/5 Apply technologies that are each in a different phase of the life cycle

1/2/3/4/5 Reduce the commitment to/dependence on one specific kind of technology

1/2/3/4/5 Emphasize applied R&D, instead of basic R&D

1/2/3/4/5 Use the tactics of the technological follower (copying new technological developments with regard to production and products)

1/2/3/4/5 Start multiproject research programmes for product development. That is, create strategic core programmes in research, which are made up of various projects

1/2/3/4/5 Develop, together with other organizations/competitors, new products in view of the high development costs

1/2/3/4/5 Develop, together with other departments, new products, in view of the high development costs

1/2/3/4/5 Incorporate and apply new technological developments in the field of production quickly and easily; implement production–technical changes frequently

1/2/3/4/5 Apply quick product development and product innovation

2. Throughput

2.1 Production system

(machinery, equipment, and devices needed to process and assemble subcomponents and basic materials into end-products)

1/2/3/4/5 Implement a modular construction, that is, a standardization of parts and equipment, but also a variety of end-products as a result of configuration changes:
- normalization of the preparation route
- normalization of parts and materials
- preservation of scale advantages
- short delivery time
- smaller stock of components
- purchasing advantages

1/2/3/4/5 Arrange parallel (programmable) production flows

1/2/3/4/5 Possibility of switching over to another line/machine/workstation (shunt flexibility)

1/2/3/4/5 Possibility of changing the machinery sequence (machine-routing flexibility)

1/2/3/4/5 Possibility of changing the sequence of operations (product-routing flexibility) within a fixed machinery arrangement

Appendices

1/2/3/4/5 Increase the usability/applicability of existing machinery and equipment (multipurpose machinery)

1/2/3/4/5 Improve the switchability of machinery and equipment:
  • shorter setup times
  • higher capacity utilization

1/2/3/4/5 Use computer-controlled, adjustable machinery; numerically controlled machines (NC) or robotization:
  • broad usability
  • low setup costs
  • possibility of changing the processing run (programming flexibility)

1/2/3/4/5 Apply CAD/CAM (computer-aided design/computer-aided manufacturing)

1/2/3/4/5 Use normalized standby devices on various machinery to reduce the setup times

1/2/3/4/5 Increase the mutual interchangeability of parts and devices

1/2/3/4/5 Specialize into end-product in the latest possible stage of the goods stream; have the lowest possible specificity per part

1/2/3/4/5 Quality measurement in the earliest possible stage of the production process

1/2/3/4/5 Reduce the (technical) lead time and, intrinsic to this, the delivery time of products

1/2/3/4/5 • reduce the number of production phases by integrating certain process steps

1/2/3/4/5 • combine certain operations (e.g. work assembly and quality control); flexible production systems

1/2/3/4/5 • emphasis on direct quality control instead of control afterwards (do things correctly the first time)

1/2/3/4/5 • shift intermediate stocks to the final stage of the production process (sharpen quickness of reaction)
  Depending on:
  ⋆ added-value composition of the stocks
  ⋆ convergence or divergence of the production process

1/2/3/4/5 • increase the capacities of machinery and work; decrease the capacity utilization resulting in a reduction of the waiting times between the successive production phases.
  Strongly depending on the type of production process:
  ⋆ capital-intensive production process:
    high (technical) capacity utilization of machinery
  ⋆ work-intensive production process:
    multiskilled personnel with a high (organizational) activity ratio, and machinery and equipment with a low capacity utilization
    Solution: part of the capacity should have a very high utilization and another part should have a very low utilization. The low-utilization part should then be able to set off unexpected deviations.

1/2/3/4/5 • shorten the (average) processing times per phase

1/2/3/4/5 • reduce variations in processing times between pieces of machinery

1/2/3/4/5 • use priority rules and high-priority procedures

1/2/3/4/5 Produce small, varying batch sizes

1/2/3/4/5 Have variable production capacities available

1/2/3/4/5 Diversify production methods, that is, broaden the operational production repertoire

1/2/3/4/5 Set up small production units
- lower setup costs
- lower starting-up costs

1/2/3/4/5 Diversify production locations, that is, the production should not be concentrated in one place

2.2 Information systems

1/2/3/4/5 Decentralize information systems; individual employees keep the files up to date and process changes

1/2/3/4/5 Apply a modular construction; decomposition in independent subsystems:
- increase the adaptability and maintainability of the data system
- data construction which can be expanded and accessed easily

1/2/3/4/5 Increase the integratability (compatibility); many possibilities for mutual gearing of the various subsystems of a data system:
- increase the mutual interchangeability of subsystems
- increase the coupling possibilities of subsystems; automatic co-changing of coupled files

1/2/3/4/5 Increase the variety of application possibilities; universal systems to be used for various production activities

1/2/3/4/5 Shorten the response time

1/2/3/4/5 Increase the transferability of information by choosing the correct presentation form, arrangement of the material, and so on

1/2/3/4/5 Increase the user-friendliness, that is, high accessibility and easy use

1/2/3/4/5 Have a backup possibility available in case of failures in the information system.

2.3 Inventories

(opening inventories, disconnection inventories, closing inventories)

1/2/3/4/5 Build up safety stocks in order to compensate for great blockages in the delivery or production of subcomponents and/or basic materials that are of major importance for the continuation of the production process

1/2/3/4/5 Build up decoupling stocks; thus two subsequent phases in the production process can be made independent of each other to a certain extent (slack resources)

1/2/3/4/5 Move intermediate stocks to the initial phase of the production process to increase the alternative usability of these stocks (increase in ability to react); shift the stock upstream (bring the decoupling point to the left)

1/2/3/4/5 Build up the stock of finished products

1/2/3/4/5 • speculative inventories; these are kept with the intention of gaining an advantage from expected price changes (keen quickness of reaction)

1/2/3/4/5 • seasonal inventories; to compensate for fluctuations in sales

2.4 Products *(in the processing stage)*

1/2/3/4/5 Shorten the lead time of products, that is, quick order acceptance, collection of material, short technical processing times, and quick delivery

Appendices

1/2/3/4/5 Vary the product assortment; expansion/cutback in the assortment (assortment flexibility)

1/2/3/4/5 Vary the quantitative composition of the product mix (mix flexibility)

1/2/3/4/5 Vary the product volume

1/2/3/4/5 Compose a complementary product mix: combination of products that are very sensitive to fluctuations, with products with a more constant volume

1/2/3/4/5 Produce the broadest possible package of products in different stages of the life cycle at a given time, causing a decrease in the sensitivity to fluctuations in the economic situation

1/2/3/4/5 Produce custom-made products (specialties); small series for key customers

1/2/3/4/5 Take down rush orders quickly and easily, with the result that planning will have to allow for exceptions; deliver additional orders at short notice

1/2/3/4/5 Be able to deliver new products quickly and easily (addition to assortment) with, consequently, changing production tasks (product-innovation flexibility)

2.5 Personnel

(permanent workforce)

1/2/3/4/5 Improve the professional competence of the staff (upgrading); management development, internal training of employees

1/2/3/4/5 Apply horizontal extension of responsibilities (job enlargement). That is, be able to perform a broader repertoire of activities:

1/2/3/4/5 • job rotation to improve the versatility of employees, specifically for very vulnerable tasks

1/2/3/4/5 • increase the transferability and interchangeability of positions

1/2/3/4/5 Apply vertical extension of responsibilities (job enrichment). That is, obtain more decision-making authority over activities to be performed:

1/2/3/4/5 • leave the setting of priorities (setting up machinery) with regard to production tasks to be performed to employees; greater controlling capacity for employees

1/2/3/4/5 • apart from an extra quality check (extrinsic), a continuous quality review by the employees involved themselves (intrinsic)

1/2/3/4/5 • increased training; too great an extension of responsibilities (without extra training) may lead to losses in efficiency and quality

1/2/3/4/5 Use crash teams ('butterflies', 'flying squads'). That is, teams whose sole purpose is to do all kinds of unexpected jobs (universally versatile personnel)

1/2/3/4/5 Create:
• key positions
• multifaceted positions

1/2/3/4/5 Apply flexible compensation plans

1/2/3/4/5 • remuneration coupled to performance

1/2/3/4/5 • profit sharing

1/2/3/4/5 • shareholding

1/2/3/4/5 Flexibility in working hours

1/2/3/4/5 • flexibility in working hours depending on the season; working hours can be adapted not only to peak load, but can also be shortened in off-peak periods

1/2/3/4/5 • shift in working hours to have expensive machinery run longer, or reduce bottlenecks in the production process

1/2/3/4/5 • make good arrangements as to overtime

1/2/3/4/5 • compensate for overtime in leisure time (time-for-time arrangement)

1/2/3/4/5 • use a flexible duty roster

1/2/3/4/5 • apply flextime (block time and flexible time); suitable for production departments with a fluctuating workload. The employees may determine their own starting and finishing times, but should be present during certain fixed periods (block time)

1/2/3/4/5 Conclude flexible employment contracts

1/2/3/4/5 • job contract: contract for an indefinite period of time, whereby the length of the period is not expressed in hours, but is determined by the activities to be performed in the job

1/2/3/4/5 • part-time contract

1/2/3/4/5 Contract employees out to other departments on a temporary basis

1/2/3/4/5 Create an internal pooling arrangement, which the departments can use depending on their workload

2.6 Financial resources

1/2/3/4/5 Increase the availability of financial resources that have not yet been allocated (uncommitted resources)

1/2/3/4/5 Restrict/expand budgets with regard to production, number of staff, and size of capital

1/2/3/4/5 Liquidate certain assets

1/2/3/4/5 Lease certain industrial equipment

1/2/3/4/5 Be able to make additional investment for certain expansion of capacity and/or new facilities easily

1/2/3/4/5 Split large investments into smaller, independent parts, depending on the availability of funds/budgets

1/2/3/4/5 Shorten the pay-back period on investments

1/2/3/4/5 Reduce fixed costs

1/2/3/4/5 Reduce indirect costs

1/2/3/4/5 Restrict long-term contracts that cannot be terminated prematurely

3. Output

3.1 Internal clients

1/2/3/4/5 Supply end-products to non-related internal (groups of) clients

1/2/3/4/5 Build up inventories of end-products with the internal client. That is, shift the stockpiling forward

1/2/3/4/5 Make agreements with internal clients at certain (attractive) conditions in order to obtain a more steady sale of products (planning fully utilizes the productive capacity)

1/2/3/4/5 Make agreements with regular (large) internal customers regarding the number and kind of products and their desired quality (e.g. in the form of annual contracts)

Appendices

1/2/3/4/5 Develop (on specification) new products, together with internal clients (co-design)

1/2/3/4/5 Arrange one contact for internal clients

3.2 External clients

1/2/3/4/5 Supply products to non-related external (groups of) clients; expansion of activities

1/2/3/4/5 Build up inventories of end-products with the external client. That is, shift the stockpiling forward

1/2/3/4/5 Make agreements with large external clients (key customers) regarding custom-made products (specialties), and so on

1/2/3/4/5 Make agreements with regular (large) external clients (key customers) regarding the number and kind of products and their desired quality (e.g. in the form of annual contracts)

1/2/3/4/5 Affect the sales pattern of external clients in order to better smooth the supply of work

1/2/3/4/5 See to one contact for external clients

3.3 Product-market combinations

1/2/3/4/5 Sell products on geographically diversified markets

1/2/3/4/5 Sell products in non-related markets

1/2/3/4/5 Sell products in markets in different phases of the life cycle

1/2/3/4/5 Reduce the barriers against leaving PMCs already penetrated (lowering exit barriers)

1/2/3/4/5 Reduce the barriers against entering PMCs not yet penetrated (by developing additional expertise or lowering the standard cost price); lowering entry barriers

1/2/3/4/5 Offer capacity as a combination of productive capacity and work assembly (particularly important for specialties)

1/2/3/4/5 Relaunch a product now in existence in new markets

1/2/3/4/5 Introduce new products in markets now in existence

1/2/3/4/5 Introduce new products in new markets

INFORMATION

> For choosing the correct procedure(s) to anticipate the turbulent environment, your department will have to have certain information. Indicate for each of the information-collecting activities below, by circling the right number, whether this activity:
>
> 1. is not done
> 2. is sometimes done
> 3. is done regularly
> 4. is done often
> 5. is done very often
>
> by your organization.

Information activities

1/2/3/4/5 Identify and define basic material and subcomponent markets

1/2/3/4/5 Draw up an analysis with regard to alternative basic materials and subcomponents

1/2/3/4/5 Draw up a vulnerability analysis with regard to the obtainability of basic materials and subcomponents; collect data on available kinds and quantities of basic materials and key components (qualitatively and quantitatively)

1/2/3/4/5 Draw up scenarios with regard to fluctuations in the supply volume of basic materials and subcomponents

1/2/3/4/5 Draw up an analysis with regard to available suppliers

1/2/3/4/5 Collect data on the quantity of the workforce

1/2/3/4/5 Collect data on the quality of the workforce (number of skills of employees)

1/2/3/4/5 Collect data on new technological developments with regard to the production process and product

1/2/3/4/5 Draw up scenarios with regard to the implementation time of these technological developments in the fields of process and/or product renewal

1/2/3/4/5 Segmenting of markets

1/2/3/4/5 Draw up an internal and external competition analysis

1/2/3/4/5 Implement a marketing information system

1/2/3/4/5 Perform a strengths, weaknesses, opportunities, and threats analysis (SWOT analysis) and consequently draw up scenarios

1/2/3/4/5 Define and analyse internal and external groups of clients

1/2/3/4/5 Register frequently and quickly desires/demands of internal and external clients

1/2/3/4/5 Systematize desires of clients, specific orders

1/2/3/4/5 Predict the demand of internal and external clients, so that this demand can be taken into account in planning productive capacity utilization; collect data on the kind and quantity of products expected to be sold per period

1/2/3/4/5 Draw up scenarios with regard to fluctuations in sales volume.

C TECHNOLOGY CHECKLIST: DETERMINATION OF THE TECHNOLOGY CHARACTERISTIC

1. Mode of production

   a. How does the production process take place?

unit production	small batch production	large batch production	mass production	process production

   b. Does the supply of work/input usually have little variation or is the range of variation very large?

   c. Does it concern simple products with simple, fixed operations or does it concern tailor-made products with specific operations and a large variation?

2. Size of batches and production capacity

   a. Does the unit/department manufacture varying batch sizes or are the production batches constant?

b. What cost factors determine this consideration?
- fixed costs (sunk costs)
- economies of scale and learning effects

c. Is the unit/department able to vary the production capacity at short notice?
- quantitatively (sales volume)
- qualitatively (composition of the volume)

3. Physical layout

a. Does the production process have a functional, group, line, or fixed-position layout (setup of machinery, equipment, and people)?
- functional layout: grouping of activities which show similarities in methods and/or equipment; process arrangement
- group layout: grouping of activities as to product group so that each working cell thus originated produces a certain family group
- line layout: operations and machines are successively lined up in sequence
- fixed-position layout: the product to be manufactured remains in the same place, and the production equipment to be used is taken to the product
- one workstation: one person does all activities for a certain product

b. How do you assess the extent of changeability of the layout design and configuration?
- have parallel production flows
- possibility of switching over to another line/station/machine
- possibility of changing the sequence of machinery
- possibility of changing the sequence of operations

c. In what phase of the production process does the differentiation of the end-product take place?

d. To what extent do the operations depend on each other?

e. How long is the processing time/lead time? What factors determine it?
- number of production phases
- size of the intermediate inventories and their place in the operational process
- capacity and capacity utilization
- processing times per phase
- priority rules and high-priority procedures

f. How long are the waiting periods between subsequent production phases and/or operation phases? Can changes be observed in these?

g. To what extent is the capacity utilized?

h. What is the delivery time? Can it be varied easily?

i. Does the organization frequently use inventories? If so, where are these found in the production process?

4. Means of transformation: production means and information systems

a. What means of production, devices, and information systems does the unit/department use in the manufacturing process?

b. Are the information systems very 'high-tech' (capital-intensive), leaving little space for individual employees, or are relatively primitive systems used (work-intensive)?
- very detailed systems with limited applications/systems to be used for various purposes

- very difficult to use / easy to use
- long response time / short response time

   c. How large is the degree of freedom allowed by material and equipment?
- very regulated (no space) / fairly regulated (little space) / reasonably regulated / scarcely regulated (much space) / not regulated (very much space)

   d. What range of measurements or variations of parts or of products can be supplied with the available equipment and production methods? That is, what is the applicability range of means (equipment, machinery) and production methods?
- limited product mix / extensive product mix
- expansion or cutback in assortment not easy / easy

5. Means of transformation: machinery

   a. To what range can the machines be employed? That is, can they also produce different, related products?
- universal / multipurpose equipment / specialized equipment

   b. To what extent are the machines switchable? That is, what are the costs and how much setup time is involved in modifying the machines?
- many / few setups required

   c. Are interchangeable parts, components or equipment available to the unit / department?

6. Routine / Custom-made

   a. To what extent does the production process have a routine character? To what extent is it custom-made?
- clearly established production tasks / changing production tasks
- limited number of setups / large number of setups
- quality control discerned as a separate phase or department (extrinsic) / quality control not clearly established (intrinsic)

   b. Are the operations fixed or variable (operational uncertainty)
- low operational uncertainty / high operational uncertainty

7. Working procedures and methods: software

   a. Do individual employees use various production methods, techniques, or skills? That is, is there an extensive operational production repertoire?
- limited / . . . . . . / . . . . / . . . . / extensive

   b. Are you up to date as far as expertise is concerned? Can you handle the tasks which you are to perform, in a way that conforms to modern standards?
- behind / . . . . . . / . . . . / . . . . / up to date

   c. Do you have the impression that in the course of time changes have occurred within your unit / department in working methods, techniques, equipment at the execution level, and so on?

Appendices

TABLE A.1. Framework linking questions to dimensions of technology

Technology: routine/non-routine	
Subdimensions	Questions
• *mode of production*	1, 2
• *physical layout*	3
• *means of transformation*	4, 5
• *operational production repertoire*	6, 7

D STRUCTURE CHECKLIST: DETERMINATION OF STRUCTURE CHARACTERISTIC

1. Basic Organizational Form

a. Can you characterize the organizational structure?

b. Bases for grouping/departmentalization:
In what way are individual positions, units, and so on clustered within your organization unit?
 • by function/by product or service/by target group/by place

c. Number of levels:
Are there many or few hierarchical levels?
 • hierarchical/ . . . . / . . . . . . / . . . ./flat organization

d. Size of units:
How large are the units, production units, departments, or sections on the work floor (span of control), and what is the size of middle management and the top of the unit/organization?

e. Functionalization of management:
Is there a strict separation between line and staff, or do they overlap in function?
staff has the right to advise, / . . . . / distinction between
line has the formal authority   staff and line is blurred
to decide
Is the emphasis in the unit/department on the line or the staff?
Is the line (management) divided into various aspects of management?
 • line/line-staff/functional/project/matrix
 • unity of command/functional features/functionalization

2. Division of labour/specialization

a. As a matter of course, there is some kind of division of labour/specialization within your unit/department. Has this division found concrete shape in detailed job and task descriptions?
 • no / . . . . / . . . . / . . . . / very systematically

b. Is this specialization also used for the division of daily work, or is it rather an indication of main points in the work and a tool in matters of personnel structuring and ranking?
   • daily activities / . . . . / . . . . / . . . . / formal only

3. Scope of task (performing and regulating activities)

a. Is the work 'finely' divided, or do the employees get rather 'large lumps' of work which they may perform independently?
   • the cycle time: time required for a worker to complete a set of elementary operations
      ⋆ long / short

b. Does this division of work relate to the number of activities that have to be carried out (activities on the work floor)?
   • horizontal specialization of work / horizontal job enlargement

c. Does this division of work relate to the separation between the performance of activities and the control or administration of these activities?
   • vertical specialization of work / vertical extension of responsibilities (job enrichment)

d. Does this division of work relate to the number of regulating activities (management activities)?
   • functionalization / defunctionalization

4. Depth of task (variation, training)

a. Can the work within the unit / department be characterized as richly varied or relatively monotonous?
   • number of different elementary operations per employee or station:
      ⋆ small / . . . . . / . . . . . / . . . . . / large
      ⋆ simple / . . . . . / . . . . . / . . . . . / complex
   • technical steering and control of the individual employees or stations along which the process takes place:
      ⋆ small / . . . . . / . . . . . / . . . . . / large

b. What is the level of skills, crafts, arts, and expertise, that is, the training time on the job, training, education and / or schooling which is / are required to be able to do the job? Have there been changes in one or more of these recently?

5. Interchangeability

a. Is the interchangeability of the people within your unit sufficiently great to be able to intercept variations in the size and contents of the various activities which are drawn to the unit / department?
   • no interchangeability / . . . . . / . . . . . / . . . . . / complete interchangeability

b. Do people easily switch in practice from one job to another?
   • never / . . . . . / . . . . . / . . . . . / very often and very easily

6. Standardization and formalization

a. Does your unit / department make use of:
   • standardization of the work process (standardization of throughput); the degree to which contents of the work are specified or programmed

Appendices

> - standardization of results to be obtained (standardization of output); the degree to which results of the work, such as products or performance are specified.
> b. To what extent has this been put down in writing? Think of job descriptions, work instructions, and general rules (extent of behaviour formalization).
> c. Does your organization use internal training, courses, and so on (standardization of skills)? Is there a fixed training programme?

7. Dependencies and coordination

> a. Do all the subactivities within the unit/department lead to one whole process, or do they concern relatively independent tasks that need little coordination?
>   - very interdependent / ..... / ..... / ..... / very independent
>   - reciprocal / sequential / pooled interdependencies
> b. How are these subactivities coordinated, if necessary?
>   - mutual adjustment / direct supervision / standardization of work process / standardization of output / standardization of skills

8. Decision-making and (de)centralization

> a. How does the decision-making within the unit/department take place?
>   - centralized / ..... / ..... / ..... / decentralized (vertical)
>   - local / ..... / ..... / ..... / scattered
>   What is the effect of the lower levels as to operational and strategic decisions?
> b. Is there much consultation among departments, production units, sections, and so on or are they individually reasonably autonomous (horizontal decentralization)?
> c. Are there certain consultative bodies within the unit (lateral relations)?
>   - liaison positions / task forces, project teams / integration managers / matrix structures

9. Planning

> a. Do people within your unit explicitly and systematically use planning? If so, to what does this planning relate and how does the planning process take place (content, process)?
> b. Do they use certain planning systems?
>   - internal goals and priority-setting: extent to which the unit itself sets its goals and sets priorities, within the given framework
>   * top-down / bottom-up: central management formulates the plan for the entire organization. Subsequently the plans are further elaborated in the various organization units; central management awaits the plans of the units and then tries to integrate them into a complete plan
>   * short-/long-term goals: (0–1) (1–2) (2–3) (3–4) (4–5) expressed in years
>   * quantitative / qualitative goals
>   - internal programming of planning and control: extent to which the unit translates operational goals and priorities into programmes and planning
>   - progress control and evaluation of results: extent to which the unit controls and evaluates the progress and the results of its actions

10. Participation

In so far as organizational activities such as goals, planning, work assembly, progress control, time accounting, evaluation of results, and so on, happen more or less systematically, is this a matter of a few people, for example, the management or the secretariat, or are as many as possible employees involved in it?
• very exclusive / ..... / ..... / ..... / very participative

11. Control systems

Does your unit use certain control systems with regard to personnel, compensation, budgets, data, and so on:
• financial control systems
  ⋆ incremental budgeting / zero-base budgeting
• compensation systems
  ⋆ short- / long-term compensation
• Management Development systems or Human Resources Development systems
• information systems
  ⋆ centralized / decentralized

12. Change in the organization

a. Are there certain frictions within the unit that raise the question of whether changes in the configuration or the functioning of the organization are necessary?
b. Have you recently been confronted with a change in your unit? If so, what kind of change? What were the reasons for it?
c. Have the problems that caused the change been solved?
d. Do you have the impression that in the course of time changes have occurred within your unit in terms of contact, consultation, and decision?
e. Do you have the impression that the formal structure strongly deviates from the actual structure?
   What is your opinion about the changeability of your unit?
   • very small / small / moderate / rather great / great

E CULTURE CHECKLIST: DETERMINATION OF CULTURE CHARACTERISTIC

IDENTITY FORMATION

1. History

Can you tell something about the history of the organization and specifically about the organization unit?
• How long has the organization existed (and your unit within it)?
• What developments has the organization unit experienced?

2. Mission

a. Please indicate in a few catchwords what the organization with which you are associated stands for.
b. Do you think that the organization has an image?

TABLE A.2. Framework linking questions to dimensions of structure

Structure: mechanistic/organic	
Subdimensions	Questions
• *basic organizational form*	1
▶ grouping	1*b*
▶ levels	1*c*
▶ size	1*d*
▶ functionalization	1*e*, 3*d*
• *planning and control system*	9, 11
• *process regulations*	2–8, 10, 12
▶ specialization	2
—scope of task	3
—depth of task	4
—interchangeability	5
▶ standardization	6
—work process/results	6*a*
▶ formalization	2*a*, 2*b*, 6*b*
▶ training and education	4*b*, 6*c*
—standardization of skills	
▶ liaison devices	7*a*, 7*b*, 8*c*
▶ horizontal decentralization	7*a*, 8*b*, 8*c*
▶ delegation	8*a*
▶ participation	10

c. If so, what is this image? (discuss symbols, logos)
   • narrow/ . . . . . / . . . . . / . . . . . /broad

3. Unit's contribution to mission

a. What does the organization unit contribute to this vision/mission?
b. Is this vision/mission shared by everyone within your unit?
   • weak/ . . . . . / . . . . . / . . . . . /strong
c. Are there different images/ideas about the mission or the image of the organization within your unit?
   • heterogeneous/ . . . . . / . . . . . / . . . . . /homogeneous
d. Does your unit strongly deviate from the organization as a whole, in so far as mentality, identity, and mission are concerned?

4. Important people

a. Are there, in your opinion, people who are currently of major importance to the organization (discuss people with a positive significance and people with a negative significance to the organization)?
b. What is their significance for the organization?
c. Which people have had significance in the past?
d. What has been their significance for the organization?

5. Important events

a. Can you mention an important crisis in which the unit has been involved (discuss the most important event)?
b. How did people respond to it?

6. Celebrations/mourning

a. What events are celebrated in the organization/unit (find out who is involved)?
b. Are there events of mourning in the organization/unit?

7. Language/specific expressions

a. What terms did you learn at the time that were used only by insiders?
b. Can you think of other specific terms of the organization which you have learned later?
c. What are winged words in the organization?

8. Stories/anecdotes

a. Can you tell a mythic story about the organization/unit with which you work?
b. What stories about the old days are still regularly told in the organization/unit, for example, to newcomers?

MANAGEMENT STYLE

9. Leadership profile

a. Do you supervise people in the organization/unit? If so, how many?
b. What education has an executive within your organization usually had?
c. Have executives been recruited mainly from within the organization's own ranks, or have they been enlisted from outside?
d. What is the average age level of an executive within this unit?
e. Can you draw a profile of those people who take up the highest positions within your organization (sex, religion, career history, family background, political and social orientation)?

10. Leadership style

Leadership often consists of a combination of directing and collaborating behaviour. Characteristics of directing (task-oriented) behaviour are:
- emphasis on task performance
- one-way communication
- control

Appendices

Characteristics of collaborating (relation-oriented) behaviour are:
- emphasis on the mutual relationship
- two-way communication
- employees being involved in decision-making
  - a. How would you characterize your style of leading?
    - mainly directing (task-oriented/instructive); indicating step by step what employees should do, and keeping close supervision of the task performance
    - mainly collaborating (relation-oriented/participative); making decisions, together with the employee, and supporting him/her in the task performance
    - directing and collaborating (consultative); asking for the contribution of employees in making decisions, and following the task performance closely
    - neither (delegative): leaving decisions and responsibility for performing the tasks to the employees
  - b. In what way do you yourself receive leading?
  - c. How much freedom of action has, in your opinion, an executive within the organization to vary his leadership with regard to directing and collaboration?
    - none/little/not much/much/complete
  - d. In what outwardly visible forms is leading expressed (think of sample behaviour, ritual events, such as meetings, celebrations)?
  - e. What should an executive in this unit not do?

11. Philosophy about leading

  - a. Is there in the organization unit a philosophy of leading people? If so, what is this philosophy?
  - b. Do you experience in practice that leading is given in this way? If so, please explain this with several examples. If not, how is leading given?
  - c. How, in your opinion, is leading given to you in terms of good and bad?

12. Planning approach

  - a. How are the goals actually established? How should this be done according to you?
    - top-down/ . . . . . / . . . . . / . . . . . /bottom-up
  - b. Are the established goals unchangeable and constant, or are they changed regularly? If they are changed regularly, within what period does this happen?
  - c. Are the goals, established explicitly or implicitly, mainly:
    - quantitative/ . . . . . / . . . . . / . . . . . /qualitative
    - detailed/ . . . . . / . . . . . / . . . . . /rough
    - short-term/ . . . . . / . . . . . / . . . . . /long-term
      (0–1) (1–2) (2–3) (3–4) (4–5) expressed in years

13. Management attitude

  - a. Can changes be observed in management techniques or approach used within the organization unit?
    - fixed procedures and activities (routines)
    - procedures of urgency and priority rules (heuristics)
    - ad hoc activities (improvisation)
  - b. If so, is the willingness to use new management techniques large or small?
    - low/ . . . . . /reasonable/ . . . . . /high

UNWRITTEN RULES

14. Discipline dominance

a. What is the background (as for training and experience) of the average employee of your organization unit?

b. What is the average age level approximately?

15. Socialization of respondent

a. Please think of when you entered this organization/ organization unit. What were your most important discoveries during the first three months concerning working in this unit?

b. Did certain things happen to you in the organization/organization unit which made you say: 'I belong to it?' (If necessary, help the interviewee by giving some examples).

16. Socialization of newcomers

a. What are the ways in which the organization unit indicates which people belong to it?

b. Suppose you get a new colleague in your department/section/unit tomorrow. What is the most important thing that you would like to make clear to him/her about this organization?

c. When is it said of a newcomer that he fits into the organization/organization unit? (Ask for profile description)

d. When is it said of a person that he is not going to make it? (Note how he deals with things that happen within this organization)

e. Is there some kind of internal introductory programme for new employees?
   • no / . . . . . / . . . . . / . . . . . / very systematic

17. Socialization by social policy/HRM

a. Is there a philosophy regarding career planning and career policy within the organization? If so, what is this philosophy?

b. Is this philosophy followed in actual practice? Is there any system for internal career planning for employees?
   • no / very little / something / systematic / very systematic

c. Is there any systematic rotation of people within your organization unit, so that they can easily understand the whole and become more easily interchangeable?
   • no / . . . . . / . . . . . / . . . . . / very systematic

d. Is the performance of employees assessed?
   • no assessment / . . . . . . / sometimes / . . . . . . / always

e. Are the assessment discussions more than a formality?
   • formality / hardly worthwhile / sometimes functional / functional / very functional

f. Is the assessment system directed towards the short or the long term?
   • short term / . . . . . / medium term / . . . . . / long term
      (0–1) (1–2) (2–3) (3–4) (4–5) expressed in years

Appendices

18. External training

a. Is taking external training and courses stimulated?
- in no way whatsoever / ..... / ..... / ..... / strongly stimulated

b. Is there a great willingness to take such courses/training?
- low/ ..... /reasonable/ ..... /great

19. Formal-actual

a. What are the biggest mistakes you can make within this organization?

b. What is particularly appreciated within this organization?

c. What are, according to you, some of the most important rules (written or unwritten) that are valid within this organization?

d. How does the organization/organization unit with which you are associated appreciate the following proposition: 'The rules of this organization may not be broken, even if someone thinks this would be in the greatest interest of the organization'?

e. Do you have the impression that, within your unit, changes have occurred over time in values, norms, expectations, ideas, and feelings towards work?

f. Do you have the impression that other norms and ideas are necessary? If so, do the existing norms and values act prohibitively?

g. Do you have the impression that the actual organization strongly deviates from the formal organization?

20. Tolerance for ambiguity

a. Could you characterize the relationship between you and your colleagues in a few catchwords?
- formal/informal
- every man for himself/collaborative
- predictable/surprising

b. How would your colleagues, for instance, react
- if you make a noticeable mistake?
- if you dress differently from usual?
- if you put up a special performance?

c. How do people think about deviating views/new ideas? Do such ideas have a chance at all within the organization unit?

d. Do employees bring in new ideas/possible improvements? Does your unit have a few creative people?

EXTERNAL ORIENTATION

21. Focus

a. Is the 'future' something that is germane within the organization unit? If so, how do people think about it?

b. Who do you consider to be the direct and indirect people interested in your organization unit (stakeholder analysis)?
- limited/extensive

22. Closed/open organization

a. How sensitive is, in your opinion, the organization unit to developments that occur in the market, the social environment, other organization units/departments, and so on? How is this sensitivity expressed?

b. What is the opinion within your organization unit about renewal/changes in the work process, products to be delivered and/or services to be rendered?
- dominance of process (means oriented)/ dominance of product (product oriented)
- product-bound (technology push)/customer-bound (market pull)

c. What is the most negative image that is possible in the outside world about this organization unit (something that might happen)? Think in this respect of both the external environment and other units within the organization.

d. What is the most positive image possible (something that might happen)?

e. Do you think that the (internal/external) environment will remain stable, or does not need a reaction?

f. Do many outsiders (clients, employees from other departments) come to this organization unit?

23. Planning attitude

Four attitudes can be distinguished with regard to planning:

- attempts are made to maintain the existing achievements (market share, customers, type of product); planning is directed towards maintaining the existing situation (reactive)
- the environment is considered to be uncontrollable, so the organization does not undertake any actions. Planning is, therefore, useless (inactive)
- data from the past are used to predict future developments in order to anticipate them; planning in order to be able to anticipate (proactive)
- a desired future is designed without taking the past into account; planning to reach the ideal situation (interactive)

Which of the four attitudes is dominant within your organization unit?

TABLE A.3. Framework linking questions to dimensions of culture

Culture: conservative / innovative	
Subdimensions	Questions
• *Identity formation*	1–3, 4–8 (facultative)
► communality (strong/weak)	3, 3b
► scope (narrow/broad)	2, 2c
► homogeneity (homogeneous/heterogeneous)	3, 3c, 3d
• *Management style*	9–13
► leadership style	9, 10, 11
► planning approach	12
► management attitude	13
• *Unwritten rules*	14–20
► discipline dominance	14
► socialization	15, 16, 17, 18
—newcomers	15, 16
—social policy (HRM)	17
—education/training	18
► attitude formal-actual	19
► tolerance for ambiguity	20
• *External orientation*	21–23
► focus	21
► closed/open	10c, 18, 22
► planning attitude	23

Appendix II
Diagnostic Results of the Multi-Case Longitudinal Study

The data collected by means of the standardized questionnaires and quick survey (see Appendix I) in cases X, Y, and Z were analysed with the FARSYS I computer program. This appendix provides a representation of the turbulence profiles, flexibility profiles, and the organizational characteristics of cases X, Y, and Z resulting from the pre-measurements, and the new flexibility profiles resulting from the post-measurements. For a more elaborate discussion of the measurement procedures, we refer to Volberda (1992).

Appendices

PRE-MEASUREMENT

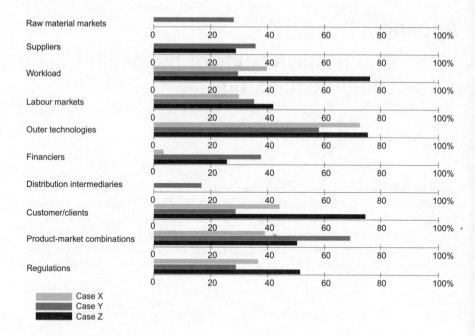

Fig. A.1. Environmental turbulence profile

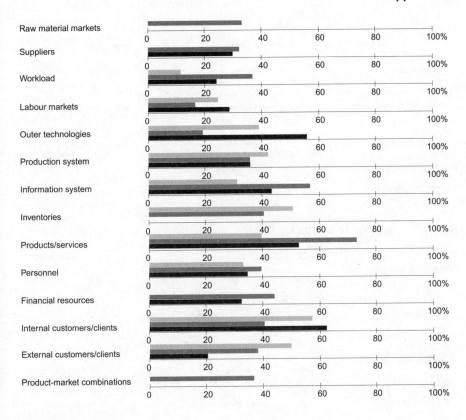

Raw material markets

Suppliers

Workload

Labour markets

Outer technologies

Production system

Information system

Inventories

Products/services

Personnel

Financial resources

Internal customers/clients

External customers/clients

Product-market combinations

Case X
Case Y
Case Z

Fig. A.2. Flexibility profile (pre-measurement)

Appendices

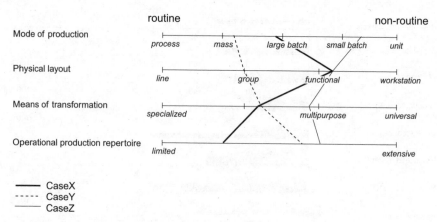

	routine					non-routine
Mode of production		process	mass	large batch	small batch	unit
Physical layout		line	group	functional		workstation
Means of transformation		specialized		multipurpose		universal
Operational production repertoire		limited				extensive

——— CaseX
- - - - CaseY
——— CaseZ

Fig. A.3. Technology characteristic

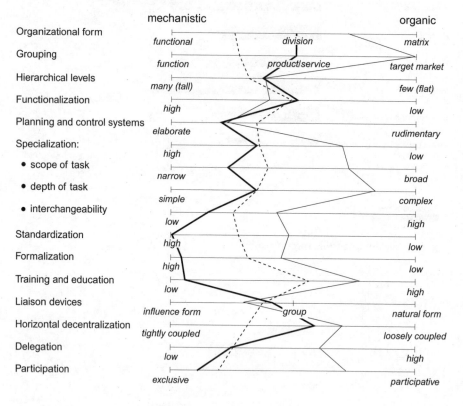

	mechanistic		organic
Organizational form	functional	division	matrix
Grouping	function	product/service	target market
Hierarchical levels	many (tall)		few (flat)
Functionalization	high		low
Planning and control systems	elaborate		rudimentary
Specialization:			
• scope of task	high		low
• depth of task	narrow		broad
• interchangeability	simple		complex
Standardization	low		high
Formalization	high		low
Training and education	high		low
Liaison devices	low		high
Horizontal decentralization	influence form	group	natural form
Delegation	tightly coupled		loosely coupled
Participation	low		high
	exclusive		participative

——— Case X
- - - - Case Y
——— Case Z

Fig. A.4. Structure characteristic

314

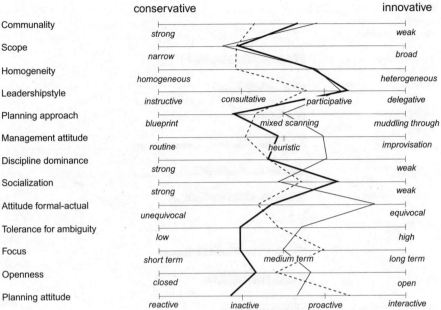

Communality

Scope

Homogeneity

Leadershipstyle

Planning approach

Management attitude

Discipline dominance

Socialization

Attitude formal-actual

Tolerance for ambiguity

Focus

Openness

Planning attitude

conservative   innovative

strong		weak
narrow		broad
homogeneous		heterogeneous
instructive	consultative participative	delegative
blueprint	mixed scanning	muddling through
routine	heuristic	improvisation
strong		weak
strong		weak
unequivocal		equivocal
low		high
short term	medium term	long term
closed		open
reactive	inactive proactive	interactive

—— Case X
- - - Case Y
—— Case Z

Fig. A.5. Culture characteristic

POST-MEASUREMENT

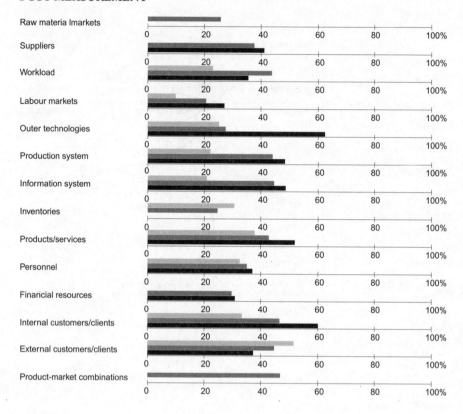

Fig. A.6. Flexibility profile (post-measurement)

References

Aaker, D. A., and Mascarenhas, B. (1984), 'The Need for Strategic Flexibility', *The Journal of Business Strategy*, 5/2, autumn, 74–82.

Ackoff, R. L. (1971), 'Towards a System of Systems Concepts', *Management Science*, 17/11: 661–71.

—— (1974), *Redesigning the Future*, New York: Wiley.

—— (1977), 'Towards Flexible Organizations: A Multidimensional Design', *Omega*, 5/6: 649–62.

—— (1981), *Creating the Corporate Future*, New York: Wiley.

Adler, P. S. (1988), 'Managing Flexible Automation', *California Management Review*, spring, 34–56.

Aharoni, Y., Maimon, Z. and Segev, E. (1978), 'Performance and Autonomy in Organizations: Determining Dominant Environmental Components', *Management Science*, 24/9: 949–59.

Albert, S. (1984), 'A Delite Design Model for Successful Transitions', in J. Kimberly and R. Quinn (eds.), *Managing Organizational Transitions*, Homewood, Ill.: Irwin, 169–91.

Aldrich, H. E., and Pfeffer, J. (1976), 'Environments of Organizations', *Annual Review of Sociology*, 2: 121–40.

Allaire, Y., and Firsirotu, M. E. (1984), 'Theories of Organizational Culture', *Organization Studies*, 5/3: 193–226.

Amit, R., and Schoemaker, P. J. H. (1993), 'Strategic Assets and Organizational Rent', *Strategic Management Journal*, 14: 33–46.

Andrews, K. R. (1971), *The Concept of Corporate Strategy*, Homewood, Ill.: Dow Jones-Irwin.

Angle, H. L., and Van de Ven, A. H. (1989), 'Suggestions for Managing the Innovation Journey', in A. H. Van de Ven, H. L. Angle, and M. S. Poole (eds.), *Research on the Management of Innovation*, New York: Harper & Row, 663–97.

Ansoff, H. I. (1965), *Corporate Strategy*, New York: McGraw-Hill.

—— (1974), 'Corporate Structure: Present and Future', *Working Paper 74-4*, European Institute for Advanced Studies in Management, Brussels.

—— (1978), 'The Changing Shape of the Strategic Problem', in D. E. Schendel and C. W. Hofer (eds.), *Strategic Management: A New View of Business Policy and Planning*, Boston and Toronto: Little, Brown & Company, 30–44.

—— (1980), 'Strategic Issue Management', *Strategic Management Journal*, 1: 131–48.

—— (1988), *The New Corporate Strategy*, Chichester: Wiley.

References

Ansoff, H. I. and Brandenburg, R. G. (1971), 'A Language for Organization Design: Parts I and II', *Management Science*, 17/12: B705–31.

—— Eppink, D. J., and Gomer, H. (1975), 'Management and Discontinuity, Problems of Managerial Decisiveness', *Working Paper 75–29*, European Institute for Advanced Studies in Management, Brussels.

Appelbaum, E., and Schettkat, R. (1990), *Labor Market Adjustments to Structural Change and Technological Progress*, New York: Praeger.

Argyris, C., and Schön, D. (1978), *Organizational Learning*, Reading, Mass.: Addison-Wesley.

Arrow, K. (1962), 'The Economic Implications of Learning By Doing', *Review of Economic Studies*, 29, June, 155–73.

Ashby, W. R. (1964), *An Introduction to Cybernetics*, London: Methuen.

Babüroglu, O. N. (1988), 'The Vortical Environment: The Fifth in the Emery-Trist Levels of Organizational Environments', *Human Relations*, 41/3: 181–210.

Baden-Fuller, C., and Stopford, J. M. (1994), *Rejuvenating the Mature Business*, Boston: Harvard Business School Press.

—— and Volberda, H. W. (1997), 'Strategic Renewal in Large Complex Organizations: A Competence-Based View', in A. Heene and R. Sanchez (eds.), *Competence-Based Strategic Management*, Chichester: Wiley, 89–110.

Bahrami, H. (1992), 'The Emerging Flexible Organization: Perspectives from Silicon Valley', *California Management Review*, summer, 33–52.

Bain, J. S. (1968), *Industrial Organization*, New York: Wiley.

Barnett, W. P., Greve, H. R., and Park, D. Y. (1994), 'An Evolutionary Model of Organizational Performance', *Strategic Management Journal*, 15: 11–28.

Barney, J. B. (1986), 'Organizational culture: Can it be a Source of Sustained Competitive Advantage?' *Academy of Management Review*, 11: 656–65.

Bartlett, C. A. (1993), 'Strategic Flexibility, Firm Organization, and Managerial Work in Dynamic Markets', in *Advances in Strategic Management*, ix, Greenwich, Conn.: JAI Press, 293–98.

—— and Ghoshal, S. (1988), 'Organizing for Worldwide Effectiveness', *California Management Review*, autumn, 54–74.

—— —— (1993), 'Beyond the M-Form: Toward a Managerial Theory of the Firm', *Strategic Management Journal*, 14, Special Issue, 23–46.

Bate, P. (1984), 'The Impact of Organizational Culture on Approaches to Organizational Problem-Solving', *Organization Studies*, 5/1: 43–66.

Bateson, G. (1936), *Naven*, Cambridge: Cambridge University Press.

Becker, S. W., and Whiskler, T. L. (1967), 'The Innovative Organization: A Selective View of Current Theory and Research', *Journal of Business*, 40: 462–69.

Beckhard, R., and Harris, H. T. (1977), *Organizational Transitions: Managing Complex Change*, Reading, Mass.: Addison-Wesley.

Bedeian, A. G. (1980), *Organizations: Theory and Analysis*, Hinsdale, Ill.: The Dryden Press.

Beer, S. (1985), *Diagnosing the System*, New York: Wiley.

Bendix, R. (1956), *Work and Authority in Industry*, New York: Wiley.

References

Berg, P. (1986), 'Organization Change as a Symbolic Transformation Process', in P. J. Frost, L. F. Moore, M. R. Louis, C. L. Lundberg, and J. Martin (eds.), *Organizational Culture*, Beverly Hills, Calif.: Sage, 281–301.

Bettis, R. A., and Prahalad, C. K. (1995), 'The Dominant Logic: Retrospective and Extension', *Strategic Management Journal*, 16/1: 5–14.

Blank, P. D., and Turner, A. N. (1987), 'Gestalt Research: Clinical Field Research Approaches to Studying Organizations', in J. W. Lorsch (ed.), *Handbook of Organizational Behavior*, Englewood Cliffs, NJ: Prentice-Hall, 109–25.

Boerlijst, J. G., Krabbendam, J. J., Schilfgaarde, P., and Willenborg, J. A. M. (1985), *Flexibele automatisering*, 's-Gravenhage: SMO informatief.

Bolwijn, P. T., and Kumpe, T. (1990), 'Manufacturing in the 1990s—Productivity, Flexibility and Innovation', *Long Range Planning*, 23/4: 44–57.

Bouma, F., Rutges, A., and Volberda, H. W. (1994), 'Flexibiliteitsdiagnose en herontwerp: software gereedschap ter ondersteuning van de organisatie-adviseur', *Bedrijfskunde*, 66/1: 83–92.

Bourgeois, L. J., III (1980), 'Strategy and Environment: A Conceptual Integration', *Academy of Management Review*, 5/1: 25–39.

—— (1981), 'On the Measurement of Organizational Slack', *Academy of Management Review*, 6/1: 29–39.

—— and Brodwin, D. R. (1984), 'Strategic Implementation: Five Approaches to an Elusive Phenomenon', *Strategic Management Journal*, 5: 241–64.

Bower, J. L. (1970), *Managing the Resource Allocation Process*, Boston, Mass.: Harvard Business School Press.

Bowman, E. H. (1973), 'Epistemology, Corporate Strategy, and Academe', *Working Paper 73–45*, European Institute for Advanced Studies in Management, Brussels.

Boynton, A. C., and Victor, B. (1991), 'Beyond Flexibility: Building and Managing the Dynamically Stable Organization', *California Management Review*, autumn, 53–66.

Bradach, J., and Eccles, R. (1989), 'Markets versus Hierarchies: From Ideal Types to Plural Types', in W. R. Scott (ed.), *Annual Review of Sociology*, 15: 97–118.

Braybrooke, D., and Lindblom, C. E. (1970), *A Strategy of Decision: Policy Evaluation as a Social Process*, New York: Free Press.

Brunsson, N. (1982), 'The Irrationality of Action and Action Rationality: Decisions, Ideologies and Organizational Actions', *Journal of Management Studies*, 19/1: 29–44.

Burgelman, R. A. (1983), 'A Process Model of Internal Corporate Venturing in the Diversified Major Firm', *Administrative Science Quarterly*, 28, June, 223–44.

—— (1991), 'Intraorganizational Ecology of Strategy Making and Organizational Adaptation: Theory and Field Research', *Organization Science*, 2: 239–62.

—— (1994), 'Fading Memories: A Process Theory of Strategic Business Exit in Dynamic Environments', *Administrative Science Quarterly*, 39: 24–56.

Burns, T., and Stalker, G. M. (1961), *The Management of Innovation*, London: Tavistock.

Burton, R. M. (1984), 'Variety in Strategic Planning: An Alternative to the Problem Solving Approach', *Columbia Journal of Business*, winter, 92–8.

—— and Damon, W. W. (1975), 'Limitations to Decentralization for Long Range

References

Planning and Control in Multinational Corporations', Working Paper, European International Business Association, Jouy-en-Josas, Dec.

Burton, R. M. and Naylor, T. H. (1980), 'Economic Theory in Corporate Planning', *Strategic Management Journal*, 1/3: 249–63.

Business Week (1993), 'Is Microsoft Too Powerful?' 1 Mar., 85.

—— (1994), 'Motorola: Training for the Millennium', 28 Mar., 158–62.

—— (1996), 'The Fall of an American Icon', 5 Feb., 32–9.

Buzacott, J. A., and Yao, D. D. (1986), 'Flexible Manufacturing Systems: A Review of Analytical Models', *Management Science*, 32/7: 890–905.

Camerer, C., and Vepsalainen, A. (1988), 'The Economic Efficiency of Corporate Culture', *Strategic Management Journal*, 9: 115–26.

Cameron, K. S. (1986), 'Effectiveness as Paradox: Consensus and Conflict in Conceptions of Organizational Effectiveness', *Management Science*, 32/5: 539–53.

Carroll, J. (1967), 'A Note on Departmental Autonomy and Innovation in Medical Schools', *Journal of Business*, 40/4: 531–4.

Castrogiovanni, G. J. (1991), 'Environmental Munificence: A Theoretical Assessment', *Academy of Management Review*, 16/3: 542–65.

Chaffee, E. E. (1985), 'Three Modes of Strategy', *Academy of Management Review*, 10/1: 89–98.

Chandler, A. D., Jr. (1962), *Strategy and Structure*, Cambridge, Mass.: MIT Press.

Chase, R. B., and Aquilano, N. J. (1977), *Production and Operations Management, A Life Cycle Approach*, Homewood, Ill.: Irwin.

Child, J. (1972), 'Organizational Structure, Environment and Performance: The Role of Strategic Choice', *Sociology*, 6/1: 1–22.

Ciborra, C. U. (1996), 'The Platform Organization: Recombining Strategies, Structures, and Surprises', *Organization Science*, 7/2: 103–18.

Clark, B. (1972), 'The Organizational Saga in Higher Education', *Administrative Science Quarterly*, 17: 178–84.

Clark, K. B. (1985), 'The Interaction of Design Hierarchies and Market Concepts in Technological Evolution', *Research Policy*, 14: 235–51.

Clegg, S. R. (1990), *Modern Organizations—Organization Studies in the Postmodern World*, London: Sage Publications.

Cohen, W. M., and Levinthal, D. A. (1990), 'Absorptive Capacity: A New Perspective on Learning and Innovation', *Administrative Science Quarterly*, 35: 128–52.

Cohn, S. F., and Turyn, R. M. (1984), 'Organizational Structure, Decision Making Procedures, and the Adaption of Innovations', *IEEE Transactions on Engineering Management*, EM31, Nov., 154–61.

Collis, D. J. (1994), 'How Valuable are Organizational Capabilities', *Strategic Management Journal*, 15: 143–52.

Coyle, T., and Page, T. (1994), 'Learning to Change in SmithKline Beecham', *Business Change & Re-engineering*, 1/4: 10–19.

Craig, T. (1996), 'The Japanese Beer Wars: Initiating and Responding to Hypercompetition in New Product Development', *Organization Science*, 7/3: 302–21.

Crozier, M. (1964), *The Bureaucratic Phenomenon*, Chicago: University of Chicago Press (English translation).

—— (1973), *The Stalled Society*, New York: Viking Press (Translation of *La société bloquée*).

Cyert, R., and March, J. (1963), *A Behavioral Theory of the Firm*, Englewood Cliffs, NJ: Prentice-Hall.

Daft, R. L., and Lewin, A. Y. (1993), 'Where are the Theories for the "New" Organizational Forms? An Editorial Essay', *Organization Science*, 4/4: i–vi.

D'Aveni, R. (1994), *Hypercompetition: Managing the Dynamics of Strategic Maneuvering*, New York: The Free Press.

Davidow, W. H., and Malone, M. S. (1992), *The Virtual Corporation*, New York: HarperCollins.

Davis-Blake, A., and Uzzi, B. (1993), 'Determinants of Employment Externalization: A Study of Temporary Workers and Independent Contractors', *Administrative Science Quarterly*, 38: 195–223.

Deal, T. E., and Kennedy, A. A. (1982), *Corporate Cultures*, Reading, Mass.: Addison-Wesley.

De Leeuw, A. C. J. (1986), *Organisaties: management, analyse, ontwerp en verandering: een systeemvisie*, Assen/Maastricht: Van Gorcum (2nd edn.).

—— (1989), 'Bevoegdheden en verantwoordelijkheden—Oude wijsheden voor het organiseren', *Human resource management*, II.A.2.9-1, No. 3: 101–11.

—— and Volberda, H. W. (1996), 'On the Concept of Flexibility: A Dual Control Perspective', *Omega*, 24/2: 121–39.

De Meyer, A., Nakane, J., Miller, J. G., and Ferdows, K. (1989), 'Flexibility: The Next Competitive Battle—The Manufacturing Futures Survey', *Strategic Management Journal*, 10/2: 135–44.

De Vries, J., and Van de Water, H. (1992), 'Quality Circles, the Production Function and Quality of Working Life: Results of a Study in Seven Large Companies', *International Journal of Quality & Reliability Management*, 9/4: 30–45.

Dill, W. R. (1958), 'Environments as an Influence on Managerial Autonomy', *Administrative Science Quarterly*, 2/4: 409–43.

Dougherty, D. (1989), 'Interpretive Barriers to Successful Product Innovation', *Report No. 89–114*, Cambridge, Mass.: Marketing Science Institute.

Drucker, P. (1985), *Innovation and Entrepreneurship*, New York: Harper & Row.

—— (1993), *Post-Capitalist Society*, Oxford: Butterworth-Heinemann.

Dumaine, B. (1989), 'How Managers can Succeed through Speed', *Fortune*, Feb., 54–9.

Duncan, R. B. (1972), 'Characteristics of Organizational Environments and Perceived Environmental Uncertainty', *Administrative Science Quarterly*, 17/3: 313–27.

—— (1976), 'The Ambidextrous Organization: Designing Dual Structures for Innovation', in R. H. Kilmann, L. R. Pondy, and D. P. Slevin (eds.), *The Management of Organization Design*, i, New York: Elsevier North-Holland, 167–88.

Dyer, W. G., Jr. (1986), 'The Cycle of Cultural Evolution in Organizations', in R. H. Kilmann, M. J. Saxton, and R. Serpa (eds.), *Gaining Control of the Corporate Culture*, San Francisco: Jossey-Bass, 200–29.

321

References

Eccles, R. G., and Nohria, N. (1992), *Beyond the Hype: Rediscovering the Essence of Management*, Cambridge, Mass: Harvard Business School Press.

Eisenhardt, K. M. (1989), 'Building Theories from Case Study Research', *Academy of Management Review*, 14/4: 532–50.

Elfring, T., and Volberda, H. W. (1996), 'Schools of Thought in Strategic Management', in T. Elfring, H. Siggaard Jensen, and A. Money (eds.), *Theory Building in the Business Sciences*, Copenhagen: Munksgaard International Publishers, 11–47.

Emery, F. E. (ed.) (1969), *Systems Thinking*, Harmondsworth: Penguin.

—— and Trist, E. (1965), 'The Causal Texture of Organizational Environments', *Human Relations*, 18: 21–31.

Eppink, D. J. (1978), *Managing the Unforeseen: A Study of Flexibility*, dissertation thesis, Ermelo: Administratief Centrum.

Etzioni, A. (1968), *The Active Society*, New York: The Free Press.

Evans, J. S. (1991), 'Strategic Flexibility for High Technology Manoeuvres: A Conceptual Framework', *Journal of Management Studies*, 28/1: 69–89.

Fast, N. D. (1979), 'The Future of Industrial New Venture Departments', *Industrial Marketing Management*, 8: 264–73.

Fayol, H. (1949), *General and Industrial Management*, London: Pitman.

Feldman, S. P. (1988), 'How Organizational Culture Can Affect Innovation', *Organizational Dynamics*, summer, 57–67.

Fiol, C. M., and Lyles, M. A. (1985), 'Organizational Learning', *Academy of Management Review*, 10/4: 803–13.

Fortune (1994), 'GM's $11,000,000,000 Turnaround', 17 Oct., 30–42.

—— (1995), 'GM: Some Gain, Much Pain', 20 May, 46–50.

—— (1996), '3M Fights Back', 5 Feb., 42–7.

Frazelle, E. H. (1986), 'Flexibility: A Strategic Response In Changing Times', *Industrial Engineering*, Mar., 17–20.

Fredrickson, J. W. (1983), 'Strategic Process Research: Questions and Recommendations', *Academy of Management Review*, 8/4: 565–75.

—— (1984), 'The Comprehensiveness of Strategic Decision Processes: Extension, Observations, Future Directions', *Academy of Management Journal*, 27/3: 445–66.

—— and Mitchell, T. R. (1984), 'Strategic Decision Processes: Comprehensiveness and Performance in an Industry with an Unstable Environment', *Academy of Management Journal*, 27/2: 399–423.

Friedlander, F. (1983), 'Patterns of Individual and Organizational Learning', in P. Srivastva (ed.), *The Executive Mind*, San Francisco: Jossey Bass, 192–220.

Gabor, D. (1969), 'Open-Ended Planning', in E. Jantsch (ed.), *Perspectives of Planning*, Paris, OECD.

Galbraith, J. R. (1973), *Designing Complex Organizations*, Reading, Mass.: Addison-Wesley.

—— (1982), 'Designing the Innovating Organization', *Organizational Dynamics*, winter, 3–24.

Galunic, D. C., and Eisenhardt, K. M. (1996), 'The Evolution of Intracorporate Domains: Divisional Charter Losses in High-Technology, Multidivisional Corporations', *Organization Science*, 7/3: 255–82.

Garud, R., and Kotha, S. (1994), 'Using the Brain as a Metaphor to Model Flexible Production Systems', *Academy of Management Review*, 19/4: 671–98.

Garvin, D. A. (1993), 'Building a Learning Organization', *Harvard Business Review*, 71, July–Aug., 78–91.

Gatignon, H., and Robertson, T. S. (1985), 'A Propositional Inventory for New Diffusion Research', *The Journal of Consumer Research*, 11/4: 849–67.

Gerwin, D. (1993), 'Manufacturing Flexibility: A Strategic Perspective', *Management Science*, 39/4: 395–410.

Ghemawat, P. (1991), *Commitment: The Dynamic of Strategy*, The Free Press: New York.

Gillespie, D. F., and Mileti, D. S. (1977), 'Technology and the Study of Organizations: An Overview and Appraisal', *Academy of Management Review*, Jan., 7–16.

Ginsburg, A., and Buchholtz, A. (1990), 'Converting to For-Profit Status: Corporate Responsiveness to Radical Change', *Academy of Management Journal*, 33/3, Sept., 445–77.

Grant, R. (1996), 'Prospering in Dynamically-Competitive Environments: Organizational Capability as Knowledge Integration', *Organization Science*, 7/4: 375–87.

Green, S. (1988), 'Strategy, Organizational Culture and Symbolism', *Long Range Planning*, 21/4: 121–9.

Greiner, L. E. (1972), 'Evolution and Revolution as Organizations Grow', *Harvard Business Review*, July–Aug., 37–46.

Gresov, C. (1984), 'Designing Organizations to Innovate and Implement: Using Two Dilemmas to Create a Solution', *Columbia Journal of World Business*, winter, 63–7.

Grimes, A. J., and Klein, S. M. (1973), 'The Technological Imperative: The Relative Impact of Task Unit, Modal Technology, and Hierarchy on Structure', *Academy of Management Journal*, 16: 583–97.

Hage, J., and Aiken, M. (1969), 'Routine Technology, Social Structure and Organizational Goals', *Administrative Science Quarterly*, 14: 368–79.

—— and Dewar, R. (1973), 'Elite Values versus Organizational Structure in Predicting Innovation', *Administrative Science Quarterly*, 18: 279–90.

Hambrick, D. C., and D'Aveni, R. (1988), 'Large Corporate Failures as Downward Spirals', *Administrative Science Quarterly*, 33: 1–23.

Hamel, G., and Prahalad, C. K. (1989), 'Strategic Intent', *Harvard Business Review*, May–June, 63–76.

—— —— (1994), *Competing for the Future*, Boston: Harvard Business School Press.

Hammer, M., and Champy, J. (1993), *Reengineering The Corporation*, London: Nicholas Brealey.

Handy, C. (1995), *The Age of Unreason*, London: Arrow Business Books.

Hannan, M. T., and Freeman, J. (1977), 'The Population Ecology of Organizations', *American Journal of Sociology*, 82/5: 929–63.

—— —— (1984), 'Structural Inertia and Organizational Change', *American Sociological Review*, 49: 149–64.

Hanssen-Bauer, J., and Snow, C. (1996), 'Responding to Hypercompetition: The Structure and Processes of a Regional Learning Network Organization', *Organization Science*, 7/4: 413–27.

References

Harrigan, K. R. (1985), *Strategic Flexibility*, Massachusetts and Toronto: Lexington Books.

Harrison, M. I. (1987), *Diagnosing Organizations*, Applied Social Research Methods Series, viii, Newbury Park: Sage Publications.

Harrison, R. (1984), 'Leadership and Strategy for New-Age', in J. Adams (ed.), *Transforming Work*, Alexandrai, Va.: Miles River Press.

Harvey, E. (1968), 'Technology and the Structure of Organizations', *American Sociological Review*, 33: 241–59.

Haselhoff, F. (1977), *Organisatiestrategie, een dilemma*, Alphen a/d Rijn: Samsom.

Hayes, R. H., and Pisano, G. P. (1994), 'Beyond World Class: The New Manufacturing Strategy', *Harvard Business Review*, 72: 77–86.

Hedberg, B. (1981), 'How Organizations Learn and Unlearn', in N. Nystrom and W. Starbuck (eds.), *Handbook of Organizational Design*, i, Oxford: Oxford University Press, 3–27.

—— and Jönsson, S. (1978), 'Designing Semi-confusing Information Systems for Organizations in Changing Environments', *Accounting, Organizations and Society*, 3/1: 47–64.

—— Nystrom, P., and Starbuck, W. H. (1976), 'Camping on Seesaws: Prescriptions for a Self Designing Organization', *Administrative Science Quarterly*, 21: 41–65.

Henderson, R., and Cockburn, I. (1994), 'Measuring Competence? Exploring Firm Effects in Pharmaceutical Research', *Strategic Management Journal*, 15: 63–84.

Hersey, P., and Blanchard, K. H. (1982), *Management of Organizational Behavior: Utilizing Human Resources*, Englewood Cliffs, NJ: Prentice-Hall (4th edn.).

Hickson, D. J., Pugh, D. S., and Pheysey, D. C. (1969), 'Operations Technology and Organization Structure: An Empirical Reappraisal', *Administrative Science Quarterly*, 14: 378–97.

Hill, T. (1983), *Production/Operations Management*, New York: Prentice-Hall.

Hill, W., Fehlbaum, R., and Ulrich, P. (1974), 'Konzeption einer modernen Organisationlehre', *Zeitschrift für Organisation*, 43/1: 4–16.

Hisrich, R. D., and Peters, M. P. (1989), *Entrepreneurship: Starting, Developing, and Managing a New Enterprise*, Homewood, Ill.: R. D. Irwin.

Hofer, C. W., and Schendel, D. (1978), *Strategy Formulation: Analytical Concepts*, St Paul, Minn.: West Publishing.

Hofstede, G. (1980), 'Motivation, Leadership and Organization: Do American Theories Apply Abroad?' *Organizational Dynamics*, summer, 42–63.

—— Neuijen, B., Daval Ohayv, D., and Sanders, G. (1990), 'Measuring Organizational Cultures: A Qualitative and Quantitative Study across Twenty Cases', *Administrative Science Quarterly*, 35: 286–316.

Howard, R. (1992), 'The CEO as Organizational Architect: An Interview with Xerox's Paul Allaire', *Harvard Business Review*, 70/5: 106–21.

Hrebiniak, L. G., and Joyce, W. F. (1984), *Implementing Strategy*, New York: Macmillan.

—— —— (1985), 'Organizational Adaptation: Strategic Choice and Environmental Determinism', *Administrative Science Quarterly*, 30, Sept., 336–49.

—— —— (1986), 'The Strategic Importance of Managing Myopia', *Sloan Management Review*, autumn, 5–14.

Hulsink, W. (1996), *Do Nations Matter in a Globalising Industry*, Delft: Eburon.

Hunt, J. W. (1972), *The Restless Organization*, Sydney: Wiley.

Hunt, R. G. (1970), 'Technology and Organization', *Academy of Management Journal*, 13: 236–52.

Ilinitch, A. Y., D'Aveni, R. A., and Lewin, A. Y. (1996), 'New Organizational Forms and Strategies for Managing in Hypercompetitive Environments', *Organization Science*, 7/3: 211–20.

Itami, H. (1987), *Mobilizing Invisible Assets*, Cambridge, Mass.: Harvard University Press.

Ittner, C. D., and Kogut, B. (1995), 'How Control Systems Can Support Organizational Flexibility', in E. Bowman and B. Kogut (eds.), *Redesigning The Firm*, New York: Oxford University Press, 155–80.

Jaikumar, R. (1986), 'Postindustrial Manufacturing', *Harvard Business Review*, 69: 69–76.

Jessop, B., Kastendiek, H., Nielsen, K., and Pederson, O. K. (eds.), (1991), *The Politics of Flexibility—Restructuring State and Industry in Britain, Germany and Scandinavia*, Aldershot: Edward Elgar.

Johannisson, B. (1987), 'Anarchists and Organizers—Entrepreneurs in a Network Perspective', *International Studies of Management and Organization*, 17/1: 49–63.

Johnson, G. (1987), *Strategic Change and the Management Process*, Oxford: Basil Blackwell.

—— (1988), 'Rethinking Incrementalism', *Strategic Management Journal*, 9, Sept., 75–91.

Kanter, R. M. (1982), 'The Middle Manager as Innovator', *Harvard Business Review*, 61, July–Aug., 95–105.

—— (1983), *The Change Masters*, New York: Simon & Schuster.

—— (1988), 'When a Thousand Flowers Bloom: Structural, Collective, and Social Conditions for Innovation in Organization', in B. M. Staw and L. L. Cummings (eds.), *Research in Organizational Behavior*, x, Greenwich, Conn.: JAI Press, 169–211.

—— (1994), *When Giants Learn to Dance: Mastering the Challenge of Strategy, Management and Careers in the 1990s*, London: Routledge (Reprint).

—— Stein, B. A., and Jick, T. D. (1992), *The Challenge of Organizational Change: How Companies Experience it and Leaders Guide it*, New York: Free Press.

Keesing, R. (1974), 'Theories of Culture', *Annual Review of Anthropology*, 3: 73–97.

Khandwalla, P. N. (1971), 'Influence of the Techno-Economic Environment on Firms' Organization', *Research Report*, McGill University, Montreal.

—— (1977), *The Design of Organizations*, New York: Harcourt, Brace, Jovanovich.

Kieser, A. (1969), 'Zur Flexibilität verschiedener Organisationsstrukturen', *Zeitschrift für Organisation*, 38, Oct.–Nov, 273–82.

Kilmann, R. H. (1977), *Social Systems Design: Normative Theory and the MAPS Design Technology*, New York: Elsevier North-Holland.

Kimberly, J. R. (1979), 'Issues in the Creation of Organizations: Initiation, Innovation, and Institutionalization', *Academy of Management Journal*, 22: 437–57.

Kirzner, I. (1973), *Competition and Entrepreneurship*, Chicago: University of Chicago Press.

—— (1985), *Discovery and the Capitalist Process*, Chicago: University of Chicago Press.

Knight, F. H. (1921), *Risk, Uncertainty and Profit*, Chicago, Ill.: University of Chicago Press.

References

Knight, K. (1976), 'Matrix Organization: A Review', *The Journal of Management Studies*, 13: 111–130.

Kogut, B., and Zander, U. (1992), 'Knowledge of the Firm, Combinative Capabilities, and the Replication of Technology', *Organization Science*, 3/3: 383–97.

Kopp, D. G., and Litschert, R. J. (1980), 'A Buffering Response in Light of Variation in Core Technology, Perceived Environmental Uncertainty, and Size', *Academy of Management Journal*, 23/2: 252–66.

Kotha, S. (1995), 'Mass Customization: Implementing the Emerging Paradigm for Competitive Advantage', *Strategic Management Journal*, 16, Special Issue, 21–42.

Kotler, P. (1972), 'A Generic Concept of Marketing', *Journal of Marketing*, 36, April, 46–54.

—— (1988), *Marketing Management: Analysis, Planning, Implementation, and Control*, Englewood Cliffs, NJ: Prentice-Hall.

Krabbendam, J. J., and Boer, H. (1989), 'Doorlooptijdverkorting en flexibele fabricagesystemen', *Bedrijfskunde*, 61/3: 228–33.

Krijnen, H. G. (1979), 'The Flexible Firm', *Long Range Planning*, 12, Apr., 63–75.

Lammers, C. J. (1987), 'Transcience and Persistence of Ideal Types in Organization Theory', in Nancy DiTomaso and Samuel Bacharach (eds.), *Research in the Sociology of Organizations, A Research Annual*, vi, Greenwich: JAI Press, 1–41.

Landau, M. (1969), 'Redundancy, Rationality and the Problem of Duplication and Overlap', *Public Administration Review*, 346–58.

—— (1973), 'On the Concept Of a Self-Correcting Organization', *Public Administration Review*, 33: 533–42.

Lawrence, P. R. (1981), 'Organization and Environment Perspective—The Harvard Organization and Environment Research Program', in A. H. van de Ven and W. F. Joyce (eds.), *Perspectives on Organization Design and Behavior*, New York: Wiley, 311–37.

—— and Lorsch, J. (1967), *Organization and Environment*, Boston: Harvard School of Business Administration Press.

Learned, E. P., Christensen, C. R., Andrews, K. R., and Guth, W. (1969), *Business Policy: Text and Cases*, Homewood, Ill.: Irwin.

Lei, D., Hitt, M. A., and Goldhar, J. D. (1996), 'Advanced Manufacturing Technology: Organizational Design and Strategic Flexibility', *Organization Studies*, 17/3: 501–23.

Lenz, R. T., and Lyles, M. A. (1985), 'Paralysis by Analysis: Is Your Planning System Becoming too Rational?' *Long Range Planning*, 18/4: 64–72.

Leonard-Barton, D. (1992), 'Core Capabilities and Core Rigidities: A Paradox in Managing New Product Development', *Strategic Management Journal*, 13, Special Issue, 111–25.

—— (1995), *Wellsprings of Knowledge: Building and Sustaining the Sources of Innovation*, Boston, Mass.: Harvard Business School Press.

—— Kent Bowen, H., Clark, K. B., Holloway, C. A., and Wheelwright, S. C. (1994), 'How to Integrate Work and Deepen Expertise', *Harvard Business Review*, Sept.–Oct., 121–30.

Levinthal, D. A., and March, J. G. (1993), 'The Myopia of Learning', *Strategic Management Journal*, 14, Special Issue, 95–112.

326

Levitt, B., and March, J. G. (1988), 'Organizational Learning', in W. R. Scott (ed.), *Annual Review of Sociology*, xiv, Palo Alto, Calif.: Annual Reviews, 319–40.

Levy, A., and Merry, U. (1986), *Organizational Transformation*, New York: Praeger.

Lewin, A. Y., and Minton, J. W. (1986), 'Determining Organizational Effectiveness: Another Look, and an Agenda for Research', *Management Science*, 32/5: 514–38.

—— and Stephens, C. U. (1993), 'Designing Postindustrial Organizations: Combining Theory and Practice', in G. P. Huber and W. H. Glick, *Organizational Change and Redesign*, New York: Oxford University Press, 393–409.

Liebeskind, J. P., Lumerman Oliver, A., Zucker, L., and Brewer, M. (1996), 'Social Networks, Learning and Flexibility: Sourcing Scientific Knowledge in New Biotechnology Firms', *Organization Science*, 7/4: 428–43.

Likert, R. (1961), *New Patterns of Management*, New York: McGraw-Hill.

Lindblom, C. E. (1959), 'The Science of "Muddling Through" ', *Public Administration Review*, 19, spring, 79–88.

Linneman, R. E., and Chandran, R. (1981), 'Contingency Planning', *Managerial Planning*, Jan.–Feb.

Lorange, P., and Vancil, R. A. (1977), *Strategic Planning Systems*, Englewood Cliffs, NJ: Prentice-Hall.

Lorenzoni, G., and Baden-Fuller, C. (1995), 'Creating a Strategic Center to Manage a Web of Partners', *California Management Review*, 37/3: 146–63.

Louis, M. (1983), 'Organizations as Culture Bearing Milieux', in L. Pondy, P. Frost, G. Morgan, and T. Dandridge (eds.), *Organizational Symbolism*, Greenwich, Conn.: JAI Press, 39–54.

Low, M. (1989), 'Administrative Form, Organizational Commitment and Performance: A Comparison of the Bureaucratic and Constituency Models', Dissertation Proposal, The Wharton School of the University of Pennsylvania, Oct.

MacMillan, I. G. (1985), 'Progress in Research on Corporate Venturing: 1985', *Working Paper*, NY University, Center for Entrepreneurial Studies.

Maljers, F., Baden-Fuller, C., and van den Bosch, F. (1996), 'Maintaining Strategic Momentum: The CEO's Agenda', *European Management Journal*, 14/6: 555–61.

Mandelbaum, M. (1978), *Flexibility in Decision Making: An Exploration and Unification*, Ph.D. dissertation, Toronto: University of Toronto.

March, J. G. (1981), 'Footnotes to Organizational Change', *Administrative Science Quarterly*, 26: 563–77.

—— and Simon, H. (1958), *Organizations*, New York: Wiley.

Martin, J., and Siehl, C. (1983), 'Organizational Cultures and Counter-Culture: An Uneasy Symbiosis', *Organizational Dynamics*, 11: 52–64.

Mascarenhas, B. (1982), 'Coping with Uncertainty in International Business', *Journal of International Business Studies*, 13/2: 87–98.

Maturana, H., and Varela, F. (1980), *Autopoesis and Cognition: The Realization of the Living*, London: Reidl.

Mayo, E. (1933), *The Human Problems of an Industrial Civilization*, New York: Macmillan.

Meredith, J. (1988), 'Installation of Flexible Manufacturing System Teaches Management Lessons in Integration, Labor, Cost, Benefits', *Industrial Engineering*, Apr., 18–27.

References

Metcalfe, L. (1981), 'Designing Precarious Partnerships', in P. C. Nystrom and W. H. Starbuck (eds.), *Handbook of Organizational Design*, i, New York: Oxford University Press, 503–30.

Meyer, A. D. (1982), 'How Ideologies Supplant Formal Structures and Shape Responses to Environments', *Journal of Management Studies*, 19/1: 46–61.

Meyer, J., and Rowan, B. (1977), 'Institutionalized Organizations; Formal Structure as Myth and Ceremony', *American Journal of Sociology*, 83: 340–63.

Meyerson, D., and Martin, J. (1987), 'Cultural Change: An Integration of Three Different Views', *Journal of Management Studies*, 24/6: 623–47.

Miles, R. E., Coleman, H. J., Jr., and Creed, W. E. D. (1995), 'Keys to Success in Corporate Redesign', *California Management Review*, 37/3: 128–45.

—— and Snow, C. C. (1978), *Organizational Strategy, Structure, and Process*, New York: McGraw-Hill.

—— —— (1986), 'Organizations: New Concepts for New Forms', *California Management Review*, 28/3: 62–73.

—— —— (1992), 'Causes and Failure in Network Organizations', *California Management Review*, 34/4: 53–72.

—— —— (1994), *Fit, Failure and the Hall of Fame*, New York: Free Press.

Miller, D., and Chen, M. (1994), 'Sources and Consequences of Competitive Inertia: A Study of the U.S. Airline Industry', *Administrative Science Quarterly*, 39: 1–23.

—— and Friesen, P. (1980), 'Archetypes of Organizational Transition', *Administrative Science Quarterly*, 25/2: 268–300.

—— and Ross, M. (1975), 'Self-Serving Biases in the Attribution of Causality', *Psychology Bulletin*, 82: 213–25.

Ministry of Economic Affairs (1994), *Platform Globalization* (in Dutch), Den Haag: Ministerie van Economische Zaken.

—— (1996), *Competitiveness Audit* (in Dutch), Den Haag: Ministerie van Economische Zaken.

Mintzberg, H. (1973), 'Strategy-Making in Three Modes', *California Management Review*, 16/2: 44–53.

—— (1978), 'Patterns in Strategy Formation', *Management Science*, 24: 934–48.

—— (1979), *The Structuring of Organizations*, Englewood Cliffs, NJ: Prentice-Hall.

—— (1990), 'Strategy Formation: Schools of Thought', in J. W. Frederickson (ed.), *Perspectives on Strategic Management*, Boston: Ballinger, 105–235.

—— (1994), *The Rise and Fall of Strategic Planning*, New York: The Free Press.

—— and Waters, J. A. (1985), 'Of Strategies, Deliberate and Emergent', *Strategic Management Journal*, 6: 257–272.

—— and Westley, F. (1992), 'Cycles of Organizational Change', *Strategic Management Journal*, 13: 39–59.

Morgan, G. (1981), 'The Schismatic Metaphor and its Implications for Organizational Analysis', *Organizational Studies*, 2/1: 23–44.

—— (1986), *Images of Organization*, Beverly Hills, Calif.: Sage Publications.

Morroni, M. (1991), 'Production Flexibility', in G. M. Hodgson and E. Screpanti (eds.), *Rethinking Economics*, Aldershot: Edward Elgar, 68–80.

Muller, H., de Samblanckx, S., and Matthys, D. (1987), 'The Expert System Approach and the Flexibility-Complexity Problem in Scheduling Production Systems', *International Journal of Production Research*, 25/11: 1659–70.

Nadler, D. A. (1981), 'Managing Organizational Change: An Integrative Perspective', *The Journal of Applied Behavioral Science*, 17/2: 191–211.

Nelson, R. R., and Winter, S. G. (1977), 'In Search of a Useful Theory of Innovation', *Research Policy*, 6: 36–76.

—— —— (1982), *An Evolutionary Theory of Economic Change*, Cambridge, Mass.: Harvard University Press.

Nemetz, P. L., and Fry, L. W. (1988), 'Flexible Manufacturing Organizations: Implications for Strategy Formulation and Organization Design', *Academy of Management Review*, 13/4: 627–38.

Newman, W. H., Summer, W. H., and Warren, E. K. (1972), *The Process of Management: Concepts, Behavior and Practice*, Englewood Cliffs, NJ: Prentice-Hall.

Nicholls, J. (1980), 'The Alloplastic Organization', *Journal of General Management*, autumn, 61–79.

Nonaka, I. (1994), 'A Dynamic Theory of Organizational Knowledge Creation', *Organization Science*, 5/1: 14–37.

—— and Takeuchi, H. (1995), *The Knowledge-Creating Company*, New York: Oxford University Press.

OECD (1994), *Employment Outlook*, Paris: OECD.

Ouchi, W. G. (1979), 'A Conceptual Framework for the Design of Organizational Control Mechanisms', *Management Science*, 25/9: 833–48.

—— (1980), 'Markets, Bureaucracies and Clans', *Administrative Science Quarterly*, 28: 129–41.

—— (1981), *Theory Z: How American Business can Meet the Japanese Challenge*, Reading, Mass.: Addison-Wesley.

Parthasarthy, R., and Sethi, S. P. (1992), 'The Impact of Flexible Automation on Business Strategy and Organizational Structure', *Academy of Management Review*, 17/1: 86–111.

Pascale, R. T. (1984), 'Perspectives on Strategy: The Real Story Behind Honda's Success', *California Management Review*, 26/3: 47–86.

—— (1990), *Managing on the Edge*, London: Penguin Books.

—— and Athos, A. G. (1981), *The Art of Japanese Management: Applications for American Executives*, New York: Simon & Schuster.

Pasmore, W. A. (1994), *Creating Strategic Change: Designing the Flexible, High-Performing Organization*, New York: Wiley.

Pennings, J. M. (1985), 'Introduction: On the Nature and Theory of Strategic Decisions', in —— (ed.), *Organizational Strategy and Change*, San Francisco: Jossey Bass, 1–34.

—— and Gresov, C. G. (1986), 'Technoeconomic and Structural Correlates of Organizational Culture: An Integrative Framework', *Organization Studies*, 7/4: 317–34.

—— and Harianto, F. (1992), 'Technological Networking and Innovation Implementation', *Organization Science*, 3/3: 356–82.

Penrose, E. T. (1959), *The Theory of Growth of the Firm*, New York: Wiley.

Perrow, C. (1967), 'A Framework for the Comparative Analysis of Organizations', *American Sociological Review*, 32: 194–208.

329

References

Perrow, C. (1970), *Organizational Analysis: A Sociological View*, London: Tavistock.
—— (1974), 'Is Business Really Changing?' *Organizational Dynamics*, summer, 31–44.
—— (1986), *Complex Organizations—A critical essay*, New York: Random House (3rd edn.).
Peters, T. J. (1987), *Thriving on Chaos*, New York: Knopf.
—— (1992), *Liberation Management*, London: Macmillan.
—— and Waterman, R. H., Jr. (1982), *In Search of Excellence*, New York: Warner Books.
Pine II, B. J. (1993), *Mass Customization: The New Frontier in Business Competition*, Boston: Harvard Business School Press.
Piore, M., and Sabel, C. (1984), 'Why Companies Might be Moving Steadily towards Specialization and Flexibility', *International Management*, Oct., 97–100.
Poole, M. S., and van de Ven, A. H. (1989), 'Using Paradox to Build Management and Organization Theories', *Academy of Management Review*, 14/4: 562–78.
Porter, M. E. (1980), *Competitive Strategy: Techniques for Analyzing Industries and Competitors*, New York: Free Press.
Powell, W. W. (1987), 'Hybrid Organizational Arrangements: New Form or Transitional Development', *California Management Review*, 30/1: 67–87.
—— (1990), 'Neither Market nor Hierarchy: Network Forms of Organization', in *Research in Organizational Behavior*, xii, Greenwich, Conn.: JAI Press, 295–336.
Prahalad, C. K., and Bettis, R. A. (1986), 'The Dominant Logic: A New Linkage Between Diversity and Performance', *Strategic Management Journal*, 7/6: 485–501.
—— and Hamel, G. (1990), 'The Core Competence of the Corporation', *Harvard Business Review*, 68, May–June, 79–91.
Prigogine, I. (1976), 'Order through Fluctuation: Self-Organization and Social System', in E. Jantsch and C. H. Waddington (eds.), *Evolution and Consciousness: Human Systems in Transition*, Reading, Mass.: Addison-Wesley, 93–133.
Pugh, D. S., Hickson, D. J., Hinings, C. J., McDonald, K., Turner, C., and Lupton, T. (1963), 'A Conceptual Scheme for Organizational Analysis', *Administrative Science Quarterly*, 8: 289–315.
Quinn, J. B. (1980), *Strategies for Change—Logical Incrementalism*, Homewood, Ill.: Irwin.
—— (1985), 'Managing Innovation: Controlled Chaos', *Harvard Business Review*, 63/3: 73–84.
—— (1992), *Intelligent Enterprise: A Knowledge and Service Based Paradigm for Industry*, New York: The Free Press.
Reichwald, R., and Behrbohm, P. (1983), 'Flexibilität als Eigenschaft productionswirtschaftlicher Systeme', *Zeitschrift für Betriebskunde*, 53: 831–53.
Richardson, J. (1996), 'Vertical Integration and Rapid Response in Fashion Apparel', *Organization Science*, 7/4: 400–12.
Ritsema van Eck, E. J. (1984), 'Doorlichting en Diagnose', Working Paper, Themagroep Besluitvorming, Faculteit Bedrijfskunde RUG.
Roberts, E. B. (1980), 'New Ventures for Corporate Growth', *Harvard Business Review*, July–Aug., 134–42.
Roethlisberger, F. J., and Dickson, W. J. (1939), *Management and the Worker*, Cambridge, Mass.: Harvard University Press.

Rogers, E. M. (1983), *Diffusion of Innovations*, New York: The Free Press.

Romme, A. G. L. (1996), 'A Note on the Hierarchy-Team Debate', *Strategic Management Journal*, 17/5: 411–17.

Rose, R. A. (1988), 'Organizations as Multiple Cultures: A Rules Theory Analysis', *Human Relations*, 41/2: 139–70.

Rosenberg, N. (1972), *Technology and American Economic Growth*, New York: Harper Torch Books.

Rumelt, R. P. (1987), 'Theory, Strategy, and Entrepreneurship', in D. J. Teece (ed.), *The Competitive Challenge—Strategies for Industrial Innovation and Renewal*, Cambridge: Ballinger Publishing Company, 137–58.

—— (1995), 'Inertia and Transformation', in C. A. Montgomery (ed.), *Resource-Based and Evolutionary Theories of the Firm*, Boston: Kluwer Academic, 101–32.

Sanchez, R. (1993), 'Strategic Flexibility, Firm Organization, and Managerial Work in Dynamic Markets', in *Advances in Strategic Management*, ix, Greenwich, Conn.: JAI Press, 251–91.

—— (1995), 'Strategic Flexibility in Product Competition', *Strategic Management Journal*, 16, Special Issue, 135–60.

—— and Heene, A. (1996), 'A Systems View of the Firm in Competence-Based Competition', in R. Sanchez, A. Heene, and H. Thomas (eds.), *Dynamics of Competence-Based Competition*, Oxford: Elsevier Science, 39–62.

Sanders, G., and Neuijen, B. (1987), *Bedrijfscultuur: diagnose en beïnvloeding*, Assen/Maastricht: Van Gorcum.

Schein, E. H. (1985), *Organizational Culture and Leadership*, San Francisco: Jossey-Bass.

Schön, D. A. (1971), *Beyond the Stable State*, New York: Random House.

Schroeder, R., van de Ven, A., Scudder, G., and Polley, D. (1986), 'Managing Innovation and Change Processes: Findings from the Minnesota Innovation Research Program', *Agribusiness*, 2/4: 501–23.

Schumpeter, J. A. (1934), *The Theory of Economic Development*, Cambridge Mass.: Harvard University Press.

Scott, B. W. (1965), *Long-Range Planning in American Industry*, New York: American Management Association.

Scott, W. R. (1987), *Organizations—Rational, Natural, and Open Systems*, Englewood Cliffs, NJ: Prentice-Hall (2nd edn.).

Selznick, P. (1957), *Leadership in Administration—A Sociological Interpretation*, New York: Harper & Row.

Senge, P. (1990), 'The Leader's New Work: Building Learning Organizations', *Sloan Management Review*, autumn, 7–23.

Shepard, H. A. (1967), 'Innovation-Resisting and Innovation-Producing Organizations', *Journal of Business*, 40/4, Oct., 470–77.

Simon, H. A. (1947), *Administrative Behavior*, New York: Macmillan.

—— (1960), *The New Science of Management Decision*, New York: Harper & Row.

Smircich, L. (1983), 'Concepts of Culture and Organizational Analysis', *Administrative Science Quarterly*, 28: 339–58.

References

Smircich, L. and Stubbart, C. (1985), 'Strategic Management in an Enacted World', *Academy of Management Review*, 10/4: 724–36.

Smith, A. (1957), *Selections from the Wealth of Nations*, edited by George J. Stigler, New York: Appleton (originally published in 1776).

Smith, A. D. and Zeithaml, C. (1996), 'Garbage Cans and Advancing Hypercompetition: The Creation and Exploitation of New Capabilities and Strategic Flexibility in Two Regional Bell Operating Companies', *Organization Science*, 7/4: 388–99.

Smith, K. K. (1982), 'Philosophical Problems in Thinking about Organizational Change', in Paul S. Goodman and Associates (eds.), *Change in Organizations: New Perspectives on Theory, Research, and Practice*, San Francisco: Jossey-Bass, 316–74.

Smith, V. (1994), 'Institutionalizing Flexibility in a Service Firm', *Work and Occupations*, 21/3: 284–307.

Stalk, G. (1988), 'Time—The Next Source of Competitive Advantage', *Harvard Business Review*, July–Aug., 41–51.

—— Evans, P., and Shulman, L. E. (1992), 'Competing on Capabilities: The New Rules of Corporate Strategy', *Harvard Business Review*, Mar.–Apr., 57–69.

Starbuck, W. H. (1965), 'Organizational Growth and Development', in J. G. March (ed.), *Handbook of Organizations*, Chicago: Rand McNally.

—— (1982), 'Congealing Oil: Inventing Ideologies to Justify Acting Ideologies Out', *Journal of Management Studies*, 19/1: 3–27.

—— (1983), 'Organizations as Action Generators', *American Sociological Review*, 48: 91–102.

Steers, R. M. (1975), 'Problems in the Measurement of Organizational Effectiveness', *Administrative Science Quarterly*, 20, Dec., 546–58.

Stevenson, H. H., and Gumpert, D. E. (1985), 'The Heart of Entrepreneurship', *Harvard Business Review*, 64, Mar.–Apr., 85–94.

—— and Sahlman, W. A. (1986), 'Importance of Entrepreneurship in Economic Development', in R. D. Hisrich (ed.), *Entrepreneurship, Intrapreneurship and Venture Capital*, Lexington, Mass.: Lexington Books, 1–26.

Stewart, R. (1983), 'Managerial Behaviour: How Research has Changed the Traditional Picture', in Michael J. Earl, *Perspectives on Management—A Multidisciplinary Analysis*, Oxford: Oxford University Press, 82–98.

Stinchcombe, A. L. (1965), 'Social Structure and Organizations', in J. G. March (ed.), *Handbook of Organizations*, Chicago: Rand McNally, 142–93.

Stopford, J. M., and Baden-Fuller, C. W. F. (1994), 'Creating Corporate Entrepreneurship', *Strategic Management Journal*, 15/7: 521–36.

Swamidass, P. M., and Newell, W. T. (1987), 'Manufacturing Strategy, Environmental Uncertainty and Performance: A Path-Analytic Model', *Management Science*, 33/4: 509–24.

Taylor, F. W. (1911), *The Principles of Scientific Management*, New York: Harper & Row.

—— (1947), *Scientific Management*, New York: Harper.

Teece, D. J. (1984), 'Economic Analysis and Strategic Management', *California Management Review*, spring, 87–110.

—— Pisano, G., and Shuen, A. (1997), 'Dynamic Capabilities and Strategic Management', *Strategic Management Journal*, 18/7: 509–33.

Thompson, J. D. (1967), *Organizations in Action*, New York: McGraw-Hill.

Tichy, N. M. (1983), *Managing Strategic Change*, New York: Wiley.

—— and Sherman, S. (1994), *Control Your Destiny or Someone Else Will*, New York: Harper Business.

Toffler, A. (1985), *The Adaptive Corporation*, New York: McGraw-Hill.

Trist, E. (1981), 'The Evolution of Sociotechnical Systems as a Framework and as an Action Research Program', in A. van de Ven and W. Joyce (eds.), *Perspectives on Organizational Design and Behavior*, New York: Wiley, 19–75.

Tushman, M. L., and Anderson, P. (1986), 'Technological Discontinuities and Organizational Environments', *Administrative Science Quarterly*, 31: 439–65.

—— and Romanelli, E. (1985), 'Organizational Evolution: A Metamorphosis Model of Convergence and Reorientation', in L. L. Cummings and B. M. Staw (eds.), *Research in Organizational Behavior*, vii, Greenwich, Conn.: JAI Press, 171–222.

Ulrich, D., and Lake, D. (1990), *Organizational Capability*, New York: Wiley.

Upton, D. M. (1993), *McDonald's Corporation 1992: Operations, Flexibility and the Environment*, HBS case number 9–693–028, Boston, Mass.: HBS Case Services.

—— (1995), 'What Really Makes Factories Flexible?' *Harvard Business Review*, July–Aug., 74–84.

Utterback, J. M., and Abernathy, W. J. (1975), 'A Dynamic Model of Process and Product Innovation', *Omega*, 3/6: 639–56.

Vaill, P. (1982), 'The Purposing of High Performing Systems', *Organization Dynamics*, autumn, 23–40.

Van Cauwenberg, A., and Cool, K. (1982), 'Strategic Management in a New Framework', *Strategic Management Journal*, 3: 245–64.

Van de Ven, A. H. (1986), 'Central Problems in the Management of Innovation', *Management Science*, 32/5: 590–607.

—— and Garud, R. (1988), 'A Framework for Understanding the Emergence of New Industries', in R. S. Rosenbloom and R. A. Burgelman (eds.), *Research on Technological Innovation, Management and Policy*, iv, Greenwich, Conn.: JAI Press.

—— and Poole, M. S. (1988), 'Paradoxical Requirements for a Theory of Organizational Change', in R. E. Quinn and K. S. Cameron (eds.), *Paradox and Transformation: Toward a Theory of Change in Organization and Management*, Cambridge, Mass.: Ballinger, 19–63.

Van Donk, D. P., de Vries, J., and van de Water, H. (1991), 'Towards a Conceptual Framework of the Production Function', *International Journal of Operations & Production Management*, 11/1: 32–40.

Van Ham, J. C., Pauwe, J., and Williams, A. R. T. (1987), 'Flexibiliteit en stabiliteit vanuit individu en organisatie', in A. Buitendam (ed.), *Arbeidsmarkt, Arbeidsorganisatie, Arbeidsverhoudingen, Sociaal Beleid*, ch. 6, Deventer: Kluwer, 74–90.

Volberda, H. W. (1992), *Organizational Flexibility: Change and Preservation—A Flexibility Audit and Redesign Method*, Groningen: Wolters-Noordhoff.

—— (1996a), 'Toward The Flexible Form: How To Remain Vital in Hypercompetitive Environments', *Organization Science*, 7/4: 359–74.

—— (1996b), 'Flexible Configuration Strategies within Philips Semiconductors: A Strategic Process of Entrepreneurial Revitalization', in R. Sanchez, A. Heene, and H. Thomas (eds.), *Dynamics of Competence-Based Competition*, Oxford: Elsevier Science, 229–78.

References

Volberda, H. W. (1997), 'Building Flexible Organizations for Fast-moving Markets', *Long Range Planning*, 30/2: 169–83.

—— and Baden-Fuller, C. (1996), 'Strategic Renewal from an Evolutionary Perspective: Four Dynamic Mechanisms', *Management Report Series*, No. 266, Rotterdam School of Management, Erasmus University.

—— and Cheah, H. (1993), 'A New Perspective on Entrepreneurship: A Dialectic Process of Transformation within the Entrepreneurial Mode, Type of Flexibility and Organizational Form', in H. Klandt (ed.), *Research in Entrepreneurship*, Aldershot: Avebury, 261–86.

—— and Van Bruggen, G. (1997), 'On the Concept of Environmental Turbulence: A Scaling Experiment', *NOBO Proceedings*, UT Service: Enschede.

Walker, C. R. (1962), *Modern Technology and Civilization*, New York: McGraw-Hill.

Weber, M. (1946), *From Max Weber: Essays in Sociology*, edited by H. H. Gerth and C. Wright Mills, New York: Oxford University Press.

Weick, K. E. (1979), *The Social Psychology of Organizations*, Reading, Mass.: Addison-Wesley (2nd edn.).

—— (1982), 'Management of Organizational Change Among Loosely Coupled Elements', in P. S. Goodman and Associates (eds.), *Change in Organizations: New Perspectives in Theory, Research, and Practice*, San Francisco: Jossey-Bass, 375–408.

—— (1985), 'The Significance of Corporate Culture', in P. J. Frost, L. F. Moore, M. R. Louis, C. C. Lundberg, and J. Martin (eds.), *Organizational Culture*, Beverly Hills, Calif.: Sage, 381–89.

Wernerfelt, B. (1984), 'A Resource-Based View of the Firm', *Strategic Management Journal*, 5: 171–80.

Wheelwright, S. C. (1984), 'Manufacturing Strategy: Defining the Missing Link', *Strategic Management Journal*, 5/1: 77–91.

Womack, J. P., Jones, D. T., and Roos, D. (1990), *The Machine that Changed the World*, New York: Rawson Associates.

Woodward, J. (1965), *Industrial Organization: Theory and Practice*, London: Oxford University Press.

Wortmann, J. C. (1989), 'Flexibiliteit en Logistieke Informatiesystemen', in W. M. J. Geraerds (ed.), *Flexibiliteit in Logistiek*, Alphen a/d Rijn: Samsom.

Wrapp, H. E. (1967), 'Good Managers Don't Make Policy Decisions', *Harvard Business Review*, 45/5: 91–9.

Yin, R. K. (1989), *Case Study Research: Design and Methods*, Applied Social Research Methods Series, v, Newbury Park: Sage Publications (rev. edn.).

Zaleznick, A. (1977), 'Managers and Leaders: Are they Different?' *Harvard Business Review*, May–June 67–78.

Zelenovic, D. M. (1982), 'Flexibility—A Condition for Effective Production Systems', *International Journal of Production Research*, 20/3: 319–37.

Index

Index

batch production 126–7, 131, 132–3, 135, 297–8
Bate, P. 102, 163, 164, 174
Bateson, G. 61, 75, 113
Becker, S. W. 70
Beckhard, R. 232, 244
Bedeian, A. G. 124
Beer, S. 153, 180
behaviour
  behavioural humanists 23
  entrepreneurial 62–73, 80, 223
  opportunistic 35–9, 43, 80, 243
  regulation 151–5
Behrbohm, P. 85, 89, 91, 93, 95–6, 100
beliefs *see* culture and beliefs
Bell *see* Regional Bell Operating Companies
Bendix, R. 29
Benetton 28, 118, 133, 202
Berg, P. 165
'*Bestands-Flexibilität*' 95
Bettis, R. A. 40
Blanchard, K. H. 171
Blank, P. D. 230
blueprint/synoptic planning approach 171–3
Boeing 132
Boer, H. 132
Boerlijst, J. G. 16, 132
Bolwijn, P. T. 63, 82
Boonstra, C. 112
Boston Consulting Group 29
bottom-up
  emergent perspective 113
  initiatives, facilitating 38
Bouma, F. 245, 262
boundary of unit of analysis 231–2
bounded rationality 22, 24
Bourgeois, L. J., III 32, 56, 147, 186
Bouw, P. 61
Bower, J. L. 38, 112
Bowman, E. H. 15
Boynton, A. C. 39, 82, 89, 107, 110
Bradach, J. 115
brain metaphor 25, 26
Braybrooke, D. 33
breakthrough innovations 68
British Telecom 203, 230
broad operational production repertoire 125, 133–5
broad scope 168
broad-minded external orientation 165, 179–81
Brodwin, D. R. 32, 147
Bruggen, G. van 197
Brunsson, N. 167
BT (British Telecom) 203, 230
Buchholtz, A. 49
building blocks of flexibility analysed 234–7
bureaucracy 20–1, 212
Burgelman, R. A. 112, 214, 272
  organization design 144, 168
  postmodern organization 38, 48, 66, 72

Burns, T. and Stalker, G. M. 102, 209, 281
  competition 191, 192
  organization design 144, 168
  postmodern organization 44–5, 46, 52, 70–1
Burton, R. M. 33, 34, 35, 159
business process reengineering 123
Buzacott, J. A. 82

CAD (computer-aided design) *see* computer-aided technology
CAM (computer-aided manufacturing) *see* computer-aided technology
Camerer, C. 102, 115, 163, 167, 174, 177
Cameron, K. S. 75
Canada 203
Canon 40, 115
capabilities
  dynamic 108–11, 199–201
  flexible 235, 239–41
  management 39, 100–1
  meta-capabilities 199–201
  and opportunistic behaviour 35–9, 43, 80
  see also creating flexible capabilities
capacity
  absorptive 109, 110, 201–3
  adaptive 90
  control 97–9, 104
  production 297–8
Carroll, J. 168
Castrogiovanni, G. J. 187, 188, 189
categories of organizations 230
Caterpillar 198
Cauwenberg, A. van 38, 40, 41
Chaffee, E. E. 31, 32, 36, 40
Champy, J. 95
Chandler, A. D. Jr 32, 112, 270
Chandran, R. 33
change 303
  acceleration 11–17
  changeability 26, 128, 129
  competitive 11–17, 97
  design and configuration 128, 129
  in dominant management-thinking 17–26
  and environment 45–6
  evaluating 88
  identifying external 88
  incremental 64–6, 70, 73, 80, 87, 273, 281
  interchangeability 150–1, 301
  management thinking 17–26
  and preservation, tension between 73–9
  reflective *see* learning
  speed 101, 105
  and stability 90, 91–2
  trajectories 239–45
  triangles 239–41
  unforeseen 85, 90, 93
  unreflective 55
  see also dynamism; transformation

336

Index

Index

Index

Index

Index

tolerance for ambiguity 175, 178
top-down:
  deliberate managerial process 112–13
  planning 147
total flexibility 87
Touraine, A. 46
towards flexible form 209–23
  revitalization of large established firms 216, 219–22
  routinization of entrepreneurial firms 215–19
  typology of alternative flexible forms 211–15
Toyota 14, 47, 114, 115, 119, 201
traditional
  authority 20, 29
  basic organizational form 137–46
  leadership and cultural barriers 165, 169–73
training 152, 154–5, 307–8
trajectories of change and transformation 239–45, 275–9
transformation
  dual trajectories of 275–9
  means 125, 130–3, 242
  trajectory 265–8
  see also change
transition:
  continuous 190
  and FAR 227, 239–45, 250–1, 255–6
  team 244
triangles:
  change 239–41
  diagnostic 237–9
Trist, E. 22–3, 150, 157, 190
trust 115
T-shaped capabilities 115
Tulip 269
turbulent environment 190–7
  control in 96–7
  defined 190
  hypercompetition 197–8
  reducible, neutralizable and fundamental 240
  scan/profile 234–5, 283–8, 312
'turnaround' see revitalization
Turner, A. N. 230
Turyn, R. M. 65, 110
Tushman, M. L. 3, 68, 70, 78, 206, 208, 273
typology of alternative flexible forms 211–15

Ulrich, D. 104
uncertainty 33, 68, 196
underused assets 88
unequivocal attitude, formal–actual 175, 176–8
unforeseen change 85, 90, 93
Unilever 71, 273–4
unit production 126, 133, 135
United Parcel Service 200
universal equipment 131
universal means of transformation 125, 130–3
unlearning and relearning 200

unpredictability 193–5, 196–7, 248
unreflective change 55
unwritten rules 242, 307–8
  and cultural barriers 164, 165, 174–8
UPS (United Parcel Service) 200
Upton, D. M. 13, 14, 82
Utterback, J. M. 63, 66, 69, 213, 217
Uzzi, B. 82

Vaill, P. 170
values
  core 166
  cross-value capabilities 114–16
Van Ommeren Tank Storage 5, 146, 264, 265
Vancil, R. A. 32
Varela, F. 25, 105–6
variation/variability/variety 26
  cyclical model 47–8
  in operations 134–5
  of response, increasing 200
Ven, A. H. van de 3, 113, 243, 271
  organization design 139, 146, 150
  postmodern organization 30, 59, 74, 77–8
Vepsalainen, A. 102, 115, 163, 167, 174, 177
vertical
  integration 213, 215–16, 223
  management 112–14, 115
  specialization 150
vicious circle of process regulations 149
Victor, B. 39, 82, 89, 107, 110
visioning 200
Volkswagen 4
Vries, J. De 29

Wal-Mart 30, 223
Walker, C. R. 189
Wang Computers 107
warning time 91, 201
Water, H. van de 29
Waters, J. A. 35, 42, 115, 179
weak identities 166–8, 169
Weber, M. 12, 20–1, 211
Weick, K. E. 114, 274
  competition 186, 198
  organization design 143, 158
  paradox of flexibility 86–7, 90, 92
  postmodern organization 40, 47, 50, 60, 61, 69, 71
  towards flexible form 209, 210
Welch, J. 34, 112, 270
Wernerfelt, B. 64
Western Electric 183
Westley, F. 272
Wheelwright, S. C. 82
Whiskler, T. L. 70
Winter, S. G. 64, 65, 202, 215, 273, 279
Womack, J. P. 14
Woodward, J. 23, 44–5, 123, 124, 125–6, 131, 132
work-cell layout 129